Police Power and Race Riots

Police Power and Race Riots

Urban Unrest in Paris and New York

Cathy Lisa Schneider

PENN

UNIVERSITY OF PENNSYLVANIA PRESS

PHILADELPHIA

Published by
University of Pennsylvania Press
Philadelphia, Pennsylvania 19104-4112
www.upenn.edu/pennpress

Printed in the United States of America
on acid-free paper

10 9 8 7 6 5 4 3 2 1

A Cataloging-in-Publication record is available from the
Library of Congress

ISBN 978-0-8122-4618-6

Dedicated to the memory of

My mother, Frieda Schneider (1921–2008)
My brother, David Michael Schneider (1960–2004)
My friend and mentor Chuck Tilly (1929–2008)

Until the killing of black men, black mothers' sons, becomes as important to the rest of the country as the killing of a white mother's son. We who believe in freedom cannot rest until this happens.

—Ella Baker (1964)

Contents

Introduction

A riot is somebody talking. A riot is a man crying out "Listen to me mister. There's something I've been trying to tell you and you are not listening."
—Federal Communications Commissioner Nicholas Johnson (speaking after the 1968 riots in Washington, D.C.)[1]

On the night of July 18, 1964, three weeks after Lyndon Johnson signed the Civil Rights Act, New York City police lieutenant Thomas Gilligan shot and killed James Powell, a fifteen-year-old black student, outside his high school in upper Manhattan. An altercation had ensued when Patrick Lynch, the white janitor of a nearby building, sprayed black high school students with a garden hose as they left the school. Lynch shouted racial epithets at the boys, and Powell and two other high school students chased him back to his building. Officer Gilligan arrived on the scene, pivoted, and shot Powell three times. The high school students screamed and cursed at the police, some throwing bottles and cans. "Come on," they taunted Gilligan, "shoot another nigger."[2] Dozens more police arrived on the scene.

The following day hundreds of Harlem residents gathered in front of police stations but were met with walls of tactical police. Scuffles broke out as police wielded batons and shot into the crowds. Meanwhile residents threw bricks and bottles, pulled fire alarms, overturned cars, looted stores, and occasionally attacked white bystanders. After three days the disorder spread from Harlem to Bedford-Stuyvesant in Brooklyn. More than six thousand officers were called in to quell the disturbances. By the sixth day of what would become the first major urban uprising of the 1960s, more than five hundred people had been injured, including thirty-five policemen, and another black man was dead, of gunshot wounds. Property damages were assessed at several million dollars.

In the weeks that followed, similar outbreaks occurred in Rochester, Philadelphia, and several smaller northeastern cities. The following year violence in the Watts ghetto in Los Angeles exploded, leaving thirty-four dead. Riots in Chicago, Cleveland, Dayton, San Francisco, Atlanta, and Omaha erupted in 1966. In 1967 Puerto Rican riots broke out in New York, concentrating in East Harlem and South Bronx. Black neighborhoods in Boston, Nashville, Cincinnati, Newark, and Milwaukee followed suit. Detroit experienced the largest and most deadly disturbance; there police violence left forty-three dead: "By one count the 1964–1968 period produced 329 important riots in 257 cities, with 52,629 persons being arrested for riot-related offenses, 8,371 injured, and 220 killed—mostly black civilians."[3] Only twice in the next five decades (excluding local and relatively isolated, if significant, neighborhood skirmishes and confrontations between residents and police) would minority residents set a major American city aflame.

On October 27, 2005, in Clichy-sous-Bois, outside Paris, police chased one black Mauritanian and two North African (Tunisian and Kurdish) teenage boys, Bouna Traoré, Zyad Benna, and Muhittan Altun, into an electrical substation outside Paris. The boys had tried to avoid an identity check and were pursued by officers carrying stun guns. Cornered, the boys scaled an eight-foot wall covered with barbed wire and skull and crossbones warning of the dangers of electricity. Seeing the boys inside the generator, the commanding officer notified headquarters that reinforcements would not be needed, the boys would not live long now.[4] The police officers then abandoned the site. Inside the grid, the terrified boys clung to each other for eleven minutes, weaving back and forth and looking for a way out. When Bouna accidentally hit the generator, he and Zyad, who was holding his hand, died instantly. Muhittan, although holding Zyad's hand, was saved by the power surge. Severely burned, he retraced his steps, rescaled the wall, and ran, crying hysterically, into the arms of Bouna's stunned and unprepared older brother, Siyakha, who was on his way to buy food to end the family's Ramadan fast.

In the days that followed, young men from the town marched through the streets cursing and throwing garbage at the police. A massive nonviolent march was followed by more police actions including the shooting of tear gas into a mosque filled with women and children. Following the tear gas incident, then minister of the interior Nicolas Sarkozy, having unjustly accused the three teenagers of criminality two days before, gave an inflammatory radio address denying the responsibility of the police or the need for investigation. Hurt and angry, young people retaliated, setting cars and buildings aflame. Fires spread from one poor minority suburb (*banlieue*) to another, until 280 suburbs, cities, and towns across France were ablaze. For three weeks youths of predominantly North African and African descent set fire to an estimated 10,000 cars and attacked 255 schools, 233 other public buildings, and scores of private businesses. Despite the arrest of nearly 5,000 people, the police subdued the burning *banlieues* only after the government imposed a curfew—a means last used against Algerian Frenchmen during the Algerian war.[5]

These two series of events, taking place on opposite sides of the Atlantic, in strikingly different settings and half a century apart, nonetheless display some startling similarities. In both, police violence resulted in the death of one or more minority teenagers. In both, the ensuing uprisings began where the boys had been killed but soon spread to neighboring sites and then distant towns and cities. Following both events, the respective states used the riots to justify harsh new criminal policies targeted at poor minority youths—launching a war on drugs in the United States and harsh new criminal policies in France.

These parallels raise three critical questions. First, why did police forces in such dramatically different settings interact with distinct minorities in such similar ways? Second, why did these interactions lead to riots in New York and hundreds of cities across the United States during the 1960s and in Paris and across France in 2005? Third, why have riots been so rare in New York and most of the United States since the 1970s, even where police brutality and racial profiling have grown? This puzzle is all the more striking since the socioeconomic divide in American cities, like New York, ranks among the world's widest, whereas the divide in French cities, like Paris, ranks among the narrower. As Michael Katz observes, "Today the most intriguing questions are not why the riots [of the 1960s] occurred but why they have not reoccurred. . . . With the exception of Liberty City Miami in 1980 and South-central Los Angeles in early 1992, American cities have not burned since the early 1970s. Even the botched response to Hurricane Katrina did not provoke civil violence. The question becomes all the more intriguing, in the light of October 2005, when riots erupted in at least three hundred towns across France."[6]

How can we explain the conundrum that Katz identifies? The short answer to this puzzle is that many of the factors that make life unbearable in American slums have little to do with riots. Misery is ubiquitous; riots are exceedingly rare. This is not surprising as a) poverty and unemployment dishearten rather than mobilize and b) people often blame themselves for economic failure. Police violence, in contrast, and the killing of unarmed minority youths by white police in particular spark moral outrage, activate racial boundaries, crystallize grievances along a single us/them boundary, and provoke riots.

No feature of a racially divided society is a more potent symbol of racial domination or instills the message of subjugation more forcefully than police. The frequent identity checks, the stop-and-frisks, the disrespect and brutal manner with which police address minority youths, and, worst of all, the utter impunity that allows the most racist and sadistic officers to commit gross violations of human rights and homicide: all these constantly and painfully remind youths of their subordinate status. As the French rapper Monsieur R notes, police "just by the way they look at you they give you the feeling that you are a second-class citizen, even if you were born here. Children are stopped for inspection five times, just on the way from their home to the metro! And I'm talking of a walking distance of less than 10 minutes. . . . Today in France the police logic is simple. . . . Here, if you're black or Arab, it doesn't matter if you have money or a good job, you'll remain black or Arab your whole life."[7]

In unequal, racially divided societies political elites rely on police to enforce categorical boundaries. When political rhetoric, distorted media attention, and public policy activate[8] those boundaries, police violence against subordinate groups intensifies. Police violence further polarizes social relations around an us/them divide. Under such conditions an egregious incident of police violence may trigger riots and urban unrest. If social movements, courts, or other institutions offer alternative paths to justice, no matter how limited, riots are rare. Riots are the last resort for those who find all other paths to justice blocked.

Policing Racial Boundaries

All states draw boundaries that, as Eric Wolf puts it, "define rights to membership, construct justificatory ontogenies for their cadres and lay down criteria for denying participation and benefits to groups deemed unwelcome, unworthy or deleterious."[9] State building, by definition, entails the creation of unequal, bounded categories—Frenchman/German, citizen/

noncitizen, and national/non-national. Extreme categorical inequality results when powerful groups conquer less powerful groups and force them into submission. During and following such historical processes members of powerful groups tell stories about members of less powerful groups to justify their own privileged position. As Adolph Reed notes, "Ascriptive ideologies are just-so stories with the potential to become self-fulfilling prophecies. They emerge from self-interested common sense as folk knowledge: they are 'known' to be true unreflectively because they seem to comport with the evidence of quotidian experience. They are likely to become generally assumed as self-evident truth, and imposed as such by law and custom, when they converge with and reinforce the interests of powerful strata in the society."[10]

Categories simplify and facilitate exploitation (the expropriation of profits, labor power, and resources) and opportunity hoarding (the exclusion of others from access to valuable resources and opportunities). They "lock such differences into place by delivering greater rewards to occupants of the ostensibly superior category," notes Charles Tilly.[11] Because the categories solve pressing organizational problems and are costly to change, they often outlast their original purpose. Categories constructed for the purposes of slavery, conquest, or colonialism can later be used to reinforce unequal systems of remuneration, for example, "assisting employers in assigning workers to jobs for which they were racially suited."[12] One Pittsburgh company in the 1920s, Reed notes, classified thirty-six different racial groups by their supposed capacity for twenty-two distinct jobs, each demanding different atmospheric conditions, levels of speed and precision, and day- or night-shift work. Similarly, Anibal Quijano and Ramon Grosfoguel and Chloe S. Georas describe "colonialities of power," in which social practices are "implicated in relationships among people even when the colonial relationships have been eradicated."[13]

Adaptation reinforces categorical inequality when social networks form on either side of a categorical boundary. Those on one side of the boundary "claim solidarity with others on the same side . . . and invoke a certain sort of relationship to those on the opposite side," notes Tilly.[14] Over time both sides "attribute hard and durable and even genetic reality to the categories they inscribe. Wherever they come from the categories have serious social consequences."[15] That is not to say that racial categorizations are static and ahistorical, or that racism, as David Goldberg puts it, "is singular and monolithic, simply the same attitude complex manifested in varying circumstances."[16] Rather preexisting, yet malleable categories are used by a wide array of actors to navigate or control a complicated and evolving environment.

Several problems remain for state authorities. First, polarization can have "the unintended consequence of defining, legitimating and provoking group identity and mobilization, forging struggles for inclusion between state agents and emerging political actors," as Anthony Marx notes.[17] Second, racial, ethnic, or religious segregation may unintentionally provide a space for resistance, as Niall O Dochartaigh and Lorenzo Bosi observe in their study of the civil rights movement in Northern Ireland: "[B]oundaries drawn and maintained by states can act as a source of power for oppositional forces by creating and consolidating homogenous bounded spaces that can act as resources for resistance."[18] It may also, as Sebastien Roché observes, contribute to the diffusion of riots: "When the minority at the national level becomes a majority in a neighborhood, the balance of power tends to be inverted."[19] Faced with such challenges, "privileged groups may indirectly encourage police killings," David Jacobs and Robert M. O'Brian note, "by demanding that restraints be removed so the police can maintain order."[20]

The control of racial and spatial boundaries is an essential component of police work. "The desire to render society transparent, to know everything about everyone extends back at least as far as the European Enlightenment," notes Clifford Rosenberg. "Faced with the impossibility of realizing these ambitions," he continues, "police forces have had to give priority to some categories of people or places to watch over. . . . police forces have always worried about foreigners, aliens, outsiders and marginal types."[21] Governments and dominant groups expect police to make these distinctions and pass laws to facilitate this process. In 1925, for instance, the French minister of the interior told the prefect of police, "[W]e want to weed out the bad ones, but we cannot give them the impression that we are treating them like foreigners, undesirable foreigners at that, and requiring passports for that reason. . . . We can demand passports under other pretexts, but not to protect ourselves from them; we must appear to be protecting them."[22]

Police forces do not invent these categories. Rather they use categories that mirror those of the society in which they are embedded. They commonly match preexisting exterior categories such as race or ethnicity to interior categories such as citizenship rights, obligations, and forbidden behaviors. These classifications serve as shorthand, allowing officers to summarize "complex and ambiguous situations in a short period of time."[23] Some neighborhoods are designated as in need of protection and others as foreign or dangerous. "Both the racial characteristics of the suspect and the suspect's neighborhood influence police decisions to stop, search or arrest a suspect," Jeffrey Fagan, Amanda Geller, Garth Davies, and Valerie West observe: race and neighborhood interactively "animate the formation of suspicion among police officers."[24]

In racially divided societies, police, like occupying armies, mark stigmatized minority neighborhoods as enemy territory. "Enforcement through bounding," note O Dochartaigh and Bosi, "has the key advantage of simplicity. . . . Boundaries provide a simple and powerful method of communication, pouring huge and often complex information into a single symbol that distinguishes between the vast and complex variety of the internal and similarly complex external. To bound space is to communicate huge volumes of information in a single symbol."[25]

The categories such boundaries inscribe are largely fungible. Tilly notes, "[S]eemingly contradictory categorical principles such as age, race, gender and ethnicity operate in similar ways and can be organizationally combined or substituted within limits set by previously established scripting and local knowledge."[26] In New York and Paris, police paint blacks, Puerto Ricans, Arabs, and Berbers as racialized others. One French officer who railed against "little jerkoffs," for instance, told Didier Fassin, "The blacks are just like the Arabs, except they've no brain."[27] Similarly two high-ranking members of a French left-wing police union told me a story that linked both blacks and Arabs to a host of ominous threats:

> The problem here began after the war in Algeria. The Arabs could not stay there because they had collaborated with France. They ended up congregating in small areas. Housing prices went down and black immigrants now found it very cheap and gathered there too. This concentration created an underground world. . . . Yet for us as police it is good, it is easier to bust. If they were spread around the city it would be difficult to police. If you let them live together, you do not even have to go into the cité. You can put police at either end and close it. It is a way to localize and crystallize delinquency in

a single place. But, if you live there and see all blacks and Arabs on the pavement you can imagine people say "what are the police doing?"[28]

"Only in extremely unequal societies where particular groups are denied full membership," notes Pieter Spierenburg, "do police act in a disrespectful and brutal manner with unarmed citizenry."[29] Paul Chevigny concurs: "The term punishment is never used unless the person on whom the penalty is inflicted is clearly subordinate to the one imposing the penal act."[30] Fassin observes,

> Police violence, whether physical or moral, is exercised in a radically and institutionally unequal manner. On one side are individuals who have not only the monopoly of the legitimate use of force, but also exclusive access to effective use of it given the circumstances. On the other are individuals who are doubly captive, owing to both the physical coercion they undergo and the latent threat weighing on them if ever they should have the bad idea of talking back. Whether detained, handcuffed or simply surrounded by officers, the person exposed to their power is rendered structurally inferior: he is bound to submit, and any protest or rebellion can only lead to even greater submission. Violence is therefore almost always strictly unilateral. But it is also targeted. It is not applied to all.[31]

Comparative studies of policing tend to emphasize the impact of different state structures and institutional cultures on policing strategies. "Policing styles are influenced by the political system," argue Donatella Della Porta and Herbert Reiter. "Institutional features such as police organization, the nature of the judiciary, law codes and constitutional rights—may play a role in defining the opportunities and constraints."[32] But if institutional structure and culture were key, then police in France—a country with a strong central state apparatus, a national police force, common law tradition, and elimination of racial categories in census and law—should interact with black and Arab residents very differently than American police—locally controlled, in a federal state with statutory law and multicultural traditions—interact with blacks and Latinos.

Yet we see strikingly similar interactions between police and minority populations in Paris and those in New York. The structure of inequality at large and the demands placed on police by powerful social classes, dominant racial groups, and the state are more important than the culture and organization of the institution. "The problem is not to know whether the police act identically everywhere within a national territory or across borders," as Fassin points out, "but whether the type of relation they have with a certain public, the way in which political incentives influence their practice, the effects of various systems of evaluation and sanctioning on their conducts, or the justification they provide for their deviant behaviors are generalizable."[33]

Debating Riots

In the first major study of seventy-five riots occurring in the United States between 1964 and 1967, the U.S. Commission on Civil Disorders (aka the Kerner Commission) in 1968 reached the stark conclusion that "our nation is moving towards two societies, one black, one white—separate and unequal."[34] While members of the commission observed that "almost invariably the incident that ignites disorder arises from police action," they were careful to emphasize that "the disorder did not erupt as a result of a single triggering or precipitating incident. Instead it was generated out of an increasingly disturbed social atmosphere, in which typically a series of tension-heightening incidents over a period of weeks or months became linked in the minds of many in the Negro community with a reservoir of underlying grievances."[35] The solution would require nothing less than "the realization of common opportunities for all. . . . From every American it will require new attitudes, new understandings, and above all a new will."[36]

The findings were simultaneously too vast and too limited. The list was too vast. While blacks and Latinos suffered immense hardships and injustice, they did not burn buildings or loot stores to protest every wrong. The commission listed the following twelve most cited grievances in descending order by intensity: 1) police practices; 2) unemployment and underemployment; 3) inadequate housing; 4) inadequate education; 5) poor recreational facilities and programs; 6) ineffectiveness of the political structure and grievance mechanisms; 7) disrespectful white attitudes; 8) discriminatory administration of justice; 9) inadequacy of federal programs; 10) inadequacy of municipal services; 11) discriminatory consumer and credit practices; and 12) inadequate welfare programs.[37] Of those grievances, numbers

2, 3, 4, 5, 8, 9, 10, 11, and 12 are arguably worse today, while neighborhoods are quiescent. Their most cited grievance—police practices—was given the least attention and led to the least reform, while the change in grievance mechanisms (number 6) may be the single best explanation for the lack of riots today.

It is unlikely that extreme deprivation caused the riots. Susan Olzak and her coauthors, in a massive multiple regression of 1,770 racial and ethnic collection action events and 154 race riots in the United States between 1960 and 1993, found little evidence that riots were caused by extreme deprivation. Instead they found that riots occurred where the situations for blacks were improving, where neighborhoods had become less segregated, and where poverty had begun to decline.[38] Riots erupt when life improves for the poor and oppressed, they argue—an equally questionable conclusion.[39]

The conclusions reached by the Kerner Commission were too limited. The riots were triggered not simply by weeks or months of tension-producing incidents but by a long history of violent policing of racial boundaries that had only intensified in the civil rights era. In a prescient study of seventy-five riots that erupted in black neighborhoods between 1913 and 1963, Stanley Lieberson and Arnold Silverman found that in those cities where ghetto residents rioted, blacks had lower rates of unemployment, better jobs, and higher wages and the wage differential between blacks and whites was smaller.[40] Yet it was not the improvements, they insisted, that precipitated the riots. It was police violence. Moreover, in those cities where ghetto riots erupted 1) the police force was white; 2) the local government was white, elected through a system "less sensitive to the demands of the electorate"; and 3) the businesses community was white.

Local government, they pointed out, is "one of the most important institutions to consider in an analysis of race riots. Municipal policies, particularly with respect to police, can greatly influence the chances of a race riot."[41] Riots are "more likely to occur where social institutions function inadequately, or when grievances cannot be resolved, or resolved under the existing institutional arrangements . . . such that a disadvantaged segment is unable to obtain recognition of its interests and concerns through normal political channels."[42] In other words, Lieberson and Silverman's findings coincided with number 1 and number 6 of the Kerner Commission's list of twelve grievances.

In 1970, Harlan Hahn and Joe Feagan reported similar findings in their study of riots in New York and Detroit. With "few exceptions, every major incident of urban violence was triggered by police. . . . it is likely that hostility of Negroes towards white authority has been kindled by abrasive contacts with ghetto police."[43] Similarly, Robert Fogelson found that "with a few exceptions . . . the nineteen sixties riots were all precipitated by police actions."[44] Yet none of these authors produced a full-length book on police riots, or on the interaction between the two; and no one attempted to generalize these findings and apply them to riots outside the United States.

The Kerner Commission findings were clearly overdetermined. Lieberson and Silverman's, Hahn and Feagan's, and Fogelson's findings, on the other hand, were drawn from studies of American cities that had similar characteristics. It was difficult to know if their findings were replicable in a different context. A cursory examination of riots in Great Britain, however, gives some added support to their conclusions. Before I turn to studies of riots in Great Britain, however, I consider a final study of the American riots, one that provides a clue as to why some residents and not others respond to police violence with riotous actions.

In 1968 Edward Ransford conducted a survey of residents of the Los Angeles Watts neighborhood, many of whom had participated in the 1965 riots. All residents surveyed expressed an overwhelming sense of powerlessness born of "extreme discrimination barriers . . . a belief that all channels for social redress are closed."[45] Although black militants shared this sense of political powerlessness, they exhibited a much lower level of individual powerlessness. Melvin Seeman later theorized that the black militants Ransford studied were less likely to riot because activism had enhanced their sense of self-worth: "The militants [were less] likely to be low in powerlessness when this refers to their sense of personal efficacy but high in powerlessness in the sense of being aware of (and fighting against) blocked social control (discrimination and bureaucratic arrangements)."[46] While both Seeman and Ransford stress the importance of personal efficacy in dissuading black militants from participation in riots, there is another explanation: Black activists participated in organizations that both prized disciplined strategic action and offered an alternative repertoire to pursue justice. Participation in successful collective actions increased activists' confidence in their own *collective* capacity and made them less susceptible to the pull of flaming streets.

British Police Studies

Not long after race-related riots declined in the United States, the first major riots erupted in Great Britain. They began innocuously enough when in March 1981, following the "Black People's Day of Action" parade, conflicts between police and predominantly black youths burst forth into small-scale confrontations. At the beginning of April, the metropolitan police initiated Operation Swamp 81, a campaign that included a massive sweep of the black neighborhood Brixton. Over 1,000 men were stopped and frisked in a matter of days. On April 10, police chased a badly bleeding young black man who had passed by them apparently after having been stabbed by a group of boys. When a police officer tried to take the wounded youth to a waiting car (allegedly to get him to a hospital), a crowd gathered to protect the young man. The officer called for police backup. Rumors began to spread that the police had let the youth die in custody, and the crowd began to turn on them. As more backup police arrived, young people pelted them with bricks and bottles. Lootings and then fires followed. In two days 28 buildings and 120 cars were set aflame and 117 stores were damaged and/or looted. Before the riots ended, 65 civilians and 229 police officers were injured.

Then in July riots tore through Handsworth, Birmingham; Southall, London; Toxteth, Liverpool; Moss Side, Manchester; Leeds and Leicester; Halifax in Southampton; Bedford in Gloucester; Wolverhampton and Coventry; and Bristol and Edinburgh. A national commission was formed to look into the cause of the riots. The official report of the commission, known as the Scarman Report after the presiding magistrate, determined that the riots "were not planned but a spontaneous outburst of built-up resentment sparked by particular incidents, . . . a loss of confidence and mistrust in the police and their methods of policing, . . . and racial disadvantage and racial discrimination."[47]

In 1985 a new wave of violent confrontations between black youths and white police officers tore through Brixton, the Handsworth suburb of Birmingham, the West Midland areas of Coventry and Wolverhampton, and then the St. Paul's district of Bristol after a black taxi driver was arrested by a white police officer for a parking ticket. The worst riots occurred in the mostly black Broadwater Farm housing estate in the predominantly white Tottenham district of London. Residents complained that police had occupied the area and harassed, abused, and otherwise treated violently and disrespectfully the area's residents. Police shot rioters with plastic bullets, and the police constable Keith Blakelock was murdered with a machete. Another 20 civilians and 223 police officers were injured.[48] The 1985 riots, like the preceding 1981 riots, had come on the heels of a spectacular rise in repressive drug and street crime policing.

The two waves of riots acted as a catalyst, generating a surge of new research. They also shifted the direction of the field from a highly theoretical academic discipline to a broader policy-oriented one. Most studies, however, continued to focus on the micro-processes and institutional culture of the police, a methodological approach heavily reliant on participant observation. David Waddington, Simon Holdaway, Clive Norris, Nigel and Jane Fielding, Charles Kemp, and Robert Reiner are among the most important British scholars in the field. David Waddington developed a "Flashpoint model" listing six factors that together explained why minor altercations could spiral out of control: 1) structural—poverty, unemployment, relative deprivation, and racial discrimination; 2) political/ideological —a group's political legitimacy, power, and influence or lack thereof; 3) cultural—the rules, norms, and self-definition a group develops and the compatibility of those norms with those of the police and society at large; 4) contextual—history of negative interactions between a minority group and the police, leading to a breakdown in communication; 5) situational— specific spatial and symbolic characteristics of the site of conflict; and 6) interactional—personal miscommunication, signaling, and misreading of particular actions.[49]

Waddington's emphasis on conflicting interpretation of events rather than the events themselves and his insistence that the precipitating event might be quite minor make specificity difficult. Waddington recognizes that structural inequality has a deleterious impact on the relationship between police and racial minorities, but he does not identify the processes or mechanisms that structure inequality along race or ethnic lines, or the ways that police actions are rooted in and perpetuate categorical inequality. Moreover studies have provided scant support for his model. In a study of police stops and seizures, Norris and his coauthors found no evidence to support the claim that black youths behave more disrespectfully toward police than do white youths.[50] Police officers were two and a half times more likely to stop blacks than their presence in the population suggested, even when blacks were significantly *less* likely than whites to show disrespect toward the police. Police stopped whites when they were inebriated, so those stopped behaved less respectfully. They stopped blacks, in contrast, on speculative rather than evidentiary grounds. Blacks were thus far more likely to behave respectfully.[51] Police actions, in other words, had nothing to do with the behavior of blacks. Rather police were biased a priori against blacks, and blacks correctly read the situations at hand.

Racial and ethnic prejudices are embedded in police occupational culture and work, insists Holdaway. Police officers speak in racially derogatory terms even toward their own black and Asian colleagues. Black and Asian officers "must affirm rather than challenge the values of their colleagues. . . . Black officers find a greater measure of acceptance among colleagues when they demonstrate physical prowess when dealing with an offender."[52] Holdaway illustrates the ways in which police work is embedded in systems of inequality and how police work depends on categorical mapping. Yet he pays insufficient attention to broader political processes. As Robert Reiner points out, British researchers became too close to the police they studied. The result was that they ignored "the wider context of social, political and economic change . . . concentrating on funded, short scale projects, examining trees while failing to remark on the forest."[53]

French Studies of Riots and *Banlieues*

The 2005 riots also sparked a wave of theorizing in France. Most explanations fell into one of two categories. One set of work was based on statistical analysis of the correlates of riots. In a broad comparative study of neighborhoods in which riots broke out and those where they did not, for instance, Hugues Lagrange observed that riots erupted where a high percentage of African immigrants, large families, and youths resided. Africans, he claims, were more likely to have larger families (sometimes although not always due to polygamy), and children from large families tended to do poorly in school (lacking basic skills) and were more likely to engage in criminal and delinquent activities and riots.[54]

Fabien Jobard concurs in a series of articles drawn largely from Lagrange's data.[55] Disputing claims made by unnamed American authors, Jobard argues that the French riots were not race riots, like American or British riots, since the rioters did not attack people or stores belonging to other races or ethnic groups (although he admits there were no such stores in the *banlieues*) or claim to speak on behalf of a race. Instead, he argues, in his analysis of the 208 people tried in Bobigny for rioting, that while polygamous families were rare (3 percent of case files),

> [t]he average size of the families to which they belonged was typically very large: the average number of brothers and sisters was actually 4.6, while as many as one-fifth of the relevant families contained seven or more children. A family size of this kind is indicative of the presence of a large number of families from sub-Saharan Africa—a feature of French life highlighted by correlations produced by Lagrange. The geographical locations of the riots, especially in the west of France, are also closely aligned to major settlements of the new sub-Saharan migrants (and, indeed, such locations are characterized by the concentration of large families).[56]

Concentrating their efforts on preventing the riots from spreading, Jobard insists, police in 2005 failed to crack down on rioters, allowing youths to remain "free to continue their activities unhindered in smaller territories surrounded by police forces."[57] In 2005, Jobard argued that there was no evidence that French police were racially biased when they stopped "a given individual or group of individuals regardless of the signs of racism that may be observed here and there."[58] In a later study, however, conducted with René Lévy in collobaration with John Lamberth and Rachel Nield from the Open Society Foundation, they found significant racial disparities in the frequency with which police stopped pedestrians. Researchers recorded police stops at several metro stations outside shopping areas downtown. They found that police stopped Arab youths 7.8 times and black youths 6.0 times more often than they did white youths.[59] Jobard and Lévy were careful to point out, however, that style of dress was a better predictor of being stopped than ethnicity alone. Police responded to the study by insisting that young people coming in from the *banlieues*, dressed in the style of ghetto youth, were more likely to shoplift (although they provided no evidence to support this claim). Since there had been no studies to dispute (or support) the police officers' claims, and Jobard and Lévy had studied only shopping centers, the widely publicized study did not change policy makers' perspectives on police reform. More critically, the study underestimated the degree of racial profiling by failing to record stops in *banlieues*: neighborhoods virtually occupied by police, with few stores or shopping areas.

The second set of studies was based on ethnographic research in the *banlieues*. The work of Didier Lapeyronnie, for instance, demonstrates both the strengths and weaknesses of this methodological approach. On the one hand, through years of work with neighborhood youths, Lapeyronnie discovered that police violence and racial discrimination caused more anger and frustration among *banlieue* youths than poverty or unemployment. In a 2006 article in *Déviance et société* he argues that riots were a form of collective action, sparked by police violence and a perception of conflict between us and them:

> This common negative experience generates an "us" which manifests itself in opposition to the police, indeed permanent conflict with them. The "we" thus negatively constituted by hostility toward the police is not devoid of significance. . . . In activating the "us" and forcing the change of the legitimacy of the imperative frameworks, the incident also renders the revolt both expected and legitimate. . . . The death of young people at the site of police interventions always elicits strong individual and collective emotion and crystallizes the feeling of "us," victims of injustice, in opposition to a "them," an unjust police force.[60]

On the other hand, like many ethnographers, Lapeyronnie reifies space and place, projecting motives and character faults to an entire neighborhood. He exaggerates the isolation of neighborhood residents and describes their lives as if they ended at the neighborhood edge. As such, he narrows his sites on a microcosm of dysfunctional interpersonal relationships, cultures, and behaviors. Much like the works of others who have looked at the "culture of poverty," Lapeyronnie's study is reminiscent of the Chicago school—a view of the city as a "mosaic of little worlds which touch but do not interpenetrate,"[61] where "the primary [source] of social integration and order"[62] is the geographic community and poorly integrated neighborhoods foster an array of bad behaviors. In 2001 Lapeyronnie attributed riots to maladjustment: "Discomfort and self-doubt become a permanent condition and often end in self-destruction. Alcohol, drugs, and narcotics consumption are only the most banal forms. *Riots*, 'rodeos' and excessively risky behavior, and finally excessive TV viewing are all part of such self-destructive behavior" (emphasis mine).[63]

Despite the fact that his 2006 article seems to be a relational analysis of riots as forms of collective action provoked by police violence, Lapeyronnie fails to trace these dynamics either in the conclusion to the article or in his 2008 book.[64] Instead he returns to the same neofunctionalist analysis that dominates his earlier work: residents of the *banlieues* appear to have a singular set of emotional and mental processes.[65] He says,

> Through the emotion that is felt, the individual directly demonstrates his attachment to the "us" and the solidarity which connects him to those who share the same feeling, the same mindset. For a moment, he distances himself from the triviality of his own reality in order to submit himself to a "force" completely outside of himself. Because of the riot, the affirmation of "self" melts into the affirmation of "we." The individual charges himself with an energy which allows him to move to action, a sort of electricity, says Durkheim, an "emotional energy" which is also moral for him since it is strongly linked to the attachment to life or to respect.[66]

But residents of large urban areas do not all know each other or share similar characteristics. The reification of such spaces deflects attention from the real "relationship of controller and controlled," as Robert Sack cogently notes.[67] In contrast to those who see conflicts between police and minorities as the results of dysfunctional pathologies, alternative cultures, and/or the misinterpretations of events, I argue that such conflicts are embedded in the larger structural dynamics of, and resistance to, exploitation and categorical inequality. As Elizabeth Wood so eloquently puts it, "[T]he values, norms, practices, beliefs and collective identity . . . evolved in response to the experience of the conflict itself."[68]

Still, many ethnographers depict the plight of *banlieue* and minority youths with sensitivity and empathy. David Le Poutre, Stéphanie Beaud, Michel Pialoux, Michel Kokoreff, and Christine Bachman describe a host of serious problems that minority youths in *banlieues* confront, including poverty, unemployment, poor housing, discrimination, and humiliating encounters with teachers, police, and other state officials. Kokoreff, for instance, writes of the negative, deleterious role played by the police in the *banlieues*: "The urban police no longer appear as a cause of peace; on the contrary, they arouse fear. The principal tool of the forces of order is

the identity check, which systematically heightens tension instead of reliev-
ing it."[69]

French Studies of Police

Most French specialists on policing articulate an interactive model similar
to that of David Waddington. Sophie Body-Gendrot, for instance, rejects
studies whose subtext is that "large immigrant families concentrated in
public housing estates are, themselves, the source of the problems"[70] and
yet argues that police "are tired of being humiliated, sneered at and physically attacked by disenfranchised youth."[71] Similarly, Roché describes numerous incidents of police abuse but concludes, "In my view, a police
action alone cannot explain a riot. Riots are only the pinnacle of a perennial
conflict between particular groups of young men and police. . . . From one
side to the other, insults fly, blows or more are exchanged, and masculine
intimidation becomes part of the routine. Relationships are particularly
poor with youth of foreign origin. [One study suggests that] youth of North
African immigrant backgrounds see the police as a rival gang, as a racist
force."[72]

Laurent Bonelli, Laurent Mucchielli (at times with Marwan Mohammed
or Abderrahim Ait-Omar), Farhad Khosrokhavar, and Didier Fassin have
been the sharpest critics of both the politics of crime control and police
conduct in poor minority *banlieues*.[73] Bonelli argues that the "culture of
results" encourages police to look for crimes rather than prevent them.
Perpetual identity checks lead to escalating conflict: "Each victory for one
side is a defeat for the other." When a young boy dies during a police
operation or is shot by the police, "the neighbourhood burns."[74] Khosrokhavar points out that Muslim youths are far more likely to be imprisoned
than white French for the same behavior or crime.[75] Marwan Mohammed
and Laurent Mucchielli point out that most riots in France over the past
twenty-five years have been confrontations between *banlieue* youths and
police and that police intrusions and violence rank top place among the
fears and complaints of minority youths.[76] The political elites are largely to
blame. They deliberately foster panic during election campaigns and then
deploy police against *banlieue* youths under the guise of controlling crime.[77]

Didier Fassin's engrossing and elegant ethnography of the French police
stands alone.[78] Fassin challenges the Flashpoint paradigm commonly used

by French scholars. It is not the actions of minority youths that provoke police violence, he contends, but rather the discourse and actions of French political elites, who have deliberately stoked racial fears and encouraged police to act like occupying armies in poor *banlieues*:

> Among the hundreds of such incidents I witnessed, almost the only ones in which the individuals concerned displayed insolence involved youngsters from middle-class or wealthy backgrounds, particularly students who evidently had no experience of this kind of situation and seemed unaware of the potential consequences of their behavior. Yet in none of these cases—which were anyway quite infrequent, since these groups rarely face such procedures—did the officers seek to escalate the tension in order to provoke a scene that could later be set down as insulting and resisting the police.
>
> Conversely, when checks were carried out in the projects or on the streets of the city, young people, mostly of working-class background and non-European origin, almost always kept a low profile, only speaking when they were asked a question, not reacting to the abusive or racist comments and aggressive or humiliating treatment some officers subjected them to, simply presenting their papers and submitting to the body search. Accustomed to and even blasé about these repeated irritations, knowing quite well what would happen if they protested, they appeared to be waiting until the bad moment passed, silent, expressionless, for the only way not to lose face in this confrontation was not to enter into any transaction with the police.[79]

Fassin attributes the 2005 riots and nearly every major urban disturbance from Watts to London over the past fifty years to racial profiling and police aggression in "disadvantaged neighborhoods, usually leading to the death of youth belonging to a racial or ethnic minority group."[80]

Comparative Studies

There are relatively few systematic cross-national and comparative studies of riots. Three of the strongest such approaches are those of Loïc Wacquant, Janet Abu-Lughod, and Michael Katz.[81]

Wacquant's scathing discussion of the link between neoliberalism and mass incarceration and his devastating critique of Chicago school analyses of urban poverty alone make his work worth reading. But his explanation for riots is less convincing. The American riots of the 1960s and the French riots in 2005 were the results of diametrically opposite processes, he insists. American riots were "propelled from outside by the crumbling of the caste system"; French riots were the result of the slow decomposition of working-class neighborhoods from within. The first was caused by "the restructuring of urban capitalism and the policy of social regression of the federal government set against the backdrop of continued ostracization of African Americans," and the second "by the triangular relationship between the state, social classes and the city."[82]

Banlieues, Wacquant claims, are antighettos, places of integration and state intervention. In the United States we have "racial cloistering," whereas in France the comparable pattern is one of "ethnic dispersion and diversity."[83] "Twenty-five years after the great race riots of 1965–1968, African American neighborhoods of New York, Chicago, Philadelphia and Detroit have the look of war zones [while] degraded working-class banlieues, renamed 'sensitive neighborhoods,' have been the target of a concerted renovation plan under the heading of Neighborhood Social Development."[84]

Wacquant's explanation is unsatisfying. First, he does not explain why different processes in divergent societies led to similar outcomes. If the American riots were provoked by improvements in their environment (the crumbling of the caste system), why did French riots erupt when things were getting worse (the decomposition of working-class neighborhoods)? And why did the decomposition of working-class neighborhoods provoke riots only in France and only in neighborhoods where blacks and Arabs were concentrated? The decomposition of working-class neighborhoods was certainly a more global phenomenon. Wacquant fails to offer a systematic explanation.

Second, Wacquant exaggerates the stability, homogeneity, and isolation of black ghettos in American cities, particularly during the 1960s, which is when most riots occurred. Indeed, as Wacquant has observed, American ghettos were not yet "ethnically and socially homogeneous universe[s] characterized by low organizational density."[85] Many, such as Harlem, were characterized by high density and overcrowding. Others, such as the South Bronx and Brooklyn, were working-class areas in the process of decomposition—although admittedly decomposing far more rapidly than the French *banlieues* and spurred by different socioeconomic processes (specifically highway expansion, urban renewal, mass exodus of industry, and white flight). The timing of the new migrants was similarly miserable: black and Puerto Rican migrants arrived just as the last factories were closing and blue-collar jobs were exiting the city. Massive changes to the American city were blamed on the new arrivals, giving grist to politicians who promised to protect white citizens with punitive policing measures, much as French politicians did at the turn of the twenty-first century. Indeed both American ghettos and French *banlieues,* and not, as Wacquant claims, simply the former, were "anchored and aggravated by public politics of urban triage and neglect."[86] And both were only "ethnic" in the "demand that the state, precisely, cease to treat them as such."[87]

Third, Wacquant's admittedly neofunctionalist explanation is devoid of actors. If the 1960s riots in America were, as he claims, "propelled by the crumbling of the caste system," why did blacks and Puerto Ricans abandon the streets before the caste system crumbled? If the real demands of rioting youths in France were "decent jobs, good schools, affordable or improved housing, access to basic public services, and fair treatment by the police and other agents of the state";[88] if anger was directed at police as the last "buffer between them and a society that rejects them";[89] and if the 1992 riots in Los Angeles were "as much about empty bellies and broken hearts as about police batons and Rodney King,"[90] why do American youths so rarely riot now? If the prison, as Wacquant claims elsewhere, was the main medium of social control, why was there a fifteen-year gap between the denouement of the riots and the explosive growth of the prison system? Finally, what explains the willingness of black and Arab youths in France to set their neighborhoods aflame if they lived in a country devoid of racial exploitation and their neighborhoods had been the "target of a concerted renovation plan"?

Janet Abu-Lughod's book *Race, Space and Riots in Chicago, New York and Los Angeles* is a useful point in contrast.[91] Unlike Wacquant, who treats the United States as Chicago writ large, Abu-Lughod contrasts the riots in that city to those in New York and Los Angeles. Of the three, New York had the fewest, briefest, and least damaging riots. Abu-Lughod attributes this to police training and restraint. The heterogeneity, accessibility, organization, and political power of New York's black and Latino neighborhoods were necessary conditions for the development of better policing strategies and better police resident interactions. Where neighborhoods were more segregated, as in Chicago and Los Angeles, police forces were less accountable.

A long history of black grassroots political organizing and a less violent white political establishment explain the smaller and less frequent riots in New York. Abu-Lughod's analysis supports a boundary activation model. Nonetheless there are some flaws in her analysis. First, segregation in large parts of the city, according to most indices, was worse in New York than in either Chicago or Los Angeles in both the 1960s and the 1990s.[92] Integration is not a good explanation for fewer riots in New York. Second, Abu-Lughod uses different explanations for different riots, making it difficult to derive theory from her comparative method. While she explains the riots of the 1960s as unique historical events ignited by the recession and the changing course of the civil rights movement, she attributes the 1992 riot in Los Angeles to the superimposition of race, space, and poverty. Yet Los Angeles was hardly alone. Why did so few American cities follow suit, or in Katz's words, "not burn"? Why did riots instead erupt in Paris in 2005, Manchester in 2011, and Stockholm in 2013?

Despite Abu-Lughod's recognition that police violence sparked riots in five out of her six cases (she blames the assassination of Martin Luther King Jr. for the other), she barely explores the phenomenon. She claims that police training and restraint discouraged riots in New York, and yet police abuse spiraled during the 1990s. These gaps aside, Abu-Lughod's keen insights and attention to the role of racial segregation and police violence in provoking riots, and the mitigating role played by social movement organizations in preventing them, provide a rich avenue for theorizing.

In "Why Aren't U.S. Cities Burning?," "Why Don't American Cities Burn Very Often?," and *Why Don't American Cities Burn?*,[93] Michael Katz addresses the central paradox straight on. Income inequality in the United States, he notes, swung sharply upward after 1973:

The proportion of African American men out of the regular labor force soared. Among twenty-six to thirty-year-old black men, labor force non participation leaped from around 9 percent in 1940 to 30 percent in 2000. . . . The number incarcerated skyrocketed, jumping 82 percent during the 1990s; 49 percent of prisoners compared to 13 percent of the overall population were black. On any given day one of three twenty to twenty-nine-year-old black men was either in jail or on probation, parole or both. Nor did allegations of police violence disappear as, for instance, in reactions to the 1997 brutalizing of Abner Louima while in the custody of New York City police.[94]

One study, he notes, found that "the spatial concentration of the poor rose dramatically in many U.S. metropolitan areas. The number of poor people living in high-poverty areas doubled; the chance that a poor black child resided in a high poverty neighborhood increased from roughly one-in-four to one-in-three; and the physical size of the blighted sections of many central cities increased even more dramatically."[95] Yet riots erupted only in France.

Katz also explains this puzzle by focusing on boundary changes, which he argues, à la Tilly, "strongly affect the likelihood, intensity, scale and form of collective violence."[96] Since Katz is principally interested in why American cities no longer burn, he focuses on boundary deactivation, specifically three far-reaching changes to the structure of race relations in the United States that have deactivated racial boundaries and made riots less likely and less frequent. Katz labels them the ecology of power, the management of marginalization, and the incorporation and control of immigrants.[97]

Boundaries accentuate and cement inequality, Katz observes, by accelerating the accumulation of advantages and resources. When such boundaries are challenged, as they were when blacks migrated north to American cities, violence is often the result: "Between 1950 and 1970 the black population of many cities skyrocketed: in Newark from 17 to 54 percent, in Chicago from 14 to 34 percent, and in Detroit from 16 percent to 44 percent. . . . To preserve existing boundaries whites often turned to violence—a response documented with painful detail by many historians. The point for this discussion is that civil violence erupted at the height of urban boundary challenges, when huge numbers of African Americans had moved in and whites had not yet moved out."[98]

The first change identified by Katz was to the ecology of power in American cities. In the late 1960s, white flight left many cities under the control of mayors representing newly empowered black and Latino majorities. Between 1965 and 1980 the number of black elected officials jumped from 100 to 1,813.[99] Although deindustrialization and cuts in federal spending decimated the power and capacity of these mayors, black opposition movements now often faced black mayors and even black police. "The new ecology of urban power dampen[ed] the potential for civil violence by pairing class and racial segregation with the devolution of control over space to previously marginalized groups."[100]

Second, the management of marginalization (operating through five separate mechanisms—selective incorporation, indirect rule, mimetic reforms, consumption, repression, and surveillance) further derailed mobilization. Many blacks found employment in the public or quasi-public sector, and their selective incorporation into the middle class was fragile and dependent. Mimetic reforms further diverted class action into more manageable arenas. The decentralization of school districts replaced the struggle for community control, election campaigns replaced protest movements, and, as Katz approvingly cites Katznelson, "modest but sufficiently tantalizing distribution [substituted] for redistribution."[101]

The combination of white abandonment, selective incorporation, and mimetic reform allowed powerful white Americans to rule black America through powerless black leaders: real power remained in the hands of the white establishment. "But indirect rule meant that civil violence or other claims on city governance would be directed towards African American elected officials, African American public bureaucracies and African American police."[102] Increasing consumption and blacks' indebtedness further decreased motivation and arenas for political action. Mass incarceration, parole and felony disenfranchisement, and police actions designed to pit black gangs against each other weakened black resistance.

Third, the incorporation of immigrants lessened the risk that blacks might use violence to demand rights: "For the civil violence that rocked Paris and frightens other Europeans is a product of recent immigration, not the grievance and frustrations of historically marginalized citizens. . . . The two events—civil violence in France, peaceful protests in the United States—highlight divergent relations of immigrants to the state and to the economy. America's immigrants sought redress through government. . . . They want nothing so much as the rights of American citizens."[103]

There are, however, several problems with Katz's otherwise compelling analysis. First, new immigrants did not riot in France. Of the more than 4,000 arrested, only 120 were born outside France.[104] Those who rioted were French—black and Arab children and grandchildren of former colonial subjects, and, in the case of Algerians, former Frenchmen. While the French continued to refer to these youths as immigrants, their lives, in fact, paralleled those of blacks and many Latinos in the United States.

Second, the concept of indirect rule does not explain why black and Puerto Rican residents of New York City—a city with a white mayor who barely disguised his contempt for the black community, excluded blacks from his administration, and did nothing to increase minority representation in the overwhelmingly white police force—did not rise up in the 1990s. Even after the brutal slayings of Anthony Baez, Patrick Dorismand, and Amadou Diallo and the torture of Abner Louima the city remained quiet.

Third, repression is not a good explanation for quiescence, since Katz, as well as others, uses it to explain revolts. Finally, and most critically, Katz fails to question some of the most common explanations for the American hot summer or ghetto revolts. Poverty, racism, and unemployment may cause great pain and misery, but human beings are capable of tolerating great injustice in silence. Before we can understand boundary deactivation, we need to reexamine boundary activation—those rare, singular moments when all social interactions revolve around a single us/them boundary. In other words, we need to sort through the smoldering ashes of urban unrest before we can explain the quelling of the fire.

The Argument

In countries with large unaffiliated or detachable segments of the electorate, appeals to racial fears can provide the margin of victory in tight elections. The fear of being labeled soft on crime, immigration, or security encourages a rush to the right as the major political actors engage in competitive outbidding. Political campaigns capture media attention. Sensationalist and racially distorted media stories put additional pressure on political candidates in tight races. As Lewis Dexter observes, a politician "makes the world to which he thinks he is responding."[105] The bellicose rhetoric of the campaign, as Fassin observes, "legitimizes not only the police's views of the situation but also the way they work to impose order."[106] The use of phrases such as "war on crime" or "war on drugs" evokes a military logic and leads to increasingly violent policing in poor minority neighborhoods.

Racially targeted police violence inflicts an ugly wound: it undermines the legitimacy of the state and sends the message that the lives of some of its citizens are not valued. In the absence of strong social movements with a standard nonviolent repertoire or state action (real or potential) on behalf of injured communities, a particularly egregious incident of police violence, such as the killing of an unarmed youth, may incite riots. Most riots begin as nonviolent gatherings and pleas for justice by families, friends, and neighbors of the victims. Police repression of such gatherings encourages others to join the fray. Network ties between residents of an affected area and those who live in places with similar conditions lead to riot diffusion, particularly to areas where affected minorities comprise the majority of residents. Where social movements or other social or revolutionary organizations channel anger and enforce discipline, however, or where alternative avenues of redress exist, riots are rare. The process, then, often proceeds as follows:

1) Voters from the dominant majority find stigmatization and control of racialized minorities politically attractive and credible, especially when political, spatial, or social-economic change threatens established racial boundaries and creates insecurity.

2) Politicians in tight races attempt to appeal to a detachable section of the electorate by playing to racial fears.

3) The political scramble to avoid being outsegued on the crime issue leads major political actors to engage in increasingly harsh law-and-order public discourse.

4) Increased political attention to crime leads to spikes in sensationalist and racially distorted media coverage.

5) Politicians favoring harsh policing measures are elected and pass harsh punitive crime and/or anti-immigrant laws.

6) Police interpret such signals to mean they are immune from prosecution when interacting with members of subjugated groups.

7) There is a dramatic increase in levels of police brutality in stigmatized minority neighborhoods, leading inexorably to a particularly egregious act of violence—usually the killing of a young unarmed minority male.

8) The state is unwilling to hold the police officers accountable or, worse, takes the side of the police officers against the victim.

9) Lacking other options (such as established institutions to address or channel grievances, strong social or community organizations, or a repertoire of successful nonviolent protest), communities explode.

10) As knowledge of or rumors about events spread, riots diffuse to surrounding neighborhoods, then to cities and towns with similar conditions, particularly those where affected minorities constitute the majority of residents. National-level incidents (such as the assassination of Martin Luther King Jr.) and officeholders provoke more rapid riot diffusion than neighborhood-level events or officeholders.

What is key is not the sum of these elements but the way in which they concatenate: the mechanisms that link an incident of police violence to riots or, alternatively, to other forms of contentious politics. This book traces the processes and sequences of interactions and events in two cities with vastly different social and political structures, racial constructions, and political economies. Police use violence against subjugated minorities in both cities, but in one city subjugated minorities, particularly poor minority youths, respond in ways that sometimes culminate in full-fledged riots. In the other, subjugated minorities and victims of police abuse more often engage in conventional forms of individual and collective action, organizing protest marches and civil disobedience; petitioning district attorneys, federal prosecutors, political officeholders, and members of the Department of Justice; and filing civil law suits.

In 1964 riots broke out in New York when a) police violence was ignored and unofficially encouraged; b) mass migration, white flight, urban renewal programs, and highway construction devastated black and Puerto Rican neighborhoods, overwhelming the capacity of black and Puerto Rican organizations to channel anger into sustained nonviolent action; and c) blacks and Latinos were largely denied access to local courts, civilian review boards, or other forms of legal redress. Riots broke out in 2005 in Paris when a) growing police violence against blacks and Arabs was officially ignored and unofficially encouraged; b) the discourse of republican equality did not allow open discussion of racial dynamics, much less the development of civil and social organizations to address these dynamics; c) revolutionary organizations such as the Front de Libération Nationale (National Liberation Front of Algeria, or FLN) had long ceased to exist; d) courts refused to hold police officers accountable for violence used against North and sub-Saharan African immigrants or black and Arab youths, and those who charged police officers with civil offenses were far more likely to be sentenced for rebellion than to win their cases.

The structure of policing shaped the geography of urban unrest. In the United States, the decentralized structure of the police, with each unit under the control of a local mayor, led to a segmented, staggered pattern of riots during the 1960s, which crisscrossed the country for half a decade. Riots erupted most violently in Los Angeles, Detroit, Chicago, Washington, D.C., and Newark, cities where residential patterns were most segregated and police abuse most profuse. By the late 1970s riots had become rare. Still in some cases—most notably Liberty City, Florida, in 1980 and Los Angeles in 1992, where racial boundaries were particularly contentious and where police operated with virtual impunity—they reoccurred. Yet even those extremely damaging riots were isolated geographically, as the federal government intervened to subdue the rioters and hold local police accountable for their actions.

In France, in contrast, the centralized structure of policing produced a different pattern of urban unrest. Since the police were national, it was the national government that determined local reactions. The centralized structure of policing ensured, as Katz observes, that "[a]ntagonism towards the police reinforce[d] the distrust of the national government. . . . [In 2005] their protests, neither planned nor coordinated, reflected frustration, rage, alienation, and a lack of confidence in or access to official political channels. In this they resembled African Americans in the 1960s more than immigrants to the United States late in the twentieth century."[107] When then minister of the interior Nicolas Sarkozy announced on the radio that "his police had done nothing wrong" and threatened to take action against delinquents and hooligans, he provoked rapid riot contagion throughout France within days of his statement.

The logic of inquiry, as Gary Goertz and James Mahoney note, is looking for the "cause of effects" (starting with real events and moving backward).[108] Three elements, I argue, are present in most ghetto riots: activated categorical boundaries; violent transgressions across categorical boundaries by police or other security forces (or vigilantes protected by security forces) usually leading to the death of an unarmed youth (in interethnic riots the violence transgression is committed by members of dominant groups; in opportunistic riots, a pattern of violence against subordinate groups is suddenly disrupted when the repressive capacity of the state precipitously declines); and failure of state officials to hold police or security forces accountable. These three variables combined make riots more likely.

A wider array and combination of variables avert riots. The explanation is asymmetric, as Goertz and Mahoney observe of most explanations in qualitative research: "The causes of failure outcomes are not necessarily equivalent to the absence or negation of the causes of success outcome."[109] American scholars have attributed the decline of riots to a host of factors. On the one hand, the expansion of Great Society programs, the election of blacks to political office, and the integration of police departments are said to have co-opted activists and deactivated racial boundaries. On the other hand, the decline of riots has been attributed to the mass incarceration of black and, to a somewhat lesser degree, Latino males. As Pamela Oliver notes, "The crucial thing to understand is that a repressive strategy initially triggered by massive urban unrest and other social movements was maintained and expanded long after the riots abated. It was not aimed at preventing unrest by repressing riots: it was preventing unrest by repressing potential rioters. People were not arrested and incarcerated for dissent or even for rioting: they were arrested and incarcerated for crimes."[110] Mass incarceration prevented riots, she notes, "by removing people from the system before they commit[ed] the undesired action."[111]

While all of these factors may have reduced the likelihood of riots, none of these explanations answers our puzzle. The first set of factors has deactivated racial boundaries in many cities but does not explain why riots did not erupt in New York during the 1990s despite escalating racial tensions and police violence, when a white mayor, a white administration, and a white police force held sway. Similarly, mass incarceration may have devastated inner-city neighborhoods but cannot account for either the sharp decline in riot frequency since the mid to late 1970s (long before the massive climb in incarceration rates) or the mammoth explosion in 1992 in Los Angeles (when California incarceration rates were substantially higher than the average and New York's were substantially lower). Indeed, California, having one of the higher incarceration rates in the country, is among the most riot-prone states, perhaps due to the devastating impact that mass incarceration has had on activist networks.

Two factors have received far less attention but have transformed the way in which blacks and Latinos in New York, and in much of the rest of the nation, now respond to police homicides. Together they have dramatically reduced the likelihood of riots. First, social movements born in the cauldron of the great race riots of the 1960s now intentionally and unintentionally channel anger into more organized forms of collective action. Social movements provide a standard repertoire of action. Activists who had cut their teeth on the great race riots of the 1960s led black and Puerto Rican power movements in the 1970s and in the 1980s formed networks of community-based organizations on once riot-strewn streets. By the 1990s they were organizing around a host of critical local issues: struggles over control of local school and area policy boards; the creation of joint planning councils; and the availability of low-income housing and community gardens. In addition they organized against racial profiling and police brutality. Gregg Carter claims that the riots stopped because "you can only burn down your neighborhood so many times."[112] Similarly a neighborhood activist on the Lower East Side told me, "If you look at areas like Watts and Newark, they are still rebuilding from the riots that took place then." To a certain extent that is true, but other avenues had to become available. Now when police kill, activists and social movement organizations converge. They give solace to the families and friends, lead mass marches, demand indictments and federal interventions if those fail, and help families file civil suits. Some even sit on civilian review boards.

Second, the passage of significant civil rights laws has opened the courts to black and Latino plaintiffs and made the federal government a potential ally.[113] "Victims of discrimination," note Rogers Smith and Desmond King, increasingly seek "relief in the federal courts."[114] Courtroom battles have replaced street struggles. Demands for individual reparations have replaced demands for social justice. Not-guilty verdicts in criminal trials for homicide are not the end of the road. The Justice Department can try police officers for the violation of victims' civil rights. Families frequently file civil suits. Between 1977 and 1998 only three New York City police officers were convicted for homicide while on duty.[115] Yet during the 1990s New York spent approximately twenty-five million dollars a year to settle police violence cases out of court.[116] Legal proceedings provide a clear course of action and reduce feelings of impotence, and they take years to pursue. At the end of the process (whatever the verdict) the energy of families, communities, and social movement activists has been depleted. As Vincente "Panama" Alba, the director of the Coalition to Fight Police Brutality, told me, "People burn out, get frustrated. The mobilization necessary to do justice in one case is extraordinary. It is difficult to go on and on."

In sum, the civil rights movement and the riots that followed changed the environment for families and friends of those killed by police. On the one hand, wars on drugs and crime have led to the incarceration of two million mostly young black and Latino men and the penal supervision of another seven million. On the other hand, community organizations have developed a standard repertoire for dealing with police violence. Victims and their families now fight police violence through a combination of organized street demonstrations and legal justice. Although homicide convictions of on-duty police officers are exceptional, growing numbers of attorneys specializing in civil actions have convinced many cities to routinely settle police brutality cases out of court. Together these factors have reduced the likelihood of riots, even where white mayors, white administrations, and white police forces hold sway.

The deactivation of racial boundaries has also made riots rare in Marseille, the only city in France that did not burn in 2005. Despite the city's endemic poverty, unemployment, and crime and its large immigrant and Muslim populations, political leaders in Marseille rejected the dominant French republican assimilationist paradigm. They created integrated spaces for deliberation and interaction and recognized and consulted regularly with leaders of ethnic organizations to improve relationships between police and minority youths (largely by letting police develop long-term relationships with neighborhoods rather than shifting them about). This and Marseille's integrated downtown streets and beaches made racial boundaries less polarized than those of Paris, Lyon, or other major cities. But Marseille's political system is riddled with corruption and ties to organized crime. Ironically, even mafias deactivate racial boundaries and make riots less likely, as I explain in Chapter 4, by creating a weblike political structure in place of a bifurcated boundary. They also punish those who engage in undirected violence or strike out on their own. (Organized criminal groups often play a similar role in the United States.)

Defining Riots

This is a study of modern urban riots, what have sometimes been called ghetto riots or urban uprisings. In the modular modern urban riot unruly crowds burn, loot, or otherwise assail stores, public buildings, cars, and/or symbols of state power. They also engage in confrontations with police, usually by throwing garbage or other objects. Some rioters may attack members of dominant groups, but these are usually opportunistic encounters and not central activities. Most participants attack only property. These uprisings include elements of what Charles Tilly has labeled "broken negotiations," "scattered attacks," and "opportunism"—that is, violent reactions to transgressions or violations of unwritten (or written) social pacts or agreements; symbolic and other attacks on property (weapons of the weak); and taking advantage of disorder either to improve one's material standing or to wreak revenge.[117] As in other forms of violence, riots ensue when "actors on at least one side respond by engaging in coordinated attacks on sites across the boundary while those on the other side engage in defense against those attacks."[118] Although property damage in such riots can run high, most deaths result from police killings. In the 1960s, as Thomas Sugrue notes, "Only a handful of cities—notably, Detroit, Newark and Los Angeles—accounted for nearly all the deaths. And, most of the casualties were the result of law enforcement actions against blacks, not black violence against the police or white bystanders."[119]

The term "riot" is also used to describe forms of violence having little resemblance to the typical ghetto riot, other than activated categorical boundaries and violent transgressions across those boundaries. Rampages by dominant groups against stigmatized minorities, commonly called race riots, are closer to pogroms. They are usually either instigated or protected by the police, such as the white riot in 1900 in New York, which was set off after a black man stabbed a white off-duty policeman, and the anti-immigrant riot in Vitry, France, in 1977, instigated by the Communist mayor. Other examples include the smaller anti-immigrant riots in Germany in the 1990s.[120] Similarly, large-scale interethnic riots, with their extremely high death tolls, more closely fit what Charles Tilly has called coordinated destruction.[121] The defining feature of coordinated destruction in addition to activated boundaries is that at least one side employs specialists in violence and includes powerful, well-connected people willing to use lethal violence to acquire or maintain control over valued resources and/or extend their jurisdiction over territory. "The communities are organized only along intra-ethnic lines and the interconnections with other communities are very weak or even nonexistent," Ashutosh Varshney similarly observes, making "ethnic violence . . . quite likely."[122] The most deadly are those between groups with significant size and long-standing grievances, such as those between Hindus and Muslims in Asia. If only one side includes violence specialists, the conflict may become genocide. Donald Horowitz, one of the world's experts on such conflicts, does not believe that ghetto uprisings should be called riots at all, given how dissimilar they are in form and content to these violent conflagrations.[123]

Some ghetto riots include aspects of interethnic riots, as when minority groups attack members of other minority groups or, more uncommonly, members of the dominant majority. Some interethnic conflict between blacks and Koreans in the course of the 1992 Los Angeles riots, for instance, may have been motivated by a Korean grocer's killing of a fifteen-year-old African American girl a year before the riot and the white judge's decision (a week before the Rodney King verdict) to reduce the jury's recommendation for a sixteen-year sentence for manslaughter to a five-month suspended sentence and five-hundred-dollar fine. Yet, even here only two Asians were killed and most rioters attacked property rather than individuals. In most ghetto riots the boundary activated is not interethnic but rather drawn between stigmatized minorities (both blacks and Latinos in the United States and blacks, Arabs, and Berbers in France) and the state. Police, the only specialists in violence, do the bulk of the killings.

Ghetto riots often include elements of opportunism, as disorder opens up possibilities for personal profit.[124] As Tilly observes, individuals "looted when they saw that law enforcement had disappeared and that store owners had lost control over their premises."[125] One woman told an interviewer during the 1965 Watts riot, "Well, you could see all the stuff lying there and all those people going in and out and somebody was going to take it, so I thought I might as well take it for myself."[126] Another, churchgoing woman put it this way: "It dawned on me as I was passing a certain store that I had been paying for my present television for five years and [therefore] the store owed me five televisions. So I got three and I believe the store still owes me two."[127] A self-identified looter in Detroit in 1967 told Nathan Caplan that the blacks were "trying to get the goods from the white folks because the white folks own everything and they [blacks] were just trying to get something so they can own it."[128] Even in opportunistic looting, as Tilly notes, activated racial boundaries divided "the overwhelmingly black looters and fire bombers from the overwhelmingly white fire and police departments."[129]

Opportunity alone rarely leads to riots. Where there is a long-standing pattern of police abuse of stigmatized minorities, however, a sudden decline in the state's repressive capacity may spark riots. As with other forms of collective action, the order and magnitude of threat and opportunity lead to different patterns of mobilization. Robert Curvin and Bruce Porter, for instance, found that the pattern of participation (based on the arrest records) during the 1977 blackout riots (which erupted as the result of the decline in the state's repressive capacity, that is, opportunity) reversed that of the 1960s riots.[130] In the 1960s those arrested during the initial days had no previous arrest record. Only toward the end did those with criminal records comprise the majority of those arrested, indicating a shift to opportunistic looting. In the 1977 riots, in contrast, those arrested during the initial period tended to have criminal records and only toward the end did those without criminal records comprise a significant proportion of those arrested.[131] I will return to the 1977 riots in Chapter 1. Suffice it to say that such sudden and lengthy declines in the state's repressive capacity are extraordinary.

Methodology

This book is based on over fifteen years of intermittent ethnographic and participant observation in New York City and greater Paris. I have tried to answer the following three questions: 1) why police behaved similarly with very different minorities in very different contexts; 2) why riots erupted in Paris and New York half a century and an ocean apart; and 3) why riots did not erupt in New York in the 1990s, when a white mayor held power and wielded it through a nearly all-white police force, or in Marseille in 2005. The methodology is threefold. First, I use a series of paired structured comparisons: 1) between New York in the 1960s and Paris in 2005, when both cities had riots; 2) between Paris in 2005 and New York in the 1990s, when only Paris had riots; and 3) between Paris and Marseille in 2005, when only Paris had riots.

Second, I engage in process tracing working backward from incidents of riots and nonriots respectively, what Goertz and Mahoney have called cause of effect.[132] I use interviews and participant observations to trace the mechanisms that led incidents of police violence to culminate in riots or alternatively other forms of contentious action such as lawsuits, community protests, civilian review board complaints, the formation of new organizations, or political speeches and rallies. As Sidney Tarrow notes, "If we want to know why a particular outcome emerged, we need to understand how it occurred."[133]

Third, I used a combination of participant observation, snowball sampling, and cubist ethnography (so called because it explores a conflict from multiple angles[134]) in three neighborhoods in New York, and six *banlieues* outside Paris. I conducted my first interviews in New York as an Aaron Diamond Fellow at the Hunter College Center on AIDS, Drugs and

Community Health in the mid-1990s. The Parisian research began when I was a Columbia University Fellow at Reid Hall Paris between 2001 and 2002. In New York, I conducted research in Mott Haven, South Bronx, the section of the Lower East Side called Loisaida by Puerto Ricans and Alphabet City by whites, and South Side Williamsburg, and I worked with the following community-based groups: Musica Against Drugs; St. Ann's Corner of Harm Reduction; Lower East Side Harm Reduction; Coalition for a District Alternative (CODA); the Institute for Latin Studies; the Puerto Rican Defense Fund; the Legal Aid Society; the Puerto Rican Committee for Human Rights; Charas, South Side Action Committee in Williamsburg; the Justice Committee (originally a subsection of the National Congress for Puerto Rican Rights); Copwatch and New York Coalition Against Police Brutality and Stolen Lives. I interviewed former radical party militants from the Real Great Society, the Young Lords, the Puerto Rican Socialist Party, and to a lesser extent the Black Panthers and Nation of Islam, most of whom were founders or activists in the community groups mentioned above. In addition to the New York City Police Department (NYPD), I interviewed members of the National Black Police Association, the Police Executive Reform Foundation, and the former police chief of New Haven. In addition, I interviewed mothers and fathers of those killed by police and activists in anti-police-brutality organizations.

In Paris, I conducted research principally in the northern districts of 95 (Val-d'Oise) and 93 (Seine-Saint-Denis). In Val-d'Oise I worked primarily in Garges-lès-Gonesse, Sarcelles, and Villiers-le-Bel. In Seine-Saint-Denis I worked principally in Aubervilliers, Clichy-sous-Bois, and the Cité des Bosquets (housing project) in Montfermeil. I participated with and conducted participant observations with Veto, Movement immigration et banlieue (MIB), and Groupe de travail banlieue and interviewed members of Indigenes de republique; Movement contre les bavures policières; Sortir du colonialism; and Association, Collectif, Liberte, Égalité, Fraternité, Ensemble et Uni (ACLEFEU). From 2001 to 2005 I worked predominantly in Sarcelles, Garges-les-Gonesse, and Aubervilliers. In 2006 I began working in Clichy-sous-Bois, Montfermeil, and Villier-le-Bel. I conducted my first interview with the French police in 2001 and continued to interview police officers until 2011. I also interviewed families and friends of young people killed by police, and I interviewed one local mayor. I have avoided using the names of those I interviewed except where they have organized or spoken out publicly on the issues. In the case of active-duty police officers, I

Table 1. New York City neighborhoods

Racial and ethnic makeup

Neighborhood	% Puerto Rican	% Latino	% African American	% Nonwhite Latino
Mott Haven	50.2	65.4	31.7	2.0
Lower East Side	32.2	45.4	11.1	19.7
Williamsburg	45.2	68.9	13.9	14.1

Source: Christopher Hanson-Sanchez, *Puerto Rican Specific Data: Institute of Puerto Rican Policy Census Through 1990* (New York: Microdata Supplies, 1995).

Poverty and unemployment rates

Neighborhood	Unemployment %	% Puerto Rican unemployment	Poverty %	% Latino poverty	Latino per capita income
Mott Haven	19.3	20.4	52.0	54.1	$14,939
Lower East Side	10.1	16.6	34.7	44.0	$17,967
Williamsburg	15.5	16.8	43.0	46.0	$18,142

Source: Christopher Hanson-Sanchez, *Puerto Rican Specific Data: Institute of Puerto Rican Policy Census Through 1990* (New York: Microdata Supplies, 1995).

Community health indicators per 100,000

Neighborhood	Cumulative AIDS rates, 1992	Hospital substance abuse, 1992	Homicide rate, 1992	Homicides, 1993	Infant mortality rate, 1993
New York City	580.5	6.3	26.6	NA	10.3
Mott Haven	943.0	14.1	76.3	70	12.0
Lower East Side	1,304.5	6.9	11.6	6	8.1
Williamsburg	591.1	9.1	32.8	22	13.0

Source: New York City Health Atlas 1994 (New York: United Hospital Fund, n.d.).

have taken pains to disguise the neighborhoods and other identifying features as well. All of the interviews conducted after 2001 were conducted in French, although bilingual friends sometimes accompanied me and helped interpret. The translations of all interviews and French writings are my own, except where otherwise noted.

The neighborhoods where I conducted field research in New York were predominantly Puerto Rican, but I argue that the experiences of residents

Table 2. Parisian *banlieues*, 2009 statistics

Banlieues	*Clichy-sous-Bois*	*Montfermeil*	*Aubervilliers*	*Sarcelles*	*Garges-lès-Gonesse*	*Villiers-le-Bel*
Miles from Paris	9.8	10.7	4.5	10.1	8.8	10.8
Population	29,962	35,700	74,701	59,421	40,215	27,013
Density per km²	7,585	2,670	12, 968	7,032	7,351	3,700
Unemployment rate (%) for residents between the ages of 15 and 64	22.3	12.7 (21.6 in the housing estate Cité des Bosquets)	21.8	22.5	21.2	17.8
Average yearly income per household in euros	15,314	23,590 (13,506 in Cité des Bosquets)	14,397	16, 844	14, 350	16,045
% *Habitation à loyer modéré* (HLMs, or public housing)	30.0 NA (45.1 percent in Cité des Bosquets)	39.0	50.6	39.9	46.47	

Source: Institute National de la statistique et des etudes économiques (INSEE), at the following Web sites: http://www.insee.fr/fr/bases-de-donnees/esl/comparateur.asp?codgeo = com-95585 #; http://www.insee.fr/fr/bases-de-donnees/esl/comparateur.asp?codgeo = com-95680; http://www.insee.fr/fr/bases-de-donnees/esl/comparateur.asp?codgeo = com-93014; http://www.insee.fr/fr/bases-de-donnees/esl/comparateur.asp?codgeo = com-93001; http://www.insee.fr/fr/bases-de-donnees/esl/comparateur.asp?codgeo = com-95268; http://www.insee.fr/fr/bases-de-donnees/esl/comparateur.asp?codgeo = cv-9315; http://sig.ville.gouv.fr/zone/3159076; http://www.journaldunet.com/management/ville/.

of these neighborhoods is generalizable to residents of other stigmatized minority neighborhoods. First, at the time I conducted field research they were among the poorest neighborhoods in New York. Second, the Puerto Rican experience in New York has been similar to that of African Americans. Both groups have lived in New York City for at least one generation; the largest wave of black and Puerto Rican migrants arrived in the 1950s and early 1960s. Third, and most important for this study, blacks and Puerto Ricans have had similar interactions with police, and most of those killed by the NYPD have been either black or Puerto Rican. As Ramiro Martinez observes,

> Scholars have noted that legal cynicism and dissatisfaction with police are both intertwined with levels of neighborhood disadvantage, an effect that trumps racial differences in attitudes towards the police even after controlling for neighborhood violent crime rates. Moreover, ecological characteristics of policing also include the use of physical and deadly force at the city level, officer misconduct in police precincts and slower response times in communities highlighting research that attitudes towards the policing may be a function of a neighborhood context and even determinants in police killings.[135]

My work thus addresses an important lacuna in research on ethnicity, policing, and riots. As Martinez notes, "The scarcity of research on Latinos and policing is one of the most enduring shortcomings in the development of race/ethnicity and the criminal justice system scholarship."[136]

Moreover the categorical boundaries that New York police use to classify populations locate both blacks and Puerto Ricans on the same side of a racial divide, in diametric opposition to the city's white populations. Police in France do the same with blacks and Arabs. As Tilly observes, "Durable inequality among categories arises because people who control access to value-producing resources solve pressing organizational problems by means of categorical distinctions. For these reasons, inequalities by race, gender, ethnicity class, age, citizenship, educational level and other apparently contradictory principles of differentiation form through similar social processes and are to an important degree organizationally interchangeable."[137]

Organization of the Book

In Chapter 1 I look at the construction of racial boundaries in the United States and the violent policing of those boundaries as large waves of black migrants from the South and Puerto Ricans arrived in New York City. I trace the processes that sparked riots in 1935; in 1943; most significantly in 1964, when conflicts in New York initiated a chain of riots throughout the country; and again in 1967, when predominantly Puerto Rican East Harlem and South Bronx burst into flames. I also introduce the three neighborhoods of Mott Haven, South Bronx; Williamsburg, Brooklyn; and the Lower East Side of Manhattan (the section popularly called Alphabet City by Anglos and Loisaida by Latinos), and I track them from their founding to the macroeconomic restructuring of the late 1950s and early 1960s, the race riots of 1964 and 1967, the radical black and Puerto Rican organizing efforts from 1969 to 1973, and the immensely destructive 1977 blackout riots. I conclude this chapter by discussing the 1989 election of David Dinkins, the first African American mayor of New York, and contrasting the dynamic that led to the 1992 Rodney King riot in Los Angeles with that which prevented a small, but similar riot in the Washington Heights section of Manhattan from exploding into a citywide conflagration the same year.

In Chapter 2 I examine the construction of racial boundaries in France and the policing of those boundaries in Paris from the occupation of Algeria and the creation of a French/Muslim racial boundary through the creation of the "North African brigades" and the violent slaughter of unarmed Algerian protesters in 1961 to violent attacks by dominant groups and police on black and Arab youths. This chapter concludes with the 2002 presidential race and the strong first-round near win of the racist National Front candidate Jean Marie Le Pen.

In Chapter 3 I pose the following question: why, when so many of the worst aspects of 1960s race relations remained in New York City between 1990 and 2001—a white mayor, impoverished and still mostly segregated black and Latino neighborhoods, racially coded law-and-order rhetoric, and violent racially biased policing—did neighborhoods not burn? I begin by analyzing the 1993 mayoral race and the way that campaign activated racial boundaries in New York. I then look at boundary activation from the perspective of the police officers whom I interviewed, including those who worked in the three neighborhoods, those who worked in the city at large, those of minority extraction, and those police officers and chiefs active in

efforts to promote police reform nationally. From there I shift to neighborhood organizing efforts in the 1980s and 1990s, building on interviews I
conducted with black and Puerto Rican activists and residents of Mott
Haven, Williamsburg, and the Lower East Side and with leaders of anti-
police-brutality organizations (many of whom were radical activists in the
early 1970s and continue to live in these three neighborhoods). I conclude
this chapter with the stories of four mothers and one father of young people
killed by police (Nicholas Heyward, Amadou Diallo, Anthony Rosario,
Malcolm Ferguson, and Timur Person) and their efforts to pursue justice
for their children and to prevent others from suffering a similar fate.

In Chapter 4 I trace the processes and mechanisms that led Paris to
burn for three consecutive weeks in November 2005. I use extensive interviews with French police, with the families of boys killed by police, and
with residents of Sarcelles; Garges-lès-Gonesse; Villiers-le-Bel; Aubervilliers,
Clichy-sous-Bois; and Cité des Bosquets, Montfermeil, to explore that dynamic. Lastly, I contrast the situation in Parisian *banlieues* with that in the
impoverished neighborhoods of northern Marseille, where riots did not
erupt.

In the Conclusion I discuss changes in policing politics in New York
and Paris since 2005 and reexamine my main theoretical claims in light of
the evidence of the two cases. Finally, I delve into the implications of this
analysis for understanding more recent riots in Europe and elsewhere.

Chapter 1

Policing Racial Boundaries
and Riots in New York (1920–1993)

The Great Migration, which began in 1916, brought half a million blacks north. The boll weevil had ruined the southern cotton harvest, wiped out white landowners, dried up credit, and forced black sharecroppers and tenant farmers into debt. The simultaneous decline of King Cotton and the advent of World War I freed blacks from coerced farm labor in the South. Puerto Ricans arrived around the same time. In 1917 the Jones Act had made Puerto Ricans U.S. citizens eligible for both the draft and stateside migration to escape rural poverty. New York labor scouts (anxious to fill war-time shortages) scoured the South and Puerto Rico, recruiting and transporting workers north "in consignments running high into the hundreds."[1] The new migrants found housing in the Lower East Side, Central Harlem, San Juan Hill, Hell's Kitchen, and Greenwich Village.

In this chapter I track the history of New York City's black and Puerto Rican neighborhoods, paying particular attention to the construction of ghettos, the policing of racial and spatial boundaries, and the relationship between racial polarization, police violence, and urban unrest in the riots of 1935, 1943, 1964, 1967, 1977, 1991, and 1992. I also introduce three New York City neighborhoods: Mott Haven in the South Bronx; Williamsburg in Brooklyn; and the Lower East Side of Manhattan. I conducted ethnographic field research in these neighborhoods between May 1993 and September 1996. I trace the development of these neighborhoods from the time of the Great Migration to the riots of the late 1960s. This is followed by a look at the radical organizing efforts of the early 1970s, the eruption of riots in 1977 after widespread power outages (called the "blackout riots"), and the decline of radical organizing efforts after 1977. By the

1990s, I argue, radical black and Puerto Rican activists had turned their energies to community organizing around neighborhood needs and against police brutality. Together they knit the frayed fabric of their communities and developed an established repertoire of contention that intentionally and unintentionally made riots less probable.

The Great Depression and Communist Cross-Racial Organizing in New York

Unlike in many cities where brutal mobs drove black residents into undesirable areas on the outskirts, black and Puerto Rican migrants found housing in inner-city New York. Harlem, in particular, was centrally located and a chosen destination for many migrants. In 1900, when blacks made up less than 2 percent of the city's population, white race riots led them to concentrate in Harlem, where they could offer each other protection. Black migrants were attracted to the neighborhood's vibrant artistic and intellectual life. Harlem even elected a black state assemblyman in 1917. Even in Harlem life for blacks was hard, as Langston Hughes observed: "[S]ome Harlemites thought the millennium had come. They thought the race problem had at last been solved. . . . I don't know what made any Negroes think that—except that they were mostly intellectuals doing the thinking. The ordinary Negroes hadn't heard of the Negro Renaissance. And if they had, it hadn't raised their wages any."[2]

Many World War I veterans expected some recognition or compensation for their war-time service. W. E. B. Du Bois had encouraged blacks to enlist, pointing out that black military service in the American Revolution, the War of 1812, the Civil War, and the Spanish-American War had been followed by emancipation, enfranchisement, and increased accumulation of wealth.[3] But those who expected similar improvements after World War I were bitterly disappointed. The period following the war was characterized by "hysterical racism, the acceleration of lynchings, the revival of the clan, and more than twenty major riotous assaults by whites in Northern and border cities who rampaged in black neighborhoods, stoned blacks on beaches and attacked them on main thoroughfares and public transportation."[4] By the mid-1920s Ku Klux Klan membership was said to have reached five million, with more members outside the South than within.

Black and Puerto Rican migrants were ill prepared to weather the ravages of the Great Depression. They were four times as likely to be unemployed or on relief than whites and lived in unheated cold-water flats, often without food, and were vulnerable to vermin and disease. Some were unable to support their families and committed suicide. Others were forced into soup lines and slave markets, where they sold their services to the highest bidder. Some ten to twenty eviction cases a day were reported to the Urban League, and blacks were five times more likely to be left homeless than whites.[5]

The fledgling New York branch of the American Communist Party stepped up organizing efforts in Harlem and East Harlem during this period. They led protests against unemployment and in support of racial justice. They recruited heavily among black, Puerto Rican, and Jewish migrants. As Communists stepped up their cross-race appeals, the NYPD stepped up its attacks on blacks and Puerto Ricans spotted in white neighborhoods, forcibly separating interracial couples (claiming that prostitution was involved) and breaking into interracial meetings.[6] Police violence unintentionally "reinforced black support for party-led organizing efforts" and, communist organizers discovered, could effectively be linked "to the larger racial and class struggle."[7] They increasingly attacked "the NYPD for its violent attempts to sunder the growing unity of black and white workers."[8] The harder Communists worked to build class coalitions across racial lines, the more violently the NYPD enforced those boundaries.

The First Ghetto Riot in New York City

On March 19, 1935, a white police officer arrested a black Puerto Rican boy, Lino Rivera, after the store manager caught him shoplifting a penknife in the Kress store on 125th Street. The police officer took the boy to the basement exit and then released him. A black female customer, seeing the police bring the boy to the basement, began shouting that the police had taken the boy to the basement to beat him, a not-uncommon scenario. Other customers, hearing her scream, began to overturn counters and toss merchandise to the floor. As rumors of a beating circulated, a full-scale street battle ensued. The violence spread throughout Harlem, ending with one dead, sixty-four injured, and seventy-five under arrest.[9]

Although the police blamed the Communist Party for inciting the riot, during the hearings succeeding witnesses told stories of terrible police abuse, including charges of police intimidation of witnesses. They pointed to four brutal cases of police repression in particular, including that of Thomas Aiken, an unemployed man who had been "blinded by blows from a police officer while standing . . . in a Harlem Bread line."[10] In response, Mayor Fiorello LaGuardia formed an eleven-member biracial commission to study conditions in Harlem. In its scathing final report the Mayor's Commission on Conditions in Harlem concluded that "the insecurity of the individual in Harlem against police aggression is one of the most potent causes for the existing hostility to authority. . . . Police aggressions and brutalities more than any other factor weld the people together for mass action."[11]

The commission recommended the creation of a biracial committee of Harlem citizens to hear civilian complaints and act as a liaison with the NYPD, but the police commissioner forced the suppression of the report.[12] He called the hearings "biased and dominated by Communist agitators" and stated that the police "were needed to fight the high crime rate."[13] The police had a good relationship with the black community, he insisted, and "any resentment which does exist is borne by the lawless elements because of the police activity directed against them."[14] Police violence in black and Puerto Rican neighborhoods continued unabated, helping the Communists expand their base in "networks spawned by the riot."[15] This would not be the last time that post-riot networks were the basis for future organizing efforts.

"Residential segregation," Thomas Sugrue notes, was "the linchpin of racial division and separation."[16] In the 1920s nearly every residential development included covenants specifically precluding owners from renting to non-Caucasians. In the 1930s a series of federal housing reforms designed to forestall the wave of foreclosures during the Great Depression increased racial segregation in the city by reinforcing informal real estate practices and court-authorized covenants. The first of these acts created the Home Owners Loan Corporation in 1933 to provide loans to homeowners at risk of foreclosure. The second created the Federal Housing Authority (FHA) in 1934. These two institutions stalled the rate of foreclosures, but defining all but homogeneous white neighborhoods as high-risk investments increased racial and spatial segregation in the city. A single black family was enough to tip the status of a neighborhood from good (marked as A or B and colored green or blue) to "actuarially unsound"[17] (such neighborhoods were marked as C and D and were ineligible for FHA-backed loans). An Association of Real Estate Developers (REALTOR) brochure justified this policy: "The prospective buyer might be a bootlegger who would cause considerable annoyance to his neighbors, a madam who had a number of call girls on the string, a gangster who wants a screen for his activities by living in a better neighborhood or a colored man of means who was giving his children a college education and thought they were entitled to live among whites."[18]

The 1937 Wagner-Seagull Housing Act and the 1945 Veterans Administration Act would exacerbate these effects by underwriting mortgages only in stable (homogeneous) white neighborhoods. Other federal legislation aggravated the problem by giving local governments the authority to determine where public housing projects were to be located and who could live in each building. Public housing projects reserved for blacks and Puerto Ricans were almost always located in the least desirable locations. Slum-clearance programs intensified racial segregation, tearing down tenements and forcing blacks and Puerto Ricans into public projects in areas of concentrated poverty and unemployment and excluding racial minorities from access to housing in white districts. These acts will be discussed later, but from the beginning segregation encouraged rent gouging, reduced the availability of low-income housing, and created ghetto areas of concentrated poverty. In addition it encouraged racial profiling and police violence by allowing police to treat the residents of some neighborhoods differently from those of another and to situate blacks and Puerto Ricans spatially apart from whites.

As African Americans fled Manhattan in search of better or cheaper housing in Brooklyn, white residents there, as Thomas Kessner observes, "lobbied Mayor LaGuardia for greater police protection and even threatened to lead a vigilante movement against the criminals in the neighborhood in 1936. White demands for increased law enforcement encouraged a more aggressive style of policing that led to numerous complaints by black citizens."[19]

World War II and the Erection of Ghetto Walls in New York

World War II and industrial labor shortages attracted a new wave of migrants to northern cities. While only 11 percent of eligible black males had fought in World War I, fully 70 percent of them, or 1.15 million, fought in World War II, the same percentage as that of whites (the number of Puerto Ricans who fought was not recorded). Sam, a black activist and former Communist and Black Panther, told me that his father had been proud to serve: "[H]e went to war and the army gave him education, travel—he saw the world—and some rank. Like many black men he continued to espouse [that] equality on the battlefield would lead to equal citizenship." However, the army remained segregated.[20] Katznelson notes,

> In the midst of a war defined in a large measure as an epochal battle between liberal democracy and Nazi and Fascist totalitarianism, one that distinguished between people on the basis of blood and race, the U.S. military was not only engaged in sorting Americans by race but in *policing the boundary separating white from black* . . . . [T]he draft selected individuals to fill quotas to meet the test of a racially proportionate military and . . . they were assigned to units on the basis of a simple dual racial system. . . . The issue of classification proved particularly vexing in Puerto Rico where the population was so varied racially and where the country's National Guard units had been integrated [emphasis mine].[21]

The black population of New York increased from 458,000 in 1940 to 547,000 in 1945 alone. As the nonwhite population grew, the city's major newspaper chains, including the *Times,* the *Daily News,* the *World Telegram,* and all the Hearst papers, capitalized on white racial fears, publishing a series of sensational front-page stories accusing blacks and Puerto Ricans of "stabbing, raping, and mugging whites in Harlem and other black neighborhoods."[22] The term "mugging," as Marilyn Johnson notes, "originated in New York, nearly always with reference to black-on-white crime. The press campaign peaked in the spring of 1943 when a so-called mugging outbreak prompted police to pull a thousand officers from clerical duty and assign them to plainclothes details in Harlem and Bedford-Stuyvesant."[23] Increased racially inflammatory media and renewed calls for law enforcement led to a massive increase in both vigilante and police violence targeted at both blacks and Puerto Ricans. The Harlem Charter denounced the crime smears to no avail. Adam Clayton Powell Sr. decried the increase in police violence, which he claimed epitomized the brutality of racial discrimination and led to anger "at every white policeman throughout the United

States who had constantly beaten, wounded and often killed colored men and women without provocation."[24] Other local black leaders compared white police to Hitler's Gestapo.

The Second 1943 Ghetto Riot

On August 1, 1943, a New York City policeman hit an African American woman while arresting her for disturbing the peace at the Braddock hotel (one of several black hotels targeted by the NYPD in its antivice campaign). Robert Bandy, a black active-duty soldier in the U.S. Army, jumped to her defense, trying to shield her from the officer's blows, and the officer turned on the soldier and shot him. As the soldier was carried on a stretcher to an ambulance, an onlooker shouted out that the police officer had shot a black soldier, and Harlem residents took action. They threw "bricks and bottles, overturning cars, fighting with police, smashing windows and looting stores."[25] The riot lasted twenty-four hours and resulted in 6 deaths, 185 injuries, and over $250,000 in property damage. The National Association for the Advancement of Colored People (NAACP) called the riot the result of "the fury shown of repeated unchecked, unpunished and often unreported shooting, maiming, and insulting [of] Negro troops."[26]

Mayor LaGuardia immediately sent black military police (MPs) into Harlem and deputized more than 1,000 black MPs to help patrol the streets, which significantly reduced casualties, particularly in comparison to those resulting from the riots that broke out in Detroit the same year.[27] As a direct result of the riots, blacks' representation in the police force of New York City was increased. In 1943 the NYPD had only 155 black police officers in a force of 600,000. This was only 22 more than it had in 1938. Moreover the number of black detectives had fallen from 10 to 5 during the same period. Now with the 1943 riots as an impetus, the city increased the number of black police from 155 to 600, but this was still a tiny fragment of the total in a city that grew increasingly black and Latino. It should also be noted that black policemen were not given any positions of power or decision-making. "For the most part, the NYPD viewed black police as 'riot insurance'—a political concession to angry black communities which would hopefully help prevent and/or control future outbreaks of racial violence, just as the black deputies had done during the 1943 riot."[28]

Little was done to address the more serious issue of police violence. Marilyn Johnson notes, "The false rumors of Bandy's death also echoed those surrounding the Lino Rivera incident that sparked the 1935 Harlem Riots. In both versions an innocent black youth [in the first a black Puerto Rican youth] was killed by a repressive white policy system designed to protect whites or white business interests in Harlem. The symbolic significance of the victims, then, was key to the unleashing of violence."[29] Both the 1935 and 1943 riots predated other ghetto riots and prefigured the revolts that would erupt throughout the country in the late 1960s.[30]

Blacks and Puerto Rican Ghettos in Postwar New York

Between 1950 and 1970, 1.5 million blacks, or 1 in 7, left the South. As a result the black population of every northern city ballooned. It rose from 17 percent to 54 percent in Newark, from 14 percent to 34 percent in Chicago, and from 16 percent to 44 percent in Detroit. Migrants who had once moved from South Carolina to North Carolina or from North Carolina to Virginia now went to New York,[31] while those from Texas and Louisiana traveled to Chicago or Los Angeles. Puerto Ricans fled desperate poverty and political repression on the island and also began to arrive in New York City in massive numbers. Forty thousand arrived in 1946; 58,000 arrived in 1952; and 75,000 arrived in 1953. As one Puerto Rican activist described his family's experience in New York (1966): "[W]e arrived into a very different environment from the one we had left; we arrived onto streets without nature, into cold apartments and factories when we had been accustomed to tropical heat. Many died of TB and other illnesses caused by the cold."

The design of most of the programs providing benefits to World War II veterans deliberately limited access for blacks and Puerto Ricans. The occupations in which African Americans and Puerto Ricans worked were excluded from labor regulations and minimum wage laws, and this combined with deliberately "racist patterns of administration [meant that] New Deal policies for Social Security, social welfare, and labor market programs restricted black prospects while providing positive economic reinforcements for the great majority of white citizens."[32] The GI Bill gave veterans access to federally guaranteed low-interest housing and student loans as well as job training and assistance in securing jobs in their fields, but few blacks could take advantage of these programs. The overwhelming majority of white colleges and universities excluded blacks from admissions, and black colleges and universities were few and starved for resources. Local job counselors without exception were white and often denied blacks access to skilled employment and training. Even in the North the United States Employment Service (USES), charged with administering the program, channeled black veterans into traditional black jobs, reinforcing "the existing division of labor by race."[33] Katznelson notes, "Because unemployment insurance was made available only to those who could demonstrate a willingness to take a suitable job, and because suitability was defined by USES, many blacks were compelled to take work far below their skill level. Carpenters became janitors; truck drivers became dishwashers; communications repair experts, porters."[34] Sixty-five percent of African Americans nationally were ineligible for Social Security.[35]

The Veterans Administration's loan guarantees of the Serviceman's Readjustment Act of 1944 and the 1949 Housing Act[36] constructed formidable obstacles to integration: underwriting mortgages in white suburban areas, bankrolling white suburbanization through discriminatory housing subsidies, equating racial segregation with neighborhood stability, and requiring developers to sign covenants against black home buyers as a precondition for financing. "The completeness of racial segregation," observes Sugrue, "made ghettoisation seem an inevitable, natural consequence of profound racial difference."[37] This was largely because "*[t]he barriers that kept blacks confined to racially isolated deteriorating inner city neighborhoods were largely invisible to whites*" (emphasis mine).[38]

Blacks and Puerto Ricans arrived just as the city shed working-class jobs. Between 1947 and 1976 five hundred thousand factory jobs were lost as industries left the city.[39] However, deindustrialization is only half the story. Comparing the experiences of poor semiskilled white southerners to those of poor semiskilled southern blacks, Katz observes, reveals the extent and impact of racial discrimination: white southerners also "encountered hostility and some discrimination, but never on a scale that matched the racial discrimination and violence that confronted African Americans. White southerners melded into the urban fabric, living where they wanted, sometimes being given jobs over African Americans with more work experience."[40]

"Racism closed the most promising doors," notes Katz. "Exploitative work, bad pay, racism, and foreclosed opportunities amounted to a formula for poverty."[41] These factors also increased the susceptibility of African Americans and Puerto Ricans to the heroin trade. Heroin dealing offered one of the few employment opportunities available to black and Puerto Rican youths. Concentrated poverty, hopelessness, despair, and sheer boredom made it hard to resist the lure of the drug. By the late 1940s, 15 percent of the census tracks in New York City, home to 30 percent of the city's youths, housed over 80 percent of its heroin users.[42] Adolescents living near drug-selling locations were two to three times as likely to use drugs.[43] The growth of the heroin trade and the new federal and state laws with their heavy penalties for drug use gave police one more justification for combing ghetto streets and assaulting black and Puerto Rican residents. Violent clashes between white police officers and young black and Puerto Rican men "accounted for a large percentage of interracial homicides."[44]

In 1961 the *Pittsburgh Courier* called New York City a Jim Crow town "when police arrested and beat Guinea's Deputy Ambassador to the United Nations after a routine traffic stop."[45] That same year police officers brutalized a prominent designing engineer who had recently been featured in a magazine article on the Emancipation Proclamation. He was attacked first in the street and then again in the station by the same officers when he attempted to file a complaint. The *Amsterdam News* covered the story in chilling detail: "We'll give you something to complain about," the identical four officers promised in the police station, "before taking him to the basement, beating him and charging him with resisting arrest."[46]

In addition to police violence, the new migrants were forced to deal with white youth gangs. As the black and Puerto Rican population grew, so did white resistance. "To preserve existing boundaries," Katz notes, "whites often turned to violence—a response documented with painful detail by many historians. . . . Civil violence erupted at the height of urban boundary challenges."[47] Eusebio Soto remembered Italian gangs attacking Puerto Rican youths in Williamsburg, Brooklyn, and the violent spiral that led to the growth of Puerto Rican gangs (1996):

> When I was 10 or 11 years old you see these gangs, man, drunk, coming down the street and hitting everyone. . . . all of a sudden [Puerto Rican] gangs come up . . . not gangs to hurt people, to protect the area, because you have gangs from up there Bushwick coming down, hitting everyone they saw. . . .

We knew nothing about gangs. They resented the idea that we were moving in. So, they sought control over whatever we did and they went into our neighborhood and we didn't even speak English. For us to see these guys come through and start beating on us for no reason at all, I say why do these people hate me, what for? And, I had to learn how to fight because I was Puerto Rican. It's not because of anything else. I had to learn how to fight to defend the idea that I was Puerto Rican. And we fought. It was war. We all had to fight to get our respect and we got respected. We got it. People would say, "Those crazy Puerto Ricans, they'll cut you. We would, ya know, ya had to do that—it wasn't that we came here looking for trouble. We didn't come from Puerto Rico in gangs. This was something that was introduced to us here. We didn't know nothing about gangs—it was purely defensive action.

Some whites embraced law-and-order candidates who promised more policing of black and Puerto Rican ghettos. Others took advantage of low-interest federally insured GI loans (which allowed them to buy suburban homes) and the massive expanse of highways (which simultaneously destroyed their neighborhoods in the Bronx and Brooklyn and made commuting possible) to flee the city. Blacks and Puerto Ricans were locked out of these mortgages and suburban communities. New York landlords "cut down on maintenance, rented to welfare and problem families, induced tenant turnover, failed to pay taxes and then either walked away or sold the building to the city for another round of slum clearance."[48] The Bronx had been a desirable location for working-class Jews, Irish, and Italians in the 1940s. By the time blacks and Puerto Ricans arrived, bulldozers had already razed the tight-knit neighborhoods to make way for highways and public housing towers. The destruction of the elevated train removed the last low-cost transit to downtown jobs.[49]

Policing the Heroin Trade

In the 1950s Italian and Jewish mobsters controlled the heroin trade. Blacks and Puerto Ricans found employment at the lowest rungs, the most poorly paying and riskiest end of the business. By the mid-1960s two organizations controlled heroin wholesales in the city: the Lucchese crime family and the

NYPD.[50] In one decade the special investigative unit of the NYPD put 180 million kilos or $32 million worth of heroin on the streets.[51] The Federal Bureau of Narcotics (FBN) was no better. The bureau already had an illustrious history, as the son-in-law of the FBN bureau chief helped heroin importer Arnold Rothstein evade income tax in the 1920s. Now in the 1960s FBN agents sold the names of informants to the major crime families, with the result that fifty to sixty informants a month were murdered.[52] According to an internal affairs report filed in 1968, one-fifth of FBN officers were involved in the trade. According to Eric Schneider, "The conclusion is inescapable, that the flow of heroin into users' veins would have been impossible without the assistance of the city's police forces and the New York offices of the FBN."[53]

The sheer duplicity of the NYPD in arresting and harassing poor users and street sellers while profiting from the wholesale distribution of heroin in their neighborhoods increased the frustration, helplessness, and anger of ghetto youths. Corruption and venality went hand in hand, as young people were shot in the back by drunken on-duty officers or pummeled in patrol cars and precinct houses. According to Schneider, "'You get a cop [who] wants to know something' said one youth explaining the use of the third degree 'maybe some information from a guy and they smack you around so you can find out.' Other times police picked a youth up and drove him around the neighborhood beating him in the back of the car without ever taking him to the precinct. Order and safety depended on self-reliance, on one's reputation for toughness, and on connections to others who might exact revenge on one's behalf, and not on the system of police and courts."[54]

One Puerto Rican former gang leader in the Bronx told me (March 1996) how police brutality had shaped his racial identity and feeling about the law: "Most families were into thinking the right way was the white way. My family had me comb my hair with coconut milk to straighten it. They listed me as white on my birth certificate. Then, I saw my father, who was always king in my house, tremble in front of a white policeman. It robbed him of his dignity. I lost respect for my father. I compensated for him by becoming more bold and more bad."

Escalating Police Violence in Black and Puerto Rican Ghettos

By 1963 residents of black northern ghettos were on edge. "Complaints about the police reached crisis proportions," notes Sugrue; "[m]uch to the surprise of members of the U.S. Commission on Civil Rights, which conducted hearings in northern cities between 1959 and 1961, black complaints about police conduct were as frequent as or more than those about unemployment, housing and education."[55] Each incident of police violence added to racial tensions. On November 17, 1963, six hundred Puerto Ricans protested in front of a police station after a New York City police officer shot and killed two Puerto Rican youths. Leaders of the National Association for Puerto Rican Civil Rights charged the police with acting "like they were running a plantation."[56]

The situation grew increasingly dire in 1964, and by summer civil rights groups had put police brutality front and center. Yet despite ongoing protests and efforts by community groups to push the city to investigate incidents of police brutality or create a civilian review board, neither Mayor Wagner nor the city council budged. Daniel Monti observes that continued rebukes "spurred the NAACP, CORE, Puerto Rican Committee for Civil Rights and Workers Defense League to set up their own civilian review board in May of 1964. Relations between police and minority citizens had deteriorated to such an extent that any significant incident could have led to a serious outburst."[57]

On April 17, 1964, six boys were playing and pushing each other on the way home from school when one knocked over a fruit stand owned by Edward De Luca on the corner of 128th Street and Lenox. When a crate of grapefruit fell on the ground, the boys began playing ball with the fruit. De Luca blew a whistle to frighten the boys, but the local police heard the whistle and came charging after the boys with weapons drawn. Some had them aimed at the roofs, frightening residents, who withdrew from the windows. As the police caught the boys, they began beating them and then turned on two adult residents who tried to defend the children. The men were Frank Safford, a thirty-one-year-old black salesman, and Fecundo Acion, a forty-seven-year-old Puerto Rican man, both of whom the police cuffed, beat in the street, and continued beating in the precinct.

Safford told James Baldwin that about thirty-five officers beat him while in custody: they "came into the room and started beating, punching us in the jaw, in the stomach, in the chest, beating us with a padded club. They beat us across the head bad, pulls us on the floor, spit on us, call us niggers, dogs, animals when I don't see why we are the animals the way they are beating us. Like they beat the other kids and the elderly fellow [Fecundo Acion]. They throw him almost through one of the radiators. I thought he was dead over there."[58] Another witness told Baldwin, "Now here come an old man walking out a stoop and asked the cop 'say, listen sir, what's going on here?' The cop turned around and smash him a couple of times in the head. He get that just for a question. No reason at all. Just for a question."[59] No one was charged with a crime, but Safford lost an eye as a result of the beatings.

Several days later a white couple who owned a secondhand store in Harlem was attacked and stabbed several times. The woman died from her injuries. Within hours four of the six boys the police had identified at the fruit-stand "riot" were picked up and accused of the murder. The railroading of the Harlem six had a profound influence on James Baldwin, who wrote of the event in a scathing piece for the *Nation*. "This is why," Baldwin notes, "those pious calls to 'respect the law,' always to be heard from prominent citizens each time the ghetto explodes, are so obscene. . . . They are dying there like flies: they are dying in the streets of all our Harlems far more hideously than flies. . . . Well they don't need us for work no more. Where are they building the gas ovens?"[60] In a later article Baldwin reflects, "The only way to police a ghetto is oppressive. None of the Police Commissioner's men, even with the best will in the world, have any way of understanding the lives led by the people: they swagger about in twos and threes patrolling. Their very presence is an insult, and it would be, even if they spent their entire day feeding gum drops to children."[61]

The First Ghetto Riot of the 1960s

On July 16, 1964, Officer Thomas Gilligan shot and killed fifteen-year-old James Powell outside a schoolyard. The shooting followed an altercation between several black high school students and the white janitor of a neighboring building (as discussed in the Introduction). When the janitor turned his garden hose on the students, in a manner reminiscent of police attacks on protesters in Mississippi, as well as a barrage of racial insults, the youths responded in anger. The janitor retreated to his building with several boys on his heels. It was then that Officer Gilligan appeared. Gilligan saw the retreating janitor, turned, and shot James Powell dead. The high school students screamed in pain and outrage. In the evening hundreds of residents gathered at the police precinct, where they encountered a solid wall of police. The officers charged the protesters, and the crowd responded with rocks and bottles. The police then attempted to rope off Harlem from 125th Street and Third Avenue to Eighth Avenue, but residents resisted by hurling garbage, stones, and anything else they could find at police. Some residents began to overturn cars and set buildings aflame. Police opened fire with live ammunition. By nightfall mass looting had ensued, and riots spread from Central and East Harlem and to the Brooklyn neighborhoods of Bedford-Stuyvesant and Brownsville.

The next day civil rights groups led marches demanding that the city investigate and take action against the police department. When those efforts came to naught, the protests moved, as Sugrue notes:

> from peaceful picketing to violent retaliation. On July 16 hundreds of "screaming youths" pelted police officers with bottles and cans in Manhattan's Yorkville neighborhood. The following day two hundred teenagers took to the streets of Harlem looting, burning, and attacking police officers. Over the next week, roving bands of youths and police clashed throughout the city. The uprising followed a pattern that would become commonplace during the mid-1960s—beginning with a police incident and ending with angry crowds in the streets.[62]

The protests continued for five days and nights.[63] Over five hundred people were seriously injured and (as described in the Introduction) one black man was shot dead by police. Activated racial boundaries, increasing police violence, and the police killing of a young unarmed youth were key ingredients. However, the first response to police violence was nonviolent. Only when the police responded to the nonviolent assembly with violence did the NAACP and CORE lose control of the crowds. As one journalist warned, "[I]t is not possible for even the most responsible Negro leaders to control the Negro masses once pent up anger and total despair are unleashed by a thoughtless or brutal act."[64]

The riots were an expression of rage, a refusal to remain cowed in the face of police violence, and a defensive response to the violent policing of racial boundaries. A white man whom I interviewed told me that two black adolescent boys, whom he often hired to help him with yard work, had pelted him with stones during the riot. After the riot the two boys came by the house again to ask for work. "You just pelted me with stones," the man said. "We didn't throw stones at you," they responded. "Of course you did.

I saw you and you were looking right at me," he retorted. "No," they said, "we weren't throwing them at you; we were throwing stones at 'the man.'" In contrast, a black man I spoke with told me it was one of the happiest moments in his life (2009). "The most peaceful I ever felt was in the middle of the riot. None of the damn rules applied. You were absolutely free from the law."

In the aftermath of the riots, Mayor Wagner finally promised to investigate the shooting of Powell and others and to create a civilian review board. Yet again he did neither. By 1965 complaints of brutality had become more numerous than before.[65] Bertrand Russell stated, "[Harlem's] inhabitants are brutalized at every moment of their lives by police, poverty and indignities."[66] A journalist observed that Harlem had "rioted five times since 1935. *Each time an incident with police lit the fuse, the police representing the face of the enemy, of economic and social repression*" (emphasis mine).[67]

The Harlem riot initiated a wave of riots that would spread first to cities connected to Harlem through family and friendship ties, and subject to similar levels of police violence and brutality, and then to distant cities throughout the country. Nestled within the national wave of riots were smaller incidents of riots diffused through towns geographically connected to the major city riots.[68] Riots first spread from New York to the nearby towns of Nyack in Rockland County, New York, and to Montclair, Patterson, Jersey City, Rahway, Livingston, East Orange, and Irvington in New Jersey—towns with a similar history of police violence. Then Rochester residents reacted following police repression of a peaceful demonstration outside a Kodak plant. Philadelphians followed with "three days of disorder after the arrest of a [black] driver and rumors that police had killed a pregnant woman."[69] Riots in six other cities exploded in 1964 and more followed in 1965, including one in the Watts neighborhood of Los Angeles, where thirty-four people died, thirty-one of them black and shot by police.[70]

In 1966 new riots broke out in East New York, Brooklyn. They also broke out in Omaha, Baltimore, San Francisco, Jacksonville, and most fiercely in Cleveland and Chicago. "Nineteen sixty-seven was the most combustible with 163 uprisings, capped by deadly clashes between black residents of Newark and Detroit and the police, the National Guard and the U.S. Army. In Newark, thirty-four people died in a weeklong uprising that laid waste to large parts of the city's central ward; in Detroit, forty-three people died in a weeklong uprising, three quarters of them rioters."[71]

The year 1967 was the year of Latino riots—Puerto Ricans rioted in East Harlem, the South Bronx, and Chicago, Chicanos rioted in California and the Southwest.[72]

The 1967 Puerto Rican Riots
in East Harlem and South Bronx

As the decade progressed things grew steadily worse for Puerto Ricans in New York City. In the 1960s the city built inexpensive co-ops on the outskirts of the Bronx, which allowed working-class whites who could not afford to buy their own homes to buy apartments in these complexes. Few Blacks and Puerto Ricans could afford to buy co-ops. The construction of Co-op City in the northeastern Bronx, in particular, encouraged a mass exodus. Better-off whites fled to the suburbs, working-class whites moved to the northeastern Bronx co-ops. As the value of housing in the South Bronx declined, owners burned "their buildings once they had been milked of profitability and stripped of assets."[73] Those who remained behind were left bereft.

The sheer extent of demographic change would have overwhelmed even the most effective social movement organizations, but those that had played key roles in the 1930s and early 1940s had been decimated by the actions of the House Un-American Activities Committee (HUAC) and Senator Joseph McCarthy. As Roberto P. Rodriguez-Morazzani notes, "The virtual outlawing of the Communist Party USA, with the passage of the McCarran Act in 1950 and the decline of the American Labor Party, closed off two important avenues for radicalism amongst Puerto Ricans in the United States. Moreover, mainstream politics was not generally open to Puerto Ricans. Neither the Democratic nor Republican parties were very much interested in having Puerto Ricans participate in the political process. In fact, exclusion from the political process was the experience of Puerto Ricans."[74]

In 1967 the first major Puerto Rican riots broke out in New York City. They began after a police officer shot a Puerto Rican man he accused of wielding a knife. "For three nights, residents of East Harlem and the South Bronx attacked stores, looting and burning them. More than a thousand police, including many Tactical Patrol Force officers[,] were sent to contain the disorder but, according to news reports, this 'only aggravated community resentment.'"[75] Once again the presence of the police, and particularly the new Tactical Patrol Force, prompted black and Latino radicals to equate the police with an occupying army.[76]

The precipitating incident occurred at noon. At 1:35 P.M. the police barricaded the block. At 8:30 the first bottles crashed over the crowd. Looting started around 10:00. At midnight one group of Puerto Ricans carrying a Puerto Rican flag tried to march to the 103rd Street precinct but was blocked by police. Others tried marching to city hall and were also blocked. The police grabbed one youth carrying a Puerto Rican flag. They grabbed another they claimed had thrown a Molotov cocktail.[77] In Mott Haven, South Bronx, "throngs of Puerto Ricans ran through the streets and broke some windows."[78] Shortly after midnight, police herded a crowd into a housing project in East Harlem, and as the hostages tried to break free, the police charged at them with clubs. The police came under sniper fire on 112th Street between Second and Third, some papers reported, and a Puerto Rican youth's neck was broken after the cease-fire. At Third and 110th Street someone drew a chalk line and scrawled "Puerto Rican border. Do not cross, flatfoot." Media sources warned that some blacks from Harlem were also seen in the area (though it is difficult to know how they made that identification). More than one hundred residents offered to go with the police in an attempt to cool the crowds, and several Latino leaders spoke to the crowds and urged them to remain calm.

Desperate to avoid further conflagration, city officials reached out to Puerto Rican and community leaders. Forty East Harlem residents met with the police inspector and hammered out the following: 1) the appointment of a Puerto Rican as a deputy police commissioner for community relations; 2) the appointment of one or two Puerto Rican professors at the police academy to educate police to the problems of the Puerto Rican community; 3) the appointment of a Puerto Rican precinct captain in East Harlem; 4) a departmental investigation of racial bigotry among the police.

The Great Society and Black and Puerto Rican Power: 1969–1973

The Presidential Commission on Civil Disorders (popularly called the Kerner Commission) concluded its investigation into the cause of the pre-1967 race riots by warning of the ramifications of ongoing police violence:

"To many Negroes police have come to symbolize white power, white racism, and white repression."[79] Similarly a New York City journalist noted that "neither New York nor any [other] American city is normal as long as thousands of black people are penned in, developing the prisoner's mentality of hate for his keepers."[80] Yet in the South where police violence was even more brazen, riots were rare. Strong social movement organizations channeled anger into established repertoires of nonviolent action. Only after the assassination of Martin Luther King Jr., the leader of the nonviolent movement, did riots erupt in southern cities.

In the years that followed the great race riots intense organizing efforts by both the left and the right changed the complexion of northern and western cities and the way black and Latino residents would respond to police violence in the future. Conservative groups used racial fears to win over a newly detachable sector of the electorate and gain ascendency in the Republican Party to challenge the bipartisan consensus that had existed since the New Deal. As Joe Soss and his coauthors note,

> Racial conservatives, galvanized by the civil rights victories, began to pursue a "law and order" campaign that identified social protest, civil disobedience, urban riots, street crime, and deviant behaviors in poor neighborhoods as related parts of a single problem: the breakdown of social order. Together, these groups formed a powerful coalition, pushing an agenda rooted in order, discipline, personal responsibility, and a moral state. As conservative and business interests mobilized, they sought more than immediate policy victories. Adopting a longer view, they invested in efforts to transform the intellectual and organizational landscape of American politics.[81]

These groups used racially coded appeals for law and order (as will be discussed later in this chapter), linking the civil rights movement to riots and crime. The onslaught would eventually pay big dividends for the conservative movement. Yet the first attempt of a conservative Republican (Barry Goldwater) to use the civil rights movement to win election to national office was unsuccessful. Lyndon Johnson beat him by a landslide. Although Johnson rejected the findings of the report he himself had commissioned, he adopted a number of the commission's recommendations, most notably the War on Poverty and the Great Society. Johnson made millions of dollars in federal aid available to cities for community-based organizations in conflict-ridden communities. The aim, notes Katznelson, was "to take the radical impulse away from the politics of race by the creation of mechanisms of participation at the community level that had the capability to limit conflicts to a community orientation, to separate issues from each other, and to stress a politics of distribution—in short, to reduce race to ethnicity in the traditional community bound sense. . . . [As popular power] movements absorbed the energies of insurgents [they] also transformed their protests and rendered them harmless."[82] Similarly Sugrue notes, "The irony of the War on Poverty was that the federal government did not, for the most part, address the economic problems that were the root cause of poverty. . . . But, unexpectedly, the federal government allied itself with local activists. . . . The Johnson administration unleashed and legitimated an insurgent movement for 'community control' that dovetailed with the growing demand for black power. . . . The long-term consequence was to wholly recast the terrain of debate over race, rights and equality in the United States from the federal to the local."[83]

In New York, Mayor John Lindsay used the money to hire black and Puerto Rican activists and neighborhood youths as peacekeepers. In the 1970s these young people employed their new organizing skills to create radical black and Puerto Rican power organizations. In the 1980s these radical activists, most of whom had cut their teeth on the 1960s riots, forged community-based organizations, some of which were dedicated to fighting police brutality. Groups such as the Black Panthers, the Nation of Islam, the Real Great Society, the Young Lords, and the Revolutionary Communist Party gave birth in the 1980s to the NYC Coalition Against Police Brutality, the Justice Committee, Make the Road New York, the Malcolm X Grassroots Movement, the National Hip Hop Political Convention, the Audre Lorde Project, the Immigrant Justice Solidarity Project, and Stolen Lives. Individual activists such as Charles Barron, a former Black Panther, became an anti-police-brutality activist and councilman; Richie Perez, a former Young Lord, founded the Justice Project; Vincente Alba, a former Young Lord, now leads the Coalition against Police Brutality; Armando Perez, a Real Great Society founder, was elected district leader; Margarita Lopez, formerly of the Puerto Rican Socialist Party, was elected councilwoman; David Santiago, a Puerto Rican Socialist and Young Lord, play critical organizing roles in the 1980s and 1990s.

My research was conducted in predominantly Puerto Rican neighborhoods, where the Real Great Society, the Young Lords, and the Puerto Rican Socialist Party were the most important community-based organizations. The Real Great Society (RGS) operated principally on the Lower East Side. When the RGS extended organizing efforts to East Harlem, two of its leaders influenced several young people who would later form the Young Lords Party of New York.[84] The Young Lords were most active in and had their most profound impact on East Harlem and Mott Haven, South Bronx. The Puerto Rican Socialist Party was strongest in Williamsburg, Brooklyn. In all these areas, over time, participation in grassroots organizing efforts increased residents' confidence in their own collective capacity.

While the focus here is on Puerto Rican organizing efforts, there is a thread that ties the Puerto Rican experience to that of blacks. First, migration to the city occurred in similar waves. Second, both groups of migrants fled rural poverty and political repression only to encounter racial discrimination in New York. Both were confined to the lowest wage labor market, the poorest housing, and inferior schools. Police viewed them in similar ways, enforcing ghetto boundaries, targeting them for drug arrests, and using high levels of violence and brutality. Black and Puerto Rican neighborhoods exploded in the 1960s. Riots erupted in black neighborhoods in 1964 but spread to Puerto Rican neighborhoods too. The reverse was true of the Puerto Rican riots of 1967. Similarly, the evolution of radical Puerto Rican organizations paralleled that of black organizations in the city. The following section is based on ethnographic field research conducted in three predominantly Puerto Rican neighborhoods. A parallel process, I argue, was taking place in black neighborhoods in the city.

The Real Great Society and Puerto Rican
Organizing on the Lower East Side

The Lower East Side had long been a cauldron of movement activity. Puerto Ricans in cigar factories and Jews in the textile industry were early and active participants in labor, immigrant, communist, and socialist organizing efforts. In 1966 a local street gang called the Assassin Lords formed a political organization they called the University of the Streets (as mentioned earlier). Armando explained (in the first of many conversations we had between 1992 and 1999, the year Armando was murdered[85]):

I was in the "Assassin Lords," another was in the "Dragons." . . . The gangs were mostly about having something to do. We would get into a gang and fight each other. . . . We came to the realization that it didn't make any sense for Puerto Ricans to be fighting each other. We decided to give something back to the community. . . . In the Lower East Side there was a huge need for day care centers. So, we applied for different grants and foundations and got funding for a day care center called "visiting mothers." It was run out of a store-front. Then we got funding for other projects, and somewhere be-tween 1966 and 1967 we received a fairly large grant. From there we started an organization called "University of the Streets." It is still located on East 7th and has a karate program, drama, theater, art, and reading[s].

After the 1967 riots, Armando and Chino Garcia formed the Real Great Society (RGS), named after President Johnson's Great Society initiative. Armando credited Johnson with providing an alternative for ghetto youths. "We have never seen anything like that since, not in [the] past 30 years," Armando insisted. "To me Johnson was the greatest president we ever had for social problems."

In 1966 *Life* magazine reviewed *The Gang and the Political Establishment,* written by a Columbia University professor about the Real Great Society. Afterward gang leaders from around the country began to contact them. "This gave us the opportunity to travel all over the country," Armando said. "We discovered we all had similar problems, especially regard-ing education and housing. We noted a pattern. We realized it was not just a problem on the Lower East Side. We had a very big struggle on our hands. . . . We got serious. We began to educate ourselves."

The 1968 Teachers Strike and the Network
of Organizations in Williamsburg, Brooklyn

Unlike the South Bronx or Harlem, Williamsburg was still a large working-class neighborhood during the 1960s. In 1969 one-quarter of all industrial jobs in New York were in Brooklyn and over 50 percent of those were in Greenpoint-Williamsburg and Newton Creek. The largest employers were the American Sugar Company, E. M. Schaefer Brewing Company, Lumber

Exchange terminal, and, until its closure in 1966, the Brooklyn Navy Yards. In 1968 the first major political mobilization in Williamsburg emerged in response to the 1968 United Federation of Teachers citywide strike (which was launched in opposition to community control of school boards). At Eastern District High School the teacher strike prompted a student uprising. Puerto Rican high school students, radical clergy, and VISTA volunteers all participated. They forced the school principal to resign. Manny Maldonado, president of the ASPIRA club (an organization designed to help and encourage Puerto Rican high school students to succeed), emerged as one of five or six student movement leaders. Martin Needleman, who worked with ASPIRA and VISTA at the time and directed Brooklyn Legal Services during the 1990s, recalled, in 1992, "A lot of what's happening in current efforts goes back to these school struggles. . . . Community activists' contacts were made then. It turned out to be an investment in our future—this community networking." Eusebio Cuso shared similar remembrances (1996):

> Little by little we got to do a lot of things together. . . . Manny [Maldonado] used to come up to David's [Santiago] house and I used to live with David. . . . They started calling us the Socialist building—they said we were all Socialists. . . . Everybody who lived in that building was into some struggle or another. So they called us the revolutionaries, the politicos, the politicians, and all that good shit. . . . The whole building was into whatever it took to better the neighborhood. Habitantes Unidos.

Out of their organizing efforts the Los Sures community housing organization was born, named for the area of Williamsburg (the South Side) where most Puerto Ricans lived. "We held meetings in buildings to form tenants associations and then began going out to the buildings trying to organize the tenants association to become a citywide community management program. As more landlords abandoned the apartments we began doing rehabilitation. We also began working with the tenant interim lease (TIL) program,[86] helping the tenants make contracts with the city to run their own buildings," noted Barbara Shliff (1993). The same network of activists she had known from the time she was a VISTA volunteer in 1968 led most of the organizing efforts.

The first board of Los Sures included most of the leaders of the 1968 school strike. Los Sures, Schliff told me, "was a voluntary organization that grew out of community needs, and then got funding. [It was an outgrowth of] the network of organizations and people that had been involved a long time; it was the hallmark of the struggle for the people's community school board." Luis Olmeda was the first chair of Los Sures. "Olmeda stressed Puerto Rican Pride and identity," noted David Santiago, when I interviewed him in 1994: "He opened up the political struggle here. In the 1970s, he led the occupation of the Kraus housing projects, and put garbage in the street to protest the lack of sanitation in the neighborhood." David Lopez, later an organizer for Musica Against Drugs (an organization founded by Manny Maldonado to help fight drug abuse and AIDS), and Carmen Calderon, from the South Side Mission, were also members of the first board of Los Sures. Williamsburg organizing efforts will be discussed later in the chapter.

The Young Lords and the Emergence of New Yorican Social Movements in East Harlem and South Bronx

East Harlem had been the setting of the largest Puerto Rican riot in the city, and Mayor Lindsay invested the most resources there. In so doing, he unintentionally spurred the creation of a network of skilled grassroots activists. These activists would play leading roles in channeling anger at police violence into organized forms of nonviolent protest in decades to come. By 1968 East Harlem was a cauldron of organizing activity. Miguel "Mickey" Melendez had participated in the riots. The city hired him as a "peacemaker." Melendez commuted in from Mott Haven, South Bronx. Armando Perez came in from the Lower East Side. Armando introduced Melendez to University of the Streets. Luis Gonzalez, another organizer in East Harlem, introduced Melendez to his cousin Juan Gonzalez, the leader of the 1969 student strike at Columbia University.

In the summer of 1969, Mayor Lindsay tried to cut funding to some of the new community-based organizations. The activists used their newly honed organizational skills to fight back. Melendez called Juan Gonzalez, currently leading the student movement at Columbia, and Felipe Luciano, leading the black student movement at Queens, and told them that Puerto Ricans in East Harlem needed their help. They arrived "with a bunch of radical compañeros from Columbia," Melendez told Ramon Gonzalez, my research assistant in 1993. They "blockaded the East River drive, and the city surrendered." Melendez, Luciano, and Gonzalez then formed a Puerto Rican student group called Sociedad Albizpo Campos. Melendez transferred to Old Westbury, a radical and experimental new college interested in the concept of University of the Streets, and became a recruiter. On a recruiting trip to Chicago, he attended a meeting of the Chicago Young Lords where they discussed the recent takeover of Clemente High School. At the end of the meeting, Melendez was introduced to "this redheaded guy with a purple beret who is named Cha Cha Jimenez [founder of the Young Lords]. Cha Cha introduces me to David Perez [one of the student leaders]." They spoke at length about the problem of "police brutality in our barrios."[87] The following year David transferred to Old Westbury, and the New York branch of the Young Lords was born.

On July 26, 1969, Felipe Luciano announced the creation of the New York branch of the Young Lords before a crowd celebrating the anniversary of the Cuban revolution in the Lower East Side's Tompkins Square Park. Soon afterward they began walking around 110th Street "with the memory of the riots that had erupted the week before on those same streets," Melendez said. They were now asking people what it was they wanted. "They said *basura* (garbage)," Gonzales told me in 1993: "So every Sunday we would sweep the streets. More and more people kept joining. We put the garbage in the middle of 3rd Avenue, and we blocked traffic with it." Gonzalez decided to call this action the first East Harlem *garbage offensive*. Once they had the garbage in the middle of the street, they set it aflame:

> I did not count the people but in my recollection there could have been five hundred or five thousand neighborhoods taking part in the garbage protests. Every single Young Lord threw a match. Every single person in the community who helped threw matches. . . . Flames went up spectacularly and people started to scream with joy. In my mind the people—timid mothers, grandmothers, everyone— were showing their support of the Young Lords' action. *This new sight brought to mind the 1967 riots . . . but this time the protest was flawlessly executed.*[88] (emphasis mine)

Finally the city sent sanitation trucks to the neighborhood and agreed to keep the area clean. The Young Lords then initiated clothing drives and breakfast programs. When a conservative pastor called the police, Gonzalez said, "We kidnapped the church. We occupied the Methodist church in order to run a breakfast program for needy children. [The message was that] this will happen to any institution in a poor community that does not respond to the needs of the people. We initiated the 'people's church.' That was the high point of the Young Lords."

One-quarter of the membership of the Young Lords was African American, and many of the group's leaders were Afro–Puerto Ricans. "We began talking about anti-black prejudice in our culture," Gonzalez recalled. The salsa musician Eddie Palmeri wrote the hit song "Justicia" about them, and Ray Barretto spoke of them admiringly in the lyrics to his salsa songs as well.

The action with the most important long-term consequence, however, was the Young Lords' successful fight against lead poisoning. They did their own testing and showed that over 80 percent of residents in East Harlem were suffering from high levels of lead. As a result legislation was passed banning lead-based paint and forcing landlords to remove existing paint.

Organizing in Mott Haven, South Bronx

In 1970 the Young Lords launched a major offensive in Mott Haven. They focused their effort on Lincoln Hospital, the worst hospital in the city. The hospital had an active group of workers and radical doctors who had graduated from medical school in 1969 and 1970. "The doctors supported us," Armando Perez (from RGS, now active in planning the Lincoln take-over) told me. "We met at an apartment at midnight in the Upper West Side, for a surprise party. When everyone arrived we said, 'surprise, we're taking over Lincoln hospital.'" They drove a truck up the ramp to the emergency room. "We heard the guards say, you can't do it. Willie [a member of the group] went to the back of the truck, opened it up, and we occupied the building. . . . It was a public relations action—we occupied it for a day to demand that they raise the minimum wage of health care workers, worker control, and a new building."

Vincente "Panama" Alba, director of the Coalition against Police Brutality, learned his activist skills with the Young Lords. He told me in 1993, in the first of many conversations, "We adopted the most militant approach—direct confrontation. We needed health care, so we took over a hospital. We worked according to a four-year plan. In four years we'll be free, in jail, or dead. We built the hospital. The older workers say, 'this hospital was built by the Young Lords.'" Later they invited everyone who was into drugs to eat free in the hospital cafeteria, initiating a long-term commitment to "harm reduction" (treating drug abuse as a health issue, focusing on reducing the harm associated with it). They enlisted the help of St. Ann's Episcopal Church, the only church receptive to their demands, in clothing drives, liberation schools, welfare rights, and tenant organizations. Some Young Lords began to do prisoner support, supporting in particular the prisoners in Attica during and following the uprising. Others moved to Puerto Rico and began to do work promoting independence there.

Police and FBI agents infiltrated the Young Lords as part of their Counter Intelligence Program, known more commonly by its acronym, COINTEL. Then terrorist cells began to emerge. "It was so depressing," Alba noted. "When the Young Lords arose in 1969–70, a lot of other things were happening," Armando observed. "There were sharp racial tensions, and it was the middle of the Vietnam War. . . . The country was in an upheaval with Americans trying to figure out 'is this worth it?' It was a different time. People felt you had to do something. There was a sense of life and death that you don't have now. The methods of social control were different."

The Decline of Black and Puerto Rican Power

By the 1970s the Panthers, the Young Lords, and other organizations were in disarray. Personal disputes and ideological divisions, poor strategic choices, and the COINTEL infiltration all did damage. Not all 1970s radicals dedicated their lives to improving their communities. Some used their organizing skills to amass personal wealth and power. In Williamsburg, Luis Olmedo used his position as chair of Los Sures to run for council in 1973. "Olmedo was a nationalist," noted local activist Saul Nieves (1996), and as such "able to take advantage. The nationalists supported anyone who supported independence. When he ran for council in 1973, he swept." He won by large margins until he was indicted for corruption. Meanwhile the neighborhood fell into disrepair.

By 1978 both Schaefer Brewing Company and Rheingold Brewing Company had abandoned the city. Unemployment in Williamsburg reached 12.1 percent, up from 5.8 percent in 1970. The loss of jobs and the deterioration of housing left the community crumbling and threatened by street gangs, drugs, and arson. Street gangs, which had provided an alternative status and identity for young people since the 1950s, gradually became involved in drug trafficking. As Cuso, the local activist and former gang member, told me in 1994, "In the 1950s the gangs were huge. . . . When they flooded the neighborhood with drugs all the gang members became drug addicts. The presidents of the gangs became drug dealers." Cuso, Maldonado, and other activists became addicted to heroin. Many later contracted H.I.V. "Poverty is the major reason for drug abuse," Maldonado said. "You have to offer people something—something to aim for. Drugs are the major economic resource in this neighborhood. There are kids out here with big bankrolls, fancy cars. It is attractive. When I grew up there was a lot of peer pressure—in the 1960s it was what was happening. A lot of kids in this neighborhood got involved—winded up using drugs, getting addicted."

In Mott Haven, Ramon Velez used his seat on the city council to win millions of dollars in federal antipoverty monies for his own community organizations. After he came under major city and state investigations in 1977, he successfully maneuvered to get his cohorts on the board of directors of the new Lincoln Hospital. He opened a multiservice center that received large city contracts and subcontracted services from other service agencies and businesses connected to the machine, allowing him and his cronies to "load their pocketbooks and enrich their bank accounts," claimed one local activist. "As the machine grew," noted another, "it undermined real movements from coming out in the Bronx."

By 1976 Mott Haven was one of the poorest congressional districts in the United States. City policy encouraged opportunistic arson. "The lag between when the landlord stopped paying taxes, providing services, and collecting rent and when the city acquired, demolished, and finally wiped the structure from its books varied from years to overnight. At each stage of the process landlords, tenants, and squatters could and often did burn their buildings."[89] Poverty, joblessness, and a desolate landscape led to desperation and spiraling crime rates, which were then blamed on and generalized to all black and Puerto Rican residents in the popular press and imagination.[90] As Evelyn Gonzalez pointedly notes, "Without the social constraints and community sanctions engendered by such networks [community ties] delinquency, alcoholism, drug abuse and violent behavior increased. . . . Once stability and safety were gone, the neighborhoods of Mott Haven, Melrose, Morrisania-Claremont, and Hunts Point-Croton Park East disappeared and the blighted area of the South Bronx grew. . . . Without neighborhoods, the older stock of the South Bronx disappeared."[91]

Harry DeRienzo, founder of Banana Kelly and later Consumer Farmer, two grassroots housing organizations active in the 1980s and 1990s, recalled, "People were [literally] burned out. Fires affected especially community boards 2 and 3. The area lost about 70 percent of its population. Everyone who could leave did." Another neighborhood activist bitterly observed, "We had politicians parceling out power. . . . Tracts of land in the community were deliberately allowed to fall apart, to pave the way for further development" and personal gain.

In the Lower East Side "the combination of private capital flight and the absence of government response made portions [of the neighborhood] . . . virtually uninhabitable. Blocks dotted with decrepit or abandoned buildings provided havens for drug users or sellers, with shooting galleries and stash houses."[92] "Social disorganization, violence and ethnic strife marked the East Village. . . . runaways slept in abandoned buildings, in doorways, in phone booths, or on rooftops, supporting themselves through begging, street selling, dope dealing, petty thievery and prostitution."[93] The Lower East Side "surpassed even Harlem as a retail drug market . . . as its proximity to transportation routes and landscapes of devastation stimulate ever larger numbers of drug users and traders."[94] Alphabet City, "an area approximately fifty square blocks located near the major tunnels and bridges into Manhattan[,] was in the words of the police, 'the retail drug capital of the world.' "[95]

The 1977 Blackout Riots

The 1977 blackout riots accelerated this trend. Unlike with the riots of the 1960s, the triggering incident was not police abuse but rather opportunity. The spatial pattern, repertoire, and characteristics of the riot differed in striking ways from those of the earlier wave.[96] As Wohlenberg notes, "[T]he first riot of the decade occurred in Harlem in 1964 and the riot syndrome— the innovation—spread outward from the initial occurrence to other cities and attained widespread adoption by 1968."[97] The blackout riots hit all neighborhoods in the city simultaneously, which made them extremely hard to police. Riots that begin in one neighborhood can often be contained if a police commissioner chooses to concentrate his forces there. Riots that explode everywhere at once are far more difficult to control. For this reason alone, the 1977 blackout riots were particularly combustible.

Another defining feature of the blackout riots was that most of those arrested on the first day had established criminal records. It was only in the later hours that residents without any previous criminal record participated in the looting (what Spike Lee remembers ruefully as "Christmas in July"[98]). During the 1960s, riots had followed the opposite course, with the first wave of arrests being individuals previously unknown to police. Moreover, the 1960s rioters had avoided looting stores owned by local blacks or Latinos. The 1977 rioters did not make such distinctions: all stores were hit at the same rate. Lacking insurance for anything but fire, many vulnerable storeowners set their own shops aflame, escalating the destruction of neighborhoods.

The blackout that triggered the 1977 riots struck during an unusually severe heat wave. The extra energy being used to cool commercial buildings and apartments taxed the poorly maintained circuit breakers, steam units, and service remote controls, none of which had been upgraded or replaced in years. When a bolt of lightning hit the Buchanan South generator, those outside the plant were unable to regulate the distribution of electricity across the units, and the employee ordered to operate the load-dumping equipment turned the master switch the wrong way or "didn't lift the protective cover from the console before trying to depress the buttons."[99] All at once, millions of New Yorkers were without lights and air-conditioning. They took to the streets, fleeing the heat and darkness of their apartments. Some thousand began looting, and others joined in.

The Bronx and Brooklyn were hit especially hard. A total of 473 stores in the Bronx were damaged and 961 looters arrested. When Mayor Abraham Beame issued the call for policemen to return to duty, he told them to report to whichever precinct was closest. That left the Bronx virtually without police. The Bronx precinct reported a total of 38 officers. "Ten times that number would have been necessary to cope with the spontaneous incidents of looting, fires and attacks on police officers," the precinct head told Jonathan Mahler.[100]

It was worse in Brooklyn, where a five-mile stretch from Sunset Park through Williamsburg, Bushwick, Brownsville, and Flatbush became the scene of massive looting. "Seven hundred Brooklyn stores were plundered; 1,088 people were arrested."[101] One of the worst-hit neighborhoods was Bushwick, bordering Williamsburg. A decade earlier Bushwick had been a working-class Italian neighborhood. When the Navy Yard closed, a white exodus began. While some Brooklyn neighborhoods received "Model City" status, allowing them to qualify for antipoverty funds, the government had relied on six-year-old census figures marking Bushwick as too rich to qualify. As bulldozers cleared tracts and destroyed tenement housing in East New York, Brownsville, and Williamsburg to make way for new low-income housing projects—many of which were never built—displaced residents found their way to Bushwick. The closing of the beer industry after the Navy Yard accelerated the process of urban decay. Racial tensions between Italians and Puerto Ricans, in particular, sometimes boiled over, as Cuso recalled. In 1977 the Eighty-third police precinct was overwhelmingly white, but those officers policed a neighborhood that was "overwhelmingly black and Hispanic with a narrow strip of Italians along its western edge. 'Our job was about arresting minorities,'" a police officer from the Eighty-third told Mahler.[102]

Even before the riots, Bushwick was the victim of arson, usually set by the landlords. Most of the homes there were "made of wood and designed with air shafts over their stairwells. They burned like furnaces. Because they were usually connected via common cocklofts, the attic space between the roof and the ceiling[,] fires virtually leaped from house to house."[103] The riots hit Bushwick worse than any other neighborhood in the city. It was hard to know who was setting the fires faster: looters or store, home, and apartment owners hoping to cash in on insurance.

It was probably no accident that the worst riots to hit the city occurred when radical politics were in decline and in the neighborhoods most devastated by housing abandonment and arson. Where community organizations remained active they were a mitigating factor. In the Lower East Side, "looters began to smash and destroy windows and interiors of various commercial premises . . . along Avenues A, B and C, from Houston up to Tenth Street," Mahler notes.[104] But "genuine community spirit . . . may have helped keep the stealing to a minimum," Robert Curvin and Bruce Porter point out.[105] Residents of Loisaida, between Avenues A and D, went to the streets to protect the vulnerable businesses. "Bonds between poor people and shop keepers, surely extraordinary in urban life, seemed to be taken for granted."[106]

By this time the Real Great Society had changed its name to CHARAS–El Bohio Cultural and Community Center (the acronym derived from the first names of its founders). Armando Perez and Chino Garcia and other CHARAS members were in the streets trying to keep everyone calm. Another local activist, Artie Santiago, told Curvin and Porter that while he might have been the first in the community to go down to the police precinct to protest an arrest of a community member, his feelings toward the looters were decidedly different. As soon as the lights went out, he and others took to the streets to talk to young people: "We talked about the fact that we had been through the riots and all we had gotten out of it was a devastated neighborhood. . . . The rioting was not a protest, just a bunch of clowns taking advantage of a situation to benefit themselves. The looting was inexcusable. If the social problems are bad enough you don't need the lights to go out to rebel. We can't afford these kinds of riots anymore. There's nothing left here. The economy is no longer in the neighborhood. We've helped destroy our own neighborhoods in past riots. I know because I've been in them."[107]

Twenty-four hours later the power was restored and the city was returning to normal. However, 3,776 people had been arrested and were now being held in suffocating conditions in the overcrowded and infamous "tombs" jail; with a street temperature of 102 degrees, internal temperatures easily hit 120. One looter died in a basement cell, while Mayor Beame urged prosecutors to mete out stiff punishments, set high bails, and refuse any plea bargaining with anyone having a previous felony conviction.[108]

Neighborhoods Begin to Rebuild

Gradually activists began the slow, arduous work of rebuilding and reconstructing neighborhood networks. In the Lower East Side, CHARAS developed a wide array of initiatives including a local credit union, solar energy for urban use, and a housing program that provided the first sweat-equity buildings in the United States. The group became a national model for low-income home ownership, community gardens, the University of the Streets

Performance Space, and the first Lower East Side recycling center. Its sweat-equity project was the model for the city's Adopt a Building program. Members of CHARAS created the Joint Planning Council, which fought to preserve abandoned properties for families in need, and collaborated with the Nuyorican café (formed in 1973 by Miguel Algarin) and Puerto Rican writers and poets such as Miguel Piñero. Puerto Ricans, Armando pointed out, have the lowest self-esteem of any group. Culture work is an important part of building that esteem. Armando rejected the argument that the riots were an authentic rebellion and the Great Society programs were a form of co-optation: "If you look at areas like Watts and Newark they are still re-building from the riots that took place then."

In Williamsburg, too, activists began to reorganize. In 1976 the tenants of 149 South Fourth Street voted unanimously to take over management of their building and become the first Los Sures tenants to elect to buy their building. Cuso notes (1996), "People started taking over buildings, and the ones that were almost falling, people grabbed them and they didn't fall. People who needed housing would get into those buildings and today all those buildings are renovated, man. You know the neighborhood and the people here. All of a sudden they gave a damn. And they started doing little things, not big tremendous things but little things."

In the Bronx, however, no significant reorganizing efforts were under way before the 1980s. "There are a lot of similarities between the Lower East Side and Williamsburg," a Lower East Side activist told me. "They are both close-knit communities, with strong networks and a history of strug-gle." The networks were weaker in the Bronx and the devastation of the neighborhoods greater. But the remnants of the Young Lords there created both the first and, later, the broadest coalition of anti-police-brutality orga-nizations in the city. Richie Perez created the Justice Committee of the National Congress for Puerto Rican Rights, and Panama Alba created the New York Coalition Against Police Brutality.

The Decline of Riots

In this book, I have paid a great deal of attention to the building of commu-nity organizations. From the mid-1980s on, I claim, these organizations channeled anger at police violence into courts and other nonviolent forms of protest. There is another more common explanation for the decline in the number of riots in the United States. Scholars have pointed to the devastating impact of the mass incarceration of black and Latino men. By removing a large percentage of men from inner-city neighborhoods, confining them first to federal and state institutions, and then leaving them under penal supervision for years on end, the state removed the very men most disposed to organize or engage in riots.[109] While this explanation is powerful, it is incomplete.

First, New York has one of the lowest incarceration rates in the country. Most of those detained during the 1990s were accused of misdemeanors, not felonies. A high percentage of these cases were simply thrown out of court. The average length of sentence for those convicted was three and a half years. The rate of return to the neighborhoods was quite high and might have disposed the former prisoners to a more antagonistic relationship with the police and with the state. While those under penal supervision may legitimately have feared that any violation of their parole would land them back in jail, their sentences were usually not long enough for this alone to be a significant deterrence. More crucially, California has a far higher incarceration rate and had a far higher incarceration rate than New York when Los Angeles exploded in 1992. Moreover, the disparity between incarceration rates in New York and those in California has grown significantly (particularly since California passed the three strikes law in 1993, giving life sentences for those convicted of three nonviolent felonies). New York now has one of the lowest incarceration rates in the country and California has one of the highest. Yet riots erupt with some regularity in California and are quite rare in New York. If mass incarceration were the explanation it should be the reverse. Instead of preventing riots, the punitive turn in criminal justice has multiplied the number of negative encounters between police and minority youth and in California, in particular, eviscerated the social organizations and networks that might have provided victims of police abuse an alternative path to pursue justice.

Competitive Outbidding and Increased
Police Brutality in New York

In 1980 Ronald Reagan won a landslide victory using racially coded attacks on the urban poor, blaming "Great Society policies for coddling criminals, rewarding bad choices with handouts and so on—for a rising tide of irresponsibility, promiscuity, violence and welfare dependence."[110] Both Barry Goldwater and Richard Nixon had unsuccessfully tried to use the issue as a battering ram. Goldwater had argued that Democratic support for civil rights had made women and children unsafe on the streets: "In the great struggle to advance human civil rights even a jail sentence is no longer a dishonor but a proud achievement. Perhaps we are destined to see in this law-loving land people running for office not on their stainless records but on their prison record."[111] He lost in a landslide to Lyndon Johnson. Nixon expressed satisfaction at his ability to use crime as a wedge issue in 1968: "[I]t hits it right on the nose. It's all about law and order and the damn Negro–Puerto Rican groups out there."[112] Before the Watergate scandal pushed the Republicans into political exile, Rockefeller tried to run to Nixon's right in the Republican presidential primary by proposing the Rockefeller drug laws, the most draconian legislation in the country for first-time drug offenders. The 1973 laws made the sale of as little as two ounces (56 grams) of heroin or cocaine and the possession of four ounces of cannabis (113 grams) Class A felonies (the same category as homicide) and set the penalty equivalent to that of second-degree murder: fifteen years to life. Nonetheless, Rockefeller lost his presidential primary campaign.

Reagan was the first to successfully turn a punitive stance toward crime and poverty into a landslide victory, winning support not only from Southern white racists (what Nixon had called his southern strategy) but also from many working-class Democrats outside the South. Believing that they had been outsegued, and hoping "to take the corrosive issues of race, crime and welfare off the table,"[113] congressional Democrats looked for an opportunity to get ahead of the Republicans on a security issue. When Len Bias, a black University of Maryland star basketball player, died of a powder cocaine overdose, congressional Democrats used the tragedy to seize the spotlight. Returning from the July recess, Tip O'Neill thundered, "Write me some good goddam legislation. All anybody up in Boston is talking about is Len Bias. The papers are screaming for blood. We need to get out in front of this now. This week. Today. The Republicans beat us to it in 1984 and I don't want that to happen again. I want dramatic new initiatives for dealing with crack and drugs. If we can do this fast enough we can take the issue away from the Reagan White House."[114] A media frenzy followed: "Dramatic footage of Black and Latino men being carted off in chains, or of police breaking down crack house doors, became a near nightly news event. In July 1986 alone the three major TV Networks offered 74 evening news segments on drugs, half of these about crack," note Craig Reinerman and Harry Levine.[115] As Robert Jervis observes, "[A]n issue is considered newsworthy to the extent that it is being treated by the media, and they and politicians take their cues from each other."[116]

Congressional Democrats were so anxious to get the bill through Congress that they literally cut and pasted it together so hurriedly that several paragraphs fell off before passage and were subsequently lost. Congress neglected to hold hearings, consult with experts, or investigate the impact of previous mandatory sentencing schemes, such as the Rockefeller Laws in New York: laws which had done nothing to prevent the scourge of crack cocaine from entering New York or leaving a wave of homicides in its wake. The committee relied on one investigator, Jehru Brown, from Washington, D.C.'s metropolitan police department, to determine the quantity of narcotics that qualified as mid-level versus high-level trafficking. Years later the congressmen learned that Jehru Brown had lied about being an officer with the metropolitan police department, had lied about graduating from Howard University's School of Pharmacy, had lied about being a pharmacist, and had lied about being a homicide detective. Brown had testified in four thousand narcotics cases and in all probability had lied in every case.[117] As the bill went to committee, Eric Sterling notes, "The Democrats could not stop the Republicans from out flanking them to recover the mantle of toughness. . . . After the bill passed the House . . . the Republicans in the Senate took their swing at it. . . . On the mandatory minimums they raised the maximum penalties and changed the drug triggering quantities. The 10-year mandatory minimum now carried a maximum of life in prison instead of 30 years. The 5-year minimum now carried a maximum of 40 years instead of 20 years. The 10-year crack trigger was reduced from 20 grams to 5 grams."[118] Congress later added a conspiracy clause applying the identical sentence to anyone connected to or possessing knowledge of the activities of the person caught with the drug.

The 1986 Anti–Drug Abuse Act, an act of crass political opportunism passed in haste during an election year, had a titanic impact on poor black and Latino communities. As Todd Clear notes, "None of the stories being told about prison changes in the United States would be possible without the seismic changes that were made in the drug laws. . . . The number of people incarcerated for drug crimes increased tenfold between 1980 and 2001. No other type of offense had incarceration numbers rise at anything close to that rate."[119] By 1993 more than one million people had been arrested for drug abuse violations, 75 percent for simple possession, and more than half were black or Latino.[120] In New York the racial disproportion of arrests was even higher, and close to 90 percent of all drug arrests were of blacks or Latinos. The war on drugs multiplied the quantity of hostile encounters between police and black and Latino youths.

The Last Riots in New York

By 1989 New York City neighborhood activists were struggling to deal with multiple scourges: a nationwide recession leading to the sharpest decline in income growth since 1982 and the highest unemployment rate since 1980; increases in drug addiction and a new disease spreading rapidly among IV injection drug users, their partners, and children as well as gay men; and huge increases in homicides in black and Puerto Rican neighborhoods as gangs vied for control over the lucrative crack trade. A slew of corruption scandals implicating key figures in his administration added to Mayor Ed Koch's embarrassment. Unable to solve myriad problems, Koch blamed blacks for all the city's woes. Blacks, he claimed, were responsible for both the crack epidemic and the explosive increase in crime during his administration. The solution was a dramatic expansion in the power and prerogatives of the NYPD.

An increase in police violence followed inexorably. When police officers choked to death a thirty-five-year-old black businessman and community leader named Arthur Miller in Crown Heights, evidence pointed to state collusion. The deputy medical examiner found "no evidence of savage or excessive beating," and the U.S. attorney for the Eastern District of New York found "insufficient evidence" that Miller's rights had been violated.[121] Anger at Koch's racial insensitivity came to a head when sixteen-year-old Yusuf Hawkins, a black youth visiting his girlfriend in the Italian neighborhood of Bensonhurst in Brooklyn, was chased and beaten to death by a group of Italian teenagers carrying baseball bats. Instead of riots, however, communities mobilized nonviolent actions and organized politically. One large group of black protesters, led by Al Sharpton, marched through Bensonhurst and was greeted with racial epithets and flying watermelon chunks. Mayor Koch responded to the incident by suggesting that blacks should stay out of Bensonhurst. As anger in the black community rose, the black borough president David Dinkins appealed for calm. "Blacks had a right to march anywhere in the city," he insisted.[122]

Mayor Koch's "inflammatory racial rhetoric"[123] shifted the momentum of the primary campaign and helped Dinkins win the Democratic mayoral primary. In the general election, however, Dinkins faced a powerful opponent, one willing to mobilize racial tension to win elections. Rudolph Giuliani, the new district attorney, arrived in New York straight from the Reagan White House, where he had been the youngest associate attorney general in history and a key figure in the construction of the carceral state. He had already built himself a reputation as a fearless prosecutor willing to pursue the leaders of major crime families in New York City, under the single rubric of the Racketeer-Influenced and Corrupt Organizations Act (although the idea for tying together the five crime families under one racketeering case had been suggested to Giuliani's predecessor in the early 1980s and was already under way in 1982 as a result of the undercover mission of Donnie Brasco). Giuliani also took credit for the prosecution of the junk-bond kings Ivan Boesky and Michael Milken, although the former case had been well under way before Giuliani took office and in the latter he relied on information supplied by the staff at Merrill Lynch. Even "the principal case that Mr. Giuliani personally tried during his six-year tenure, that of Stanley M. Friedman, the Bronx Democratic leader accused of corruption, had its genesis in an investigation conducted by the F.B.I. in Chicago."[124]

Dinkins relied on his multiracial appeal, popularity with white Manhattan liberals, and support from the labor unions. What turned the corner on his campaign, however, was a massive grassroots organizing campaign in black and Latino neighborhoods. Major Owens in Brooklyn had been a leader of black community organizing efforts during the 1968 citywide teachers' strike in Ocean-Hill/Brownsville, another neighborhood where the struggle for local control of schools has created a network of experienced grassroots organizers. Owens, who had come to office by fighting the Brooklyn Democratic machine and some of the older black establishment politicians, was a strong Dinkins backer. Bill Lynch had served as a chief senior staffer and campaign manager to Owens and now played the same role for Dinkins. In Williamsburg, David Santiago and other veterans of the 1968 Eastern District school strike created the South Side action committee, which spearheaded the Latinos-for-Dinkins campaign. In the

Bronx, including Mott Haven, Freddie Ferrar and Jose Serrano were strong Dinkins backers.

Yet Dinkins's campaign contained within it an almost insurmountable tension, notes Phillip Thompson III, "between the muted racial rhetoric dictated by his inter-racial coalition-building strategy and the need for a strong articulation of black demands and perspectives—a 'black testimonial'—to attract activist black volunteers and mobilize his black constituents."[125] Blacks and Latinos wanted more jobs, better wages, and more programs for the poor and homeless. Whites wanted more police, lower taxes, and less crime. "Black communities," Thompson points out, "tended to view crime and civic disorder as reflecting a need of jobs and social programs; whites tended to view crime as showing a need for more frequent and more severe punishment."[126] Whites expressed great confidence in the police, while for blacks, police brutality was still a critical issue. In the 1989 mayoral race Dinkins won by a mere 47,000 votes out of 1.8 million in a city where Democrats outnumbered Republicans 5 to 1. Dinkins won almost 90 percent of the black vote and over two-thirds of the Latino vote, but his shallow support among white voters would continue to be a significant handicap. White liberals, however, provided his margin of victory (see Table 3).

Dinkins and the War on Crime

David Dinkins came to office at the height of the crack wars. Ed Koch had made crack a referendum on the city's black population, not on his own term in office. As a black mayor, Dinkins could not deflect attention from the issue. His first act was to massively expand the ranks of the police department by nearly 40 percent under a program he called "Safe Cities, Safe Streets." Most of the new police recruits would not finish training until after Dinkins had lost the 1993 election, depriving Dinkins of the visual comfort of more police officers on the street. Even so Dinkins massively expanded community policing and the use of beat cops, and crime rates began to fall by his second year in office. Both crime and homicides peaked in 1990, largely due to the eighty-seven killed in an arson attack on the Happy Land social club, and declined steadily every year after that.[127] Crime would remain, however, Dinkins's Achilles' heel. Then in 1991 a small riot broke out in Crown Heights, Brooklyn.

Table 3. Percentage of votes obtained by assembly district type in the 1989
New York City mayoral primaries and general election

	Primaries			General election		
	Dinkins %	Koch %	Turnout %	Dinkins %	Giuliani %	Turnout %
Black assembly districts	84.8	10.3	56.7	89.0	10.4	65.9
Mixed minority districts	65.1	26.8	48.3	76.7	22.4	56.8
Latino districts	60.4	31.8	47.0	73.6	25.4	56.9
White liberal districts	46.5	44.0	52.6	50.7	47.8	59.4
White Catholic districts	29.7	62.2	46.7	25.8	71.9	68.8
Outer-borough Jewish districts	25.9	67.2	56.4	29.3	68.6	67.5
Total	50.8	42.0	52.4	50.4	48.0	63.6

Source: New York City Board of Elections. See also John Mollenkopf, *A Phoenix in the Ashes*
(Princeton, N.J.: Princeton University Press, 1994), 182.

Crown Heights Riot

Racial tensions had long plagued this neighborhood, which had a divided
population of blacks (about 85 percent), mostly West Indian, and Hasidic
(Orthodox) Jews. The Hasidic community was a closed one, and there were
no ties or informal social relations across the West Indian/Hasidic boundary. Moreover the black community believed that the Hasidim were granted
special treatment by police and other public officials. These suspicions appeared validated after an incident on August 19, 1991. The third car of a

three-car motorcade (carrying a Hasidic rabbi and three other Hasidic men) sped through a red light, ricocheted off a passing car, reamed into the sidewalk, and hit two young black children, instantly killing seven-year-old Gavin Cato. The police, who had been escorting the motorcade, assumed control of the situation. When the Hasidic community ambulance arrived, the police officers instructed the ambulance driver to take the four Hasidic men since a crowd had begun to attack them. A New York City ambulance arrived soon after to transport the two black children to the hospital.

When the Hasidic ambulance took the uninjured Hasidic men and left the black children behind, a rumor spread that the Hasidic EMT workers had refused to treat the injured children. Rage began to build among West Indians. The episode was just one more piece of evidence that the police did not protect black children. When the rabbi driving the third car was not charged with a crime (it was ruled an accident), black youths began attacking buildings, looting stores, and setting fires, many yelling vile anti-Semitic epithets. Although the killing of Gavin Cato had been an accident, the role of the police, in escorting the Hasidic motorcade and in sending the ambulance away with the Hasidic men, and the failure of the city to bring charges against Gavin Cato's killer activated racial boundaries and sparked an interethnic riot (if a one-sided one). As frightened Hasidim hid in their homes, black neighborhood youths stormed through the streets. In the most violent incident of the night twenty-nine-year-old yeshiva student Yankel Rosenbaum was stabbed to death. The riots continued throughout the night and through the next four days.

By the third day, frightened Hasidic Jews felt as if the mayor and the police had abandoned them: They had come to believe that Dinkins had deliberately given orders to the police to hold back. This suspicion was unsubstantiated in a later investigative report: "There is absolutely no evidence of this," said the report's author, Richard Girgenti, the state's criminal justice director.[128] Still, the report claimed, the mayor had not responded adequately to calls for help from the Jewish community. Furthermore the New York City Police Department had failed to "implement timely and appropriate tactics" to quell the riots. Finally, it claimed, the police had given "misleading information to the mayor's office suggesting they were in control of the rioting," and the mayor had "failed to question the police assessment until the third day of the riots."[129]

Black leaders were offended at what appeared to be a lopsided emphasis on the wrongs committed against the Hasidim. "The city needs to apologize, but not for that one night," said Richard Green, of the Crown Heights Youth Collective. "Crown Heights occurred because of 20 years of neglect and estrangement."[130] Giuliani, he claimed, needed to apologize. "Dinkins walked the streets of Crown Heights, and prevented it from spreading," Green said. "He put his life on the line." "Everyone's child is dear to them," the Brooklyn activist Mildred Johnston said. "If Yankel's life was worth an apology and a financial settlement, the same should apply to Gavin's life. They were both human beings." Carmel Cato, who witnessed his son's death, called justice one-sided: "If they want to do something, they should remember this family."[131] "This is an outrage," said the Reverend Dennis Dillon, of Harvest Christian Center. "This is not about him caring about the people of New York—it is about [Giuliani's] political future."[132]

The L.A. Riots and the Washington Heights Riot in 1992

Seven months later arguably the largest, most violent riot in U.S. history hit Los Angeles. Its genesis was a home video shot on March 3, 1991, showing five white police officers beating an unarmed black man already prone after being Tasered and kicked in the head. The video aired repeatedly on national television. Due to the publicity surrounding the case, the trial was moved to Simi Valley, and the jury was drawn from San Fernando Valley, a predominantly white and secondarily Latino area. The jury consisted of ten whites, one Latino, and one Asian; the latter two selections proved ominous for the future of Los Angeles. On April 29, 1992, the jury acquitted all five officers of assault and three of the five of using excessive force. The jury was hung over the charges levied on the fourth officer. The jury reached its decision after being allowed to witness two minutes of the ten-minute video.

For the next six days Los Angeles was consumed in violence. Since the riots hit multiple Los Angeles neighborhoods simultaneously, under the best of circumstances it would have been difficult to bring them under control rapidly. But the Los Angeles Police Department, apparently miffed at being blamed for the violence, withdrew. Ultimately the city was pacified only after the U.S. National Guard, Army, and Marines were deployed.

Unlike the 1960s riots, where police were responsible for most of the killings, in the 1992 Los Angeles riot, police were responsible for less than a quarter, only 11 of the 53 deaths attributed to the disturbances.[133] As many as two thousand residents were seriously injured, thirty-six hundred stores and buildings were set aflame, and more than ten thousand businesses were damaged, costing the city close to one billion dollars in damages. Most of the violence was concentrated in South Central, an area populated by both blacks and Latinos. Half of those arrested and nearly one-third of those killed were Latino. There is some evidence that blacks set many of the buildings on fire in the initial hours of the riots and that Latinos followed with opportunistic looting. Koreans and Asians owned many of the damaged and looted stores, but Latinos owned 12 percent of the looted stores, and those storeowners were almost uniformly denied federal funds for rebuilding.[134] Several Korean storeowners defended their stores with guns and live ammunition.

The relatively high degree of interethnic conflict in the Los Angeles riots distinguished them from those of the 1960s. Yet there also were many incidents of black and Latino residents saving the lives of whites, Asians, and each other. Only two Asians were killed in the six days of riots, even while many of their stores were looted or damaged by arson. The L.A. riots resembled those of the 1960s in three significant ways. First, Los Angeles had among the most venal and brutal police in the country and the nearly all-white police force had acted like an occupying army "engaged in trench war with its residents."[135] Second, a police officer had beaten an unarmed, handcuffed African American man, and the abuse had been filmed and was thus incontrovertible. Nearly everyone in the United States had seen the video. Third, the riots began only after the all-white jury refused to hold the officers accountable. Moreover, the Rodney King verdict followed on the heels of another case, in which a white judge had rejected a jury's recommendation and suspended the sentence of a Korean woman for fatally shooting an unarmed fifteen-year-old African American girl in her grocery.[136] The two judicial decisions, only one week apart, sent an unmistakable message to the black community. The state was uninterested in protecting the lives of blacks, including innocent black youth.

Although New York did not go up in flames following the Los Angeles riots (black and Puerto Rican leaders and activists organized nonviolent protest marches and Mayor Dinkins marched alongside them), rising racial tensions did lead to a one-week rebellion later that year. Both the cause and the resolution of the Washington Heights riot are instructive. On July 3, 1992, Jose Garcia, an immigrant from the Dominican Republic, was shot in the back during a confrontation with New York police officer Michael O'Keefe in the largely Dominican neighborhood of Washington Heights. O'Keefe claimed that he had struggled with Garcia, who was armed and high on cocaine, before he fired twice, killing him.[137] The police backed O'Keefe, saying that Garcia, who was on probation for drug charges, had concealed a .38 caliber revolver. Witnesses, however, insisted that Garcia was unarmed and pleading for his life when he was shot.

For six consecutive days, riots spread from Washington Heights at 183rd Street to 135th Street in Central Harlem. Residents smashed car windows and set the vehicles aflame, destroying over one hundred. Others threw garbage cans at the police, and some reportedly shot at police and squad cars. One NYPD helicopter reportedly returned to Floyd Bennett Field with a bullet hole. Scores of officers were injured, as were ninety civilians, one fatally. A police officer was heard to yell, "Napalm the hood" into his police radio, to the dismay of the mayor and the police commissioner.

Mayor Dinkins deployed over two thousand police officers to quell the disturbance, all the while pleading with residents for calm. Walking through the area, Dinkins promised a full investigation of the incident, and he urged residents to "keep the peace."[138] The governor put the New York National Guard on alert. Police experts said that this and the speedy response of New York City police to the disturbances stood in sharp contrast to the situation in Los Angeles.[139] Police Commissioner Lee Brown, an African American, had been actively courting minorities and had increasingly assigned units to foot patrol in various neighborhoods, in contrast to Los Angeles, where the police patrolled from the relative safety of squad cars.[140] The NYPD also abstained from the use of armored cars or other military kinds of equipment.[141] That is not to say that the NYPD was free from suspicion. At the time a number of officers were under investigation for drug trafficking and even murder.[142] The local Spanish-language newspapers carried frequent and prominent reports of incidents of police brutality.[143] It was believed that the second resident of the neighborhood to die was pushed to his death from a roof by police.[144] As one journalist critically observed, "[that] the police can abuse their power or be other than a friendly force in the community may seem far-fetched to some. But, in communities like Washington Heights, harassment, corruption, prejudgment of residents and unwarranted beatings of suspects are common. The local precinct, the 34th, is one of two in the city under investigation for corruption."[145] Similarly, Tim Wall, a former community organizer working with the Citizens Committee for New York City, notes, "My experience leads me to believe that more of this goes on than you know unless you live in one of these neighborhoods."[146]

Police officers heavily criticized Mayor Dinkins for his decision to meet with the victim's family. They claimed that the meetings gave credence to the accusations of police brutality and that by meeting with the family Dinkins was taking sides against Officer O'Keefe.[147] Dinkins pointed out that he had steadily increased the budget of the NYPD since his inauguration, while he had cut the budget of virtually every other city agency. It was ridiculous and unfair, he noted, "to say that if you comfort a family, that you have taken sides against the police officer."[148] It is likely that the actions by Dinkins and Lee Brown, the African American police chief, prevented a larger conflagration, but the police blamed Dinkins. "Why is it that I am the enemy of the police officers?" Dinkins asked; "[I am] the one who has stood up and produced more for this Police Department than anybody in recent years. Now you may continue to feel the way you do until the day you die and the day I die, but sir, you are wrong. You are dead wrong. And so, I am going to continue to do what I think is right."[149] The *New York Times* reported the following conversation between Dinkins and Officer Thomas Barnett:

Barnett: "This is a dangerous place, and what you did that day was bad."

Dinkins: "What is it that I did that day that was bad?"

Barnett: "When you went and confronted that drug dealer's family, you left a sour taste in all the officers' mouths."

Dinkins: "What do you mean I confronted? You mean I comforted them."

Barnett: "Yes."

Dinkins: "So did the Cardinal."

Barnett: "He's wrong, too, but you're here now."

Dinkins: "No, no, no, no, no."

Barnett: "That's our feeling."

Dinkins: "I understand that's your feeling, but you're wrong."[150]

Cardinal O'Connor, the head of the Roman Catholic Archdiocese of New York, strongly defended Dinkins. "Not once did I hear him say or imply anything that I considered disloyal to the police force, and I say that as a man fiercely loyal to and grateful for the police force. Had I heard the Mayor say or imply anything disloyal, I would have publicly disagreed and walked out," O'Connor wrote in his weekly column.[151] "Who else has visited and revisited Washington Heights over and over again since the shooting? Not once, to my knowledge, has he ever suggested that Officer O'Keefe is guilty. Not once has he suggested that the people have the right to riot if Officer O'Keefe is declared innocent by a grand jury."[152]

On July 23 another incident sparked a one-day uprising in Washington Heights, increasing fears that another might ensue should Officer O'Keefe not be indicted. Cardinal O'Connor said that he felt it would be cruel if there were no accountability or if the public were denied full disclosure about the case: "And infinitely more cruel were the public unable to accept that disclosure and go about its business in peace."[153] The cardinal's fears proved prescient about the grand jury, although not about the neighborhood's response. Indeed that September the grand jury failed to indict O'Keefe, but there was only the briefest neighborhood outcry. This was due, in part, to the corroborating evidence presented at the trial, inculpating the victim—including a radio transcript of Officer O'Keefe's panicked call for backup and a videotape of the victim juggling cocaine bags shortly before the shooting. The mayor's and police chief's quick and compassionate responses calmed residents too.

In the wake of the Washington Heights riot, in July 1992 Mayor Dinkins appointed Judge Milton Mollen to head the City of New York Commission to Investigate Allegations of Police Corruption and the Anti-Corruption Procedures of the Police Department. The commission was asked to examine and investigate "the nature and extent of corruption in the department; evaluate the department's procedures for preventing and detecting that corruption; and recommend changes and improvements to those procedures." Although the final report was not issued until 1994, shortly after Dinkins had lost to Giuliani, throughout the rest of Dinkins's term in office, a steady stream of humiliating revelations of police corruption and venality dominated the media. The commission's final report began as follows:

> The problem of police corruption extends far beyond the corrupt cop. It is a multi-faceted problem that has flourished in parts of our

city not only because of opportunity and greed, but because of a police culture that exalts loyalty over integrity; because of the silence of honest officers who fear the consequences of "ratting" on another cop no matter how grave the crime; because of willfully blind supervisors who fear the consequences of a corruption scandal more than corruption itself; because of the demise of the principle of accountability that makes commanders responsible for fighting corruption in their commands; because of a hostility between the police and the community in certain precincts that breeds an "Us versus Them" mentality; and because for years the New York Police Department abandoned its responsibility to ensure the integrity of its members.[154]

David Dinkins's concerned response to the death of a young Dominican man and his promise of a fair and speedy trial calmed the Latino community, dampening the rage that might otherwise have found outlet in widespread riots. Yet, even after Dinkins left office and a new, white mayor took his place, even when the new mayor displayed open hostility toward the black community, rejecting the findings of the Mollen Commission while defending the NYPD unconditionally during a period of escalating police violence,[155] New Yorkers would not riot again.

Chapter 2

Policing Racial Boundaries
and Riots in Paris (1920–2002)

Until 2005 most French scholars insisted that racism was a distinctly American phenomenon. French workers, Michelle Lamont argued, "define the poor and black as 'part of us,' using the language of class solidarity."[1] Although they reject North Africans, it is because they believe that Muslims "violate the principles of republicanism and are culturally incompatible with the French."[2] Patrick Weil argued that with the notable exception of Vichy, France had a long republican tradition of recognizing only individuals and their relationships to the state, although admittedly this tradition did not extend to France's colonial empire abroad.[3] Pierre Bourdieu and Loïc Wacquant went so far as to accuse Americans of "cultural imperialism" for using distinctly American racial categories to examine issues of class and immigration in French *banlieues*.[4] Even now most French scholars and nearly the entire political establishment fail to acknowledge racial inequality or racial discrimination on the part of the state or any part of its security apparatus.[5]

There are several flaws, however, in this line of reasoning. First, French political rhetoric commonly refers to the problem of immigrants and *banlieue* youths. Yet most of those termed "immigrant" were either born in France or are naturalized citizens.[6] "Immigrant" and "*banlieue* youth" are code words and mark the same categorical boundaries as race or ethnicity. Young people of black, Arab, or Berber heritage are referred to as immigrants even when they are third generation or were born in overseas French territories with French citizenship. The term "immigrant" almost never refers to actual immigrants from Europe, the United States, Australia, or New Zealand. One-quarter of Frenchmen have at least one immigrant grandparent, and yet they are considered to be fully French (*de souche*, or of French roots). As Gérard Noiriel notes, "[F]rom a genealogical perspective the living memory of the immigrant experience is greater today among the French than among Americans."[7]

Second, studies have consistently underestimated the degree of racial segregation in French cities, as both Didier Fassin and David Lapoutre have pointed out in their respective ethnographies of Quatre-Mille in La Courneuve (one of the poorest *banlieues* surrounding Paris) and the French police. Since France does not collect data on race or ethnicity, it is impossible to make comparative claims, especially with American and British cities (where data on race and ethnicity are collected by the census bureau and other public agencies). Fassin notes,

> Data on citizenship, usually the only indicator recorded in the analysis, substantially understate the reality of the presence of these groups because individuals who have acquired French citizenship are not counted. . . . Although there remain households of European origin, the majority of residents—whether they hold French nationality or not—are of African origin, either black or Arab, and they themselves complain that their communities are increasingly concentrated in these areas. Moreover, the segregation of these groups is markedly higher than it would be if this was simply the consequence of their socioeconomic level, indicating it is due not only to this latter factor, as is often said, but also to racial discrimination in housing, which adds to the discrimination in employment and more broadly, in access to most resources.[8]

Wacquant's study of Quatre-Mille, for instance, relied on a 1982 survey of citizenship to show that French *banlieues*, in contrast to America ghettos, were ethnically diverse.[9] In contrast, Lapoutre, who taught for ten years at a school in Quatre-Mille, cites a 1992 survey that queried 945 youths. Only 10 percent of those surveyed identified themselves as French *de souche*. Fifty-one percent self-identified as Arab; 30 percent as black from Africa, the Antilles, or Comoro; 5 percent as Hindu; 3 percent as Yugoslavian, Portuguese, or Italian, and the rest as Asian.[10] When Lapoutre asked young people about the overall racial and ethnic makeup of the neighborhood, they could think of only three or four families who were not ethnic or racial minorities. Moreover the youths believed that the purpose of French republican denial of race was to hide French guilt over colonialism and the postcolonial treatment of its former colonial subjects.

Third, French colonial subjects were French nationals, not immigrants. Algeria, in particular, as Todd Shepard observes, was a district in France for 130 years, and Algerian Muslims had French nationality.[11] They were excluded from full citizenship by virtue of their "civil status" as Muslims (whether or not they practiced Islam). Only after they served in the front lines in two world wars did France offer Arabs and Berbers of Algerian origin the, albeit distant, possibility that they could become full citizens. In fact for a brief period France acknowledged its long history of racial discrimination against Muslims and even took measures to remedy the inequality it caused. In 1956, as Shepard notes,

> The architects of integration admitted that official failure to grapple with the reality of mass exclusion of "Muslim" Algerians from citizenship had institutionalized discrimination: that is more than just failing to efface existing factors that had made them different from other French nationals; the state had produced novel distinctions in the guise of pursuing republican universalism. . . . Integrationists proposed a historical analysis: Since 1830, France had established a system that produced new differences and reinforced the privileges of one group, French with common civil status, over nationals with other civil statuses [such as Muslim]. Integration policies aimed to reverse the inequalities that this institutionalized discrimination had produced.[12]

When France signed the Évian Accords in 1962, however, the integrationist efforts, which included the equivalent of affirmative action replete with enforced quotas, ended with the war itself. So did France's acknowledgment of the history of racial exclusion.

Fourth, a majority of French citizens believe that there is extensive racial discrimination in their country, as do a far higher percentage of stigmatized minorities. Seventy-nine percent of French citizens in European Union (EU) barometer studies claimed that "discrimination based on ethnicity" is "very or fairly widespread,"[13] the second highest percentage of any country in the EU, narrowly following the Netherlands. Moreover 67 percent believe that the institution that most discriminates is the police force.[14] In other words, argues Fassin,

To sum up: French people, particularly those belonging to a minority, are convinced that racial discrimination occurs most frequently in interactions with law enforcement agents; police officers, whatever their rank, are firmly of the view that they are no more racist than the rest of the population, or probably even less, and that they are unjustly accused of discriminating among the public when it is in fact they who are the target of racial stigmatization; social scientists, often using statistical studies as evidence, explain that not all differentiation is discrimination, that not all discrimination is racial, that racial discrimination is not necessarily the product of racist intent, and that racist prejudices do not automatically lead to practices of racial discrimination—in short, that the issue is highly complex (though at least they are examining it, which, we should remember, was not the case until recently in French research).[15]

Constructing Racial Boundaries in Algeria

From the moment the dey fell in Algeria in 1830, French authorities were determined to make Algeria part of France. It was difficult to square, however, the absorption of the country and the rejection of its citizens with fidelity to republican values. To do so they engaged in a series of complicated maneuvers. First, the Senatus consulte of July 14, 1865, declared all residents of Algeria French nationals, while restricting Muslims to a civil status whereby they would remain governed supposedly by the laws of Islam.[16] Later, in 1870, the décret of Cremieux gave French citizenship to Algerian Jews, while an 1881 decree created a separate *indigénat* to govern Muslims. The *indigénat* included "thirty-three infractions that were not illegal under French common law but were punishable in Algeria when committed by Muslims," such as avoiding forced labor, speaking disrespectfully to a French official, failing to answer questions, defaming the republic, and traveling without a permit.[17] It was not until 1913 that the travel permit requirement for Muslims traveling between Algeria and France was eliminated.

A 1903 statute allowed Muslims whose mayor certified that they had renounced their religion and civil status and passed a morals background test to apply for French citizenship. Once his dossier was forwarded and approved by the chief of police, the governor-general, the minister of justice in Paris, the Council of State, and finally the president of the republic, who must sign a formal decree, a former Muslim or Arab could become a French citizen. Initially few French Muslims applied, but once the number of applicants rose, so did rejections, which eventually reached a rate of 75 percent.[18] Still, the process allowed France to maintain the fiction that all Muslims, if they chose to do so, could become full citizens. Shepard notes, "In Algeria, as in all of France, the law sustained the pretense that ethnicity and race did not matter, a state of affairs that continued until the Algerian revolution. The fact that local civil status was based on descent, which the Lambrecht Decree of September 1871 confirmed, suggests how tenuous such race-blind claims were."[19] The French/Muslim boundary, much like the black/white boundary in the United States, acted as the principal binary of racial exclusion and exploitation in France. When migrants from other colonies began to arrive in France, they occupied the same side of the categorical divide as Algerians—that of racialized other.

Race, Immigration, and World War I

The first records of Algerian migrant laborers appeared in France in 1831. By 1905 several thousand North Africans were working in European coal mines and 3,000 were working in France.[20] The largest wave of migrants arrived during World War I, when France drafted over half a million African and North African troops to fight. Between 1914 and 1918, 250,000 Algerians, 35,000 Moroccans, 18,000 Tunisians, and 175,000 black Africans were recruited for the war effort.[21] By 1917 almost one in forty Algerians had served in the French army.[22] Another 200,000 colonial workers from Algeria, Morocco, Tunisia, the French protectorates, Senegal, and Mali were recruited to fill war-time labor shortages, almost 120,000 from Algeria alone.[23] Migrants who arrived of their own volition served under the jurisdiction of the Conseil de guerre, a military court that could try them for unwillingness to work. Forced laborers lived in specific quarters built for this purpose and were not permitted to eat outside of these living areas.[24]

As a reward for their service to France, the French parliament passed a measure on February 4, 1919, reducing some of the obstacles to full citizenship for Algerian men, though not the requirement that they give up their civil status. France accommodated neither Muslims' demands for equal rights nor racist demands that Algerians be sent home. France's needs were too great. It had lost over one million men on the battlefields and more among the four million wounded, many of whom died without descendants. France had suffered the highest per capita loss of any country.[25] Most of the countryside to the north and east was completely destroyed, and the loss of more than half of all able-bodied men sent France into a spiral of economic crises. It also reduced the capacity of France to produce a sufficient number of new citizens to replace this population loss. In addition to a shortage of men, France was plagued by a phenomenon known as *la dénatalité française*—an unusually low ratio of births per family in comparison with the rest of Europe.[26]

Over a million immigrants were recruited after the war to fill France's desperate need for labor. Belgians worked in the coal, steel, and textile industries and resided in northeastern France, while Italians worked in low-skilled jobs and resided in southeastern France. In 1931 Polish immigrants accounted for half of all foreign workers in the mining industry and had become the largest immigrant group.[27] Russians and Jews from Germany and Eastern Europe arrived seeking refuge from political persecution.[28] Another 120,000 workers came from North Africa. In 1924 alone 71,028 Algerian and 10,000 Moroccan workers arrived in France. Colonial authorities, fearful that out-migration to France provided an alternative for workers unwilling to accept near-starvation wages, successfully pressured the French government to require that all Algerian "Muslims" obtain work permits before entering France.[29] (This was not unlike southern planters' fears of black migration to the northern United States.)

Policing Paris in the Interwar Period

In the mid-1920s, 10 percent of the Parisian population was foreign born, as were 20 percent of its workers.[30] Parisian police enforced new laws regulating residence and mobility of foreign nationals and French Muslims.[31] "Nowhere," notes Rosenberg, "did the effort to track foreign nationals start sooner than in Paris, or take place on a comparable scale."[32] A special police brigade was formed to deal exclusively with French Muslims. The "North African police brigade," as it was called, was renowned for corruption and venality. Sixty percent of those picked up were charged with "violations of immigration rules, petty theft, public drunkenness, and vagabondage."[33] Less than 2 percent were charged with violent crimes. Desperate poverty, however, in Algeria continued to fuel migration. In 1929 alone seventy thousand workers arrived from Algeria.

The Great Depression and political instability caused a temporary halt in this migrant stream. In 1934 several small fascist organizations (Solidar-ité française, Action française, Jeunesses patriotes, and Croix de feu) began to agitate against the center-left Third Republic. In the wake of the murder of the conman and Jewish financier Alexandre Stavisky (alleged to have ties with members of the government), confrontations between fascist crowds and police grew deadly. Fascists used the incident to provoke a crisis in the center-left government. The Radical Party government outlawed these organizations, but the Croix de feu continued to mobilize under a new name, the Parti sociale française.[34] The left also increased mobilization dur-ing this period. A nationwide general strike in 1936 brought the Popular Front and Leon Blum to power.[35]

Labor unions, militants of the left-wing parties, supporters of Spanish republicans, Jewish refugees, and North Africans, particularly Algerians, ex-pected a sharp change in their status with the victory of Leon Blum. The Algerians were the most bitterly disappointed. Messali Hadj, leader of the Étoile Nord-Africaine (North African Star) and a Communist, expected the party to honor its promises of support. But the Popular Front did little more than a preliminary inquiry, and even the Communists failed to follow through, claiming that Algeria was not a nation but rather "a nation in the process of formation."[36] The Popular Front did agree to expand the politi-cal rights of twenty-one thousand indigenous male Algerian elites but in 1937, at the behest of colonial authorities in Algeria, dissolved the Étoile, using the same law it had used to ban the fascist groups.[37] Hadj broke definitively with the Communist Party and formed a new, more radical organization in Algeria, the Parti du peuple Álgerian. "Immobility and re-pression were to be the memories of the Popular Front among Algerian nationalists," notes Rod Kedward, "but the readiness for reforms within colonialism had been there."[38]

As the Great Depression spread through Europe, the conflict between labor and capital grew acute. Bankers and industrialists funded fascist orga-nizations such as Solidarité française, Action française, Jeunesses patriotes, and Croix de feu. Middle-class support for the Popular Front dwindled. The senate refused to give the government more authority to take broader economic measures, and Blum, who saw it as a vote of no confidence, resigned. The Radical Party leader Édouard Daladier assumed power. Under pressure to avoid war at all costs, Daladier signed accords with Hitler in Munich. Only the Communists spoke out in protest. Deladier used Communist opposition to break with the Popular Front and reject the Spanish and Jewish refugees who had counted on at least intermittent Popular Front support.[39] Daladier headed the sole democratic government not to condemn the Nazi pogrom of Kristallnacht. The economic crisis and the increasing power of the far right convinced many North Africans to return home.[40]

In the summer of 1940, six hundred deputies, elected to the Popular Front Assembly only four years previously, gathered in the small town of Vichy and, with the exception of the Communists, voted to hand over all executive and legislative power to Marshal Petain. Petain struck an agreement with the Nazis that divided the country in three. Northern France, including Paris, was to be occupied directly by the Nazis. Southeastern France would be ceded to Italy, and the rest of the southern part of the country would come under the direct command of Marshal Petain. François La Roque, head of the banned Croix de feu, offered Petain uncritical support in the south. The fascist ex-Socialist Marcel Deats argued that Petain should form a single-party state resembling that in Italy and that the party should be his own Rassemblement national populaire party. In the north the French fascists were willing Nazi accomplices. Jacques Doriat merged his own Legion of French Volunteers against Bolshevism into a subdivision of the Waffen SS Charlemagne division. Nazi Germany gave them a degree of power they only dreamed of in democratic France.

French fascists were as brutal as their German counterparts. Their secret police—the Milice—were more feared than the Gestapo. Deportations of Communists, resistance fighters, Popular Front leaders including Blum and Daladier, and above all Jews to extermination camps far exceeded the numbers requested by their German superiors. Of the 75,721 people the French rounded up and deported, only 2,567 survived. Another 4,000 died in camps located inside France.[41] By 1943 France was exporting 40 percent of the country's total industrial output to Germany, including 80 percent of its vehicle production. Over 600,000 Frenchmen were sent to work in Germany. This in addition to the 1.6 million prisoners of war, including well over 65,000 troops from the African colonies, gave Germany 2.25 million French workers "effectively held hostage."[42]

The Police in Occupied France

The centralization and unification of the police, long desired by French authoritarian rulers, was completed under German occupation in 1941.[43] During the revolution the central police had been abolished and its functions deliberately decentralized. Local governments were given more direct control, something the central government from the restoration on had sought to reverse. It was not until Vichy and Nazi occupation that the police were fully centralized and under the control of a single entity, the Sûreté. Only Paris kept its own police force. The separation between the Parisian police and the regional police would persist until 1966, when the two were merged under the control of the minister of the interior.

By centralizing their control over police forces throughout France, the Nazis could deploy French police to hunt Jews and resistance fighters. In Paris the police rounded up ten thousand Jews, at the behest of the Nazis, for deportation to concentration camps. The gendarmes guarded them at the deportation center in Drancy. The techniques used were essentially the same as those they would later use to track Algerian nationals. "Senior police officers or administrators," note Jim House and Neil MacMaster, "during the course of their careers were involved in both forms of repression, drawing on a shared body of practice. A key role was played by the Interior Ministry which constantly circulated top officials between the Maghreb and Metropolitan France."[44]

After liberation many such officers continued to occupy top positions in the institution. One was Maurice Papon, who was named prefecture of Paris despite the key role he played in the arrest and deportation of 1,560 Jews, including children and the elderly, from Bordeaux to Auschwitz. Others included Maurice Sabatier (a *pied-noir*, who according to House and MacMaster would have stood trial with Papon had he not escaped by dying in 1989), Jean Chapel (appointed superprefect in Constantine, Algeria), Pierre Garat (head of Jewish Services during the occupation, who was transferred to Algeria in 1945), Pierre Somville (Papon's right-hand man and cabinet head, who transferred to Algeria in 1945), and Pierre-René Gazagne (a vicious *pied-noir* anti-Semite).[45] These officers brought with them knowledge of key features in the Vichy system of control, including

- "The creation of specialized intelligence agencies of the policing of target groups (Jews, Algerians)

- The total control of minority populations
- Elaborate card-index files (*fichiers*) to identify and locate individuals
- Mass round-up operations involving street level stop and search checks or the surrounding and isolation of urban sectors, with house to house searches
- Special police investigative units
- Mass holding centers and camps for those rounded up, often with screening identification units
- Exceptional and discriminatory legislation aimed to identify and detain minorities (night curfews, special identity cards, administrative arrest)."[46]

The Whitening of the Resistance Narrative and Colonial Rule

Communists, French and Eastern European Jews, Muslims, Spaniards, and other immigrants along with a small minority of non-Communist French and some Socialists and Gaulists (many in exile) composed the bulk of the French Resistance. The number of French collaborators far exceeded the number of Resistance fighters. When French forces joined the Allied invasion in North Africa and Europe, black and North African troops fought beside them, as they had done in 1940, often on the front line. Black Africans constituted 9 percent of the French forces, or 100,000 troops.[47] Over 10,000 were killed in European battles, 20,000 in North Africa, and 17,500 in POW camps, a total of 12 percent of those recruited.[48] Hundreds of thousands of North Africans, including 200,000 Algerians, fought for France as well, and tens of thousands gave their lives.

Like their black and Puerto Rican counterparts in the United States, North Africans and Africans expected their situation to improve as a result of their service in the war. Yet, like their American counterparts, they were bitterly disappointed. First, Charles de Gaulle permitted only 250,000 troops in the final offensive, selected white troops. African and North African troops were deported back to the colonies. Many were held in camps without blankets or clothes for the cold weather.[49] In Dakar, Senegal, one repatriated contingent was denied even the most minimum form of recognition. When 1,280 soldiers, now stripped of weapons, rose up and demanded back pay and demobilization premiums, they were met with gunfire. Thirty-five were killed on site, another 35 injured, and scores taken prisoner. Despite the pleas of Frenchmen who had served in the same units, they were not pardoned, and 5 died in prison.[50] Blacks and Arabs were then written out of both Resistance and victory narratives.

Second, in Africa and North Africa, Nazi and Vichy collaborators were made colonial administrators. There they used familiar forms of repression against colonial subjects. It was difficult in the wake of the Holocaust, however, to deny French Muslims the same rights as other nationals. To address the problem, the new October 1946 constitution reaffirmed equality between the civil codes but now extended French Union citizenship to all French subjects. The maneuver created a new set of difficulties. On the one hand, it soon became clear to those advocating for indigenous rights that the new federal structure was a mask for continued colonial occupation. On the other hand, French settlers in the colonies, and particularly in Algeria, protested the expansion of citizenship rights to Arabs and blacks. France attempted to resolve the conflict by distinguishing between indigenous civil rights in Algeria and other colonies (which would remain severely circumscribed) and civil rights in the French mainland, which were considerably broadened.

Article 3 of the new statute for Algeria of September 20, 1947, stated that "those Muslims residing in metropolitan France enjoy all the rights attached to the quality of French citizenship."[51] Yet even in France, Muslims remained under the auspices of Koranic law, a sleight of hand that left them under the control of the existing local justice administration. Their identity cards carried the designation "French Muslim," making it clear that the holders were not entitled to the same rights as other Frenchmen. Despite their service on the front lines during the war, often as cannon fodder for French troops, North Saharan and sub-Saharan veterans received a tiny fraction of the pensions and disability payments awarded French nationals. When war broke out in Algeria, even those small payments were suspended.

France Officially Acknowledges
Its History of Racial Discrimination

On May 8, 1945, a victory parade in Sétif, Algeria, grew into a march for independence and then deteriorated into a riot when the government attacked. While the riot was bloody, it paled in comparison to the indiscriminate violence employed by the French, who fired into crowds from tanks, dropped bombs from helicopters, and shelled the town from ships. The French estimated that Algerian deaths numbered between ten thousand and fifteen thousand, while Algerians claimed that the French killed over forty-five thousand. Fierce repression was used against anticolonial movements in Morocco and Tunisia as well, and in Madagascar the French massacred over one hundred thousand.[52]

Messali Hadj had been the leader of the pro-independence Algerians in France. After his split with the Communists in 1946, he emerged as a leader of the Triomphe de libertés démocratiques (TLD) in Algeria. The TLD was targeted during the massacre in Sétif. Hadj also headed the Organisation Spéciale (OS), which was decimated by arrests three years later. When the Front de libération nationale (National Liberation Front, FLN) and its military wing, the Armée de libération nationale (National Liberation Army, ALN), were formed in late 1954, they rejected further efforts at reform and bypassed Hadj. Hadj and his followers then created the Mouvement national Algérian (MNA), but the FLN attacked the new organization. The struggle between the FLN and the MNA later spread to the mainland, where it cost four thousand lives in France alone.[53]

The FLN and the ALN announced their presence in Algeria on November 1, 1954, with a series of bomb blasts in cafés and restaurants in Algiers that left eight people dead. "Bloody All-Saints Day" marked the beginning of the French Algerian war. Initially, France fought against all liberation movements. As Andre Siegfried put it in an editorial in *Le Figaro,* "It is not just the status of colonialism which is at issue but the destiny of the white race, and with it that of Western civilization of which it is the guarantee, the only guarantee."[54] Yet France eventually withdrew from its colonies: first from Vietnam (after great bloodshed) and then from Tunisia, Morocco, and West Africa. Algeria was different. "Algeria is France," claimed Mendès-France after negotiating French withdrawal from Tunisia and Morocco.[55]

The claim was hard to square with the poverty, illiteracy (85 percent), and low access to education suffered by indigenous Algerians.[56] With this in mind, French authorities (while simultaneously escalating counterinsurgency measures) expressed a surprising willingness to recognize France's long history of racial discrimination and, most stunningly, pursue policies to remedy both discrimination and the inequality that past discrimination had created. Shepard notes,

French bureaucrats and politicians in the 1950s and early 60s adopted a radical approach to Algerian difference in the Republic. . . . Starting in 1955, the liberal Gaullist governor Jacques Soustelle theorized and pursued policies aimed at "integrating" "Muslims" into the nation. So-called integrationists attempted to break the tight connections between colonial oppression and France's self-proclaimed universalism. . . . Integration explicitly recognized, as well, that true political equality demanded the reduction of economic inequalities. . . . [To achieve this goal] without accepting FLN claims about an organic Algerian nation, integrationists broke with republican tradition by accepting that France needed to take origins into account.[57]

To achieve these ends France embarked, first in Algeria in 1956 and then in France in 1958, on a series of radical new policies, both more expansive and encompassing than those the Americans would later call "affirmative action." These included quotas starting at 10 percent, and going as high as 70 percent in Algeria, for all government hires in every branch of the civil service. From the highest ranks of judges and police chiefs to the lowest, positions were to be filled by French Muslims of Algerian origin. Far from finding these affirmative action policies contrary to republican values, the Constitutional Council found, in one of its earliest rulings, "exceptional preferences to be constitutional."[58] French authorities changed the designation "French Muslim of Algerian origin" or "French with local status" to "French of North African origin," to be juxtaposed against "French of European origin," acknowledging both the reality of the distinct experiences of the two communities and the equal rights both communities merited as French nationals.

The reform efforts were far too late to counter the extraordinary violence accompanying the rapidly expanding war. FLN killings of 123 civilians in Philippeville led the French to massacre several thousand FLN suspects (the French say 1,200, the FLN 12,000). Soustelle now demanded all-out war and, under pressure from the Algerian Assembly, abandoned the reforms. Robert Lacoste, a Socialist, replaced Soustelle, abolished the Algerian Assembly, divided Algeria into five administrative districts, and ruled the country by decree, but to no avail. Convinced that they had support in Kabila, the French began to recruit Berbers to fight against the FLN. On October 1, 1956, a group of Berber recruits turned their guns on their

French commanders, ambushing them close to the village of Iguer n'Salem before escaping to the hills. France responded by dramatically escalating the level of violence used against Algerian draft resisters. In January 1957 General Jacques Massu arrived in Algeria with the task of decimating FLN networks. Massu, as he later admitted in his memoirs, institutionalized mass torture on a scale hitherto unknown. "The parallels to the Nazi tactics during the Occupation, was no deterrent to the French perpetrators. Their justification was the same as the Gestapo's chilling logic and calculation: Massu argued that torture was the only way to unmask an unidentified enemy."[59] The more brutal and extensive French tactics were, the more the FLN was able to extend its support networks. FLN bombs exploded in cafés, clubs, and restaurants throughout Algiers. The French committed more troops.

For the first time French magazines published searing exposés of torture tactics being used in Algeria, and protests began to grow in France. Three events between 1956 and 1958 played key roles and brought France unfavorable international attention as well. The first was the rerouting of an airliner carrying three FLN leaders from Rabat to Tunis by the French military command. The airliner was forced to land in Algiers, where the leaders were arrested and taken from the plane. The second was French military occupation of the Suez Canal, in conjunction with Israel and Britain, which was criticized by the United Nations, the United States, and the Soviet Union. The third was the bombing of the Tunisian village of Sakhiet Sidi Yousef by the French governor-general Robert Lacoste because of his suspicion that ALN leaders might be hiding there. Seventy villagers were killed.[60]

As disillusion with the war took its toll, French president René Coty appointed as prime minister Pierre Pflimlin, who was widely seen as supporting withdrawal. The news sparked a riot among *pied-noirs* in Algeria. On May 13, 1958, a coalition made up of the Algerian deputy and reserve airborne officer Pierre Lagaillarde; the French generals Raoul Salan, Edmond Jouhaud, and Jean Gracieux; and Admiral Philippe Auboyneau, supported by General Jacques Massu's Tenth Airborne Division and Jacques Soustelle's activist allies, carried out a coup in Algiers and threatened to topple the government of France. General Salan assumed leadership of the Committee of Public Safety, announced that the army had "provisionally taken over responsibility for the destiny of French Algeria," and called for President René Coty to immediately appoint de Gaulle to head a national unity government with extraordinary powers to prevent the "abandonment

of Algeria." Two days later de Gaulle announced that he was ready to assume the powers of the Republic.

Then on May 24, French Algerian paratroopers occupied Corsica and
began preparations for the seizure of Paris. They threatened to remove the
French government unless parliament immediately declared de Gaulle
leader of France. Only a handful of French political leaders refused—
among them François Mitterrand, Pierre Mendès-France, Alain Savary, and
theCommunist Party. De Gaulle demanded he be given wide emergency
powers for six months, until he could present a new constitution to the
French people for approval.

On September 28, 1958, a referendum took place, and 79.2 percent of
those who voted supported the new constitution and the creation of the
Fifth Republic. The National Assembly made de Gaulle premier, and de
Gaulle then dissolved the Assembly and the Fourth Republic. He called a
referendum for the creation of the Fifth Republic and won 80 percent of
the popular vote. Mendès-France and François Mitterrand joined the three
hundred thousand demonstrators marching to the place de la République
to register their rejection of a "fascist" coup from Algiers. Right-wing par-
liamentarians may have organized the entire episode, cognizant that the
appointment of Pflimlin would stir revolt. But French public opinion had
already turned against the war, and the attempted coup only further alienated the French from the radical settler community. On September 16,
1959, de Gaulle announced that Algeria would be granted the right to self-
determination. Massu declared from Algeria that the army would no longer
support de Gaulle. He called for the creation of paramilitary squads to
defend Algeria. These efforts culminated in the birth of the right-wing terrorist group Organisation de l'armee secrète (OAS). The rebels staged another uprising in Algiers, and in April 1961 the French army in Algeria
again threatened to invade and occupy Paris. De Gaulle narrowly managed
to suppress the revolt.

The War at Home and the Policing
of Racial Boundaries in Paris

The Rassemblement pour l'Algéria (a wing of the OAS) moved the struggle
to France, while supporters of the FLN created a network of *porteurs de
valise* to transport money, arms, and other forms of support. As the war in

Algeria raged, so did racial tensions in France. The number of Algerian immigrants living in France increased by 32.5 percent a year (compared to an average increase in the total immigrant population of barely 1.3 percent annually in the same period), and the number living in Paris alone increased tenfold, from 20,000 to 210,000. Unlike the European immigrants who were recruited and assimilated through government programs, migrants from the colonies were left to their own devices, finding housing in makeshift shantytowns close to their places of work. One migrant interviewed by Abdelmalek Sayad responded with surprise at the enormous trust employers put in their European employees. He contrasted that with their treatment of Algerian immigrants: "When it comes to us, you have to prove that you've earned your money, otherwise you've stolen it, and you become suspect. You have to show them that you have enough to live on, otherwise you're a thief or a beggar, and it's the same in both cases: it's not allowed, especially when you're an immigrant. A foreigner, an immigrant is meant to be working; if an immigrant isn't working, why not? What use is he? What is he doing here?"[61]

Saint-Denis and Aubervilliers had large shantytowns, as did Nanterre, where over ten thousand Algerians "created a semblance of home and community among the rats, mud, rags and misery."[62] The Parisian préfet de police Charles Luizet "instructed its beat cops to take a generous interpretation of the anti-vagabond law"[63] and warned that North Africans "having retained certain customs of their countries like to meet each other in the street in order to undertake endless discussions. Moreover, these North Africans engage in illicit dealings on a fairly high level."[64] The French government disbanded the North African brigade at the end of the war, noting that the institution was "aberrant, corrupt, and violent. . . . A number of its agents were themselves petty thieves who had their own run in with the law. Some appear to have recruited North Africans to serve in Colonel François de la Rocque's Parti Social Français. Worst of all, during Vichy, officers from the brigade appear to have forced colonial subjects to collaborate with the Milice."[65] Adrian Tixier-Vignancour, the new minister of the interior, created a new institution in its place, the Conseillers techniques pour les affaires musulmanes (CTAM), in 1946.

Police reports from this era refer to the dangers posed by the poor housing situation for Algerians, singling out Saint-Denis and Goutte-d'Or for "preventative raids."[66] The Paris municipal council even discussed the possibility of reconstituting the North African brigade. While the prefect denied that his intention was to re-create the brigade, the CTAM and anti-vagabond raids were a continuation of past practices.[67] In 1947 the Communists backed a general strike launched from Marseille. The Socialist minister of the interior (as will be discussed in further detail in Chapter 4) used the strike to purge the police of former Communist resistance fighters and appoint Jean Joseph Félix Ernest Baylot as prefect of Marseille. Baylot used the Guerini mob to assault strikers whom the regular police protected. His success in suppressing the Marseille strike, and purging Communist officers, led Tixier-Vignancour to move Baylot to Paris to deal with the Algerians.

Baylot had been closely affiliated with Vichy. His first act as prefect was to rout the remaining Communist police officers, replacing them with former collaborationists.[68] Maurice Papon was serving as prefect of police in Constantine, Algeria, where he had been appointed after the fall of Vichy. In Constantine, Papon had gained "extensive experience of colonial intelligence and policing operations against the nascent insurrectionary nationalists."[69] Baylot now appointed him as general secretary to the Paris prefect of police in 1951. On July 14, 1953, some 4,500 Algerians marched under Algerian flags in Communist demonstrations. At place de la Nation police opened fire. Six Algerians and one French trade unionist were shot dead, and 150 were wounded.[70] Baylot claimed that the Algerians had rushed the police and that one or more Algerians had fired the first shots to provoke a confrontation. Baylot used the conflict to petition the minister of the interior for permission to reconstitute the North African brigade, permission that was granted, although the brigade was given a new moniker, the Brigade des aggressions et violences (BAV), or "anticrime task force."[71] The only qualifications needed to serve in the new brigade, or the police more broadly, notes Laurent Bonelli, "was to be sure that the policeman had no empathy with the Algerian National Liberation Front; and more broadly with the Arabs. No other skills were needed: neither qualification nor honesty nor the need to behave properly."[72]

Every night the BAV performed hundreds of identity checks, stopping Algerians or those with Arab facial features, yet the identity checks resulted in only two or three arrests.[73] The brigade also engaged in nightly neighborhood sweeps. In the first week of August 1955, Algerians protested in front of the Goutte-d'Or police station against a police officer's use of his firearm while interrogating a pickpocket in the rue de la Charbonnière market. The police accused the Algerians of rioting after some demonstrators damaged cars and businesses. The police sealed off the neighborhood and engaged in a massive roundup. At nightfall they stopped all Algerians in the eighteenth arrondissement and raided several smaller Algerian neighborhoods. The press noted that this operation marked "the purification of the North African milieu in the capital."[74] Four hundred of the detained Algerians were summarily deported.[75]

In March 1958 Parisian police, angered by the government's failure to award bonus pay, stormed the National Assembly shouting anti-Semitic slogans. To appease the police, the government called Papon back from Morocco, where he had been serving as Rabat's prefect of police since 1954. Under Papon's direction the colonial police had engaged in "unprecedented punitive repression,"[76] issuing the order to shoot on sight. "This *rattisage* or cleansing of the medina by security forces showed the key features of the operations which Papon later deployed against the inhabitants of the shantytowns of Constantine and Paris," note House and MacMaster.[77] In Morocco, Papon mastered a new skill, "the sociological profiling of urban populations, which involved the use of census data to map the location of particular classes and ethnic groups,"[78] which he would use as the new Paris prefect of police.

When Papon arrived, approximately 180,000 Algerians were living in greater Paris, concentrated in shantytowns, microghettos, and urban enclaves. The FLN had set up an elaborate system of clandestine networks in the shantytowns to raise money for the war, eliminate potential rivals, and guard against police informants. "The impenetrable warren of lanes provided a natural redoubt for FLN militants, a place in which arms and documents could be concealed, while leaders could avoid police raids by escaping through secret exits or by constantly moving residence between townships."[79] To weaken this network, the government began razing the shantytowns and replacing them with worker hostels (Société nationale de construction de logements pour les travailleurs), temporary housing estates (*cités de transit*), and public housing projects (Habitations à loyer modérées [HLMs]).[80] A 1953 law that required all companies with more than ten employees to invest 1 percent of their total payroll in housing programs was used to finance the projects.[81] The construction of HLMs in distant suburbs contributed to the increasing racial and spatial polarization of the city. The government also acceded to Papon's request that the government remove the measures restricting the police's ability to penetrate Algerian networks. An ordinance of October 7, 1958, allowed the police to hold Algerians for up to fifteen days without charges and then deport them to army-run camps in Algeria.[82]

In 1961, however, these measures failed to prevent the Algerian war from spilling into Paris. The OAS continued to plant bombs in metro stations, and the FLN and Hadj's MNA engaged in pitched battles for control of the movement. Police use of torture and extrajudicial killings increased exponentially, and the FLN responded with several targeted assassinations of police officers. In June, however, the FLN unilaterally called a cease-fire. Papon and the French police responded by expanding and deepening the counterinsurgency offensive. The Parisian branch of the FLN begged the national leadership for permission to meet the increasing violence with violence of its own, but the leadership was adamant that *"there would be no armed riposte to police violence and that anybody found with even so much as a safety-pin on them will be condemned to death"* (emphasis mine).[83]

It was the FLN directive, with its warning of lethal punishment for those who disobeyed, that explained the response to what happened next. Police killings of North Africans increased in the month of September to thirty-seven (to seventy-five, according to Jean Luc Einaudi[84]), up from seven in August and three in July.[85] On October 5 Papon called for a citywide curfew for all Algerians. His troops were to stop all Algerians in violation, whom they could recognize by their facial features.[86] His communiqué contained an ominous warning: "In view of bringing an immediate end to the criminal activities of Algerian terrorists, new measures have just been taken by the Prefecture of the Police. . . . Muslim Algerian workers are advised most urgently to abstain from walking about during the night in the streets of Paris and in the Parisian suburbs, and most particularly during the hours of 8:30 P.M. to 5:30 A.M."[87]

The FLN responded to the violence by calling for an act of nonviolent civil disobedience. Algerian families, including women and children, were to march peaceably but in direct defiance of the curfew. They chose October 17, 1961, as the date. Papon responded to the announcement by ordering his troops to begin arresting all young men who looked Algerian or whose identity cards indicated they were Muslim.[88] He visited many police precincts imparting the following messages: "Settle your affairs with the Algerians yourselves. Whatever happens you are covered"; "For one blow give them ten"; "You don't need to complicate things. Even if the Algerians are not armed, you should think of them always as armed."[89]

On the evening of October 17, thirty thousand to forty thousand un-armed men, women, and children, many in their best Sunday attire, were met by about seven thousand police and members of special republican security companies armed with heavy truncheons or guns. They "let loose on demonstrators in, among other places, Saint Germain-des-Prés, the Opéra, the Place de la Concorde, the Champs Elysée, around the Place de l'Étoile and, on the edges of the city, at the Rond Point de la Defense beyond Neuilly."[90] Protesters were shot, beaten, garroted, and thrown half alive, along with the dead, into the Seine, their legs and hands bound. Thousands of Algerians were rounded up and brought to police stations, where they were beaten and tortured and/or killed, several dozen in front of Papon.[91] As many as six thousand others were held in sports stadiums, where torture continued, and some died running a gauntlet of police clubs. One small group of police bore witness in print: "At one end of the Neuilly bridge police troops and on the other, CRS riot police slowly moved towards one another. All the Algerians caught in this trap were struck down and systematically thrown in the Seine. At least a hundred of them under-went this treatment. The bodies of the victims floated to the surface daily and bore traces of blows and strangulation."[92]

Arrests and killings continued throughout the month.[93] Journalists were warned against covering the demonstrations and kept away from the deten-tion centers.[94] After the events, the police account of events—Algerians had opened fire—was distributed in the media, although no one questioned why no policeman had died. For the next thirty-six years no journalist or politician mentioned the event. The cover-up was complete. Only after Papon was arrested in 1999 for complicity in the deportation of Jews from Bordeaux in 1942 did the Lionel Jospin government admit the killing of forty protesters and acknowledge that the police had been excessive in their behavior. Although there has never been a complete accounting of the dead, most scholars put the number around two hundred.[95] An exhibit on the war by the Musée de l'Armée (Army Museum) put the number at hundreds.[96]

Injuries, many serious, ran far higher. At one protest meeting doctors reported that the figures from seven hospitals suggested that 448 had been seriously wounded. The FLN's own inquiry recorded 2,300 injuries, many from those rescued from the Seine.[97] Given the fear among Algerians in the city, it is likely that the FLN figure may be closer to the truth. Many of those rescued had not even been at the rally or anywhere nearby. Papon had simply used the march as a pretext to launch an almost genocidal campaign. One survivor, who lost an eye and a testicle from a beating at the police station, recalled hearing, while he was lying prostrate, Papon "issue orders: Liquidate this vermin for me, these dirty rats. Get to work. Do your business."[98]

The event left deep scars in the collective memory of Algerians and other former colonial subjects and their descendants in France. In 2002 the mayor of Paris installed a plaque in the first official mourning for the dead. In 2005 several new French films dealt with the issue, including one titled *Cache,* or "Hidden," and another called "Dark Night, October 17, 1961." Yet, as Rosenberg notes, "the abuse endured by North African migrants between the wars and the violent repression of peaceful demonstrators on the notorious night of 17 October 1961 was both logical and direct."[99] An African American journalist living in Paris incorporated the events of October 17 into his novel *The Stone Face.*[100] In it an African American ex-patriot watches a policeman clubbing an Algerian man. "Although he had fallen to the pavement, the policeman kept on swinging his long white nightstick down on the man, who was trying to protect his head from the blows with his arms. The man was screaming in a language Simenon [the hero] could not understand."[101] The beating of the Algerian by police causes Simenon to identify increasingly with Algerians in France. The blows call to mind his own beatings at the hands of police in the United States. "As he draws closer to Algerian residents he finds himself swept up in the roundups of October 17, only to be released soon after as an error, someone who did not belong. The naked logic of the police shatters Simenon's comfortable Parisian existence, forces him into conflict with the rest of the black American community in Paris, and is the catalyst that leads him to return to the United States to fight for civil rights."[102]

In December 1962 a judge heard the case of several young men who had been hospitalized after police had picked them up, beaten them, and thrown them in the Seine. One survivor testified that he had been picked up after work by five police officers, all holding machine guns, while he waited at the bus stop:

> The police officer examined the papers of everyone waiting for the bus. . . . [After handing the officer my papers] the officer ignored what I had just done and ordered me to get into the car. . . . In the car the officer continued to beat me, hitting me with the machine guns in the face and the head and all parts of my body. . . . I lost

consciousness. . . . When I regained consciousness I was afraid and kept my eyes shut. The car stopped and two police officers took me by the head and the feet to the bank of the Seine and threw me in the river. They stayed by the river for a time, and I was able to hide on the river's edge in the water until they left.[103]

Unable to work afterward, he lost his job. His doctors told him to file a complaint at the precinct. The officers at the police station just laughed. The same week seven cadavers had been found floating in the river. At the trial the police denied they had ever heard of any of them. The case was dismissed.

Despite the police massacre, Algerians did not riot. First, the severity of the repression, the mass killings and the deportations, a mere fifteen years after the Holocaust must have generated a great deal of fear. Second, the FLN had issued a stern warning that the punishment for striking out on one's own, and engaging in unplanned attacks, was death. Given the large number of fatalities among the followers of Messali Hadj, these warnings could not have been taken lightly. Third, the FLN's primary strategic goal was winning the war in Algeria. They had badly lost the battle in Paris; they could not afford to compromise the war. Most important, riots are spontaneous, unplanned outbursts by those who see no alternative avenue of redress. In this case the FLN tightly controlled Algerian neighborhoods, determined the choice of tactics and targets, and did so with the goal of winning the war in Algeria.

Several weeks later the Communist Party called for a demonstration against the OAS terrorist actions in France, which included the planting of bombs in subways and one in André Malraux's apartment, which had blinded a four-year-old girl. The police shot directly at the demonstrators, killing eight people, three of them women and one a child. The "political and public outcry against these French deaths at Charonne, contrasts starkly with the absence of major public protest at the deaths of Algerians on October 17, 1961,"[104] notes one historian, when twenty times that number were killed.

Racial Boundaries in the Aftermath of the Algerian War

In a period of seven years, France sent 2.1 million soldiers to fight in Algeria and somewhere between 300,000 and 430,000 Muslims.[105] The FLN killed somewhere between 12,000 and 16,000 Muslims, 2,700 Algerians of European origin, and somewhere between 10,000 and 17,000 French soldiers.[106] On March 16, 1962, leaders of organizations representing the two sides met in Évian to draw up plans for peace. The terms of the agreement were to be based on the claim—advocated by the FLN, its sympathizers in France, de Gaulle, the OAS, and the far right and one that French authorities had until then rejected—that "Algerians as a group were so different . . . from other French citizens, that they could not be accommodated within the French Republic."[107] The new French consensus appeared to be that expressed by de Gaulle to General Marie Paul Allard in 1959: "[Y]ou cannot possibly consider that one day an Arab, a Muslim, could be the equal of a Frenchman."[108]

By "inventing decolonization," in Shepard's words,[109] French authorities could retreat into the comfortable certainty that France had always lived up to its republican ideals. France was free of the troublesome, racist, backward, and reactionary terror-wielding colony and with it any recognition of, or policies to abate, racial discrimination in France. The integrationist debate was simply erased, as if it had never existed. No group fought harder to preserve this fiction than the Jewish community. No group suffered more than French Muslims. These diametrically opposite experiences help explain the nature of the divide between these two communities in Parisian *banlieues* today.

Initially, Prime Minister Guy Follett had argued that the Jews would be given French citizenship, but the leaders of the Jewish community strongly objected. They did not want simply to reinstate the Cremeau decree, giving them citizenship as Jews, a decree which had been lifted during Vichy. Experience had convinced them that their lives depended on not being singled out. They became the most passionate advocates for assimilation and republican values. Shepard notes,

> To counter the clear implication of this "communities" policy, Algerian Jewish leaders denied any importance to their history as a group. They turned to a history in which French laws had made them all as individuals French citizens, emphatically reasserting the assimilationist rhetoric central to what the historian Pierre Birnbaum describes as "Franco-Judaism." "Like all French people," as one of the preeminent community organizations, the Alliance Israélite universelle (AIU), laid out in a position paper on minority

status, they should be considered as "individuals," not belonging to "an ethnic community."[110]

Muslims, however, were not recognized as members of the French nation, much less as individuals. René Cassin, president of the Alliance Israélite universelle, argued that history had "explicitly made all Algerian 'Muslims' one people, just as, here implicitly, decolonization should make them—although currently French citizens—not-French."[111] By subsuming all Muslim groups in one category—Algerians—and subsuming themselves in the category "French," Jewish community leaders reified the categorical boundary separating themselves and Algerians of European origins from Algerian Muslims. It did not matter if a Jewish family had lived in the mountains for a century and practiced polygamy, or if the family now lived in Israel and had never set foot in France. Algerian Jews were undisputedly French. Muslims, in contrast—even those who had fought with the French army against the Algerian independence movement, had defended France in one or both world wars, had lived most of their lives in France, spoke better French than Arabic, and did not observe Islam—were decidedly Algerian. Although the Évian Accords had assured Muslim Algerians that they would be able to choose to retain French citizenship, all of that was forgotten once the exodus began.

Classifying all Muslims as Algerians and all Jews and Algerians of European descent as French was not only contrary to republican values and everything France had argued for thirteen decades; it also welcomed into France the very same people whose terrorist actions had turned the French public against the war. And it left those Algerians who had served in the French army in mortal danger. Yet French authorities did exactly that and without any explicit rationale. "In the exodus," notes Shepard, "virtually all policies and practices linked to integration disappeared, swept away by executive fiat in 1962."[112] The affirmative-action quotas that had been reserved for Muslims and other underprivileged minorities were now set aside for the *pied-noirs*, who were deemed people in distress. The goal was to help the French settlers make the transition to their new home, rather than address the effects of past discriminatory practices. Only a few suggested that France offer the Harkis the same treatment as other repatriates. As Sartre put it in a scathing essay titled "The Sleep Walkers," "All anyone wanted to hold onto was this: It's over with Algeria, it's over. . . . We gave all power to a dictator so that he could decide, without asking us, the best means to end the affair: genocide, resettlement, and territorial partition, integration, independence, we have washed our hands, it is his deal."[113]

Algerians as New Immigrants in France

At the end of the war, Algeria's economy was in ruins. The colonial government had driven two and a half million peasants into Centres de regroupements, surrounded by barbed wire and mined fortifications. When they were released in 1962, they lacked even the most basic prerequisites for living off the land. Another migrant interviewed by Sayad recalled, "Algeria, land of unemployment. Algeria, no work, no factories. Algeria, where there are lots of hands, so many hands that there is no work for them. When you have nothing in your hands, no trade, and don't know how to do anything, you're not going to turn up in Algiers looking for work. . . . You come to France. There is work in France, everyone knows that. You never hear it said that so and so, that this one or that one has left, isn't working, is unemployed. It just doesn't happen."[114]

Between 1962, when the war ended, and 1965 a total of 111,000 Algerians entered France. "No other European society had received such a large settler community from its colonial empire," notes Perry Anderson. "A million pieds-noirs expelled from the Maghreb, with all the bitterness of exiles. No other European society had received such a large influx of immigrants from the very zone once colonized: two and a half million maghrébins. That combination was always likely to release a political toxin."[115]

On April 10, 1964, Algeria and France signed an agreement limiting migration and establishing a trimester review of the permitted quota based on the economic situation in both countries. The agreement was similar to those signed in 1963 between France and Tunisia and between France, Mali, and Mauritania and the 1963 agreement between France and Senegal. But these agreements did not prevent the number of immigrants from continuing to grow, rising from 1,574,000 at the end of 1955 to 2,323,000 at the end of 1965. Between 1966 and 1975 three times as many immigrants arrived in France as had the preceding decade. In 1972 the number of foreigners in France reached 6 percent of the population, or 3.6 million. The number of North Africans alone reached 1.1 million, including nearly 800,000 from Algeria.[116]

Maxim Silverman calls this period *l'immigration sauvage*. Employers desperate to fill large labor shortages and impatient with formal paperwork skirted official channels and recruited labor directly. They sought legal recognition after the fact if at all. The number of migrants who came through formal channels fell to 21 percent in 1965 and 18 percent in 1968. In contrast, 65 percent of the new migrants were recruited directly by firms seeking cheap labor, and regularized after the fact.[117] This pattern was the reverse of that of previous waves of European immigration. It deprived the new migrants of access to the government services and housing that had previously facilitated integration and assimilation. Making matters worse, violence against Algerians, in particular, reached such crisis proportions that when faced with the unwillingness of French authorities to prosecute the perpetrators, the Algerian government (fearing for the safety of its citizens) suspended further immigration to France.

The French police, for their part, continued with the same system and personnel, including Papon as prefect, in the decade following the Algerian war.[118] Although the BAV was merged into the regular police force, most of its members were deployed to North African neighborhoods.[119] A police report written by Papon's lieutenant, Pierre Someveille, laid out their concerns in blatant terms: "The presence of nearly 200,000 persons originally from Algeria and African countries of French expression in the Paris region . . . poses a problem to the public authorities whose solution should be to deploy a policy limiting entries combined with expulsion measures and systematic repatriation of all inadaptable or undesirable elements. . . . The control of these ethnic groups in the social, sanitary, administrative and political domains proves more urgent each day."[120] Although the Algeria war was over, police violence against Algerians, in particular, did not subside. One of the most egregious incidents of police abuse was the kidnapping and disappearance of Ben Barka. Barka, "a labor organizer, mathematics professor," notes Amit Prakesh, in his powerful doctoral dissertation, "was in Paris to meet a filmmaker to discuss a documentary project on decolonization when he was apprehended in front of the Brasserie Lipp on the boulevard Saint-Germain by two members of the Prefecture of Police and members of the DST [Direction de la Surveillance du Territoire] and SDECE [Service de Documentation Extérieur et de Contre-Espionnage]. He was placed in a police car and was never seen again. The case is still open."[121] That this case alone did not cause a riot may have been due to the conviction of both policemen and Papon's forced resignation from the prefecture in 1967 following the trial.

On July 1, 1968, France unilaterally limited the number of Algerian immigrants to eleven hundred a month, and in December the country signed another agreement with Algeria making employment a condition of entry and capping immigration at thirty-five thousand a year.[122] The twin issues of immigration and racism now moved rapidly up the political agenda.[123] Most notably, 1965 marked the rise of Jean Marie Le Pen as manager of the presidential campaign of the far-right candidate Jean-Louis Tixier-Vignancour. Tixier-Vignancour had been a member of Action française in the 1930s, a veteran of the Vichy propaganda ministry in the 1940s, a supporter of the neo-fascist journal *Défense de l'Occident* in 1952, and an advocate for the OAS, General Salan, and Jean-Marie Bastien Thiry. Thiry was executed in 1962 for attempting to assassinate General de Gaulle after Algeria was granted independence. Le Pen had been a fascist street brawler in Paris in the 1940s and a torturer in Algeria in the 1950s.[124] In the 1964 presidential race, Tixier-Vignancour pulled 5 percent. Later he and Le Pen had a falling-out. Tixier-Vignancour believed that the party needed to reach out to mainstream conservatives to survive. Le Pen disagreed and ruptured the alliance.

The May 1968 Uprising

In 1968 France exploded into violence. The events building up to the violence were innocuous, especially in comparison to the slaughter of Algerian protesters seven years earlier. Yet police violence and the de Gaulle coup, the latter the result of the conflict in Algeria, were significant grievances. The 1968 rebellion would draw the political boundary that would impact future struggles around immigration rights, police reform, and democratic representation. Much as was the case with the student movement in the United States, imperial and colonial wars from Algeria to Vietnam were motivating factors. On the one hand, the French students strongly identified with both liberation movements in the former French colonies and civil-rights struggles in the United States. On the other hand, unlike their counterparts in the United States who had been deeply influenced by and connected to civil-rights struggles, French students ignored racial discrimination in France. The failure of the students (many of whom would become scholars or politicians) to acknowledge the links between race and class and the role of discrimination in ensuring a cheap and docile labor force in France would remain a blind spot for the French left.

On March 22, 1968, 150 students occupied an administration building at Nanterre University to discuss class discrimination, cuts in funding to the university, and the arrest of five students—one from Nanterre—accused of planting bombs in Chase Manhattan Bank and American Express offices. One student, Daniel Cohn-Bendit (French born but of German Jewish parents), had been accused of printing a flawed recipe for Molotov cocktails on the back page of the student paper. The administration responded to the protest by calling the police, who subsequently surrounded the campus building. The students left without much ado after publishing their concerns. The university administrators, however, insisted on a disciplinary hearing and threatened several students, including Cohn-Bendit, who had been arrested by police on March 27, with expulsion. Incensed, other students at Nanterre protested, and on May 2 the administrators closed the university.

On May 3 students at the Sorbonne struck in solidarity with their fellow students at Nanterre. The university rector, Alain Peyrefitte, instructed police to clear the Sorbonne courtyard. Kedward calls it the "single most important moment in the first chain of events."[125] The police then arrested the protesters who had already agreed to leave. As the packed police vans wound their way through campus, angry students tried to block their way. The police responded to student taunts with tear gas and more arrests. By day's end the police had arrested 574 students, including 179 minors, 45 women, and 58 foreigners. Among those arrested were Daniel Cohn-Bendit, Alain Krivine of the Jeunesse communiste révolutionnaire, and Jacques Sauvegot of the Union of French University Students (UNEF).[126] The UNEF and the Union of University Teachers called for action. When on May 6 more than 60,000 students and teachers marched in protest, the police charged the crowd, indiscriminately using truncheons and tear gas, "in the most violent clashes since the Algerian war was recorded on camera," notes Kedward.[127]

Televised police violence helped the movement generate sympathy beyond the university gates. High school students and teachers as well as increasing numbers of young workers now joined the protests. At the Arc de Triomph the students read a list of demands. First, all criminal charges against arrested students must be dropped. Second, police must vacate the universities. Third, both the university at Nanterre and the Sorbonne should resume their normal schedules of classes. De Gaulle responded by calling for reinforcements and heavier, more repressive police actions. On Friday, May 10, students in the Latin Quarter tore apart cobblestone streets and built makeshift barricades with the paving stones. The police retreated momentarily but returned in force, wielding batons, beating students, and shooting tear gas into the crowd. When they blocked students from crossing the bridges, pitched battles ensued and continued throughout the night. By morning 274 police and 116 demonstrators had been injured and 128 vehicles had been damaged and 60 set aflame in what would become a standard repertoire of protest in France.

On May 11 over a million people marched through Paris in protest. The police vacated the Sorbonne, allowing the radicalized students to occupy and christen it the "people's university." In the days that followed, students formed over four hundred popular action committees nationally. Workers too entered into direct conflict with the regime. The major union confederations called for a twenty-four-hour general strike on May 14 to protest government repression and express solidarity with the students. Sud-Aviation near Nantes was the first to combine the strike with the occupation of the factory. On May 15 the Renault plants in Cleon followed suit, and workers in other Renault factories, including the one in Boulogne-Billancourt outside Paris, occupied their plants the following day. Georges Séguy, the Communist secretary-general of the Confédération générale du travail (CGT), credited the students with weakening the government and giving workers the opportunity to voice their complaints: "[W]orkers understood that the government was put to the test and weakened by the confrontation [with the students] and that the moment had come to settle accounts."[128] Similarly the leader of the Confédération générale des cadres (CGC), André Malterre, said that the student strikes had opened the way for the factory occupations "by revealing the weakness of the government."[129]

By May 16 workers had occupied roughly fifty factories, and by May 17 over two hundred thousand workers were on strike. On May 18 that number ballooned to two million. A new strike was called for May 20. This time over five million workers participated. The transportation, energy, communication, and financial services were all affected, as were the educational and metallurgical sectors. In the industrial *banlieues* of Argenteuil and Bezons (in Val-d'Oise), "strikers became more subversive. A few workers ignored the CGT's condemnation of illegal sequestrations and expelled management from factories."[130] When on May 25 the CGT accepted Renault's offer of a 35 percent increase in the minimum wage, a 10 percent increase in salary for all its members, and reductions of two hours a week for those working over forty-eight hours and one hour for those laboring between forty-five and forty-eight hours, shop stewards rejected the accord and called for a continuation of the strike.[131] Eleven million French workers, approximately two-thirds of the French workforce, stormed the factories in the largest nationwide wildcat strike in the history of any industrialized nation; most had been called by local CGT militants.[132] The CGT leaders withdrew from the accords.

There is some dispute over the nature of the wildcat strikers. Michael Seidman points out that few of the leaders belonged to the far-left Trotskyite and Maoist groups dominating the student movement and that the ties between students and workers were actually quite weak. Rather, unionized workers had taken the opportunity provided by the students to launch a strike of their own. CGT militants were responsible for sixty-eight of the seventy-seven wildcat strikes. Militants in the conservative Catholic union Confédération française démocratique du travail (CFTD) had called six, and those in the Trotskyist Force ouvrière (FO) had called three. Relatively more mature workers had organized the bulk of the work stoppages. Those between the ages of thirty and forty had called fifty-one of the eighty-eight strikes. Those between the ages of twenty and thirty had initiated twenty-four, and those under twenty had called seven.[133] The strikers were overwhelmingly white and French, unlike the workforce. Although a quarter of French workers were immigrants, immigrants played a minimal role. Only 9 percent of the strikers were foreign: three Spanish "anarchists"; two "insolent" Algerians; and several Poles, Italians, and Portuguese.[134]

Melvin Seeman argues that the more extreme actions such as the kidnappings of management, occupations of the factories, expulsions of employers, and violence against nonstriking workers were taken by less experienced activists, who joined the movement only after it was well under way. Similarly, Philip Converse and Roy Pierce observe that "although hardly politicized, they were quite willing to join the excitement, sweeping by them, and the streets contained large proportions of people whose normal involvement in politics was non-existent."[135] Riding the crest of a mass movement empowered protesters but created wild pendulum swings from inaction to radicalism. Edward Ransford had come to a similar conclusion in his study of the Watts riot, notes Seeman. Ransford found that members of black militant organizations were less likely to riot.[136] He attributed this to their heightened sense of personal efficacy. Their organizations had won victories previously and thus offered the possibility of future success. As Kurt Weyland observes, "Well established organizations can maintain collective action over time and pursue a strategy of cumulative gradual reform, which entails lower cost and risk. By contrast spontaneous masses need to win now if they want to win ever: they therefore rapidly move to full-scale conflict to achieve this victory."[137]

With his government on the verge of collapse, de Gaulle met with military commanders to coordinate the actions of loyal military units. In a radio address (the national television service was on strike), he announced the dissolution of the National Assembly and called for a referendum to be followed by new parliamentary elections for June 23, 1968. He ordered workers to return to work and threatened to institute a state of emergency if they did not. On June 5 the remaining strikers returned to work or were ousted from their plants by the police. The national student union called off street demonstrations. The government banned a number of leftist organizations. On June 6 the police retook the Sorbonne. De Gaulle triumphed in the legislative elections held later in June, and the crisis came to an end. Cohn-Bendit, on a visit to Germany, found his entry barred when he attempted to return home. The government had declared him an undesirable alien.

By the 1970s the political right was stronger than before and the radical students and workers were in retreat. For all its size and militancy, most of the movement's achievements proved ephemeral. Worse, despite its commitment to third-world liberation struggles, the student movement failed to engage the urgent issue of civil rights in France, specifically the rights of Algerian nationals and other black and Arab immigrants from France's former colonies—issues that would define political battles in years to come. By failing to address the urgent issue of civil rights, the student movement allowed the far right to frame the twin issues of race and immigration for the country at large. In October 1969 a new right-wing party emerged out of the ashes of the now-banned fascist political group Occident. The new party, or Ordre nouveau (new order), included an array of Vichy leaders, many of whom openly expressed nostalgia for German occupation. The most influential of them was the Nazi collaborator François Duprat. Duprat claimed that the "time was right to set up a National Front, open to all extremist sects which would contest elections on a program somewhere short of fascist revolution as a means of putting fascists in contact with potential recruits."[138] But the National Front was not fully formed until 1972, one year before the Ordre nouveau was banned.

The big influx of North African immigrants in the 1960s became an organizing tool for the Ordre nouveau. In 1966 immigrants began to fight increased deportation proceedings through a new organization, the Fédération des associations de solidarité avec travailleurs immigrés (FASTI or coalition of organizations in solidarity with immigrant workers).[139] The Ordre nouveau used the increased visibility of North African immigrants, the bitterness many French felt over the Algerian war, and the May 1968 uprising to reach out to conservative voters. In 1972 its leaders created the National Front for French Unity, with Le Pen at its helm. In addition to the Nazi collaborator, Vichy leader, and Holocaust denier François Duprat, the National Front included Victor Barthélomy, the former general-secretary of Doriat's Parti popular français, who played a leading role in efforts to form a single Fascist Party during the occupation and establish a Nazi Europe after working with Mussolini in Italy. Doriat and Barthélomy were critical to the establishment of "a press, a cadre and a structure with a degree of local implantation."[140] Together with Tixier-Vignancour, Maurice Bardeche (a leading French fascist intellectual before and during the war and Holocaust denier after), and Oswald Mosley (the founder of the British Union of Fascists), they formed the Mouvement social Européen before collaborating with Le Pen in the Algérie française and Tixier-Vignancour campaigns.

Other members of the national leadership of the new front included François Brigneau, former member of Marcel Déat's Collaborationist National Popular Rally (RNP); Roger Holeindre, former member of the OAS; Roland Gaucher, former member of Déat's RNP; Léon Gaultier, former general secretary of the Waffen SS Division Charlemagne; Gilbert Gilles, former adjutant in the Waffen SS Division Charlemagne and former member of the OAS; Pierre Bousquet, former corporal in the Waffen SS Division Charlemagne; André Dufraisse, former member of the Parti populaire français who also served in the Division Charlemagne; Jacques Bompard, former supporter of the OAS; and others of similar background. Concerned that the National Front's Nazi and Vichy origins would isolate it, Duprat advised that "explicit references to National Socialism be dropped."[141] To further distance the party from the Nazi genocide, Duprat organized the publication and distribution of the basic texts of Holocaust denial. After Duprat's violent death from a car bomb in 1978 Le Pen took up his mentor's cloak. In place of appeals for racial purity, Le Pen spoke of Europe's superior culture and civilizing mission and advocated the "humanitarian" repatriation of immigrants.

In 1973 Le Pen called "for a tough regulation of foreign immigration and in particular of immigration from outside Europe,"[142] blaming Arabs for falling wages, rising unemployment, increased crime, and the oil crisis. Azouz Begag observes, "In the public imagination oil was associated at one and the same time with Arabs and with unemployment. These lines of thought became so intertwined that Maghrebins ended up being blamed for unemployment and became a scapegoat for the economic downturn. Anti-Arab racism took on alarming proportions."[143] Although Le Pen received only 0.74 percent of the vote in the next year's presidential election, the immigration issue was already moving up the political agenda. Anxious not to be upstaged by Le Pen, the newly elected president, Valéry Giscard d'Estaing (1974–81), designated a new cabinet position: secretary of state for foreign workers. The first to hold this position, André Postel-Viney, suspended both primary immigration and family reunification before leaving office six months later, reducing the number of permanent immigrant workers from 204,702 in 1973 to 67,415 in 1975.[144] The ban on primary immigration was never lifted. The ban on family reunification was lifted after being ruled unlawful by France's highest administrative court, the Conseil d'état, in 1978.

D'Estaing's third secretary of state for foreign workers, Lionel Stoléru, argued that immigration was antithetical to the interests of the nation and offered immigrants ten thousand francs each to return to their country of origin.[145] While the offer was intended for North and sub-Saharan Africans (an increasingly prominent section of the immigrant population), only the Spanish and Portuguese took Stoléru up on his offer. (Both groups were happy to return home after the fall of their nations' respective dictatorships.) Stoléru also passed a circular (the Marcellin-Fontanet) permitting the police to expel any immigrant who failed to furnish proof of active employment or decent housing. "Police stepped up their presence in the ZUPS (housing projects) where these young people lived. Thousands of them would soon see the inside of police stations, courts and prisons. Many were expelled from France to the 'home' country of their parents, where they had never set foot. Most came back to France illegally, living clandestinely in their hometown."[146]

Immigrants protested these measures and engaged in hunger strikes in Valence, Toulouse, Paris, La Ciotat, Lyon, Bordeaux, Strasbourg, Mulhouse,

Lille, Nice, Montpellier, Aix-en-Provence, and St. Etienne; walked off the job at the Boulogne-Bilancourt factory of Renault (outside Paris) in April 1973; and organized protest marches in Paris. "These were the first signs of a widespread mobilization," notes Silverman, "by foreign workers against discriminatory legislation and racism."[147] In the universities, North African students created the Mouvement des travailleurs Arabes in 1972. Police responded to the growing mobilization of black and Arab immigrants with increasing brutality. Begag notes, "Relations with law enforcement worsened. This degradation was further aggravated by the racism of the policemen 'repatriated' from Algeria after independence in 1962, many of whom had been recruited into the law enforcement services of metropolitan France, where they set about settling scores with the Arabs who had launched a war to gain independence and had then come and installed themselves in France."[148]

In 1976 young people in the poorest immigrant *banlieues* began to organize, with the help of social workers. Their relationship with police grew more violent. In 1977 in Vitry-sur-Seine, a southern suburb of Paris, approximately thirty young people attacked three policemen in rage. D'Estaing convened the Peyrefitte Commission to report on violence. He began the report with a warning: "a feeling of *insécurité* (insecurity) . . . can itself engender violence in a society where the rule of law is no longer upheld."[149] The commissioners blamed "the ecology of public housing projects marked by social anomie and class segregation" and deplored the immense bleak towers and lack of green spaces. "The city today has its Indians and its reservations," they warned.[150]

The commission's use of the word "insecurity" to refer to the feeling of unease provoked by a lawless society became standard political parlance. Over time the term grew in significance politically, even when it did not correspond to actual crime. Between 1959 and 1979 penal sentences for juvenile offenders doubled, rising from 15 to 32 percent.[151] In June 1979 the police in Nanterre, a northern suburb of Paris, arrested dozens of young North Africans in a sweep that did not include a single white French youth. A group of young lawyers expressed outrage at the incident.[152] The same year a terrible incident of police brutality in the Lyon suburb of Vaulx-en-Velin further enraged Maghrébin youths. Seventeen-year-old Abdelkrim Tabert had developed a strategy for taunting police, winning the admiration of other neighborhood youths. He would steal a moped and deliberately drive past the police. On September 15, 1979, a police patrol tried to arrest him. They surrounded him at a friend's apartment. Realizing that he was trapped, he slit his wrists. A shot was fired and rumors spread rapidly throughout the *banlieue*. As the police dragged Abdelkrim wounded and bleeding, his brothers and friends ran behind them. Soon several hundred North African youths surrounded the police holding Abdelkrim. Fighting broke out and a police superintendent was beaten. Police reinforcements arrived along with firemen, and the young people responded by throwing bottles, stones, garbage, and bicycle parts.[153] Throughout 1979 confrontations between young people and police in the *banlieues* of Marseille, Paris, and Lyon were frequent. In 1980 the "Rock against Police" movement was created in Paris. On April 19, 1980, over one thousand young people assembled in a small plot in the twentieth arrondissement to dance to music and vent their hatred of police.[154]

Housing Segregation in Paris

Housing also emerged as a major issue in the 1970s, especially after the deaths of five African workers from asphyxiation in apartment fires. Fifteen thousand residents of immigrant hostels marched in strike in 1975, protesting both rents and rigid rules governing life in the hostels. The strike lasted until 1980, becoming the longest strike ever outside the workplace.[155] Most hostels were located in dilapidated inner-city neighborhoods and were often run by speculators, slumlords, and racketeers. In other cases workers moved into bidonvilles or shantytowns to make room for arriving family members. Most homes in these areas were little more than shacks, lacking basic sanitary facilities, sewers, running water, and electricity. In the mid-1960s over seventy-five thousand people were still officially classified as living in these bidonvilles (and most estimate the actual number to be as much as three times that), and the numbers continued to grow throughout the early 1970s.[156] The hostel-style accommodations created in 1956 to house Algerian workers were woefully insufficient as the workers' family members began to join them in Paris. In 1975, the French government shifted its strategies toward resolving the housing crisis. It stopped investing in the construction of hostels and began investing considerable funds in the construction of better-quality public housing for immigrant families.[157]

However, the creation of new housing lagged far behind the phasing out of existing housing. The impetus behind the building of HLMs in distant suburbs was fear of the threat posed by the network of Algerian bidonvilles inside Paris. Yet some public officials had more benevolent motives and believed that placing HLMs in the *banlieues* near the factories where the workers were employed would reduce overcrowding in the city and give workers access to greenery and open spaces. In practice, however, there was little greenery and few parks were created. The construction of HLMs in the *banlieues* moved immigrants from the city center. One Algerian woman I spoke to in Aubervilliers remembered her childhood in Paris with nostalgia: "I could walk for hours and hours. Paris is such a beautiful city to walk in, and everything was accessible. Out here in the *banlieues* there is nothing. It is ugly here, and it takes so long to get to Paris. I never seem to have the time." Another French Algerian woman I spoke with remembered the move quite bitterly: "I grew up in the Marais. It wasn't till we moved to the *banlieue* that I learned I was different. There I learned that foreigners are poor."

By the 1970s the economic downturn had led to the closing of most factories in the *banlieues*. As the HLMs filled with immigrants, French tenants abandoned the area. "The French whose standard of living had been improving began to leave the suburbs," note Renee Zauberman and René Lévy, and "the public agencies responsible for the allocation of public housing filled them with former shantytown and slum-dwellers, along with new immigrants and large families, thus encouraging spatial and social segregation."[158] The problem was accentuated by the distance of the *banlieues* from the city center and the government's failure to build public transit to the area, pairing, as Paul Silverstein notes, "socioeconomic marginalization . . . with spatial isolation."[159] The urban transportation network failed to keep pace with the growth of the suburban population. The metro reached a small minority of the closest suburbs, while the farther suburbs were served, if at all, by local train service. As was the case with the urban renewal policies pursued in the United States, the result was the increased segregation of poor immigrants and racial minorities in areas of concentrated poverty.

Police Reform and the Activation of Racial Boundaries in the First Socialist Administration

In 1981 the Socialist candidate François Mitterrand swept into office promising, among other reforms, to legalize immigrant organizations and grant residency permits to all foreign workers who had entered France before January 1, 1981. His election ended a hunger strike that several clergy had

begun the previous month in the Lyon *banlieue* housing project Les Minguettes to protest the deportation of youths of North African origin. Mitterrand also vowed to abolish capital punishment, maximum-security quarters
in prison, and deportation laws and to enact sweeping revisions of the Penal
Code and Code of Criminal Procedure. Last, he pledged to drastically reform the police force.

Many of Mitterrand's supporters had been students in 1968, and police
reform was high on their agenda. The last wave of recruitment of police
had been during the Algerian war, when the sole qualification was hatred
of Arabs. The lack of accountability and professional standards had led to
massive corruption: "Many policemen were involved in illegal activities,"
notes Bonelli; "some were pimps and most of them usually drunk during
their service."[160] The director of the national police told him that "when he
arrived to Paris in the early 80's, as a young officer, he was the only one
not drinking and making sport of his service."[161] The government (taking
advantage of a wave of retirements) implemented two major reforms. First,
it institutionalized professional standards for the selection and training of
new recruits. Second, it purchased new, more modern office equipment,
vehicles, and weapons. "It is almost impossible to compare police behav-
iour in the 70's with that of today," Bonelli insists. "This does not mean
that there is no racism or alcoholism anymore in the police; but they have
disappeared as structural factors."[162] That might have been true had these
reforms not taken place during a period of increasing racial segregation and
competitive political outbidding on immigration and security.

In fact the government's promise of immigration and police reform
energized critics on the right and the left. Right-wing politicians attacked
the new government for being soft on crime and immigration and for pursuing policies that threatened the security of middle- and working-class
French families. As Fassin notes, "The historic victory of the left in the
general elections of 1981, after 23 years of conservative domination, provoked the restructuring of the French political landscape, with the rapid
rise of the far right and the weakening of the traditional right. The National
Front built its success principally on two issues, immigration and security,
often mixing the two by presenting immigrants, or their children, as the
major source of insecurity."[163] To maintain relevance the traditional right
took up both issues with increased fervor.

Some Communist mayors, anxious to avoid being out-segued by the
right on immigration, crime, and security, began accusing immigrants of
engaging in drug trafficking and other forms of crime.[164] The national

Communist leaders soon followed suit and issued a call for the repatriation of immigrants and rejected proposals to grant them voting rights in national elections.[165] As politicians from left to right scrambled to out-tough each other on crime and immigration, the issue dominated the news. One Communist mayor in Vitry went so far as to incite a pogrom against immigrants after he bulldozed their homes. Fassin notes,

> In mid-twentieth-century Paris, the Algerian population, in spite of being French nationals, were seen as undesirables, and well documented raids on the neighborhoods where they were concentrated went along with a whole trail of violence, harassment, racist insults and illegal detentions. The continuity running through these repressive practices towards certain sectors of society, from laboring classes to working-class populations, and from colonial subjects to immigrants and minorities, should not be underestimated: the activity of law enforcement has always been focused on groups whose economic and social vulnerability was easily inverted into the threat of crime and a peril to security.[166]

In the Les Minguettes suburb of Lyon, youths devised a game they called a *rodeo*. They would taunt the police, steal a car, provoke a chase, and, just as the police came near, jump out, set the car aflame, and run. In the summer of 1981 there were 250 *rodeos*. When the police killed a young man during such a *rodeo*, the neighborhood reacted aggressively. One young man told Silverstein, "It was from the moment of police provocations that the youth began to become aggressive. . . . The rodeos were to respond to everything they had undergone, they and their parents. . . . The rage they had in themselves was directed at the cars."[167] Similarly, Fassin points out, "What is manifested in these frantic flights is past experience of interactions with the police, and their occasionally playful aspects should not mask the real base of irrepressible fear. In short, a sort of immune reaction which, unlike that produced by vaccination, allows the danger to which one is exposed to be recognized, but does not protect one from it."[168]

The Rise of Le Pen

In 1980 Le Pen had been unable to get the five hundred signatures he needed to run against Mitterrand. Two factors facilitated the rise of the

Front National (FN), claims Antonis Ellinas. The first was Mitterrand's decision in May 1982 to call the presidents of three public television channels and ask them to grant Le Pen airtime, a cynical ploy to pull right-wing voters away from his rivals.[169] The second was the surprising success of the National Front in local elections. In the 1982 cantonal elections the National Front scored some surprising successes. In the small town of Dreux the party's general secretary Jean-Pierre Stirbois and his wife won 12.6 and 9.3 percent of the vote respectively. By 1983 the National Front had garnered 11.3 percent of the vote in municipal elections in Paris with Le Pen's slogan "Paris for the Parisians."[170] In a by-election in Dreux that same year, the National Front won 16.7 percent of the vote. From that time forward the National Front could count on substantial media attention.

Aware that Le Pen was making inroads, Mitterrand again maneuvered to cut the support base of the traditional right by changing the rules governing parliamentary elections from single-member to proportional representation. The following year Le Pen's National Front won 11 percent in the European elections. With the increased power of the National Front, the immigrant issue moved front and center. A spate of violent attacks by white Frenchmen on young immigrants soon followed. In 1983 an older white Frenchman shot seven young people in a suburban Parisian *cité*, injuring several residents and killing a nine-year-old North African girl and a fifteen-year-old North African boy. Police killings of minority youth also increased, and included one child as young as nine.[171]

North Africans responded to these violent transgressions—thinly veiled rhetorical attacks by political elites and more violent overt attacks in their neighborhoods—with a peaceful nonviolent protest march of *Beurs* (Algerians born in France) for "equality and against racism." The marchers departed from the same site where Algerians had been thrown in the Seine two decades before, and the march culminated in a sit-down strike in the Talbot plant. Some members of the government portrayed the event as the actions of violent Islamists, what would become an increasingly common refrain and catchall explanation for every disorder in *banlieues*.

In 1984 Le Pen "appeared on one of the most popular and sought after French television shows, *The Hour of Truth*."[172] After the broadcast, support for Le Pen doubled from 3.5 percent to 7 percent.[173] By the end of the month his support had reached 18 percent in polls.[174]

The rise of the National Front changed the parameters of partisan competition over how to deal with immigration. . . . Between 1983 and 1985 there was a programmatic shift of the moderate right on cultural politics. . . . Candidates from both the UDF [Union pour la Démocatie Française] and the RPR [Rassemblement pour la République]—and even from the Socialists—pledged to stop the "invasion" of foreigners and linked immigration with unemployment and crime. In the summer of 1983 the Gaullist mayor of Paris, Jacques Chirac, led an immigration clampdown, noting [that] the "threshold of tolerance" had been passed and that France no longer had the means to support those who "abused her hospitality."[175]

Mitterrand and the Socialists responded by backtracking on immigrants' rights. Instead of granting immigrants the vote in municipal elections, as they had promised during the campaign, they offered them "aid to reinsertion" programs to help them return to their home countries, a policy shockingly reminiscent of Stoléru's "aid to return."

In 1984 Convergence 84 organized a march against racism, a march that led to the creation of SOS Racism. The organization later allied itself with the Socialist Party, a move that alienated it from *banlieue* youths. *Beurs* marched again in 1985 and this time helped found another antiracism organization, France Plus. But whites continued to move to the right on the immigrant issue. In the 1986 parliamentary elections the conservative RPR won handily, and Mitterrand was forced to name Jacques Chirac as prime minister. The National Front won 10 percent, or thirty-five of the seats in the Assembly, and in several crucial municipalities the traditional conservative candidates even allied with them.

Chirac took up "the nationalist and anti-immigrant mantle paraded so successfully by Le Pen" with a vengeance.[176] He made Charles Pasqua, a hard-liner close to the National Front, minister of the interior in charge of the police. "Illegal immigrants," Pasqua warned, would be "deported in train loads."[177] The remark was chillingly delivered just as Klaus Barbi stood trial for the deportation of trainloads of Jews to extermination camps. The parliament shifted decision-making power over expulsions from the judiciary to local police chiefs, and Pasqua instructed the police to conduct on-the-spot identity checks.[178] The new immigration laws and the new police powers to enforce them encouraged both racial profiling and police violence. An older Algerian man told Sayad,

They are always asking you questions. Are you French and in what sense? If you're not French, why not? And now the identity checks have started again, the look in the cop's eyes, you see that—that moron and it can't be said that he looks like a genius asks you: "your papers." . . . Deep inside he'd have liked to be the only one who was French, the good Frenchman, along with all the other Frenchmen like him. They say he has "French roots." What roots? Roots aren't pretty but they are roots. I suppose other French people just have French branches, French foliage. You can see all that going through the cop's mind, even if his eyes don't shine with intelligence.[179]

Within a week of Pasqua's appointment, there were three notorious incidents of police violence. Nakome B'owole, an immigrant from the Congo, was shot in the face after being detained at the police station for stealing a pack of cigarettes. The next day Rachid Ardjouni, the eighteen-year-old son of an Arab immigrant, was shot in the head by police pursuing him for disturbing the peace. That same evening Pascal Tais, a Moroccan drug addict, was found dead in a police cell after "having suffered a ruptured spleen, broken ribs, and a punctured lung."[180] In three months three times as many immigrants were expelled as had been expelled in the entire previous year, including 101 legal Malian immigrants.[181] As the country cracked down on current immigrant residents, it closed its doors to new ones. Between 1982 and 1989 the number of asylum seekers, mostly from war-torn sub-Saharan Africa, increased from 22,500 to 61,400, but the approval rate for granting asylum decreased. Many of those already living in France legally had their petitions for visa renewals denied, making them *sans papiers*—literally "people without papers"—easy targets for police. The *sans papiers* later organized a small protest movement.

Race polarization helped the National Front increase its share of the vote in the 1988 presidential election to a record 14.38 percent. Mitterrand was reelected, however, and the Socialists regained their majority in the National Assembly. Michel Rocard, the new prime minister, attenuated some of the more drastic elements of Pasqua's legislation and humanized some of the rules for expulsion. But Chirac, as the new mayor of Paris, maintained his hostility toward non-EU immigrants, suggesting in 1990 that the problems of French workers were related to lax immigration controls. "How would you like it," he asked,

if you were a French worker who worked along with your wife and together earned 15,000 francs and you lived in public housing next to a man with three or four wives, twenty children, who took home 50,000 francs a month from welfare, without working. And if in addition, you had to deal with the noise and the smell, well the French worker goes crazy. And it is not racist to say that. We have done more than enough to unite immigrant families. It is time to pose the debate in our country, which is truly a moral debate, to know if it is natural that foreigners, who do not participate in national solidarity or pay taxes, should have the same benefits as the French.[182]

In reality, the number of foreign nationals in France had fallen by 9 percent in 1990 and by 5.6 percent in Paris. Chirac was only the mayor and had little control over national policy, but he tapped into an increasingly insecure white France vulnerable to demagogic appeals and increasingly racially polarized, for what had changed was the proportion that arrived not from Europe but from France's erstwhile colonial empire. In 1975 European nationals accounted for 57 percent of the foreign population; in 1990 their percentage had declined to 49 percent.

The distance between the *banlieues* and the city center, accentuated by poor public transit, rendered the lives of most Arabs and blacks invisible to most whites and fed into racial stereotypes. Silverstein notes,

Radially laid out, the commuter and train lines connect the suburbs directly to Paris, leaving only bus service and the occasional tramway to link suburb to suburb. Those that do connect the suburbs to Paris are heavily surveilled, with fixed cameras and roving patrols of police, military gendarmes, and conductors empowered to make arrests. The result is the relative physical and symbolic separation of *cités* from each other and from Paris proper. The concomitant stigmatizing effects of this isolation, alongside the physical dilapidation and economic impoverishment of the housing projects, have made residence in certain *cités* an impediment to being hired for a job, thus reproducing the unemployment that underwrites much of the social stigmatization of the housing projects in the first place.[183]

It also increased discriminatory policing, as Fassin observes, "by allowing police action to be focused on specific neighborhoods, and by rendering this reality invisible to the majority."[184]

Early in the summer of 1990, Thomas Claudio, age twenty-one, was killed during a motorcycle chase with police in the Mas de Taureau housing complex or *cité* outside Lyon. For three consecutive nights young people battled with police, looted stores, and in what would become a standard repertoire, set cars aflame. The riots took the left by surprise. The neighborhood had been a recipient of expansive social programs including housing renovation and social assistance, and the local Communist mayor had devoted 60 percent of the local budget to the creation of sports and education for youths. The neighborhood was "an image of perfection. . . . For the Socialist MP, Jean-Jacques Queranne, for the Communist mayor Maurice Charrier, for rightwing Lyon Urban community president, Michel Noir, the rehabilitation undertaken in this district of Lyon since 1985 was quite simply exemplary."[185] That police violence might be the problem escaped notice.

Continuing police violence and the refusal of authorities to hold violent police accountable sparked riots in Vauls-en-Vélin (a suburb of Lyon) on October 6–7, 1990, and in Sartrouville (in the Seine valley near Paris) on March 26–27, 1991; additional confrontations between youths and police took place in Parisian suburbs such as Val-Fourré (in May 1991 after Aïssa Ihich, eighteen, an asthma sufferer, was asphyxiated after being severely beaten by police) and Mantes Les Jolie (in June 1992 after Youssef Khaif was fatally shot by a policeman who mistook him for another driver).[186] Instead of addressing the issue of police violence, the Socialists pushed through further anti-immigrant measures. The number of visas granted fell to 2.3 million in 1994, from 5.6 million in 1987. The number of visas issued to Algerians, in particular, fell from 571,000 to 103,000 over the same period. Consulates rejected even well-founded applications because they were no longer legally required to give their reasons for doing so.

In 1993, the conservative Union pour une Mouvement Populaire (UMP) won the parliamentary elections and Édouard Balladur became prime minister. Balladur appointed Pasqua, yet again, minister of the interior. This time Pasqua tried to strip children born in France of their citizenship. Under the infamous Pasqua laws, children of immigrants would not be eligible for citizenship until age eighteen, when they could apply for citizenship, although the state was under no obligation to grant it. The Socialists later modified this policy, allowing young people to apply for citizenship at eighteen and automatically granting it except under certain conditions, such as when an applicant had a prior prison sentence. The loopholes, especially that involving prior prison sentences, left a proportion of young men virtually stateless. The incarceration rate of foreigners in French prisons more than tripled between 1975 and 1995, making foreigners six times more likely to be confined and seven times more likely to be arrested than French nationals. Discounting immigration offenses, foreigners were still three times more likely to be confined than French nationals. They were most disproportionately arrested for nonviolent crimes; 40.6 percent of those were arrested for forgery, 29.2 percent for narcotics offenses, and 85 percent for cannabis. More than half hailed from three countries: Algeria, Morocco, and Tunisia.[187] Similarly the number of minors sent to prison increased by 45 percent between 1993 and 1995, reversing a ten-year decline.[188]

Pasqua also introduced, on August 10, 1993, "a major expansion of the police's scope for conducting checks, not only in the absence of any crime, but also regardless of the individual's behavior. It represented a turning point in the deployment of law enforcement in poor neighborhoods, making police discretion legally admissible in this matter, almost without limits."[189] The most far-reaching of all Pasqua's reforms, however, was the creation of the Brigades anti-criminalité (BAC), literally anticrime squads composed of plainclothes officers in unmarked cars that to all intents and purposes acted as paramilitary squads outside the chain of command and with almost total impunity. Fassin notes, "The idea of paramilitarization gives a sense of this tendency to supplement the regular police, or replace them with squads whose mission, clothing, arms, style of intervention and relationship to the hierarchy place them at the fringes of the official structure. This logic readily leads to recruitment along specific lines that favor radical politicization. The anticrime squad I studied offers a noteworthy illustration. Released from most of the usual constraints and duties of regular law enforcement[,] it did not hold back from open expression of its far right leanings."[190]

In the 1995 presidential race, the National Front won a record 15.2 percent of the vote and Chirac won the presidency. The National Front maintained its strong showing in the 1997 parliamentary elections. The political system skewed right, and the perspectives of immigrants and their children were excluded from the debate. Police were rewarded for tough actions in minority neighborhoods and with minority youths and were made aware that there would be no personal consequences if their actions caused serious harm to black or Arab young people.

During the mid-1990s, police actions against *banlieue* youths outside Paris grew more deadly, and these young people often responded with the burning of cars and buildings and increasing confrontations with police. Youths and police clashed in June 1995 in Noisy-le-Grand after the police killed a local youth, Kacem Belhabib, in a motorcycle chase; in 1996 after Etienne Louborgne from Guadeloupe was shot in the head by police in his taxi at Charles de Gaulle airport and when Eduaurd Salumu Nsumbu from the Democratic Republic of the Congo died in police custody near place de Pigalle; in December 1997 in Dammarie Les Lys after Abdelkader Bouzine, sixteen, was shot in the head while driving; in 2003 after Xavier Dem, twenty-three, and later Mohammad Berrichi, twenty-eight, were killed by police; and in 1998 when twenty-two-year-old Farad Boukhalfa was shot in the head in his home in Cormeilles-en-Paris, Val-d'Oise, by a police officer who had traced his car after an alleged traffic offense.[191]

In almost every case charges against the police officers were dismissed. French African and North African youths protested and on occasion demonstrated their anger by torching cars, public buildings, schools, fire stations, synagogues, and/or supermarkets. One study by a member of the French union of judges found that each eruption of youth violence was precipitated by an incident of police abuse.[192] Another study found that seventeen out of twenty-four incidents of urban unrest were caused by the killing of young people by police or prison authorities, and almost half of those youths were chased to their deaths by police after they fled identity checks.[193] Prison youths interviewed by Michel Wieviorka, Philippe Bataille, Karine Clémént, Olivier Cousin, Farhad Khosrokhavar, Séverine Labat, Éric Macé, Paola Rebughino, and Nikola Tietze during this period claimed that rage resulting from racial injustice motivated their crimes far more often than either poverty or economic need.[194]

In 1999, France became the only European Union country singled out for using torture by the Council of Europe.[195] The finding was directly related to the case of Ahmed Selmouni, who was repeatedly beaten with a baseball bat and a truncheon and was forced to run through a corridor with police officers positioned on either side to trip him. "He was also urinated on and threatened with a syringe and a blow lamp."[196] The police officers involved in the case were not placed under investigation until 1997, "although the events had taken place in 1991, and [they] did not appear before the Correctional Court of Versailles until February 1999—only six weeks before the case was heard by the European Court in Strasbourg."[197]

The police responded with marches and parades of police cars protesting the European court's decision to "side with a drug dealer."

Selmouni's case was unusual only by degree. Under a condition known as *garde à vue,* French police were permitted to hold suspects for up to forty-eight hours (now ninety-six) before they were charged, and a suspect was permitted to consult with an attorney for only thirty minutes of that period. According to reports issued by the European Committee Against Torture, between 1990 and 2000 French police routinely beat about 5 percent of those held (averaging about one hundred a month), and almost all those beaten were of African or North African descent.[198] Hospitals verified the accounts of victims, who suffered traumatic lesions consistent with the severe beatings they claimed to have received at the hands of police. Medical records from the emergency wing of the Hôtel Dieu (the only hospital in Paris that treats prisoners under *garde à vue*) show that 11 percent of patients "admitted to the emergency room were suffering from injuries caused by police officers—including fractured jaws, severe spinal bruising and multiple lesions."[199]

Even worse, police homicides rose. Between 1977 and 2002 police killed 175 young people, almost all North African or African from the *banlieues.*[200] Other youths were killed in the prisons by prison guards. In 1996 and 1997 alone there were 475 deaths recorded and 268 official suicides of prison inmates in France. Between 1997 and 2002 there were 500 prison suicides—a rate more than ten times that in U.S. prisons. Almost all of the deaths were young people of North African or African descent.

In 1997 the Socialists won a majority in parliament and Lionel Jospin became prime minister. Le Pen's popularity, however, continued to rise. The National Front captured 14.9 percent in the 1997 parliamentary elections and 15.2 percent in the regional elections of 1998. Escalating racial tensions were evident in the Eurobarometer poll that year, where 16 percent of the French admitted they were "very racist," 32 percent admitted they were "quite racist," and 27 percent agreed they were "a little racist."[201] Nonetheless the Socialists pushed through a police reform known as *police de proximité.* In a program based on the American idea of community policing, the Jospin government expanded the use of beat cops to patrol neighborhoods on foot in order to work with the communities and avoid polarization in police community relations.

The program was moderately successful. Maria, a Muslim woman from a *banlieue,* had positive memories of the *police de proximité.* These officers would speak with *banlieue* residents and try to get to know them and in turn become familiar to them. But the *police de proximité* was an auxiliary police force with little impact on the behavior of the national police, who continued to be among the most brutal in Europe. Susan Terrio notes, "Police viewed community policing as an impediment to career advancement because it was not controlled by the Interior Ministry and did not fit union rules that limited the work week to three days during daylight hours. They were trained to confront crime, not petty delinquency. Interacting with youth in bad neighborhoods was not 'police work' but the province of 'janitors or nannies.' "[202]

While the *police de proximité* did nothing to reduce routine police abuse or the use of lethal violence by the BAC, Jospin made the unit even less relevant by proposing harsher criminal justice measures and blaming immigrant parents for an increase in juvenile delinquency. Government leaders threatened to cut off child welfare payments for those who abdicated their responsibility. By treating the issue as if it transcended party lines, notes Fassin, Jospin "contributed to making security a major issue."[203] Indeed Jospin gave the public the misleading impression that it was they who had forced the political elite to pay attention to the issue instead of vice versa. In September 1998 eight prominent left-wing intellectuals, historians, and philosophers, including the former revolutionary Regis Debray, made matters worse when they published a letter in *Le Monde* expressing concerns that "law abiding, legitimate Parisian French" were threatened by "suburban, lawless and demoralized France." "Is it racism," they asked, "to say that the most violent neighborhoods are those where illegal immigration is highest" or "to demand that parents take responsibility for their children in return for the social welfare assistance they receive?"[204]

Chapter 3

Boundary Activation
without Riots: New York (1993–2010)

> My son would be alive if the officers had parked their cars,
> talked to him like he was a human being. . . . No he was
> black and that was enough.
>
> —Kadiatou Diallo

Rudolph Giuliani opened his 1993 mayoral campaign (having lost the previous race, in 1989, to now-mayor David Dinkins) by addressing a mob of some ten thousand "raucous beer-drinking, overwhelmingly white police officers who had just finished a march on City Hall to protest a Dinkins-backed proposal for civilian oversight over police-misconduct complaints."[1] Many officers spewed racial epithets and carried signs condemning Dinkins in grossly racial terms, including one that read, "Dump the washroom attendant." Another depicted a cartoon version of Dinkins with large lips and an Afro. To cheers of "Rudy, Rudy Rudy," Giuliani waved his arms violently and launched "a profanity-laced diatribe against Dinkins." He accused Dinkins of being so soft on crime that he "might as well have held a ceremony in which he turned the neighborhood over to the drug dealers."[2] Some police broke through the barricades and stormed the steps of city hall, trapping workers inside. Others occupied streets, harassed motorists, overturned cars, and blocked traffic on the Brooklyn Bridge.[3]

Between 1993 and 2001 New York City experienced a concatenation of mechanisms similar to that which had produced riots elsewhere. During the 1993 mayoral race Giuliani deliberately stoked racial fears, although, perhaps critically, his rival Mayor Dinkins did not engage in competitive

outbidding. Nonetheless racial tensions were heightened and racial boundaries activated. Following his narrow victory, Giuliani implemented zero-
tolerance policing, pressured police to meet quotas in arrests, gradually
eliminated community policing, and refused to punish police no matter
how violent or egregious their actions. During his time in office there were
numerous incidents of police killing of unarmed blacks and Latinos, including one as young as thirteen, and a brutal torture of a detained man, who
had a broom handle shoved up his rectum. And yet New York City neighborhoods did not burn.

I argue that two factors transformed the way New Yorkers responded
to police killings, which in tandem significantly reduced the likelihood of
riots. First, activists who came of age during the cauldron of the 1960s race
riots learned organizing skills through programs designed to forestall further unrest. By the mid-1980s these activists were organizing around a host
of critical local issues, among them fighting racial profiling and police brutality. In so doing they channeled anger into more organized forms of collective action. Second, the passage of significant civil rights legislation
opened the courts to black and Latino plaintiffs and made the federal government a potential ally.[4] Activists, along with the families and friends of
victims, took advantage of these new channels to pursue justice through the
courts, including civil actions against the city. Legal proceedings provided a
clear course of action. By the end of lengthy court battles, win or lose, the
energies of all had been depleted.The most common reactions to police
violence in the 1990s and after 2000 were 1) protests and rallies; 2) appeals
to district attorneys and other elected leaders to pursue criminal indictments and, if this failed, federal interventions; 3) civil suits, the successful
conclusion of which often resulted in the creation of new organizations to
address the issues; and 4) participation in said organizations.

This chapter is organized in four parts. In the first I discuss the 1993
mayoral race and the activation of racial boundaries during and following
this contentious election. I pay particular attention to changes in policing
strategies. In the second part I discuss my interviews with police. I divided
those interviews into three categories: interviews with white NYPD officers;
interviews with minority NYPD officers; and interviews with police officers
advocating reform. In the third part of this chapter I turn to neighborhood
organizing efforts, looking at the constellation of actors and repertoires that
shaped how communities responded to police violence in the 1990s. In the
fourth part I discuss seven incidents of police homicide in depth, based on

extensive interviews with fathers and mothers of young people killed by police. I trace the dynamics that led these families and communities to engage in mass marches, court battles, and other forms of contentious politics.

The 1993 New York City Mayoral Election and Policing Racial Boundaries: Dinkins/Giuliani Redux

Crime had already begun its downward slide when Giuliani and Dinkins squared off for the second time in the 1993 mayoral race. Even so, the crack wars had led to a mounting death toll in poor neighborhoods, and Giuliani again made crime control the heart of his campaign. Not content with simply going after crack dealers or violent criminals, Giuliani targeted the homeless, beggars, and "squeegee men" (who washed motorists' wind-shields, often against their will, and asked for payment in return). His campaign was designed to play to New Yorkers' worst fears about their city. As Kevin Baker notes, he turned the race between himself and the black mayor "into [a] moral parable" in which the categories of victims and persecutors were inverted: "The well-off are continually beset by the poor, the privileged by the disinherited, the white by the black. . . . with the use of select code words . . . Giuliani was able to subtly link [a host of quotidian] frustrations to a racial root cause. . . . In Giuliani's world whites, already harassed at every turn by squeegee men, trash storms, and peddlers[,] were on the verge of losing control of the city entirely—maybe were even at the precipice of some sort of apocalyptic racial massacre."[5]

The local media played into Giuliani's hands. "Crack was the hottest combat reporting story to come along since the end of the Vietnam War," notes Robert Stutman, former director of the Drug Enforcement Agency's (DEA) New York office.[6] The same was true for national media coverage. Stories in which blacks appeared as criminals increased 23 percent between 1990 and 1997, and blacks were shown as perpetrators three to four times more often than whites.[7] The combined impact of national and local media coverage and the campaign itself convinced 84 percent of New Yorkers that crime had increased between 1989 and 1993 when in fact it had fallen. Fifty-eight percent of New Yorkers told pollsters that they felt less safe in 1993 than they had in 1989.[8]

Figure 1. Number of homicides, New York City, 1980–2000

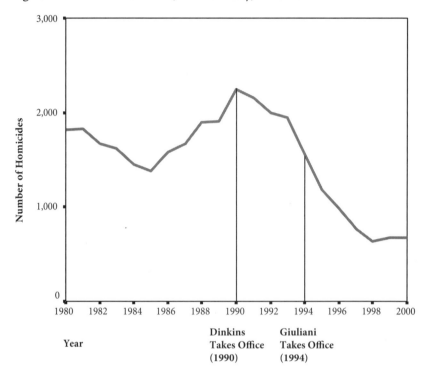

Source: New York State Division of Criminal Justice Services, "Criminal Justice Indicators, New York City," http://www.criminaljustice.state.ny.us/crimnet/ojsa/areastat/area st.htm, accessed on November 6, 2002.

Giuliani's margin of victory was as narrow as his loss had been four years earlier, 50.7 to 48.3 percent. High voter turnout in Staten Island (where a referendum on succession drew voters and passed by a 2 to 1 margin) and low voter turnout in the Bronx and Brooklyn gave Giuliani the edge, but Dinkins had lost support among whites (see Tables 4 and 5). White New Yorkers listed fear of crime as their number one concern in 1993.[9] They voted overwhelmingly for Rudolph Giuliani and claimed that crime was their reason for doing so.[10] Black New Yorkers, those most likely to be affected by violent crime, rated poverty as their first concern, and 95 percent of them voted for Dinkins.[11] They believed that Democrats were better able to address the crime issue and that education, after-school programs, and jobs were the way to do it.[12]

Figure 2. Property and violent crime rates, New York City, 1980–2000

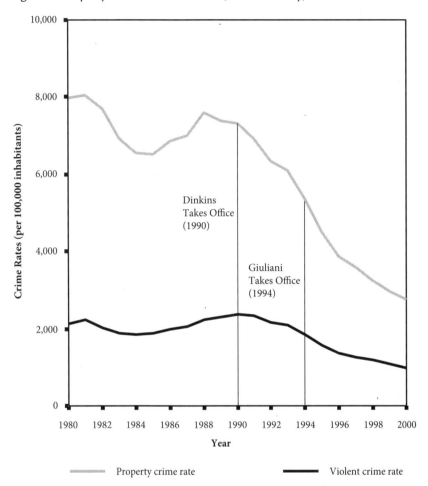

Source: New York State Division of Criminal Justice Services, "Criminal Justice Indicators, New York City," http://www.criminaljustice.state.ny.us/crimnet/ojsa/areastat/area st.htm, accessed November 6, 2002.

William Bratton had been Dinkins's chief of transit police, and Giuliani selected him as his police commissioner. Bratton was an innovative police commissioner. Like Dinkins and his police commissioner Lee Brown, Bratton was a strong supporter of community policing. If "the police fail to build confidence and personal relationships with the people in the

Table 4. Comparison of percentages of votes obtained in the 1989 and 1993
New York City mayoral elections: Shift in vote for Dinkins

	1989 % vote for Dinkins	1993 % vote for Dinkins	% change Turnout	% vote change for Dinkins
Black assembly districts	89.2	88.7	− 2.4	− .05
Mixed minority districts	76.7	74.1	− 2.07	− 2.6
Latino districts	74.3	73.5	− 5.6	− .08
White liberal districts	50.6	48.6	− .1	− 2.0
Outer-borough Jewish districts	28.9	26.8	.2	− 2.1
White Catholic districts	25.9	22.6	1.2	− 3.9

Sources: New York City Districting Commission (1989) and Associated Press (1993). See also
John Mollenkopf, *A Phoenix in the Ashes* (Princeton, N.J.: Princeton University Press, 1994),
211.

community," he insisted, "they've lost some capacity for fighting violent
crime."[13] Bratton took advantage of the extra officers recruited by Dinkins
(who had only now graduated from the academy), as well as two of Bill
Clinton's major crime control initiatives—the Community Oriented Policing Services program (which put aside $8.8 billion to fund the hiring of
one hundred thousand new police officers over six years) and the Violent
Crime Control and Law Enforcement Act of 1994 (which funneled another
$30 billion into local law enforcement) to increase the number of beat cops
in crime-ridden neighborhoods.

He also introduced three new elements to his crime-fighting strategy.
The first was the use of a computer program known as CompStat, which

Table 5. Comparison of 1989 and 1993 New York City mayoral race

	% of voters who voted for				% of voters who are	
	1989 % voted Dinkins	1989 % voted Giuliani	1993 % voted Dinkins	1993 % voted Giuliani	% of 1989 vote	% of 1991 vote
Blacks	91	7	95	5	28	29
Latinos	65	34	61	39	13	12
Whites	28	72	22	78	56	56
White liberals	51	47	51	49	29	30
White moderates	22	78	15	85	39	43
White conservatives	13	86	3	96	23	27
Jews	35	65	32	68	16	17
White Catholics	18	82	12	88	24	30
White Protestants	30	70	18	82	8	6

Sources: New York Times/CBS exit poll 1989, Voter Research Poll 1993. See also Karen F. Kaufman, "Racial Conflict and Political Choice: A Study of Mayoral Voting Behavior in New York and Kansas," *Urban Affairs Review* 33, no. 5 (1998): 666.

mapped the areas where most crimes occurred. The second was the decentralization of police authority, giving local precinct commanders more independence and more responsibility. Bratton used CompStat to hold local police commanders accountable for reducing crime rates in their districts. The third element, "quality of life," policing later christened "zero tolerance" by Giuliani, was that most often associated with both Giuliani and Bratton. The idea stemmed from an influential article written by George Kelling and James Wilson called "Broken Windows."[14] The article claimed that neighborhood deterioration followed the first broken window. If the window was not replaced, it would set in motion an inexorable process of neighborhood decay and growing crime. The solution was to prevent neighborhoods from deteriorating by cracking down rapidly on quality-of-life crimes, before they, in William Bratton's words, "led inexorably to more serious crimes."[15]

Quality-of-life policing, however, was only an untested theory. There was no evidence that those who committed quality-of-life crimes (such as drinking from an open beer can on one's front steps, painting graffiti on a wall or sidewalk, or smoking a joint) were more likely to commit larger crimes or that cracking down on petty delinquency would deter serious crime. Although both Giuliani and Bratton claimed the drop in crime in

New York was due to quality-of-life policing (a natural experiment), later studies were unable to replicate that success or confirm its responsibility for crime drops in New York, especially after controlling for poverty, stability, and race.[16] Quality-of-life, or zero-tolerance, policing encouraged police to target minority neighborhoods and residents for life-style crimes that either, as Luc Sante observes, were "limited to and taken for granted by the poor"[17]or widespread in the society at large. As William Stuntz notes, "Too much law amounts to no law at all: When legal doctrine makes everyone an offender the relevant offenders have no meaning independent of law enforcers' will. The formal rule of law yields the functional rule of official discretion. . . . Discretion and discrimination travel together."[18]

Nine days into his administration, Giuliani clashed with the Black Nation of Islam mosque in Harlem. The dispute arose when the police attempted to storm the mosque in response to a false 911 call. Half a dozen members of the congregation barred their way, literally pushing the officers back down the stairs. In the process one officer was injured, while another lost his radio and gun. The mayor demanded that the mosque turn over the suspect in the injury of the police officer. The mosque refused, saying that it was the police who should apologize.[19] The mayor's handling of the incident added insult to the injury that the black community felt over the shooting death of seventeen-year-old Shu'aib Abdul Latif in a basement confrontation with police the same week. Abdul Latif, who was arrested in March on charges of drug possession, was unarmed, police officials admitted.[20]

When Bratton skipped the meeting with Muslim leaders, C. Vernon Mason, a close associate of Reverend Al Sharpton and one of the most bombastic black activists in the city, said that the events "sent a clear message to black officials in the first 12 days of the Giuliani administration: We have a dead young man who was murdered and a mosque desecrated and now we have an insult."[21] Reverend Sharpton accused Giuliani of "trying to throw a signal to those who supported him that he's going to draw some line in the sand with the political leadership of the black community" and said that "if he wants to do that he's the one being divisive not us."[22] Eventually Giuliani and the police abandoned further pursuit of the suspect accused of injuring the police officer. A few weeks later Giuliani ended all the inclusiveness measures instituted by Dinkins—minority offices, ads in minority newspapers, bid advantages for minority firms—holding court without a single black adviser.

Zero-tolerance policing further damaged the strained relationship between the mayor and the black and, to a lesser extent, Latino communities. It also undermined the legitimacy and effectiveness of the police.[23] "Ostensibly targeted at 'disorderly' neighborhoods," Jeffrey Fagan notes, the new policing strategy was used to virtually occupy "minority neighborhoods, characterized by social and economic disadvantage."[24] Police violence intensified, and within months several high-profile police killings galvanized black and Latino communities. The first was the shooting of Nicholas Heyward, a thirteen-year-old black youth, in Brooklyn on September 27, 1994. The housing officer said that he had mistaken Nicholas's toy gun for a real gun. Then on December 22 Officer Francis X. Livoti killed twenty-nine-year-old Anthony Baez. Baez had been playing football with his brothers outside his mother's house in the Bronx when his football hit Livoti's police car. Livoti got out of his car and grabbed Baez in an illegal chokehold and held him despite the pleas of his brothers that Baez had asthma. Baez died, the coroner said, from a crushed windpipe. A few weeks later, on January 11, 1995, two detectives, one a former bodyguard of Giuliani, shot dead eighteen-year-old Anthony Rosario and twenty-two-year-old Hector Vega, apparently disarmed and lying on the ground. Giuliani blamed the boys' mothers. (I will return to these cases when discussing my interviews with the mothers and fathers of these young men.)

In 1996, barely two years into his administration, Giuliani replaced Bratton with Howard Safir. On August 9, 1997, Abner Louima, a Haitian electrical engineer, was picked up outside a club in Brooklyn. The police had received a call about a disturbance in the parking lot. The officers grabbed Louima, pushed him inside the patrol car, and pummeled him with clubs. When they got to the station, they stripped him and crushed his testicles. Then Justin Volpe took a toilet plunger and sodomized him. After waving the excrement-stained instrument in Louima's face, he then paraded it through the station telling his sergeant that he "took a man down tonight." Louima, who had committed no crime, spent months in the hospital suffering serious organ damage. After a great deal of publicity and mass mobilizations, Lieutenant Volpe was indicted, convicted, and sentenced to thirty years without parole. Then on February 4, 1999, Safir's final year, four white policemen shot Amadou Diallo, a young immigrant from Guinea, forty-one times when he reached for his wallet while standing in the doorway to his apartment building in the South Bronx. (This case too will be discussed at length at the end of this chapter.)

In 2000 Giuliani replaced Safir with Bernard Kerik. Years later Giuliani recommended Kerik to head the new Department of Homeland Security. The nomination sparked an investigation, which resulted in a sixteen-count indictment against Kerik for kickbacks, fraud, and corruption and for accepting gifts from companies linked to organized crime. The charges centered on the Interstate Industrial Corporation, which investigators believed had ties with organized crime and had paid for some $250,000 worth of renovations to Kerik's home in Riverdale. Kerik eventually pleaded guilty to two counts of tax fraud, one count of making a false statement on a loan application, and five counts of making false statements to the federal government while being vetted for senior posts. He was sentenced to four years in the penitentiary.

Despite Giuliani's reputation as a mayor tough on crime, major felony convictions fell throughout his term in office, largely due to the shoddy quality of the evidence. Misdemeanor arrests and convictions increased by 50 percent.[25] Eighty percent of those arrested for misdemeanors were black.[26] By 2001 over half of black high school dropout males in the city were in prison (although the increase in imprisonment was considerably smaller than the national average).[27] The largest increase in imprisonment was for drug crimes. Eighty percent of the fifteen thousand prisoners locked up on drug charges during Giuliani's term were never convicted of a violent felony. In addition 92 percent of them were black or Latino. Blacks and Latinos constituted 49 percent of New York City's population but accounted for 90 percent of all New York City prison admissions. New York City, in turn, accounted for 70 percent of all admissions to New York State's penitentiaries.

Racial profiling was responsible for a large part of the racial disparity in incarceration rates. In 1999, 88 percent of those stopped and frisked on suspicion of drug charges by the NYPD were black or Latino, although those groups constituted only 49 percent of New York City's population.[28] Giuliani was untroubled by the disparity. "Although 89.2 percent of the suspects stopped and frisked are black or Hispanic," he retorted, "that number corresponds to the percentage of blacks and Hispanics identified by witnesses as criminal suspects."[29] In 1999 Human Rights Watch delivered a blistering report. Zero-tolerance policing, the report pointed out, in giving police officers discretion over whom to stop, search, or arrest, had "expanded the potential for brutality, harassment, and racial and sexual profiling."[30]

Figure 3. Number of arrests by type of crime, New York City, 1980–2002

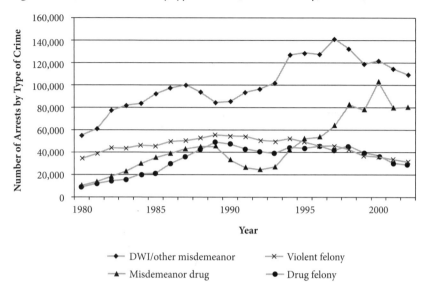

Source: New York State Division of Criminal Justice Services, "Criminal Justice Indicators, New York City," http://www.criminaljustice.state.ny.us/crimnet/ojsa/areastat/area st.htm, accessed October 28, 2003.

The number of brutality complaints tripled in one decade. Damages paid by the city to alleged victims of police misconduct jumped dramatically from $13 million in 1992 to $24 million in 1994, $26 million in 1995, and $20.5 million in 1996, before doubling again to $40.8 million in 1999 and $35.9 million in 2000.[31] All told the city "paid a cumulative total of roughly $176.9 million to dispose of more than 3,500 police misconduct lawsuits" between 1994 and 2000.[32] Many of those cases involved minorities who were killed by firearms discharged by police officers or who died while in police custody: "Nearly all of the victims in the cases of death in custody (including shootings) . . . were members of racial minorities."[33] The number of minorities killed by firearms discharged by police officers increased 34 percent, from 23 to 31 between 1993 and 1994, and did not decline until 1997.[34] The Amnesty International report refuted claims that the increase in complaints was due either to an increasingly litigious society or an increased willingness of victims to come forward. On the contrary, the report noted, "civil lawsuits may in fact under-represent the true level of police misconduct. Several sources, including the CCRB [Civilian Complaint Review Board], have said that more aggressive policing in the past few years had led to an increase in complaints of ill treatment."[35]

It is also questionable whether zero-tolerance policing and racial profiling caused New York's drop in crime. No other city that emulated these policies experienced similar success. Although the topic is beyond the scope of this book, criminologists have proposed several alternative explanations. One theory is that the solidification and subsequent decline of the crack trade led to a return to pre-crack-war levels of violence. Alfred Blumenstein observes that "crack was a new cheap drug outside the control of the older established dealers. You had a lot of kids recruited to sell it and when they got recruited they armed themselves and then their friends got guns too to protect themselves, leading to an arms race among crack dealers."[36] As the trade declined and turfs became solidified, New York experienced an equal decline in violence. Yet crime, and especially homicides, eventually dropped lower than pre-crack-war levels.

A second theory is that the stop-and-frisks helped get guns off the street, especially when paired with stringent gun controls.[37] Yet stop-and-frisks netted few weapons (fewer than a buy-back program from a church). Safir, however, claimed that dealers fearful of getting caught with a weapon ceased to carry them. A third theory focuses on the increase in beat police officers and community policing. New York, as criminologists such as Michael Jacobson, Franklin Zimring, and former Harvard Law professor William Stuntz point out, had a much lower rate of imprisonment than the rest of the country but higher numbers of police, beginning with Dinkins's safe-streets program. Having more police on the streets alone may have caused the crime decline.[38] CompStat may have increased the effect by deploying police in hot spots where crimes were most common. A fourth theory is that shift to debit cards decreased the amount of cash carried by pedestrians and decreased the profitability of street robberies accordingly, while a fifth emphasizes the impact of better medical care on falling homicide rates. Finally, neighborhood organizing may have had an impact. Robert Sampson, for instance, has recently argued that the growth of community-based organizations can reduce crime.[39] In any case, increasing a community's trust in the police has been shown elsewhere to be as effective as stop-and-frisks in reducing crime, without all the negative fallout of the latter.[40]

Interviews with Police

It was difficult to get interviews with on-duty police officers. Most told me they were not permitted to grant interviews. One told me that her commander forbade it. Below are the interviews I was able to obtain, between the years 2002 and 2010. Several are with on-duty officers whom I met in an informal, non-work setting, and they were gracious enough to speak with me as long as I guarded their identity. Others were retired officers who had been on the force when Giuliani was mayor. Still others were former police from other cities who now were involved in efforts to change the ways in which police interact with minority communities.

White Police Officers

New York police officers were by and large intensely loyal to the mayor. They appreciated his unconditional support, although they were unhappy with the dismissal of Bratton and the elimination of community policing. One white Bronx officer told me that he thought CompStat was helpful to crime fighting: "Bratton and the Mayor always pushed. I did patrol, whatever the conditions, [and] we went where crime was happening." But when the mayor replaced Bratton, the conditions for police deteriorated considerably. It is important to get squeegee men and others off the street before they commit more serious crimes, the officer said, and "having cops on the beat was one really good reason street conditions improved. If you're out talking to people going to their meetings, they are more comfortable with you. It connected cops to business people in areas, and to tenants and residents. We did problem solving, developing the kind of trust that cops in cars don't have. Commissioners Lee Brown and Ray Kelly [both under Dinkins] started that. When Kerik came in, community policing ended."

A reform officer concurred: "Bill Bratton had a more liberal sense of how to do problem solving." Giuliani opposed community policing for political reasons: "If police did problem solving, how could he make political hay out of it? How could he make hay out of peace? It is easier to launch a drug war and have police seize a large number of kilos. How do you take a picture of nothing happening? But it is a lazy amateurish policy. NYPD officers were paid the same if they just drove around and made an arrest every once in a while, but we know that crime reduction [is] driven by engagement with [the] community."

They gave three main explanations for racial profiling and police violence. The first was that black and Puerto Ricans committed more crimes. One white officer told me that there were fundamental cultural differences between blacks and whites:

> Race is always a distinguishing factor, no way around that. Which comes first—blacks are targeted by police, and as a result have higher arrest rates? Or is it that black crime rates are higher, and that drives arrests? You have to ask what is the culture in different communities? If African Americans are imprisoned 10 fold more than whites, it is because these are the communities that have street crime. . . . If you take the numbers as raw proportions the complexity is lost. There is only a piece of it that is due to ingrained racism, to preconceived notions that lead police to look at people a certain way.

Similarly another white Bronx police officer insisted that high black arrest rates are the result of "people caught doing things [that they are] not supposed to do. It is easy to say race."

A second explanation is that inexperienced or poorly trained officers commit blunders: "There are people fit for a job, and people not fit. The Diallo case was a tragedy. One guy lost it [and his shooting led the others to think there was shooting back]." Police work "has to do with maturity and with good common sense and being brought up well." In the Sean Bell case, he said, "the first cop started shooting, then you have 'terrorist' boxed. There is something wrong with how you are positioned. One sees bullets and thinks he is being shot at and responds, and the others repeat."

The third common explanation is that "there are good people and not so good people in every field." In a study conducted by the Police Executive Research Forum (PERF) police officers in three hundred focus groups gave similar answers.[41] Drew Diamond, a former police chief and founding member of PERF (whose interview will be discussed more below), said that this attitude makes him furious: "I can deal with a handful of racists. Why it washes over the rest of the officers is because good officers watch this egregious behavior and don't say anything, kind of like good Germans. . . .

There is a huge gap between the police view and the public view and particular minorities in terms of story-telling." As a direct result, he said, "the NYPD loses more police officers in the South Bronx because they are in more danger there. They act as an occupying force. . . . Violent predators make up less than one tenth of one percent" of the people living in those neighborhoods. "In public housing there is an even smaller percentage. . . . Maybe five guys are actually predators. Why can't police officers deal with that?"

A white officer in the Bronx concurred: "In my part of the Bronx they hate us! I remember I responded to a call with a pal, an African American guy opens the door—we say we received a call about a knife. He said: 'please leave.' We said not until we speak with your girlfriend and make sure she is OK and not dead. I noticed a 3- or 4-year-old. She runs behind the wall. What is that about? Turns out, his 4-year-old daughter is scared of cops. Another time, a mother tells the kid that it is not always bad when cops come. They hate us. We had eggs thrown at us, an air conditioner dropped near me."

Activated racial boundaries increase the distance between police officers and community residents but also strengthen solidarity ties between officers. As the same Bronx officer noted, "It is the camaraderie between cops—the friendships—that make it worth it. You know if you call for backup. In a matter of seconds [the] precinct empties out." These strong ties reinforce police officers' tendencies to stereotype the communities they police. They also make them less willing either to report their fellow officers or to criticize them. "You don't want to be a Monday morning quarterback," another officer said; "it is a high pressure job, [and] one has to react quickly. Police bring these stresses home, which is why they have such high divorce rates." Another noted, "The problem is the bad guys have stronger guns than we do. I have a 9-millimeter—they shoot desert eagles, AK 47s, everything that we don't have, and 10 times more powerful than what we have. The law seriously handicaps cops. [For instance] we know that there are guns in an apartment. If we can't find them we must stop our search and get a search warrant."

Police have strong network ties with each other and stereotype the communities in which they work. Communities hate and distrust the police. The boundary separating the police and the community is activated. One white officer I spoke to told me that he tries to fight the tendency to stereotype. He said he knows there are good people in the Bronx. He sees them "getting up at 5 or 6 to go to work. There are very hard-working people in my part of the Bronx, but unfortunately they get out-weighed by people that are bad. . . . Unfortunately things happen to cops and they become very upset. The work is very sad. There is no value to life there. It is like survival of the fittest."

Black and Puerto Rican Police

Ron Hampton and Anibal Diaz are minority police officers. Hampton is head of the National Black Police Association, and Diaz is Puerto Rican and a former NYPD officer in Brooklyn. Both described the pernicious way racism within the academy affected them and the communities they police. Minority police officers, they said, are more likely to leave the force than have a major impact in reducing racial profiling and abuse. Hampton's experiences in nearly all-white police force led him to create the National Black Police Association: "Being under stress [is] no excuse. We train police that way. We want them to police that way. It is not by accident. If we wanted police officers to be problem solvers we would train them that way. They get what they want. They were pulling people right out of Vietnam [and putting them in the police force]. They knew that they [soldiers] followed orders. Officers are afraid to talk because retaliation is real."

Hampton wryly observed that police are always saying that the department is an officer's family. They say, "[Y]ou don't say things against your family." But as his mother always said, "[W]hether or not you're a member of a family is determined by how they treat you." The police department is not a family for black policemen, he stated: "Rarely does the institution treat you as a part of a family." When he sees his fellow officers on the street, they walk right past him. When he asked one once why he had not acknowledged him, the white officer insisted that he had not seen him. But according to Hampton, that officer looked him straight in the face: "Black officers, when they are out of uniform, are invisible to white policemen." It is one of the reasons why so many black undercover police officers are shot by other police officers. As the father of a young boy shot in Brooklyn asked, "Why is it that it is always a white officer shooting a black officer and never vice versa?"

Anibal Diaz, a former Puerto Rican police officer in Brooklyn, told me a similar story. There is no question that police racially profile, he insisted; it is part of their training; they are taught to racially profile. When a recruit enters the academy he is "warned that black and Puerto Rican drivers may reach for a gun when you stop them for a minor traffic violation. Police training creates fear. It teaches police to overreact when in poor minority neighborhoods." It is the reason why four white officers shot Amadou Diallo with forty-one bullets when he reached for his wallet and ID: "Why did they need to shoot him forty-one times when officers are trained to hide during a shoot-out and there were so many places to hide?"

Diaz had been a prison corrections officer before he joined the NYPD. "It didn't take me long to find out something was wrong," he told me. "I found out in the academy that in my company class, me and three other guys, including the Sergeant, were the only ones not from a police family. The others called the Sergeant nigger to his face. When he reported it, the other guy's father would pick up the phone, and call his police chief father and he would call the Sergeant a fucking nigger." When a Puerto Rican officer reported "a white male officer calling a black female officer a black nigger," he said, the report was canned.

Diaz hates it when he hears white police officers say that only white communities want community policing, or that it is the hostility of the blacks and Latinos that is at issue. "Police do not care about black and Latino communities," he said: "There is no real war on drugs. If there were they would be going after the Cali cartel. They'd rather go after Joe Shmoe selling crack on the corner. [Going after the former] your life expectancy is diminished. It is easier. The crack cocaine disparity [in penalties] prevents us from going after big dealers. The small guy gets the highest penalty. . . . Less than five percent of those arrested for drug trafficking during Giuliani's term were major traffickers. Drug selling in minority communities is a survival mechanism, a consequence of poverty." In contrast, he said, at Columbia University "drug use is all over the school." The police know that. Diaz's daughter told him that there is so much around, it is impossible to avoid seeing it. But her friend's father is the top executive for GM. "He's off the hook. Imagine if a cop goes in there and arrests him. . . . his father gets on the phone and there are problems for the police officer. Police worry about politics and power."

Hampton made a similar point. Poor black and Latino kids are the easiest to arrest, he told me: "The kids walk right up to you and ask you if you want to buy drugs. Everything is done in public in these neighborhoods. The police department then brags to the media about their drug bust. It makes police departments and police commanders look good to have so many arrests. Political leaders like it because they can use it politically." The next day, however, the drug dealers are back. With too much emphasis on arrests, he said, what suffers is the quality of arrests. Police know that their cases are going to be thrown out. "We know we can't arrest ourselves out of the problem. Those arrested are easily replaceable." Politics is driving arrest and incarceration rates, according to Hampton:

> It doesn't stop people from getting drugs, or handguns. The police think the main ingredient of being a criminal is being black. This condemns an entire neighborhood. In order to catch that one percent of the neighborhood that are predators, they destroy one hundred percent of the neighborhood. Half of the time the drug dealers don't even live in that neighborhood. There is no real effort to deal with the problem. The police working in black communities don't know that part of their job is protecting people's civil rights. They know that when they are working in a white community.

Drew Diamond concurred. Racial boundaries not only separate police from communities; they also divide minority officers from other officers inside the department, especially those who challenge the dominant culture: "There is a myth that police are only one color, blue. But police departments are racially divided like anyplace else. There is another myth: we need to keep it inside the family—we can trust each other. It is built in, this mythical stuff, this brotherhood stuff. It is really more about protecting us [the police] from the community than about our ability to provide services to the community."

Police Reformers

Diamond told me that he came out of a group of former police chiefs called the "Harvard Police Executive." "We felt we needed to rethink current policing strategies. We began to think twenty or thirty years down the road." They were convinced that they had to stop leaving policing decisions in the hands of politicians. Mayors should not be deciding how police officers could best do their job. Mayors think from one term or election to the next. Police officers have to think long-term about their relationships with the communities they police, according to Diamond.

There are two dominant policing strategies in the United States, Diamond said. He called them City A and City B. City A, he told me, engages with the community. City B does not. In City B racial tensions between the community and police are high. City B is New York: "In City B there is a fundamental distrust between the police and [the] minority community. There is no trust, no healing. Why don't the police in City B behave like those in A? Police department A are the police of the poor, they serve the poor. In police department B police patrol the perimeter [of inner-city neighborhoods]. They see themselves at war—their enemy is poor people of color. . . . I've had officers look at a neighborhood and say, 'everyone in there is a drug dealer.' Whole families refuse to help us."

What they do not ask, he told me, is why members of the community in City B refuse to help the police. It is because City B "is engaged in a class war; police do not serve the community. They prefer sweeps, breaking down doors, and other actions that violate the constitutional rights of those in the community. When there is a backlash against the police, officers complain they are the good guys. They were out there risking their lives 'to save the community from predators.'" Police claim that such actions are the price communities need to pay for their safety and do not understand why community residents are unappreciative. But the strategy, according to Diamond, is counterproductive: "It is a violent strategy that provokes more violence."

Nicholas Pastore was the police chief in New Haven, Connecticut, when Giuliani was mayor in New York. New Haven did problem-solving policing (in other words, City A). Yet crime dropped at the same rate as in New York. Mayors and police chiefs set the rules and make all the difference, Pastore said. What needs to be taught and installed as a norm is a sense of fairness, an understanding "that few people belong in prison and that we should even help them and not clone them": "We are still acting as if cops are the King's army. . . . Police, and not just in America, harass, intimidate and control. They don't act like public servants, they don't protect, they control. They act more like bouncers. Policing has evolved into an active death penalty without due process of law. The police carry out the death penalty. The police kill five hundred a year without due process. There was one cop who said that if Rodney King had died, there would have been no lawsuit. Most police . . . would do anything to get ahead and if it means shooting, well then."

Pastore instituted new recruiting strategies. Women make better police officers than men, he stated, and recruiting women has a more transformative impact than recruiting minorities. Pastore appointed a radical lesbian sociologist from Yale as his deputy police chief. Ron Hampton recalled visiting New Haven when Pastore was chief. There were recruiting posters everywhere. One read, "Are you gay? Did you march in Stonewall? We want you in our police department." Another said, "Were you in the Black Panthers? Did you organize free lunch programs? We want you in the police department." What really makes the difference though, Pastore insisted, is changing the incentive structure, "turning it on its head," inverting the system of rewards and punishments. Instead of rewarding police for showing good numbers or high arrest rates, Pastore gave bonuses and other awards to officers who worked with the community to solve problems. In poor neighborhoods, he pointed out, every family has at least one member with a drug or other problem: "If these families think the police are going to arrest their family member and the youth is going to get a long prison term, they are not going to call the police, and the police will have no help. If, however, the police officer helps the family get him or her treatment, or other form of help, then the community will work with the police. . . . We need a new mission statement—be nice."

Building Community Networks

From the mid-1970s on, neighborhood activists reconstructed social networks, built community-based organizations, and fought for the rights of residents. They pressured the city to allow poor people to buy buildings through sweat equity. They fought against discrimination in the awarding of public housing and for control of schools and area police boards. They organized to help drug users reduce the harm associated with drug use or to help drug users get clean and sober. They demanded access to public health, especially for those afflicted with the new scourge of New York City, AIDS. In addition they fought against police brutality.

The methods they chose to fight police violence were neither riots nor the radical actions they had pursued during the early 1970s. From the 1980s on, black and Puerto Rican activists engaged in actions they once considered anathemas. They registered voters, organized to fight for the drawing of more representative congressional districts, fielded their own candidates, brought voters to the polls, and sometimes ran for local office. In addition they sued the city for racial discrimination in a host of arenas, including police violence. When police killed black or Latino youths, activists organized protest marches, pressured district attorneys and other elected officials, pleaded with the Justice Department, and helped victims find lawyers.

Organizing Mott Haven, South Bronx

Mott Haven, in the South Bronx, is among the poorest congressional districts in the country. It is predominantly Puerto Rican but includes an array of other racial minorities and new immigrants, many from Mexico or Central America. It is one of the seven neighborhoods in the city with the highest incarceration rate and has one of the highest incidents of police violence. In the 1990s racial discrimination and police violence increased the appeal of drug gangs. I interviewed a number of former gang leaders, gang members, and drug users at the time. Several told me that gang leaders were looked at as heroes, largely because they stood up to the police. One said, "They became true freedom fighters to us. They were independent. They didn't answer to the man. They crossed every line they told us not to cross. They were the ultimate rebels. Society puts a lot of effort to get things the way they are. When you try to change that you're an outlaw." Another told me, "Most of our population is in jail, not convicted, incarcerated. Street gangs are key to leadership in our neighborhood. It is the most demonized of demonized neighborhoods." One youth told me he remembered listening to kids coming out of prison when he was twelve or thirteen:

> I wanted to hear about [it] because I knew I'd be there someday. This guy was like me and he was there and I wanted to know what I should do when I go there. Imagine at 13. I was scared but to overcome fear they glorify it, they see it as their future so they glorify it as heroic. In the Bronx, only white people we see are the police, or people that own businesses. . . . Here everyone [is] proud to be Puerto Rican, but what is Puerto Rican? We don't know, we just want to wave a flag. We learn in the jails. Young people go to jail and they don't know Spanish. They come out speaking Spanish. That is why the gangs come out of the jails.

A local activist told me that she does not dismiss someone just because he or she is a drug dealer: "[T]he drug war boils down to a civil war, a class war, a war of color. The drug war segregates. We lose sense of the fact that because of the restructuring of the economy huge vacuums were created that the drug scene filled. A lot of these men have no alternatives; in scaling down the welfare state someone had to take that space."

A former heroin user told me he used to admire drug users:

> [They] seemed so cool. We glorified them. The more messed up and nodded out they were, the more they seemed to be the ultimate rebel. . . . And the drugs helped us deal with our pain. We didn't believe anything the so-called authorities said or did. We saw it all as part of [the] system. There is a spirit within [neighborhood youths] dying to surface. They do not know what to do with their anger. . . . You cannot preach to them, they zone out.

It was only after he was arrested, and the famous activist lawyer William Kuntzler represented him in court, that he learned to channel his anger into "*activism, legal action.*" William Kuntzler, he said, made the difference. "He showed me a different way to deal with anger. He treated me as an important member of my community, made me aware of weapons I had never thought of using." It is not only former gang leaders and drug users who have learned to use the legal system and to channel anger into legal activism. The South Bronx is home to the most active anti-police-brutality and justice organizations in the city (and it is also home to an array of housing organizations and tenant advocacy groups; a theater group; two Chilean activist groups that share a building—La Peña and Rebeldias, the latter also a hip-hop band with an international reputation; a syringe exchange program; and some activist Christian-based community groups). In 1980 Richie Perez, a former Young Lord, founded the National Congress for Puerto Rican Rights and the Justice Committee subsection to deal exclusively with police brutality. The Justice Committee outlasted the National Congress and continues to organize on police-brutality issues. It has a close relationship with another Bronx organization, Copwatch. Copwatch activists shadow police in the neighborhood, filming incidents of abuse with their cell phones. Many Copwatch activists, as a result, have been beaten and/or arrested. Another former Young Lord and long-time South Bronx resident, Vincente "Panama" Alba, heads the Coalition Against Police Brutality, an umbrella organization that includes an array of community groups dedicated to stopping police violence.[42] Alba stated that police brutality against people of color is a major issue in the community:

> Police kill with impunity because there is a culture that promotes the idea that these abuses are the price that must be paid for security, for having police fight crime. . . . When kids walk down the street, the police feel free to put them against the wall, strip search them, and when they find nothing, leave. The police are an occupational army in our community. Their standard of warfare and civil policy should be very different. In [this] war we are an enemy, but the civil police are supposed to protect and uphold [the] rights of citizens. The police admitted as much in the poster the PBA [Police Benevolent Association] hung after 9/11. On one side was a U.S. soldier, on the other a New York City policeman. It read "support your troops abroad and at home." The police say everyone must live by the law. But they are paid and sworn to uphold the law. They should be held to a higher standard not a lower standard.

Police also contribute to racist violence by not protecting blacks and Latinos from white racist vigilantes, Alba noted. In one case outside the Bronx in 1991, a young Dominican honors student at Queens College was descended on by a white racist gang when he visited his girlfriend in an area of Queens nicknamed "Spaghetti Park" in 1991. As he was gasping for breath, one member of the gang took a fire extinguisher and shoved it down his throat and killed him. The police blamed the youth Manny Mahi, a graffiti artist, who they said was a vandal. One of the gang members later became a police officer. Only after a mass campaign did the activists manage to get him removed from the NYPD, but he is still an officer on Long Island. In some cases parents call the police because their sons have not taken their medications for mental illness. In one case, Alba said, the police beat a man so savagely that he had to be hospitalized for facial reconstruction. Police regularly engage in torture, he told me in reference to the Abner Louima case, and it is rare when that comes to light. Usually only when police commit murder is any attention paid.

"All the uprisings in the 1960s were triggered by police violence," Alba insisted. "But the 1960s were a very different political time. . . . Police learned from history. Sad fact is that the justice movement has now taken on the characteristics of an industry." Among the examples he gave of the ways in which justice organizations prevent riots are the protest marches organized by Reverend Al Sharpton. When Sean Bell was shot, he said, "Reverend Sharpton's response was a peaceful march, under the theme 'shopping for justice.' They marched from Fifth Avenue and 34th street, using the NYPD sound system. People were rounded up to march peacefully and then to go home and wait for the next step. This effectively diffused anger."

It is difficult to get justice, Alba told me. It takes enormous effort to get district attorneys to issue indictments, to get the Justice Department to file civil rights charges, and to help families through the civil suits. "People burn out, get frustrated. The mobilization necessary to do justice in one case is extraordinary. It is difficult to go on and on."

Lower East Side

The Lower East Side has the longest history of left-wing organizing of any neighborhood in New York. While police violence against individuals is hardly unknown, many of the most notorious incidents have been attacks on those engaging in collective action. Collective action has also been the most common response. The Lower East Side is one of the few neighborhoods that did not riot in 1977, largely because local activists spent the entire night in the streets keeping the peace. In 1993 one of the leading Puerto Rican community activists was the victim of police abuse. She sued the city and won in civil court. In 1997 she ran for a seat on the city council representing the Lower East Side and won that too.

The incident with the police stemmed from a conflict initially having little to do with the Puerto Rican community. On August 7, 1988, New York police had stormed Tompkins Square Park in the Lower East Side in response to calls from several community board members concerned about squatters. "When the sun rose over Tompkins Square Park last Sunday after a long, hot, angry night," noted one *New York Times* reporter, "broken glass and bloodied brows bore witness to the most violent conflict between the police and a crowd in New York City in years."[43] As the crowd scattered, the police pursued them on horseback. In a video of the event one police officer can be seen putting his nightstick through the spokes of a moving bicycle, throwing the rider onto the concrete. The police then swarmed on the rider and beat him with clubs. When they spotted a couple, another officer said menacingly to the black woman,

"Move along, black nigger bitch."[44] When the man turned around to see the officer's badge number, barely uttering "what?," the officer beat him with his nightstick. "They were fighting very dirty," the man later told a journalist, "slamming my head against the ground. I had one cop lay-ing [sic] right on top of me. I got bruises all over and am still getting nosebleeds."[45]

The incident came to affect two Puerto Rican district leaders due to their new electoral viability and the threat they posed to several conserva-tive community board members. The community board was now bitterly divided. Previously, Puerto Rican activists in the Lower East Side had eschewed electoral organizing. They had been outstanding organizers in other arenas (as mentioned in Chapter 1). They were the first to trans-form a street gang into a radical political organization. They had been on the cutting edge of housing organizing, pioneering a program (Adopt-a-Building) to allow tenants to purchase their abandoned buildings with sweat equity. They had founded the University of the Streets, the Nuyori-can Poets Café, CHARAS, and a host of other important community-based organizations. Early on activists had become persuaded that riots only destroyed their own neighborhood and that they needed to build community power through organizing from below. Yet, noted Armando Perez, "We had been very stupid in not realizing that we could not shy away from electoral process. Williamsburg realized that very early. Here, Puerto Ricans wouldn't run for office. It is one of the reasons there were no Puerto Rican candidates. I wouldn't participate in elections. For years when they asked me to run I refused. Then this guy (Antonio Pagan) comes around with a bunch of lies. He represents himself as a Puerto Rican progressive with a nationalist agenda and to the white community he presents a conservative agenda."

Armando consulted with Margarita Lopez, a local organizer and social worker, and together they devised a long-term plan. Together with other local activists they formed CODA (Coalition for a District 2 Alternative). In 1992 they ran for two district leader positions and won both. All of this was done with an eye to changing the Democratic Party from the bottom up, Armando noted. "If we had lost we would have been history down here." So when in 1993 conservative members of the Lower East Side com-munity board asked the police to again evict squatters, they met opposition. The NYPD responded to the call (a particular interpretation of community policing) by "breaking heads like it was going out of style," Armando Perez told me. Because it was members of the community board who had called the police, Armando and Margarita decided to vote against a resolution condemning the squatters, even though they believed that the tenants "who put sweat equity into those buildings should have had first claim on renovated housing, not squatters."

On June 22, 1993, during a community board meeting to discuss the squatters' issue, the chairman of the community board called the police, this time to arrest those getting ready to speak. They did it to prevent debate on the resolution and to avoid its defeat. The police responded to their call by arresting Puerto Rican community members. "One of the individuals arrested was thrown on the floor by one police officer," Margarita told me: "This police officer began beating up this man, and at some point this man began bleeding." Margarita was sitting in the front row, and when she saw the man bleeding from a gaping wound in his head, she got up and screamed at the police officer: "He is bleeding, don't do that, don't beat him up, he is bleeding." At that moment the chairman of the board ordered the captain of the precinct to arrest her. "The captain of the precinct, together with four other police officers, surrounded me, arrested me, put handcuffs behind my back, dragged me to the front of the dais in the area where we were, [and proceeded to] throw me on the floor, kick me, and beat me." Margarita was taken to the Seventh Precinct and detained there until two o'clock in the morning, along with another community board member who had done nothing more than defend her and try to explain to the officers that she was a community board member.

"I was let go with pretty much the following charges: resisting arrest, impairing police business, and inciting to riot. But before I was let go I asked why I was arrested, what was the reason, who was the officer arresting me," Margarita told me. She asked what charge was being levied against her and then requested permission to call her lawyer. "None of these things were allowed. . . . I was put [in]to a closet, a broom closet, where a police officer strip-searched me, made me take my clothing off. I was naked, and I was strip-searched." Margarita filed a lawsuit against the chairman of the board and the NYPD. The process took a year and a half, but she eventually won her case. She was awarded eighty thousand dollars in compensatory damages, and the chairman of the board was given three days of community service. In 1997 Margarita Lopez was elected to the city council, representing the Lower East Side.

Williamsburg

Division Street marks the boundary between the Hasidic and Puerto Rican communities of the Southside of Williamsburg. Both communities are poor with large families, many of whom depend on public housing and other forms of government assistance. Until the mid-1980s the Hasidim controlled the area policy board and the school board and the majority of public residencies. They also enjoyed a relatively privileged relationship with the police, especially in comparison to the abuse Puerto Ricans often suffered. Although police violence did not cause the tension between Puerto Rican and Hasidic residents, discriminatory policing exacerbated it. Competition between the Hasidic and Puerto Rican communities over housing and resources helped Puerto Rican activists mobilize and shaped the way they organized against racial profiling and police violence.

Throughout the 1980s Puerto Ricans in Williamsburg had scored a number of impressive victories in their fight against what they believed was preferential treatment of the Hasidic community on a number of fronts. First, they mobilized electorally to take control of the area policy board. Then they built on their successful organizing effort (they won all the seats) to, in the words of David Santiago, "lay the groundwork so the community could win." They took the city to court for discrimination in the allocation of public housing and won again. Out of that successful struggle, the activists (most of whom had worked together since the 1968 school board strike) created the South Side Action Committee, of which Santiago was a leader. The committee spearheaded the Latinos-for-Dinkins campaign in 1989 and later the effort to insure Latino representation in drawing the new congressional districts. Santiago observed, "Our network of community groups is very connected to the neighborhood residents. Solidarity is expressed in concrete ways." They were also behind Nydia Velazquez's successful congressional campaign.

Puerto Rican activists in Williamsburg used similar organizing strategies to fight police violence in the 1990s: protest marches and other forms of collective action; meetings and other organizing efforts; appeals to leaders they had elected; and the legal system, which they used to challenge racial profiling and discrimination. On March 3, 1990, Puerto Rican activists in Williamsburg, Brooklyn, held a mass march in protest against the district attorney's refusal to indict three police officers accused of killing three unarmed men in separate incidents: Juan Rodriguez; Louis

Liranso, age seventeen; and Jose Luis Lebron, age fourteen (shot in the back while running from police). "We know there will be a lot of men in blue there in support of the officers and we want to have members of our community there as well to show support for the family of Juan Rodriguez," said Lara Torres, a spokeswoman for the National Congress for Puerto Rican Rights.

On April 19 police tolerance of Hasidic riots led Puerto Rican activists to decry preferential treatment. Several hundred Hasidic men had surrounded a car with three Hasidic men from a different sect inside. Police had attempted to rescue the men but were shoved aside by crowds of Hasidim who continued to attack the car, shouting and pounding it before setting it aflame. The owner of the burned vehicle complained that the police had neither rescued the men nor saved the car. Instead of arresting the men who attacked the car and men in it, the police bowed, he claimed, to the power of the Satmar leader Moses Teitelbaum.

On October 24, 1990 both Puerto Rican and Hasidic protesters descended on the Ninetieth Precinct in response to the arrest of a Hasidic man by a Puerto Rican policeman, Hector Ariza. A teenaged girl had accused a Hasidic man of attempting to fondle her on a bus. The bus driver had called the police, and the Puerto Rican policeman had made the arrest. Three hundred Hasidic men stormed the precinct in protest, throwing rocks and bottles and violently kicking a fallen policeman in the ribs. Forty-four policemen were injured, but only one Hasidic man was arrested. The next day five hundred Puerto Ricans stormed the steps of the Ninetieth Precinct. "What happened Tuesday is a reflection of the attitude of the Hasidic community," said David Santiago; "the Hasidim use their clout to intimidate police."

Hector Ariza, a Puerto Rican policeman raised in Williamsburg, had made the initial arrest. He told local Puerto Rican activists and reporters that the police were routinely ordered to give preferential treatment to the Hasidim. Several Puerto Rican leaders asked Mayor Dinkins to investigate these charges. Later the Grand Council of Guardians, a fraternal organization of black policemen, blasted the Police Benevolent Association for filing suit against the Nation of Islam for a riot that injured eight police officers, while failing to file suit against the Hasidic community for a riot that had injured forty-four policemen.

In December another fatal shooting of an unarmed Puerto Rican man inflamed the Latino community. Jose Cruz, a restaurant owner, had called the police during an attempted robbery. The police arrived and shot him instead. Cruz died of gunshot wounds to the head, trunk, and extremities, with injuries to his brain, spinal cord, heart, aorta, and esophagus. Three hundred Puerto Ricans again marched past the Ninetieth Precinct office, this time crying, "Murderers." Again, Puerto Ricans called attention to the contrast in police behavior toward their community members and that toward the Hasidic community. Later that month it was the Hasidim's turn to protest. The same Puerto Rican officer had arrested a Hasidic man after the man had kicked him in the shins. The officer had tried to break up a dispute between the man (a volunteer bus driver) and a group of Hasidic women waiting for the bus, on one side, and a black couple who had been unable to pass them on the sidewalk, on the other. That evening twenty Hasidic men protested in front of the police station, saying that the police officer was biased against them. The Hasidic man was charged with assaulting a police officer, but the police officer was later removed from duty.

For the Puerto Rican community, however, protesting police violence was no laughing matter. On January 12, 1996, police officers killed the eighth-grader Frankie Arzuega, age fifteen, as he sat in the backseat of a stolen car. The drivers of the car had hit a police officer while trying to avoid arrest, and the officer had shot into the back of the car. I spoke briefly to Arzuega's mother at a Stolen Lives induction ceremony. This was the eleventh time a police officer had shot an unarmed youth in Brooklyn, and the Brooklyn district attorney Charles Hynes refused to issue an indictment. At the memorial march for her son on the anniversary of his death, his mother said, "My son, he was 15 years old. Today is the day that he was going home when Sergeant James Hand killed him. He was a kid. He was thinking about what he was going to do in the future. He always said 'Ma, I would like to be a author.' . . . We have to be crying out there, screaming out there for justice for our kids that cops killed and they still is the cops out there, like nothing happened. . . . I'm still going to fight for justice and for the other mothers and we still going to fight."

Yet the neighborhood did not burn. Puerto Ricans responded to racial discrimination and police violence in their neighborhood using standard movement repertoires: protest marches, electoral strategies, grassroots organizing efforts, and civil suits against the city.

Mothers and Fathers of Police Homicide Victims

Most police killings during the 1990s occurred in the Bronx and Central and Eastern Brooklyn. The sons of the mothers I interviewed were all killed in the Bronx. Thirteen-year-old Nicholas Heyward Jr. was killed in the Gowanus Houses in Boerum Hill, Brooklyn (one block from where I lived in the mid-1990s). I interviewed his father. In each case social movement activists were early responders. They defined the issue (in the first case defining it as something other than police violence), they helped families get indictments, and failing that they aided in getting federal interventions. In addition they helped them find lawyers for civil suits (although for the first victim much of this help was not yet available).

During the 1990s the city paid approximately twenty-five million dollars a year to settle with families of young people killed by police. As one New York civil libertarian notes, "[T]he major way things come out is through lawsuits, but the money paid comes out of taxpayer funds, not the police budget and very rarely from police officers. It is extremely rare for an officer to be found guilty of police misconduct or excessive force."[46] Families did not always win either criminal cases or civil suits. In some cases they were unable to gather enough evidence to bring charges. Yet, in contrast to France, the possibility of legal justice was enough to deter riotous actions. Every family I interviewed had believed at the time they pursued justice in the courts that legal victories on behalf of their slain children would prevent similar tragedies in the future.

Nicholas Heyward Jr. (September 1994),
African American, Brooklyn

On September 27, 1994, Nicholas Heyward Jr. and his friends were playing with plastic guns on the roof of their apartment building. A black housing officer entered the roof, saw the boys, and shot thirteen-year-old Nicholas in the abdomen. The mayor blamed Nicholas's toy gun, which he insisted was indistinguishable from a real gun. The media followed the mayor's lead. The barrage of stories about transposable toy guns diverted activists from the issue of police violence. A storm of protest forced stores to remove toy guns from store shelves and replace them with guns with orange muzzles. Yet the toy gun that Nicholas Heyward Sr. showed me looked nothing like a real gun; it was a toy rifle ten inches long. After Nicholas's death the mayor and the media focused all their attention on his toy gun.

The Brooklyn district attorney Charles Hynes refused to indict. It had been a tragic accident, he said, and no one was at fault. The housing officer was responding to a 911 call about men with guns in the building. In the dimly lit stairwell, the officer heard a clicking noise and made a split-second decision. Seeing the gun, he shot Nicholas Heyward in self-defense. When Nicholas died eight hours later, the housing officer was broken-hearted. The D.A.'s story, however, was contradicted by eyewitnesses and by the police officer himself in his recorded deposition. According to the five children who had been playing, Nicholas dropped his toy gun when he saw the police officer and said, "We were only playing." In his deposition the officer admitted that a) the stairwell was not dimly lit, b) things did not happen in a split second, and c) he was not responding to a 911 call but had been in the building across the street as part of his routine patrol. He claimed that he had seen people running back and forth from the roof of the other building. He took the elevator to the fourteenth floor of that building. As he exited the elevator, Nicholas was running up and down the stairs. Then Nicholas aimed the toy gun (a ten-inch rifle) at the officer and started clicking it. The officer then shot the thirteen-year-old.

"This is how the system works when it comes to police killings," Heyward informed me. "It is sad that these officers are the ones that we are supposed to call to protect us. People shouldn't have to be afraid to call the police." When Nicholas was twelve, another police officer had pointed his gun at him and told him to lie down on the pavement. "I asked what was going on," Heyward told me. "I said, 'he didn't do anything; he was standing with me and my wife.'" The officer took Nicholas to the Seventy-sixth Precinct. "We waited at the precinct 3–4 hours. When they brought Nick down I could see he was very upset and wanted to leave right away. He was very nervous. The cop there said he was sorry the officer must have mistaken him for someone else. After we left the precinct I asked Nicholas what had happened. He said the cop said he would put his gun up his butt and pull the trigger. Then he told my son he would not live to be 15."

After Nicholas's death the family filed a complaint with the civilian review board, but the board refused to take the case. "They said it was proper how the city handled the death of a 13-year-old," Heyward said. The officer was not indicted and continued to work in the same housing projects until Heyward complained. Then he was transferred to Brownsville, an even poorer community. "I didn't think he should even be on the force," complained Heyward. I asked Heyward how the neighbors and community had responded to the killing of his son. "They were completely outraged and upset, but felt there was nothing they could do." In Heyward's case, as in later cases, it was a female police officer who broke the blue wall of silence. "Are all the police bad?" I asked Heyward. Although he believes that women officers might be better, he commented of the male officers, "I would have to say all of them. The few who claim to be good remain silent. If you know how can you remain silent? In our case, just like in the Baez case [discussed next], a lady police officer came forward and said it didn't happen that way. When she said that—at the trial—[her] fellow cops verbally attacked her. She had to be transferred to another unit. A lot of police officers are afraid of other officers. She was willing to step forward and for that she was targeted."

Heyward believes that change has to be made from the bottom up, not by putting black officers in blue uniforms. It is the mission of the police that has to change, he pointed out. When a police officer comes into a community, he said, "his job should be to help, and show young people a better way":

> I see police drive past someone in the street, and not help. If their job is supposed to be helping the community, it should include those addicted to drugs. The majority of those in jail are nonviolent drug cases. They are just locking up addicts. I should be able to see a police officer and greet him and talk to them and say, "How are you doing, officer?" That just doesn't happen. I honestly don't believe that the police system is going to change for the better [or] that one-day people in poor minority communities are going to come together with the police force. Police are always going to target poor minority neighborhoods.

Heyward later pursued a civil suit, but he did so before it had become standard practice. Movements had not yet become adept at helping parents find lawyers skilled at pressing suits of this kind. Heyward had to manage on his own. His first two lawyers took advantage of him. The first incorrectly filed the complaint, failing to include the parents in the affidavit. This dramatically reduced the potential sum that could be demanded. The second took his money but did not pursue the case. The third, Karl Thomas, had been an assistant district attorney when the D.A. refused to indict. Heyward ran into him in the street. Thomas told him how hurt he had felt about what had happened to Heyward's son and how badly he felt the D.A. had treated him. Unfortunately by that time the discovery phase of Heyward's suit had closed, and the previous lawyer's errors, including the court where the case was filed, severely limited their range of action. At trial the judge called Heyward and his attorney into chambers and explained to them that the way the suit had originally been written, especially its failure to name the parents as injured parties, meant that legally the case was not worth fifty thousand dollars. The Heyward family accepted three hundred thousand dollars.

There are several reasons why the community did not explode in violence when Heyward's thirteen-year-old son was fatally shot. First, his was the first fatal shooting since Dinkins left office, and despite Giuliani's aggressive campaign, it was not yet clear that the state would refuse to hold officers accountable. Second, the officer had been black, so racial boundaries were not activated. Third, the media and subsequently movement activists interpreted the shooting as a tragic accident. Consequently activist energies were focused on getting toy guns marked in orange rather than on protesting police violence.

Years later the Heywards' other son, who was six when Nicholas was killed, was pulled from his classroom and arrested for a robbery he did not commit. The charges were dropped when the grocer did not identify the youth as the robber. Nonetheless the youth continued to feel unsafe in Brooklyn and moved to Atlanta upon graduation. The persecution of family members who sued the police would become standard practice.

Anthony Baez (December 22, 1994), Puerto Rican, Bronx

Nearly three months after the death of Nicholas Heyward, Officer Francis X. Livoti choked Anthony Baez to death outside his mother's home in the Bronx, where he had come to spend Christmas. Anthony had grown up in a devout Christian family. His pastor had wanted him to become a priest, but Baez was drawn to the police. In 1992 Baez married and moved with his wife to Florida. He had applied to the police force there and was currently awaiting the results of his admission test. Livoti was a rogue cop with twelve civilian complaints filed against him, nine for excessive use of force. His commander, William Casey, had recommended he be transferred out of the department and out of active duty. In his deposition before the court, Casey said that he had made an unusually strong case against Officer Livoti because of his status as the police union delegate in the Forty-sixth Precinct. But the new commander, Louis R. Anemone, now chief of the department, rejected the 1991 recommendation, saying that the complaints were in his view unsubstantiated.[47]

The night Anthony died, "everyone was kicking and punching walls," his mother said. "We started marching from here to the precinct. I wanted to tell them there was a murderer inside."[48] By the time they arrived, over a hundred people had joined them. "I was never part of a movement," Iris Baez claims. "Livoti made me become part of this movement by murdering my son."[49] Unable to cast doubt on Anthony's character, the police blamed Anthony's health. They said that he had suffered an asthma attack. However, the claim was contradicted by the pathology report, which indicated that Baez's windpipe was crushed—he had been choked to death. The coroner ruled it a homicide.

"There was an extraordinary effort of mass mobilization to force the DA to indict," said "Panama" Alba of the Coalition Against Police Brutality. Even so, "the first case was thrown out of court because the DA's office had written second-degree manslaughter on the indictment instead of the correct charge *criminally negligent homicide*." Alba believes that the charge was deliberately miswritten. The case did not end there, however, "because thousands of people mobilized." Families, friends, and others demanded that D.A. Robert Johnson pursue a second indictment. During the trial, three of the four police officers at the scene testified that Baez had gotten up and walked away. Mario Erotokritou claimed that he did not see Livoti use a chokehold. Both Officers Daisy Boria and Robert Ball concurred that they had seen Baez get up and walk after his struggle with Livoti. That contradicted their earlier testimony that Baez had taken a few steps after Livoti released the chokehold.

Then, as in the Heyward case, the sole female officer, Daisy Boria, broke rank. She admitted that the story she and the other officers had told under oath had been concocted. She told the judge that her partner, Officer Erotokritou, had invited her to participate in a meeting outside the Forty-sixth Precinct to discuss the case. The plan had been to blame the choking on the mysterious hands of a black civilian. After Boria's testimony the judge concluded that there had been "a nest of perjury in the courtroom." Although the judge claimed that she did not believe that Livoti was innocent, she ruled that the district attorney had not proved his case. At issue was the testimony of the chief medical examiner, Charles S. Hirsch. Hirsch had testified that Baez died of asphyxia caused by compression of the neck and chest, a conclusion in line with the prosecution's theory that Livoti had crushed Baez's windpipe when he used an illegal chokehold. The acting justice Gerald Sheindlin, however, asked the coroner a hypothetical question. If Baez was "released from the neck grip, regained consciousness and struggled, whereupon he was pinned face down and one or more officers put pressure on his back . . . [c]ould he have suffered an acute asthma attack?" "Yes, Sir, it could be," Dr. Hirsch had said.[50] When the not-guilty verdict was read, Iris Baez collapsed in the courtroom. Crowds inside and outside the courtroom were in tears, stunned. "People lost confidence in the whole system," noted Iris; "why go to church, why pray? Tony did everything and he was taken away."

It took another "extraordinary level of mobilization," noted Alba, to get the federal government to step in. Livoti was convicted of civil rights violations and sentenced to seven years. The presiding judge said that "Livoti's brazen response to the death of Anthony Baez has helped to undermine public confidence in law enforcement, and has compounded the harm done to the Baez family and to the fabric of law and order as a result of his criminal conduct."[51] Alba, however, feels that the penalty was too light. "Seven years for the murder of Anthony Baez is not justice. There is no equal protection under the law. When you talk about killer cops it [takes] extraordinary effort to get justice," Alba bitterly reflected. "Because the criminalization of people in the inner city is so massive, there are massive numbers of people that have had previous negative interactions with the police. But in the death of Anthony Baez we have a case where the victim was squeaky clean."

Iris Baez said that it pained her to have to watch "Officer Livoti smirking at times during the trial, aloof and arrogant in their presence. This was the same man who had talked about how his authority had been usurped and challenged by Anthony and his brother David when they refused to stop tossing a football in front of their home."[52] The judge for her part blamed the city: "The Police Department did Mr. Livoti and the people of this city a grave injustice when it permitted Mr. Livoti to remain on active patrol knowing of his propensity toward violence."[53] Giuliani, in what would mark his signature response to police killings during the next eight years, denounced the judge: "Judge Sheindlin's comments regarding the Police Department during sentencing today are gratuitous and certainly don't reflect the department's excellent record in uncovering corruption, and disciplining and dismissing rogue cops. . . . Francis Livoti is a brutal criminal who deserves a long sentence in Federal prison."[54]

Not until five years after Baez's death, when the city council named a street after Anthony Baez, did Giuliani express to journalists some sympathy with the family: "[I]t was a terrible thing. It should never have happened. And it was a situation in which a police officer was left on the police force who should not have been on the police force."[55] Giuliani never apologized to the family, however, nor did he object when Anemone (the commander who chose to leave Livoti on the force despite nine Civilian Complaint Review Board [CCRB] complaints filed against him) was promoted. Baez later sued the city for $25 million but settled for $3 million. She used the funds to create a foundation to help other victims of police brutality. After her other son was picked up by police, however, ostensibly for running a stop sign—a charge he vigorously denies—and taken away from the other passengers and then beaten in an alley, she moved her family to Florida.

"When you [are] no longer marching in the streets, when you go home and everyone is gone, reality hits," Baez said. Livoti never showed any remorse. After his release, he opened a successful self-defense business in Albany, New York. "This is a classic example of what happens in poor communities of color, where no justice is possible," noted Panama Alba. Yet the failure to achieve justice in one arena led them to pursue it in other arenas. When the first indictment was badly filed, the family and community members demanded a second indictment. When Livoti demanded a judge rather than a jury trial (police always request either a judge or a change of venue) and the judge dismissed the case against him despite his acknowledgment that the police had perjured themselves, they asked for a federal intervention and sued the city in civil court. By the end of the process, they were all exhausted.

In both Nicholas Heyward's and Anthony Baez's cases, the victims were entirely innocent and, as Alba noted, "squeaky clean." When, however, a victim had a previous history with law enforcement, Giuliani's response was rancorous. He assailed these victims, turning the officers who killed them into objects of sympathy. The deaths of Anthony Rosario and Hilton Vega are cases in point.

Anthony Rosario and Hilton Vega
(January 11, 1995), Puerto Rican, Bronx

"The day my son was killed I was en route from Puerto Rico to New York," Margarita Rosario told me the day I interviewed her. Her nightmare began as follows: "Around 1:30 my husband woke me up," she said. "There are two police officers who want to speak to you. They said my son was involved in a robbery, a shoot-out with police and got killed. 'Are you sure he was shooting at police,' I asked." The officers said "yes" and then showed her a photo of two boys lying face up and dead.

The Bronx district attorney refused to indict the officers involved. He felt that Patrick Brosnan and James Crowe were highly regarded detectives who could have lost their lives because of a moment's hesitation. Brosnan had been Giuliani's personal bodyguard during his 1993 campaign and was named 1992 cop of the year. The detectives had responded to a call from George and Herminda Rodriquez, who had filed a complaint against three boys the previous day. They said the boys had threatened them and planned to return the following day. The officers waited in the Rodriquezes' apartment, and when the boys arrived as expected, forcing their way in at gunpoint, they defended themselves. In the shoot-out two of the three boys were killed. The official coroner backed the police officers, and the evening news carried their version of the story as well.

Margarita Rosario, however, found the officers' claims unconvincing. George and Herminda Rodriquez had been involved with Hilton Vega's girlfriend in an illegal scheme involving marriage for a green card, and they had then refused to pay her. Vega was Anthony's cousin and had asked Anthony and another youth to come along for support after Rodriquez invited him to the apartment to discuss the issue. In other words, Rodriquez had set the boys up. Unfortunately, Vega gave the two youths guns to carry for self-defense. Rosario admitted that Vega was irresponsible and contributed to the death of her son. She disputed the officers' claims, however. Brosnan, she said, had a reputation as a cowboy and had had three prior shootings under his belt. Panama Alba also believed that it was a set-up. He said that the officers had already disarmed the boys and forced them to lie on the floor with their hands on their heads. "They then shot them multiple times, so much so that the neighbors called the police."

For a long time, Rosario told me, she could not get out of bed. Finally her niece asked her if she was going to just let them speak that way about her son. "I knew my son so well. I knew it couldn't be true. I decided to get out of bed and do something." She filed a case with the CCRB. After investigating it, the CCRB concluded that the shootings had not been justified. However, Commissioner Bratton rejected the report and said that "[t]here had been a rush to judgment." Giuliani responded by firing the head of the CCRB. They "treated the investigation report as if it was just a piece of paper," said Rosario. Giuliani then attacked the youths on television and the radio. During one radio show Rosario called in to complain about the way the mayor had spoken about her son. She asked why he refused to indict the police officers. Giuliani told her that she herself was at fault, that she had raised her son to be a criminal. After that Rosario began organizing. She created Parents Against Police Brutality:

> I felt I was going to focus on this issue—police brutality. NYC learned the truth about my son—not from news media but from the flyers I was passing out on the streets and in subways. The more I went to rallies and protests the more I began to meet other families. I didn't know there were so many families with this experience. I got the idea of forming a group to bring all the families together. Connecting them gave me a sense of power and strength. No one understands my pain more than these people. What we want is to try to change the system. No family should be put through the agony and pain that we went through. In memory of my son I didn't want to see any more kids killed.

Rosario said that she got the idea of forming a group from a documentary on the life of Martin Luther King Jr. "I was watching it and it just sprung upon me, this is what I had to do." Had they simply spoken to her honestly and not covered it up, she believes, she would have accepted the verdict. Once she came out publicly, however, she began to get support. It is "hard to keep the group going," she admitted, "because families come and go. Some win lawsuits and then get gag orders. They can no longer speak." Nonetheless she believes that due to her organizing efforts many changes have been instituted in the police department. "There are more black officer associations and Latino officer associations." And, she continued, "people are less afraid to speak. When there is a police shooting we speak with the parents immediately, get them a lawyer, and help them file a lawsuit. Parents against Police Brutality had a lot to do with giving people the courage to do these things. You can't get discouraged. You must continue to try to change the system." Margarita also filed a civil suit against the city with her husband and settled for $1.1 million, to be divided between them (she and her husband divorced during the process).

There was a revealing coda to this case. In July 2013, New York Officer Brosnan and his partner Kevin Tracy were tried for pummeling two minority police officers, one black and the other Latino, outside a restaurant, following a fundraiser for a fellow officer's sick child in 1991. The fight began when Officer Tracy punched the black officer, Scott Thompson, outside the restaurant for supposedly badmouthing his friend. Tracy then knocked Thompson to the ground and continued to pound him as he lay prostrate. Officer Antonio Echevestre came to his partner's defense, and two white officers jumped him. Antonio Tetro called him a spic, as he hit him, and Officer Brosnan beat him so brutally that Echevestre suffered irreparable brain damage and loss of hearing. Only one of the white officers was punished and docked several days of vacation pay. A combination of jurisdictional and discovery issues caused a 22-year delay in the case. The two minority officers later left the force, Thompson after 20 years on the force, and Echevestre after 16. At this time there is still no verdict in the case.[56]

There are some parallels between this case and the previous two cases, as well as some important distinctions. Although Heyward, Baez, and Rosario all ultimately won civil suits, social movement mobilization was an important part of each story. In Heyward's case, the movements directed their energies to getting toy guns off store shelves; in the Baez case, efforts were focused on getting indictments and federal intervention; and in the Rosario and Vega case Margarita Rosario brought together other parents who had lost their children to police violence. In both the Baez and Rosario cases, the parents used their civil case settlements to create new organizations to fight police brutality. In the Rosario and Vega case, however, the mayor turned the tables on the victims, calling their own conduct into question. He would later use this tactic in every brutality incident where the victims had any prior contact with the criminal justice system. Given the racial bias in the war on drugs, this would be aimed at an increasing number of young black and Latino men.

Amadou Diallo (February 4, 1999), African, Bronx

The killing of Amadou Diallo, a twenty-three-year-old immigrant from Guinea, was perhaps New York's most notorious police killing. Diallo had been standing in the vestibule of his apartment in the Soundview section of South Bronx, neighboring Mott Haven, when four white undercover officers riddled him with bullets. The officers claimed they thought Diallo looked like a rapist on their most-wanted list. When they called to him, he reached for his wallet, apparently to show his identification, and the officers thought he was reaching for a gun. One officer started to shoot, and the other officers, hearing the shots, all began shooting. They shot forty-one rounds, hitting him nineteen times.

A grand jury indicted the officers on charges of reckless endangerment and second-degree manslaughter. But an appellate court ordered a change of venue to Albany, ostensibly to protect the officers from the publicity the case had received in New York City. An Albany jury acquitted the officers of all charges. Massive mobilizations were organized immediately following Diallo's death, then again following the court decision to permit a change of venue, and again following the verdict. Over seventeen hundred people were arrested in acts of civil disobedience—most often sit-ins in front of police headquarters. David Dinkins, Congressman Charlie Rangel, Congressman Gregory Meeks, Reverends Al Sharpton and Jesse Jackson, New York state assemblyman Ruben Diaz Jr., the actress Susan Sarandon, the British documentary filmmaker Louis Theroux, several former NYPD officers, more than a dozen rabbis and other clergy, and numerous federal, state, and local politicians were all arrested, although charges against the protesters were later dropped. In 2001 the Department of Justice refused to charge the officers for having violated Diallo's civil rights.

On April 18, 2000, Diallo's mother, Kadiatou, and his stepfather, Sankarella Diallo, filed a $60 million lawsuit against the city. They settled for $3 million. They used the money to create a foundation to provide scholarship funds for immigrant youths. I spoke with Kadiatou Diallo after a talk she gave at a Bronx community college. What struck her when her son was killed, she said, was the outcry in communities across the globe. She was sure that because of the attention the case received the police would no longer be allowed to kill black and Latino youths. Yet ten years later, "while there are some changes, they are not what we expected. The media interest is no longer the same. Now with an African American president they tell us you can be anything you want to be." But, Diallo pointed out, "police officers still kill blacks with impunity." According to Diallo, when witnesses dispute the police version of events, "they use racial stereotypes to discredit them. If any time in their life they were involved with the criminal justice system, they cannot be believed."

In the case of her son's death, there was nothing the police could use to discredit either Amadou or his mother. Even so, she said, the press referred to him as a street peddler when he was a student working to put himself through college. "I am only a mother. I believe Amadou would be alive if the officers had only parked their cars and talked to him like he was a human being. They would have realized he wasn't armed." Instead, she said, "they came out shooting, knowing nothing more than that he was black." Her life was forever changed, she told me: "For the past ten years [I interviewed her in 2009] I relive the horror everyday. How can I take him out of the vestibule where he was killed so he can be remembered differently? It is hard to lose a child, whether through a police shooting or criminal attack. More difficult still is to deal with the legal system and the media."

Her child was portrayed "in such a terrible way. It wasn't easy, but I truly believed my case would change things. I campaigned so that my son did not die in vain. It is for this that I joined Al Sharpton. But he has so many agendas. The families need something else." In the Diallo case, as in previous cases, friends and family engaged in a two-pronged strategy: nonviolent protest, on the one hand, and using the courts and legal system, on the other. All the families thought that the mass mobilizations would draw attention to the issues and prevent other families from suffering what they had suffered. This is what kept them going through years of street mobilizations, organizing efforts, court battles, and a great deal of despair.

Malcolm Ferguson (March 1, 2000), African American, Bronx

Malcolm spent eight or nine months in prison and upon his release told his mother about "the things they do to people in prison." He said, "I never want to go there again." He was trying to get his life together while taking care of his blind mother. Every time he passed a police officer, however, the officer would stop and frisk him. One day he was put in cuffs and the police officer broke his wrist in the process. The officer claimed that Malcolm was intending to sell drugs, but he was let go when no drugs were found on him. The district attorney threw the case out of court. Sometime later, at a rally to protest the Diallo killing, Malcolm was again arrested. This time the arresting officer told him he would be next. Two days later he was.

Malcolm's mother, Juanita Young, is a large, blind black woman. I interviewed her in her apartment on the second floor of a walk-up in a depressed section of the South Bronx, on a road covered with service stations. She told me that Malcolm was visiting his friends when it started drizzling. The friends stepped into a building to get out of the rain. Someone pushed Malcolm into the building; the boys thought someone was trying to rob them and ran. The police claim they thought one of the young men was someone who had just escaped arrest on drug possession charges. The police ran up the stairs after Malcolm, caught him on the steps, and, according to the officer who shot him, the gun accidentally fired.

Witnesses refute the policeman's version of events. According to witnesses, Young claimed, "my son turned around and stopped when he saw it was a cop." "They also said that the officer came into the building with his gun drawn." The medical examiner corroborated the witnesses' story rather than the police officer's version of events. After hearing what happened, a local councilman went to the crime scene. He too disputed the police officer's story. None of the police officers had even mentioned drugs initially, so the councilman knew that the offending officer was lying when he later said he had found drugs. Even so, the Bronx district attorney Robert Johnson refused to indict. He told Juanita that he would tell the jury that the police officer "just got a drug dealer off the street." That was the story the media carried the next day.

So Juanita Young hired a lawyer and sued the city. During the trial a female police officer testified that she had asked the offending officer why he had not shot Malcolm just in the leg. Then Young's lawyer asked the officer why he had shot Malcolm. The officer responded that, "he did not know why he had shot him." That was the testimony that led the jury to award Juanita Young $10.5 million in damages. She was also awarded $1.35 million in damages when she sued the NYPD for pushing her down the steps and breaking her wrist, one of a series of violent assaults she suffered after taking police officers to court for killing her son. In August 2009, shortly after I interviewed her, the police crashed her family barbecue. They threw her younger son on the ground, beat him, and took him to the precinct. They have continued to threaten her son, and Young thinks that she may have to leave the neighborhood.

Timur Person (January 5, 2007), African American, Bronx

Allene Person is a shy, quiet black woman. I met Allene in a Lower East Side apartment, where a friend had allowed her to temporarily reside, under the condition she not move anything in it. The owners had already boxed up their belongings, and the boxes substituted for furniture. Allene is a tiny woman, and, squeezed between these large boxes, she looked utterly defenseless. She had had three sons. The oldest is married and living in

New Jersey. The second oldest is in prison, on drug charges. Before he was killed, Timur, her youngest son, had lived with her at their home, and his salary had augmented her own. After Timur's death, she could not afford her rent and was evicted from her apartment. Since then, she told me, she has found it hard to sleep at night:

> The police never explained why they shot him. Timur and some other boys were standing outside a building when the cops showed up in unmarked cars. Timur went into the building and the cops followed him in. When they got him they shoved him down on the floor [and] the head cop shot him five times, once in the neck, once in the head. . . . My son was 5'4, or 5'5. Why did he have to shoot him?
>
> It was three days before his twentieth birthday. It was in High Bridge (the Bronx neighborhood with the highest number of killings by police). My other son's girlfriend got me and we walked to the hospital. I went into the room where there were a bunch of detectives. "We're working on him," they [doctors] told me. "Go out and wait thirty minutes." Half an hour later I went in and they said, "I am so sorry, we lost him." I asked to see him and they said he is on the way to the morgue. They said the cops identified him. They removed the bullets from him and sent him away while I was waiting.

The next day she went to the medical examiner's office. Her son was covered up. "Why," she asked, "is he covered up, he was shot in the neck?" Witnesses say the cop was sitting on him when he shot him:

> Kids were saying that one night when Timur was hanging out this cop chased him, grabbed him, and kicked him in the head and shoulder and said, "I will kill you." . . . I went to the home of my son's girlfriend and cried. My grandson had become attached to Timur. He kept saying, "Where's uncle Trap. He up, he up?" Then he said, "It's OK Grandma, I am going to take care of you. Grandma, I want to go to your school [where she is an assistant teacher]. If there is a guy bothering you I am going to bust him up. Uncle Trap told me to in my dream." He is three years old. If I wear a T-shirt with Timor's name he asks, "Are you feeling sad?"

I became so depressed I couldn't function. On the second anniversary vigil my legs wouldn't function. My social worker called Belleview Hospital, to get me into group therapy for people whose sons were shot. A friend from high school called me because I had lost my apartment since I couldn't afford the rent—my son had been paying it—and told me I could take her apartment. She told the building manager that her cousin was apartment watching [because the apartment is rent controlled]. I would like to go to the Bronx. Here I have no one to go to the store for me. I don't make friends easily because I am so quiet. I cry in my sleep. When I go to therapy and talk maybe I won't cry in my sleep. I thought it would get better but it got worse. I am a quiet person. I keep all that stuff inside.

Allene wanted to pursue her case in criminal court, but the Bronx district attorney refused to press charges. Her friend Juanita Young, Malcolm's mother, told her to begin a civil suit. Person wanted to do so but has not been able to learn the name of the police officer who shot Timur. The kids in the neighborhood call him "redneck," but the precinct officers will not tell her anything. Several organizations have offered to help her, including the Justice Committee and Parents Against Police Brutality. She has decided to join a new group, Mothers of Never Again, with her friend Danette Chavis. Allene told me, "We have so far a core group—five of us [she mentioned three others], Valerie Bell (Sean Bell's mother), Danette Chavis, Sean Williams. I gave a speech. I want the mothers to know how I feel, how I couldn't [even] open a soda bottle. They cried. A lady making a video said it was the best speech she had heard since I just talked about how I missed my son."

Gregory Chavis (October 9, 2004), African American, Bronx

On October 9, 2004, Gregory Chavis was caught in the crossfire of a shootout between the police and a drug gang. Chavis was shot in the back. As his friends were taking him to the hospital, a squad car pulled up. The officers pulled their guns and demanded that the youths lay Gregory on the ground. "They would not let them bring him to the hospital as he lay bleeding to death, despite the pleas of the friends and witnesses. He died in front of Lincoln Hospital from gunshot wounds that were not intended for him," Danette, Gregory's mother, told the audience at the Stolen Lives induction ceremony.

The lawsuit filed against the city of New York for the wrongful death of Gregory Chavis accused the NYPD of failing to seek required medical attention. But Danette Chavis did not want to talk about her son's death. She wanted to talk about police brutality in the Bronx. "Ninety-five percent of all criminal cases in the Bronx," she said, "are 'buy and bust operations' for drugs. Meanwhile the bodies are dropping day and night. While the cops do sweeps for drugs, homicides are not investigated. Nobody feels protected, nobody feels secure. . . . All the death and terror, dying before they graduate and politicians are going to Barack [Obama] and saying we need more money for education."

Danette Chavis, Nicholas Heyward, and other parents believe that pursuing legal remedies on a case-by-case basis is not the solution. In 2000, Richard Emery and Ilann Margalit Maazel reached a similar conclusion. They argued that the City's policy of giving victims financial settlement was

> no solace to the victims of police misconduct especially those who seek to translate their horrible experience into reform of a broken system, and who must helplessly face an officer who lies with impunity to a judge and jury. As ineffective as civil litigation is in punishing police officers who violate the law, it is even less effective in deterring officers from future unlawful conduct. This is true for one basic reason: police officers almost never pay anything out of their own pockets to settle civil lawsuits. Nor do they pay for judgments rendered after jury verdicts for plaintiffs. Police officers are so far removed from the process of settling cases and paying money damages that they often have no idea how much their cases settle for, or even whether they settle at all. We have deposed many officers who had been sued one, two, three times before, yet had no idea how any of those cases were resolved.[57]

In 2012 Chavis, Heyward, and other parents of young people killed by police started a petition on change.org asking the federal government to implement a national policy against police violence as part of a collective effort to hold police officers accountable.

Chapter 4

Boundary Activation
and Riots in Paris (2002–2010)

On October 27, 2005, in Clichy-sous-Bois, Siyakha Traoré, a twenty-three-year-old man of Mauritanian descent, was on his way to the grocer to break his Ramadan fast when he saw Muhittin Altun, a friend of his younger brother, running wildly and howling, "Bouna, Zyad, Bouna, Zyad." Smoke radiated from his body and his arms, and his legs and chest were severely burned. "What about Bouna and Zyad?" Siyakha asked (2006). Muhittin could only cry, "Bouna, Zyad," and point toward an electric substation (*transformateur éléctrique*) while weeping hysterically. Siyakha phoned the fire department and dashed to the site with Muhittin. "Bouna, Zyad!" he called at the substation, but to no avail. Siyakha and Muhittin waited almost thirty minutes for the firemen to arrive. When they did, they circled the substation. At the far side, police, ambulances, and scores of neighborhood residents were already gathered. Siyakha recognized his parents in the crowd.

As Siyakha made his way to the substation, the police blocked his path. He pleaded, "My little brother Bouna is inside." They relented. A fireman hoisted himself onto the wall. "There appear to be some people unconscious inside," he said. "Can you describe them?" Siyakha asked. "One is black and the other Arab," he was told. The fireman said no more for a few seconds and then entered the substation. When he came out, he whispered, "Actually, we cannot identify them." That is how Siyakha understood that his brother was dead. When Siyakha's father saw the faces of the policemen, he too understood that something grave had happened and put his head in his hands.

Muhittin said that Bouna, Zyad, and six other boys between the ages of fourteen and seventeen had been on their way home from a soccer match. They were crossing a large construction site when they saw officers of the

Brigades anti-criminalité (BAC). The police shouted at the boys to halt and show identification. The boys had not brought their papers to the game and knew that the police would haul them to the station if they were found without them. Also they were hungry; they had fasted all day for Ramadan. They decided to run. The police pursued them, with flash-ball[1] guns. As the boys neared the substation, a new group of police officers arrived from the opposite direction, heading them off. The police grabbed six of the boys.

Bouna, Zyad, and Muhittin were now alone, trapped against an eight-foot wall topped with barbed wire and large signs warning, "Caution: Electricity is stronger than you; your life is at stake." On the signs skulls and crossbones graphically illustrated the peril. Choosing between the wall and the police, the boys decided to scale the wall. For eleven nightmarish minutes inside the substation, the boys searched for an exit, holding onto each other tightly. Suddenly one of the boys hit the transformer. Bouna and Zyad were killed instantly, but Muhittin, last in line, was saved when a power surge cut electricity to the town. Severely burned, Muhittin back-tracked and rescaled the wall. There was no one outside the substation; the police had abandoned the site. Witnesses claimed, and radio transcripts submitted by the police investigative service support them, that one of the officers radioed his commanding officer when he saw the boys enter the substation:

> "I think they are about to enter the EDF [Électricité de France] substation. We need reinforcements to surround the neighborhood, or they are going to get out."
> "Yes, message received."
> "On second thought, if they entered the EDF site their skin is worth nothing now."[2]

Their mission accomplished, the police vanished. A simple call to the electric power company would have saved the children's lives, but instead the police abandoned them to almost certain death. Eighteen months would pass before the police were indicted for criminal neglect.

That evening Nicolas Sarkozy publicly announced that no investigation would be needed since the police had done nothing wrong. If the boys were hiding, he suggested, it was because they had committed a robbery. As friends, relatives, and classmates began to exchange information, condolences, and outrage, young people in Clichy and Montfermeil took to the streets and cursed the police, who had gathered in scores. Low-level confrontations ensued but were quelled. Two days later a thousand Parisians of all classes and colors united in Clichy to accompany the families to the funeral of Bouna and Zyad. They carried signs that said, "Dead for Nothing." At around 5:00 P.M. several boys ran into a mosque with the police on their tail. When the men at the door prevented the officers from entering, one officer launched a tear gas canister inside the mosque, asphyxiating hundreds of families attending sermon. Again Sarkozy denied that the police had committed any wrong. This time he ignited a maelstrom.

For the next three weeks riots spread from suburb to suburb, affecting over three hundred towns and inspiring sympathy riots in Brussels and Berlin. Over nine thousand vehicles were torched and hundreds of public and commercial buildings destroyed. The riots resulted in over 200 million in damages, 5,000 rioters arrested and 800 imprisoned, and 125 policemen wounded. "Behind the fires in the street," the boys' lawyers later observed, "were the fires in the heads of the youth."[3] Fires had been stoked by the long, violent, and contentious relationship between police and young people of North African or African descent.

Why was the relationship between police and *banlieue* youths so poisonous? Why were the young people willing to take such risks to avoid the police? Were the riots in the Parisian *banlieues* a result of the same social processes that had provoked riots in American cities where "the growing black underclass remained similarly invisible, and the police force in black neighborhoods was similarly viewed as an occupying army"?[4] What mechanisms produced such remarkably similar features in what are otherwise quite dissimilar cultural and political settings? What impact did the government's "zero-tolerance" war on crime have on young people targeted by police? In other words, what was the relationship between Parisian-style crime wars and the flames that consumed the Parisian suburbs for three weeks in November?

Initial Explanations

Initial explanations strayed far from the facts on the ground. Some bordered on the ridiculous. Noting high black participation in the riots, Gérard Larcher, acting minister of employment, and Bernard Accoyer, president of the Union pour un mouvement populaire (UMP) in the Assembly, argued that African polygamy was at the root of both urban violence and black unemployment. Several UMP senators introduced legislation to ban the already illegal practice, a measure signed by Prime Minister Dominique de Villepin. One French historian, Carrère d'Encausse (an expert on Russian history), told the Russian media that the riots were caused by the polygamous marital practice of African Muslims.[5] The French sociologist Hugues Lagrange (while admitting that children from polygamous families were not numerous enough to be the cause of the riots) conducted a study soon after that and claimed that African families were more likely to practice polygamy and have larger families and that both practices produced children who were scholastically weak, almost unemployable, and more likely to engage in crime and delinquency.[6]

Others blamed radical Islam. The philosopher Alain Finkielkraut, a former 1968 radical, told a reporter for *Ha'aretz* (an English-language Israeli daily) that "the problem is that most of these youth are blacks or Arabs, with a Muslim identity. [They are engaged in] a pogrom against the Republic. . . . What sets the West apart when it comes to slavery is that it was the first one to eliminate it. But this truth about slavery cannot be taught in schools. . . . We don't teach anymore that the colonial project also sought to educate, to bring civilization to the savages. . . . What did Europe do to Africans? It only did good."[7] The literary theorist Tzvetan Todorov told the audience attending a conference at Columbia University that the riots "were caused by the dysfunctional sexuality of Muslim youth obsessed with behaving in a macho way."[8]

Another common approach zeroed in on France's unusually high rate of youth unemployment, particularly among black and Arab young people (for fifteen- to twenty-four-year-olds of non-European parentage, unemployment rates are as high as 47 percent, more than double those of French youths of European origin).[9] Marxists blaming massive redundancies caused by neoliberalism found common cause with classical economists pointing the finger at France's rigid labor regulations.[10] A few claimed that lack of gainful employment had created a violent underclass culture in the *banlieues*.[11] The sociologist Olivier Roy, for instance, warned that "there is a sense of belonging to an underclass, despised, excluded and ignored. . . . a self-fulfilling sense of exclusion prevents many of these youngsters from entering the new economy. . . . They want to be part of consumer society, even as predators."[12]

Predictably, Nicolas Sarkozy's explanation was more venomous. "The central cause of unemployment, of despair, of violence in the suburbs," he retorted, "is not discrimination or the failure of the schools—it is drug traffic, the law of bands, the dictatorship of fear and the resignation of the Republic." Citing the national police claim that 80 percent of the youths arrested were well known by police, Sarkozy asserted that they were well-known delinquents and that the riots expressed "the intention of these people who have made offending their main activity to resist the ambition of the Republic to restore its order, the order of its laws, throughout the country."[13] He later promised to deport all those arrested.

Yet all of these approaches overlooked a significant array of facts. First, claims of polygamy were based on an unusual dearth of data. At the time the anti-polygamy measure was passed, there had been no studies of polygamy, how widely it was practiced, or what percentage of the participants in the riots were children of polygamous parents. When Lagrange looked at the data a year later, he found that only 3 percent of those arrested came from polygamous families.[14] Second, outside of polemics, no one has given any evidence that radical Islam played a role in the riots. Imams from the major mosques pleaded with these youths for calm, one going so far as to declare a fatwa against those who engaged in violence and vandalism.[15] As the International Crisis Group noted in its report on France, "It is the exhaustion of political Islamism, not its radicalization, that explains much of the violence, and it is the depoliticization of young Muslims, rather than their alleged reversion to a radical kind of communalism, that ought to be cause for worry."[16] Neither the Renseignements généraux (the undercover investigative police) nor the Territorial Surveillance Bureau found any evidence that radical Islam played a role in the riots.[17]

Third, all but 120 of the first 1,100 arrested were born and raised in France.[18] A 2006 study found that 75 percent of those tried for riot-related offenses "were minors enrolled in public school with no police records, one third of them were under sixteen years of age and two thirds were sixteen to eighteen. All were born in France."[19] A 2006 police study concluded that 87 percent of the 436 youths considered to be riot leaders had French nationality, although 67 percent were Arab and 17 percent black.[20] According to Ministry of Justice data, 320 of the 950 minors arrested for riot-related offenses had had prior contact with the justice system, but as endangered children not as offenders.[21] Only 25 percent of the adults had been previously arrested, and, of those, 40 percent had been accused of transgressions against a police officer.[22] The magistrates vehemently disputed all of Sarkozy's claims, point-ing out that "the vast majority of the rioters had the profile of first offend-ers"[23] and were also French nationals.

Fourth, while suburban youths were frustrated by poor wages and high unemployment,[24] neither underclass culture nor despair led young people to burn cars and public buildings for three weeks on end. First and foremost the 2005 riots were provoked by a terrible incident of police brutality (and impunity), a tragedy among a litany of similar tragedies.[25] Yet only one politi-cal leader proposed police abuse as a central cause of the riots or police reform as a central part of the solution, and she was the only North African senator, elected in 2004 from a district composed of several poor *banlieues*. In contrast, Nicolas Sarkozy, the minister of the interior in charge of police, blamed the three teenagers, whom he accused of committing a crime, and defended the police. In doing so he reaffirmed what those in *banlieues* across the country already believed—that their lives have no value in France.

Empirical Data

One year after the riots, Lagrange published an analysis based on arrest statistics. He found that the strongest predictor of participation in the riots was residence in Zone urbaine sensible (ZUS, or Urban Sensitive Area) projects (about 751 of the most deprived urban areas in France, 157 of which are located in the Parisian *banlieues*) where large numbers of sub-Saharan Africans had settled.[26] Since the families in these neighborhoods were often large, Lagrange concluded that his concern about large families was warranted, particularly as black youths were overrepresented among the rioters.

Two years later, however, the French Press Agency conducted a month of interviews with *banlieue* youths, many of whom had participated in the riots. On the basis of these interviews, the agency concluded that young people were angry first at the police and second at "the verbal provocations of Minister of Interior Nicolas Sarkozy."[27] These findings were similar to those of Donatella Della Porta, who coded newspaper accounts of the riots in the first few weeks. Coding speakers into seven categories (government, opposition, president, experts, associations, inhabitants, and youths) and seven causes (discrimination, exclusion, government, Sarkozy, immigra-tion, delinquency, and police), she found that while the experts and politi-cal elite highlighted all seven factors, youths cited only one as a leading cause of the uprisings: police. Likewise, inhabitants cited only one of the seven factors: "Sarkozy."[28]

Laurent Mucchielli and Abderrahim Ait-Omar found, in the twelve in-depth interviews they conducted a month after the riots, that what angered youths most was the combination of police violence and official cover-up. Sarkozy's refusal to admit police culpability in the use of tear gas proved this complicity.[29] One young *banlieue* resident noted, "I participated in the riots and I'm proud of it, it was to overthrow everything and to fuck over the cops."[30] Another said, "The humiliation by the cops and by the teachers is the same. They're people who abuse their fucking power without weighing the consequences of their acts."[31] Marwan Mohammed and Laurent Mucchielli later concluded that every outbreak of riots in France during the twenty-five-year period before 2006 had been caused, in one way or another, by the deaths of youths from the neighborhood, most often in police operations.[32]

Boundary Activation and Zero-Tolerance Policing

Although relations between police and young people of North African and African descent had been strained in France since the interwar years, tensions spiraled during and following the 2002 presidential race. Le Pen had accused his opponents of failing to protect true Frenchmen from immigrants and criminals. Rival candidates from the major political parties joined him in sounding the alarm. "France has too many immigrants and everyone in France feels insecure due to the behavior of young people in particular neighborhoods," Chirac insisted in an interview on Channel 2, "although Le Pen is mistaken in treating the two problems as one." The former Socialist minister of the interior Jean-Pierre Chevènment claimed that the Socialist Party had been too soft on crime. He formed a rival party during the campaign. Lionel Jospin, the Socialist prime minister, claimed that he had been too naive, believing he could reduce crime by reducing unemployment. He now supported "zero impunity." Yet violent crime rates in France were low and homicide had been steadily declining (see Figure 4). As Fassin bitingly observes, political ambition was "a key element in the spread of securitarian ideology, backed up by discourses that fan public fears to justify more repressive policies, a rise in police numbers and

Figure 4. Crime and concerns about security in France, 1972–2002

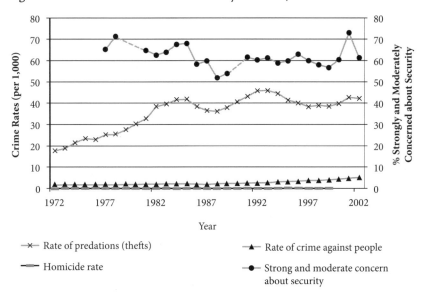

Year

—×— Rate of predations (thefts)   —▲— Rate of crime against people

▬▬▬ Homicide rate   —●— Strong and moderate concern
                                            about security

Sources: Data provided by Philippe Robert, 2003; also see Philippe Robert, "Le sentiment d'insécurité," in *Crime et sécurité, l'état des savoirs,* ed. Philippe Robert and Marie-Lys Pottier (Paris: La Découverte, 2002).

the escalating severity of penalties regardless of whether there is an objective increase in crime and criminality, and often when it is falling."[33]

During the 2002 election campaign, the number of stories featuring nonwhite criminals increased severalfold. The French public, most of whom lacked any direct knowledge of either the *banlieues* or crime, took their cue from the media. Polls over the previous decade had shown a steady decline in anti-immigrant sentiment, support for the death penalty, and fear of crime. Following the campaign, even though there had been no increase in crime, all three increased dramatically. (See Figures 5 and 6.)

While some Socialists admitted privately that a large part of the problem was the "exclusion" of North Africans and Africans from access to equal education, housing, employment, and upward mobility,[34] not one Socialist brought these issues up during the campaign. All the political candidates now appeared to agree that *banlieue* youths represented a substantial danger. Le Pen, "benefiting from the increased salience of law and order issues in the French media," Antonis Ellinas notes, "staged one of the biggest

Figure 5. Concerns with crime, xenophobia, and support for the death penalty in France, 1977–2002

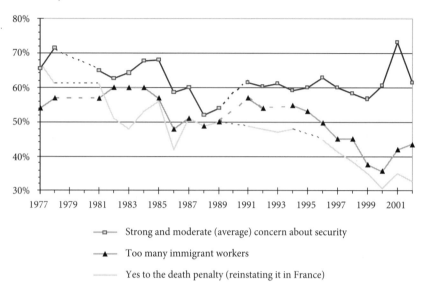

Sources: Data provided by Philippe Robert, 2003; also see Philippe Robert, "Le sentiment d'insécurité," in Crime et sécurité, l'état des savoirs, ed. Philippe Robert and Marie-Lys Pottier (Paris: La Découverte, 2002).

upsets in French electoral history by receiving 16.9 percent of the first-round vote and passing to the run-off election with Chirac."[35] Competitive outbidding on his signature issue had boosted Le Pen's popularity and with it his electoral fortune.[36]

In the days that followed, over a million people demonstrated against Le Pen in Paris alone. In the second round Chirac won easily, by over 80 percent. Yet Le Pen also increased his vote, pulling nearly 20 percent. The dominance of the security issue and its linkage in the public mind to race and immigration can be seen in the exit polls conducted by Ipsos.[37] In the first round, 58 percent of French voters put fear of crime as one of their three main concerns, and they voted overwhelmingly for the right-wing parties.[38] Seventy-four percent of Le Pen voters listed insécurité (or crime) and 80 percent listed immigration as one of their three main concerns.[39] Votes for the National Front were highest in areas of the country where

Figure 6. French media coverage of security issues between January and July 2002

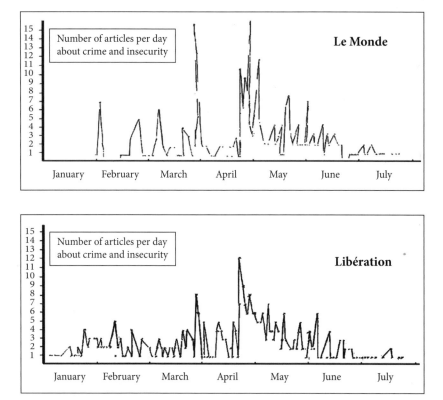

Source: Romuald Bodin and David Sorin, "Insecurité dans la presse," CLARIS (2003).

crime, immigration, and racial diversity were lowest.[40] Seventy-three per-cent of Chirac voters listed crime or security as one of their three main concerns, but only 12 percent listed immigration, a distinction also made by Chirac.[41] In both cases the voters followed the lead of the political elite. The response of the UMP to the rise of Le Pen, as Fassin notes, was to

[r]adicalize its discourse, adopting xenophobic themes translated into immigration restrictions, and producing alarm about alleged insecurity. . . . The electoral success of this strategy of rejection and fear is undeniable, since the raising of immigration and insecurity

issues played a decisive role in three consecutive general elections, allowing 17 years of continuous conservative presidency. It is noteworthy that the construction of immigration and insecurity as national priorities . . . occurred in a period when France was subject to objective threats, that of terrorism in particular, much less than other countries."[42]

One week after the election, 40 percent of those polled said they agreed with Le Pen on the security issue.[43] Twenty-three percent of respondents in another poll said they hated North Africans, and 24 percent said they hated French youths of North African origin, the highest percentage of people detesting any single group.[44] Jospin resigned, and Chirac appointed Dominique de Villepin prime minister. He appointed Dominique Perben minister of justice and Sarkozy minister of the interior in charge of the national police. Perben's 2002 Loi d'orientation et de progammation pour la justice (the so-called Perben Law), Loi pour la sécurité intérieur (the new internal security law), and Loi portant adaptation de la justice aux évolutions de la criminalité (Perben Law II) undermined recent Socialist legislation providing for a presumption of innocence, increased the period during which police could hold suspects in *garde à vue* from forty-eight to ninety-six hours for certain crimes, and weakened judicial independence. Perben also proposed legislation that would reduce from sixteen to ten the age at which a suspect would be considered a minor (although the parliament refused to lower it below the age of thirteen). Fraud on public transport services (riding the metro without a ticket) was made a felony offense punishable by up to six months in prison. In the next five years the government would add forty new procedural codes and thirty new penal codes.

The government also drew a distinction between minority men and minority women, arguing in essence, as Kimberly Morgan notes, that the government should "liberate minority women from minority men."[45] The police were to be the means for this liberation. As part of his new crime-fighting measures, Chirac promised to ensure "that the law and fundamental values are accepted. We cannot tolerate in our society that, for example, the dignity of women be denied, threatened or violated."[46] Since the primary role of government was to provide security, the police were granted substantial new resources, and the BAC lay claim to the largest share. Funding for the *police de proximite,* in contrast, was slashed.

As minister of interior, in charge of police, Sarkozy accrued two primary benefits from shifting resources to the BAC, Bonelli notes: First, "after a political campaign based on law and order, Sarkozy needed to show very clearly that 'his' police was different than the previous one, more aggressive and tougher on crime." The second reason was financial: "If you want a foot patrol, you need 3 policemen to cover a beat. 3 policemen multiplied by 20 beats means that you need permanently 60 policemen to cover a precinct. Instead of using foot patrols, you can use the BAC. You only need two vehicles and 3 policemen on board to cover the precinct. This means 6 policemen instead of 60."[47]

In return for the added resources, police officers were to show "good numbers," high arrest rates, and low crime rates. They were granted substantial leeway to do so, including the authority to intercept private communications and, in cases of suspected terrorism, to force social workers to provide local council officials with information gained during private counseling.[48] In a style reminiscent of his idol Rudolph Giuliani, Sarkozy jumped to the defense of police officers accused of abuse, while denigrating those engaged in community policing. In one notorious example, he demanded the resignation of a popular police chief in Toulouse for helping neighborhood youths form a neighborhood sports league. Police, he snidely remarked, should not behave as social workers. Officers, anxious to please Sarkozy, were faced with a conundrum. Crime rates were low, and it was difficult to show good numbers. Fassin notes,

> By establishing quantitative objectives that were most of the time unattainable, in terms of monthly arrests and clearance rates particularly, the government constrained the police to develop adaptive tactics focusing on two types of offense, which became what officers sometimes call "adjustment variables": offenses in relation to drug use and illegal residence, the offenders being, in both cases, easy prey. Indeed, the targeted practice of stopping and searching youth in the housing projects or city centers, for the former, and immigrants in public spaces like train stations, for the latter, gives a high yield in terms of arrests. This productivity has a non-negligible social cost, though, which is the banalization of racial discrimination and racial profiling, officially encouraged although illegal.[49]

Fassin describes watching police officers stop black and Arab youths to search for hashish while ignoring white students smoking in the open. All officers complained about the pressures to meet quantitative evaluation standards, but none seemed troubled by the racially discriminatory actions they took to meet them. One officer told him that they had to use drug and immigration offenses to meet their arrest quotas, but that the personal prejudices or ideological proclivities of the recruits determined which of the two they emphasized. The more xenophobic officers preferred to enforce immigration offenses. One such officer told Fassin, "I've always said there are too many illegal immigrants. . . . So whenever I can arrest one, I do."[50] Another preferred to pursue French-born youths who might be caught with cannabis: "I'm not here to arrest poor people who haven't done anything and aren't bothering anybody. . . . I prefer to take in drug users for questioning—at least they're screwing up."[51] Fassin calls it "a moral division of labor . . . based on ideological stances."[52]

This strategy allowed police to increase their arrest numbers from 67,308 in 2001 to 81,000 in both 2002 and 2003. Incarceration rates rose 9 percent during the same period, and the average length of sentence rose from 8.1 to 8.9 months. The number of inmates during the same period rose from 52,961 in 2002 to 61,500,[53] making 2003 the year with the largest inmate population in France since the Nazi occupation. By June 2004 there were 64,651 inmates in prisons designed to hold 48,802. The *maisons d'arrêt*, prisons for people awaiting trial or convicted of minor crimes carrying less than a two-year penalty, suffered most from overcrowding and operated at double their capacity.[54]

That same year, Sarkozy reiterated Chirac's emphasis on policing gender: "We need to be more proactive and demanding in matters of reception and integration. We are proud of Republican values, of the equality between men and women, of laïcité, of the French ideal of integration. So let us dare to speak of this to those we receive here. And act so that the rights of the French woman apply also to immigrant women."[55] Enforcing laïcité and liberating women provided police with yet another rationale for stopping and harassing minority youth.

Although the French do not keep statistics on race or ethnicity, Farhad Khosrokhavar, using nationality of parent as proxy, found that those who had parents born in the Maghreb made up 39.9 percent of young prisoners between the ages of eighteen and twenty-four and 35.4 percent of those between the ages of twenty-five and twenty-nine, five or six times higher than their percentages in the population (see Table 6).[56] I had a chance to visit a youth prison in Versailles. I did an informal count of prisoners in

Table 6. Percentage of male prisoners and males in ordinary households in France by age and place of father's birth

Male prisoners

Place of father's birth	18–24	25–29	30–34	35–39	40–44	45–49	50–59
France	38.8	42.4	43.7	47.7	58.6	61.3	59.6
Maghreb	39.9	35.4	26.3	24.5	13.8	11.6	14.0

Males in ordinary households

Place of father's birth	18–24	25–29	30–34	35–39	40–44	45–49	50–59
France	75.5	74.5	74.3	74.9	75.6	74.7	73.7
Maghreb	8.5	7.1	7.3	6.3	5.4	5.3	5.6

Source: Farhad Khosokhavar, *L'islam dans les prisons* (Paris: Éditions Balland, 2004), 279–80.

the outdoor recreation area. Social workers I spoke with agreed with my admittedly unscientific assessment that as many as 90 percent there might be black or Arab.

A relatively powerful and more insulated judiciary prevented a rise in incarceration rates as dramatic as had occurred in the United States. Yet "the absence of an independent investigation system left police officers virtually immune to prosecution or reprimand and in nearly open conflict with certain sections of society," an Amnesty International report concluded.[57] More disturbing was the increasing tendency of police officers to retaliate against those who registered such complaints by claiming the plaintiffs had engaged in *outrage* (insulting a police officer, something akin to the charge of contempt of court in the United States), *rebellion,* or resisting arrest. So prevalent was this form of retaliation that many lawyers felt obliged to warn clients that the cost of filing such a complaint could be months in prison, while there was little likelihood that a police officer would be convicted.[58]

The increased penalties for *outrage* and *rebellion* served a dual purpose for police. On the one hand, they allowed police officers to pile on charges and beef up their arrest rates (even while the clearance rate for serious crimes was about 10 percent).[59] One BAC officer even used a 1942 Vichy law against spitting in the streets to deliberately provoke a young person he hoped to arrest. The officer told Fassin, "It is a great thing. If I see anyone spitting, I'll slap a charge on him, and with a bit of luck it'll end with him resisting the police. It's a done deal: you hit the bastard with a 130 euro fine, he's not happy, he gets pissed and bingo! Resisting the police."[60] On the other hand, police used the charges to punish those who filed complaints for mistreatment. Only 16 out of 663 complaints investigated by authorities in 2005 and 8 out of 639 in 2006 led to the ouster of accused cops.[61] In contrast, 14,000 of the 31,800 court cases filed by police or prosecutors in 2006 for insulting police officers ended with convictions, and half of those resulted in jail terms.[62]

Between 2000 and 2009 the number of prisoners held under *garde à vue* rose 140 percent, reaching 800,000 in 2009, while the number held for over twenty-four hours increased by 73.2 percent. In 2010 the constitutional court declared the entire procedure unconstitutional.[63] In reaching a decision to overturn a procedure that had been authorized since 1993, the court observed that what had been intended as an exceptional measure had become routine: "the garde à vue and the evidence obtained as a result, have become the principal part of the prosecution case [and] the decision to place a person in garde à vue is that of the police."[64] Given the close association between *garde à vue* and abuse, young people had every reason to fear being stopped by police.

The Structure of the French Police

The French police force is among the most centralized in the world. The centralization insulates them from local politics but makes it difficult for minority residents to hold police officers accountable. As Zauberman and Lévy note, "[T]he police apparatus tends to place greater emphasis on the necessity of protecting public order, which is to say on controlling public space, than on serving users."[65] Dominique Monjardet concurs that centralized "control has transformed city police forces into local detachments of a State police, socially and functionally cut off from the city."[66] Worse, as Fassin observes, "the state to which the police are accountable has been increasingly embodied through successive ambitious Ministers of the Interior who have used them for the promotion of their political career."[67]

The French legal system distinguishes between two main police functions. The first is administrative policing, which consists of uniformed preventative patrols, with limited power to arrest, under the control of the director-general and the *préfet*, the highest-ranking public servant in each department. The second is judicial policing, or the detection and repression of specific criminal offenses, serving the *procureur* (district attorney) and the presiding magistrate. The police are divided into two branches. The first, the Gendarmerie nationale (gendarmes), is the oldest division of the police, harking back to the prerevolutionary Maréchaussée of 1536. In 1791 the Gendarmerie was reorganized as a police force with a civil mandate. Until May 2002, when it was placed under the auspices of the minister of the interior, it served as a branch of the armed forces, answering to the minister of defense. In 2002 there were ninety-eight thousand gendarmes. Gendarme troops are primarily stationed in rural areas, in regions matching those of the army. There is a small mobile unit used to respond to disasters or crises. Until the 2002—2005 reforms, gendarmes were also stationed in *banlieues*, in order to facilitate closer ties with communities. To avoid replication, the reforms restricted the gendarmes to towns smaller than fifteen thousand, to the regret of most *banlieue* youths, who hold the gendarmes in far higher esteem than the national police. In a recent poll, 84.8 percent of French respondents said they had confidence in the gendarmes. So did 83.4 percent of the residents of Seine-Saint-Denis, a district that includes Clichy-sous-Bois and Montfermeil. This is a sharp contrast with the percentage that expressed confidence in the national police—74.2 of national respondents and 64.9 of residents of Seine-Saint-Denis. This percentage dropped further among youths. Only 43.4 percent of young people in Seine-Saint-Denis had confidence in the national police.

The second branch, the Police nationale (national police), was created in 1667, originally as the police force of Paris. The Parisian police were given authority over all French police departments in 1941, during Nazi rule. In 2002 there were 132,000 national police, with a budget of $5.7 billion. The minister of the interior commands the director-general, who supervises the directorates, who oversee central and local services. The Administrative Directorate of the National Police is in charge of human resources. Higher-level officers must pass an exam in order to conduct investigations. There is some overlap with the gendarmes who also conduct investigations. The investigating magistrate and the prosecutor may work with either branch of the police. Only the national police, however, are in charge of border control and immigration enforcement. This force is comprised of several smaller specialized units. The Compagnies republicaines de securité (CRS) is charged with administrative policing and keeping order during protests and other urban disturbances. A specialized unit of the Service interadministerial d'assistance technique carries out undercover investigations of organized crime and large-scale drug trafficking. The Brigade anti-criminalité (BAC or anticrime brigade) is composed of volunteers from other units of the national police. It was created in 1994 for the sole purpose of surveillance and control of immigrants and residents of "sensitive" neighborhoods, particularly public housing projects. The BAC is the most hated police unit in the *banlieues.*

Because the French police force is centralized, new recruits are usually stationed in unfamiliar territory. Four out of five officers come from rural areas and small towns. The newest and least experienced among them are often stationed in the *banlieues.* One unofficial source put the number of minorities among rank-and-file minority policemen at about 7 percent in 2006, up from less than 5 percent five years earlier.[68] Sophie Body-Gendrot points out that this is substantially less than the 10 percent of foreign nationals in France (although her conflation of foreign and minority substantially underestimates the actual racial disproportion).[69] Most minority police officers serve in the municipal police or *police de proximité* (as detailed below), the two smallest, poorest paid, and least powerful auxiliary units (only the municipal police answer to the mayor). In contrast, only five out of eighteen hundred police chiefs in all of France are of North African origin.[70]

These problems are compounded in the BAC, which operates like a paramilitary unit outside the normal chain of command. Since police officers must apply to join the BAC, there is a great deal of self-selection among recruits. Applicants pass through an external review, increasing the likelihood that those with incompatible sensibilities will be weeded out. The head of the BAC where Fassin conducted research, for instance, was "notorious for his ideological positions with regard to immigration and minorities," and he rejected applicants who did not share his prejudices. He had never admitted a single minority or woman, due to questions about their loyalty: "You never know if, when it comes to the wire, they'll be with us or their brothers."[71] Those who applied to the squad did so with "full knowledge of the views held within the group." "All conditions were in place," notes Fassin, "for a microcosm where racism and discrimination flourished." [72] Insight into the character of BAC police can also be found in the distinctive character of the patches they wear. As Bonelli notes, "We understand very fast that they perceive themselves as predators, as hunters. Most of these patches represent wolves, tigers, snakes and eagles, very few rabbits."[73]

The *police de proximité* were created in 1995 by the Jospin government under the Orientation and Programming Security Act. They were introduced to five pilot sites in 2000 and gradually extended to sixty-two districts and eventually to all police districts in 2002, shortly before the Socialists lost the election. The government put aside an additional 5.7 percent of the overall police budget for the hiring of special police auxiliaries, mostly young people contracted for five years, in positions that put them in permanent contact with the public. The idea was inspired by community policing reforms in the United States and the United Kingdom. In France, however, the *police de proximité* were set up as a separate unit. They were assigned special uniforms but not the authority to carry arms or conduct investigations. In 2002 there were twenty-eight thousand *police de proximité*. That same year their low budget was further slashed, as "new emphasis was placed on aggressive crime reduction, performance indicators, a more intensive use of criminal intelligence, and the creation of regional integrated task forces."[74]

Last, the municipal police constitute the only unit that answers to the local mayor. There were 15,400 in 2002, and they operated in a small minority of the 36,000 municipalities. Sixty-two percent of municipal police carry firearms but "do not have any powers of arrest or investigation and do not compete with the law enforcement and order maintenance activities of the two major police forces. They represent a second tier of policing and have little training, low pay and reduced prestige."[75] Along with the *police de proximité*, this branch is the destination for most minority police recruits. Villiers-le-Bel, a *banlieue* that erupted in riots in 2010 after police ran over and killed two young people on a motorbike, has four municipal police officers.

Up until 2000 internal affairs provided the only means of monitoring police accountability. The National Security Ethics Commission Act of 2000 gave that commission responsibility for investigating ethical misconduct by both private and public security providers. The act created numerous obstacles for those wishing to file complaints, including a cumbersome complaint procedure and a commission with only three full-time clerical staff, a budget of $510,000, and no regulatory, injunction, or disciplinary powers, and whose sole means of pressure is a yearly public report. Moreover each citizen must lodge his or her complaint through a member of parliament or through the prime minister (who determines whether it falls under the jurisdiction of the commission). The process makes it difficult for poor minorities to contact the committee, as their representatives or the prime minister may refuse to pass on the complaint.[76]

The *Banlieues*

The growth of the French *banlieues* in the late nineteenth and early twentieth centuries can be traced back to Baron Haussmann's bulldozing of working-class neighborhoods to make way for the wide roads that spike outward from the heart of Paris to the periphery. He pushed the working class toward the northeastern edges of the city, while the middle-class and wealthy residents moved to the western edges, especially the sixteenth arrondissement. The spatial layout of the city became more segregated and the Parisian working class "more spatially marginalized and isolated from its neighbors; before long the majority of this class would be forced out of the city altogether," notes Tyler Stovall. Haussmann's renovations and the city's ability to attract financial capital spurred the growth of attractive, expensive housing in the center and left workers first in overcrowded dilapidated housing in the periphery. The term *banlieue*, notes Stovall, "dates back to the thirteenth century when it referred to a perimeter of one league around the city. In medieval usage the term signified a liminal space associated with social marginality, uncontrolled movement and spatialized poverty."[77]

As Paris officials built extensive rail networks for a fraction of the cost of providing public housing, they gradually incorporated smaller nearby towns into the greater metropolitan area. Seine-Saint-Denis is the oldest working-class suburban district, and Aubervilliers, Clichy, and Saint-Denis were already industrial suburban neighborhoods by the turn of the century. In contrast, the department of Seine-et-Oise was an independent township in 1790 and was broken into three smaller suburban districts—Yvelines, Val-d'Oise, and Essonne—only in 1968. Three of the neighborhoods in which I worked were in Seine-Saint-Denis (Aubervilliers, Clichy-sous-Bois, and Montfermeil) in the northeast, and the other three were in Val-d'Oise (Sarcelles, Garges-lès-Gonesse, and Villiers-le-Bel) in the north. During the

1960s Saint-Denis was home to the largest Algerian shanty, but Nanterre and Clichy also had large Algerian *bidonvilles* before the state constructed massive HLMs—large block public housing projects resembling those constructed in the former Soviet Union.

In 1976 one-third of those living in such *banlieues* were first-generation immigrants. By 1986 that number had increased to two-thirds.[78] France's ban on the collection of race and ethnicity statistics made it next to impossible to know how many of the residents were Arab or black, but there were certainly many. Most northeastern *banlieues* (which were the poorest and most conflict-ridden) lacked stores, restaurants, or cafés. Opportunities for work were few, and unemployment tended to run high—officially around 20 percent but more than double that for youths of North African and African origin.[79] Clandestine markets served as important sources of employment and supplemental cash. The proportion of young people under twenty was also high: 50 percent in some public housing projects.[80]

Sarcelles and Aubervilliers were the only two, of the six I studied, that had commercial centers. In Sarcelles the restaurants, cafés, and other commercial establishments were located close to the Jewish enclave. In Aubervilliers most commercial establishments were located close to the metro station, as it was one of the few *banlieues* accessible by metro. The others depended on buses and the RER train, the latter of which ran irregularly, stopped early in the evening, and departed from stations that were a significant distance from most homes in the area. The RER train lines were also the ones most often on strike.

Unlike in New York City, where each neighborhood has a distinct history, collective memory, and culture, Parisian *banlieues* were remarkably similar to each other. In Aubervilliers, Muslim residents told me that they knew of no whites except the very old and the very poor who still remained in the neighborhood in 2010. In Clichy-sous-Bois, Garges-lès-Gonesse, and Villiers-le-Bel, residents pointed to a white population living in better housing, often single-family homes, in a separate part of town. The buildings that housed black and Arab residents were of poor quality. In addition there had been increasing urban demolitions in these areas and fewer homes built than destroyed.

The Perspective of the Police

Several police spoke appreciatively of Sarkozy's unwavering support but complained about him pressuring them to show good *numbers* (arrest and crime rates) and his use of such statistics as the sole criteria for measuring their accomplishments. A French police captain I interviewed in 2006 (one of the rare, albeit white, police officers who grew up in the *banlieue* in which he worked) critically compared the reforms instituted by Sarkozy to those implemented during the previous Socialist government:

> In 1995, there was a grand reform of the police. They wanted us to approach young people, use less repression, and work with youth. That ended with Sarkozy. He prefers repression. The grand program of Jospin—police working on prevention—was abandoned. Now, we have more repression, less prevention, more prisons. There is strong pressure to be repressive, to show good statistics in arrests and *garde à vue.*
>
> The number-one political theme here now is "insecurity." Sarkozy says that police with higher arrest records should get higher salaries, but that is not a good solution. Now there are more petty delinquents in prison. They should distinguish between serious crimes and juvenile delinquency. Police officers have different jobs to do; not every police officer makes arrests. Some must conduct investigations. To evaluate all mathematically, to give some rewards for high arrest rates and others none is very dangerous.

Another captain told me that it was unjust to arrest *banlieue* youths for using cannabis: "It is hypocritical to go after young people who smoke marijuana when the jet set uses drugs. The drug problem is the same today as it was yesterday. It is a legislative problem. If someone is sanctioned for chewing gum, and chewing gum is illegal, we would have more chewing gum crime." Another officer told me it was next to impossible to catch people in *délit flagrant* (in the act) crime as the new policy required. The demands to show high arrest rates and at the same time catch criminals in the act steered the police toward the easiest arrests: cannabis users and undocumented immigrants.

Other police officers, however, favored the targeting of petty delinquents, even though they resented the pressure to make arrest quotas. One said, "Petty delinquency creates a sense of insecurity and fear of groups of youth hanging out. Sixty percent of those in the surrounding (white) banlieues and rural areas voted for Le Pen. They were frightened." Another

told me, "The National Front won because of delinquency in the banlieues." The ability of police to empathize with Le Pen voters stood in stark
contrast to their inability to do the same with *banlieue* residents. This was
the case even for an officer who admitted that it was "the media, especially
television, that had heightened the sense of fear and insecurity."

Policing Racial Boundaries

Racial stereotypes are an integral component of police culture. "Pervasive
racial discourse is a reality and constitutes for police officers an actual
norm, extremely difficult to escape, not to speak of opposing, for a rank
and file officer," note Wieviorka et al.[81] Zauberman and Lévy observe, "Police do not enter the police because they are racist: rather they acquire
racial prejudice through a process of acculturation."[82] Whether or not the
individual recruit enters the institution with the same racial prejudices as
the society at large, chooses to enter because he is more racist than most,
or learns racial prejudices inside the academy, the stories police tell are
riddled with racial stereotypes. Two leading members of a left-wing police
union described the relationship between race and crime several years before the riots (2001):

> You must understand, in the United States blacks are American.
> Here they are foreigners. It is our job to defend France. Our prob-
> lem here began after the war in Algeria. The Arabs could not stay
> there because they had collaborated with France. All the chiefs of
> [the] Arabic community set up huge Islamic activities in suburbs,
> and told the people that you are Islamic and Arab not French, you
> must fight France. . . . Saudi Arabia gave money for people to come
> to France and fight the French state using religion. . . . They ended
> up congregating in small areas. Housing prices went down and black
> immigrants now found it very cheap and gathered there too. This
> concentration created an underground world.
>
> Yet, for us as police it is good, [it makes] things easier to bust. If
> they were spread around the city it would be difficult to police. If
> you let them live together, you do not even have to go into the cité.
> You can put police at either end and close it. It is a way to localize

and crystallize delinquency in a single place. So when we see someone [in Paris] black or with Arabic features we stop them and ask
for their papers and then we can search them for drugs or guns.

BAC officers often expressed similar sentiments. One officer in Saint-
Denis told Roché, "When a criminal act is reported, all of the gangs that
hang around on the corner are suspects and therefore checked. If I come
across them, I check their IDs, I search them, without knowing if my colleagues have already done it. The youth complain, but they are searched for
good reason: what are they doing in the street from 2 pm to 3 in the morning? We are looking for thieves. So sure, we catch first and see later."[83]
When a Turkish businessman was severely beaten by members of a BAC
squad, one witness told the court that the head of squad had warned, "We
lost the Algerian war 40 years ago, we chickened out. We're not going to
do it again today. Take no prisoners: it's no holds barred!"[84] In this case, as
in others, Fassin points out, racist talk went hand in hand with discriminatory and abusive practice.

Even police officers who did not consider themselves racist drew
boundaries between themselves and the residents of the communities they
policed. One of the favorite stereotypes was that of Arab men as misogynists, one that meshed well with the prevailing political discourse. This
stereotype served a dual purpose, stigmatizing Arab males while placing
police in the honorable role of defending women. "There is an enormous
problem with girls," one officer told me. "One young woman was set on
fire [a terrible but singular event, committed by a jealous former boy-
friend]. There is a need to emancipate the women. The role of women is a
problem and a cultural issue." "Arabs are misogynists," another told me.
"They force women to wear veils that only allow a woman's eyes to be
seen." Another stated, "Culture and tradition make life very difficult for
women of North African origin. The women must wear veils, and only
show their eyes." Another officer blamed Muslim women's wearing of
headscarves for the increased votes for Le Pen: "In France there is a big
debate over the veil, and this is one reason why so many have voted for Le
Pen." Another frequent stereotype was that Arab youths support Al Qaeda.
"Young people say 'Hurray, Bin Laden!' There is a huge problem between
European and non-European cultures," according to one officer. Another
expressed resentment that police were forced to deal with such cultural
issues: "Our role is to investigate crime, not to deal with social issues. It is

not the role of the police to solve the latter; that is a problem of integration." Yet without being asked about cultural issues each officer had volunteered an opinion.

The most common stereotype of blacks was that they are near savages, culturally backward, and have too many wives and children, for whom they are unable to care. One officer told Fassin, "The problem is that there are people from all over, of all races. And often they live here like they live at home. Take the Africans: they have several wives and loads of children. And the kids aren't used to staying indoors, so they hang out in the street and get into bad company."[85] The head of a precinct in one of the *banlieues* told me, albeit in more subtle terms, that Africans were unable to raise their children outside an African village (2003):

> It is a question of education. The parents do not speak about education, and therefore their children are less polite and more insolent. I am from Italy but the fact that I am from another country does not give me a right to be insolent. Nationality is not an excuse. It is the adults' fault for not teaching their children. The children are 14 or 15 years old and they become the law in the family. They act like little dictators inside the family. . . . The culture in Africa is one never touches one's father, never. The chief of the village never allows it. The African family in exile loses control of their children. There are young people who are not of French origin, young people who are intelligent and understand, but the problem is not the young but the parents. It is a problem of choice in the end. Parents give their children too many rights.

When I told him my intent to live in his district, he expressed surprise: "It is very difficult to live here. It is like a desert. There is nothing here," he commented. "Why would you want to live here? I don't live here." That black and Arab youths felt the same about their *banlieues* escaped his notice. The inability to empathize with local youths was less noteworthy than more violently expressed prejudices, but it had as profound an impact on the relationship between black and Arab young people and police.

There was a near consensus among police that immigration rates were too high. "Turks, Jews, Arabs, Blacks, it is sad but there are problems within these communities," one officer told me. "The subject of immigration is taboo. Sometimes there are fights between groups with baseball bats. The problem is complicated by politics, culture, tradition, and religion. There is also a big problem in France of too many immigrants, all concentrated in the same zone. The French say 'put them in other neighborhoods but not in mine.'" The officer also told me that it should not be the job of the police to solve the communities' cultural problems: "We can deal with the delinquency en route to school, but we cannot change our role." Another said, "It is a problem having different communities and cultures living together."

None of these common stereotypes was supported by evidence. The police insisted that it was Muslim culture that conflicted with French social norms, but Muslim youths identified with French culture. The burka, which the French parliament has declared illegal, was worn by little more than three hundred women in all of France, according to the senate's original research in 2009 (although a second survey requested by Sarkozy in 2010 found a total of two thousand burka wearers, including foreign tourists). Most Africans came from urban areas, not rural villages, and few were polygamous. Most African youths respected their parents, and many did well in school. While police assumed that all blacks were African, many were born in France or in the Antilles. In addition immigration rates had been stable since 1975, and crime rates were low. Most important, the officers all seemed incapable of recognizing the diversity of the people (whatever their backgrounds) who lived in the *banlieues*.

Yet police officers saw themselves as quite diverse. "We have some very young police officers without any experience," a district police detective told me. "They have difficulty dealing with the situations they confront in the banlieues." Another said, "There are just some police who see blacks that way." But despite the fact that such officers were allowed to continue to police minority neighborhoods, no police officer admitted that there might be a problem with the institution itself.

Minority Police

The lack of minority recruitment has aggravated the problem by limiting officers' exposure to more diverse perspectives. I spoke with two North African police officers, one a *police de proximité* auxiliary and the other a member of the municipal police. Straddling the boundary between police and residents of the *banlieues*, both officers displayed deep ambivalence.

They defended the actions of their fellow police officers but expressed more sympathy with the plight of *banlieue* youths than their white colleagues did. The North African policewoman told me that life was very hard for children from the Maghreb; there was no work and both salaries and quality of life were poor. Muslims "are marked," she said. When her father arrived and used his Moroccan name, he could not find work. When he used a French name, he could. "The French dream is to have a house, social security—but the dream is not real, it only comes from having money," she told me. She understood why young people in the *banlieues* feared the police: "When I was young, the police saw my face and color, [and] they asked me for my papers. For a long time I thought police were racist. One experience like that and young people think all police are evil."

She told me that the situation was the same for police officers: "Many grew up in small villages. They think if you live in the banlieues you are bad. The police are not really racist. The young people guard the image that the police are racist. It is as if one young person insulted me and I thought the entire community was like that. And now police are more mixed—from all over. We represent the French population, more and more." She did not address the fact that most minority officers were stationed in the only two units that did not carry weapons or make arrests, or the obvious power imbalance between police and *banlieue* youths.

Many Africans, she explained, came there "thinking there will be easy money and they can return to their country with it." The reality, she said, was that

> those who look for work can find it. There is a lot of work here. All the work that the French won't do like janitorial and cleaning services. Ok, it is humiliating, but I tell them if you work hard in school you can find good work. But they want fast money like football players. It is not true that France is racist. Many young use it as an excuse. I tell them look at me. If you work hard you can leave the banlieues. I grew up in a poor neighborhood, now I live in a good apartment. I did it, so can you. We [of North African and African descent] just need to do more than the French to get the same opportunity.

The observation was a bit hard to square with the story she had just told me of her father's experiences as a "marked" man. She continued:

"The difference between young people who obey the law and those who don't are the presence or absence of parents at home after school. Only those who benefit from the presence of their parents know the difference between good and bad. When the parents are not home, older brothers or sisters can be a bad influence. The problem is that children are lost between two worlds and two cultures." She herself seemed to be struggling between two cultures, that of the police and that of the *banlieues*.

The problem was not the police, she pointed out reasonably enough. The problem was political. "We cannot just punish, punish, punish. Sarkozy says community policing (*police de proximité*) doesn't work." She believed that he was wrong and that the *police de proximité* had an important role to play. Yet the function she attributed to the community police had little to do with policing: "If we have a good reputation with the young when they have a problem they can come to talk to us." By circumscribing the role of the *police de proximité* as such, she managed to make them less threatening to the regular police (who could continue men's work) and irrelevant. She drew the distinction again, arguing that the law was both too harsh and too lax. It was too lax, she explained, repeating a common police refrain, because "[m]any young people commit crimes and never go to prison. We lose credibility. The justice has to be harder. If you commit a crime, you're punished and you don't do it again. Here the young begin with shoplifting. If you don't stop them they go on to commit greater crimes."

The law was also too harsh, she said: "Prison is not the solution. It simply introduces young people to hardened criminals." When she arrested a youth for shoplifting, she told me, she made him "stand against the wall. That is enough to frighten him into not committing the crime again." Her story about standing young people against the wall was unlikely to persuade the regular police, much less the BAC, to treat either residents of the *banlieue* or the *police de proximité* with more respect. In stark contrast, then, to the Anglo-American conception of community policing as an alternative to occupying the ghetto, the French version left the regular police unchallenged.

A North African municipal policeman I interviewed expressed similar ambivalence. When I asked him about a 2007 incident in which police ran down and killed two young people on a motorbike, setting off a spate of riots in a neighborhood he had once patrolled, he replied, "What do you do if a motorcycle runs a red light? If you don't chase it people will say the police are not doing their job. If the boys had an accident later, the police would be blamed. The police officers in that car called their chief and the chief told them to chase the boys. . . . Our job is to enforce the law. If we do not do this we are not doing our job. The police chief will call us in and say, what were you doing?"

Policing was tough work, he told me. He was at the time working in a wealthy resort area but found the work equally hard, in part because of the attitude of some of the wealthy residents: "Everyone wants you to enforce the law against someone else, but not themselves. The rich want us to enforce the law to protect them, but they get angry if we enforce the law when it is they who are breaking it. . . . It is tiresome to do the same thing day after day with no change, to be subject constantly to disapproval and pressures. Never does anyone say, 'you have done such a good job, I am going to call your police chief and tell him.' "

His experience with wealthy whites, however, convinced him that the race of the police officer was irrelevant. A white resident once accused him of discrimination. Afterward his chief told him, "Now you know how we feel." In fact, he said, he would "not treat a Moroccan differently because he was Moroccan." The story, however, suggested a false equivalency. The relationship between a Moroccan police officer and a wealthy white resident was not the moral equivalent of the relationship between white police officers and poor blacks and Arabs in the *banlieues*.

I asked him if he had experienced racism within the police force. "Not really," he answered and then continued, "Well, there are some officers that are like that." Younger officers, he said, were less racist than the older generation (an explanation diametrically opposed to the usual one of inexperienced young officers). According to him, the newer generation included more Arabs, blacks, Portuguese, people from everywhere. Yet the two branches that recruited minority officers, the municipal police and *police de proximité*, were the smallest, least powerful units, and both had their budgets slashed by Sarkozy. When I asked if he felt a great deal of solidarity with other officers, he replied, "No." His answer was remarkably different from that of white police officers, who always told me that the strong solidarity between officers made the job bearable.

The officer denied that his feelings of isolation in the police force might be due to his race, although he admitted that some officers were racist: "There are good police and bad police." The police chiefs paid attention to incidents of abuse, he said. Police who abused neighborhood residents were moved to another neighborhood until the incident was forgotten. I pointed out that this did not seem to be a good solution, moving officers who abused residents to even more vulnerable communities and waiting until the incidents were forgotten. He agreed. Later he admitted that he was not happy in the police force. The following year he resigned from his job there.

The Perspective of Residents of the *Banlieues*

> I piss on you and your police machine
> Brainless sons of whores
> Upholders of the laws
> > —*NTM (a rap band from Saint-Denis,*
> > *lyrics to their song "Police")*

Aubervilliers, Garges-lès-Gonesse, Villiers-le-Bel, and Montfermeil

During a meeting I attended in Aubervilliers in 2002, a young Muslim (of Algerian descent) angrily accused France of hypocrisy: "We demand 'Republican' *flics* (cops) to give the same discourse and attitude [to everyone], not to treat us as slaves. The young respond [to this unfair treatment]. We don't have a Republican system of justice or Republican police. . . . Justice does not take care of poor people like us. I am boiling with hatred." Another noted, "A foreigner has a state of exception from all the rights guaranteed the French—a different set of statutes for those who come from the colonies—racist laws, a different set of laws, a different justice."[86] In a workshop that a researcher conducted with police and prisoners, one prisoner turned to the police and said, "It is you who has made me a criminal."[87]

French youths of Algerian descent saw continuity between racial oppression in colonial Algeria and racial oppression in Paris. According to a religious young Muslim man in Garges-lès-Gonesse,

All the major political figures in France were colonial army officers in Algeria. Those experiences are fresh in their minds. Here it is just Algeria in France. France's record is worse than Israel's. In the National Assembly there are 560 deputies, and not one Muslim,

Arab, or African deputy. There are several in the indirectly elected, less powerful Senate. Even in Israel there are Arab deputies. . . . Here there is continuity from colonization. It has only been 40 years since the independence of Algeria in 1962. Someone like Chirac was a soldier in Algeria. It is still fresh in their minds. . . . To them we are still immigrants. . . . When the right won, the police told young people here, OK, the party is over.

Algerians also saw continuity in the forms of violence directed against them. A religious young woman of Algerian descent born and raised in Villiers-le-Bel (who had completed a Ph.D. in international law but had been unable to find work except poorly paying internships) said, "There is a long history of police violence directed at Algerians. My grandfather was tortured in Algeria. All our grandfathers were tortured in Algeria. It is what we all share. . . . [In France] we have a government that funds police to repress us. There are fewer and fewer teachers, more and more police. Young people face very aggressive police. It has gotten worse and worse every day."

A religious young Muslim woman from Garges-lès-Gonesse who was a pediatrician noted, "The police arrive in our neighborhood in large groups and are very aggressive and disrespectful. They ask everyone for IDs." One day she saw a young man marched through the streets. Another time she saw a boy take out his papers and the police purposely open them and drop them on the pavement. It was raining, so the papers got wet. He picked them up and gave them back to the officer. "Again the officer tried to push the young person to react, but the boy didn't say anything. The policeman got more aggressive and asked for papers again. Then the police took one of the boys with him. When this boy was released from *garde à vue*, he had been beaten." Another time her friend's car was stolen. When her friend went to file a police complaint, "the policeman hit her and held her for two days just for lodging a complaint."

On another occasion in Garges-lès-Gonesse, the young lawyer told me, two boys ran out of gas. "They went to get gas and brought it back and were filling their car. At that moment the police saw them filling their car and arrested them. They brought them to *garde à vue* [under the pretext that the boys were using petrol for arson] even though they saw that they were filling their car. There was an immediate tribunal. I talked to the boys' lawyer and he said Sarkozy passed a note to the prosecutor or judge and told them not to investigate, to close the case and send the boy to jail. So he is serving time in closed jail [unable to take advantage of school or work programs available to some juvenile offenders]."

Much like the Puerto Rican gang leader who told me he responded to police violence by becoming "more bad," the young people in the *banlieues* "no longer respect the law, so they break the law," the young lawyer pointed out. Police violence undermined the legitimacy of both the law and the state. "There is an institutionalization of abuse by the police," she commented. "The police are supposed to represent the law but they break the law." She told me another illustrative story: "When my brother was running to catch the bus the police stopped the bus, found him, and searched him. Luckily he is articulate and could explain to the police that he was running to catch a bus. 'Next time you are running to catch a bus and see the police,' they said, 'you stop.'"

When Algerians arrived in France, few were religious. The young woman lawyer's father was a political prisoner brought to France from Algeria during the war. When he was released, he married a French woman. France, however, rejected his application for citizenship because he had been a political prisoner. The lawyer is the only member of her family who is religious. She likes the structure, meaning, and community she finds in Islam. She does not understand why France should make her choose between her religion and her country. The law forbidding headscarves in schools has also led to discrimination against teachers and women working for the government. Another young woman, of Moroccan descent, told me that she and her friends are constantly asked where they are from. "Why," she asked, "are women wearing headscarves asked where they are from?"

It was not only religious Muslims who suffered discrimination, however. Activated racial boundaries marked entire communities as the enemy. Another young woman of Algerian origin, who works for the French senate, told me a tale of police abuse involving her entire family:

It was a snowy day and kids were throwing snowballs. One put a rock in a snowball and threw it at a cop. He ran into the building with the police chasing him. Coincidentally my younger brother was coming home from work and entered the building at the same time. The police saw him go into the apartment and the police called to my brother who was on the balcony to send his brother down. So my brother went down and they began to beat him, all of them. My older brother then went down and asked why they were beating his younger brother. He began to defend our brother and the police beat him too.

Then my mother went down to ask why they were beating her sons and they put a pistol to her head. A white neighbor saw and came out and yelled to the police, "What are you doing to Madame X?" They then arrested all of them. My brother broke the policeman's jaw during the scuffle so he was sent to jail. The lawyer told him not to file a complaint against the police, or things would go harder for him. Instead the policeman filed a civil suit against my brother. Right now, I have four brothers in jail.[88]

Stephen Pocrain, a former spokesman for Noel Mamère, the Green Party's 2002 presidential candidate, was invited to speak on a panel in Garges-lès-Gonesse on the anniversary of Malcolm X's assasination. Pocrain pointed out the commonality in the struggle that both blacks and Arabs faced:

Twenty years ago they didn't speak of Islam; they spoke of Arabs, or Beurs. It is ethno/racial exclusion. . . . Now Islam is viewed as leading to terrorism. So the discussion has changed to religion. But it is the same politics, the same carrot and stick. . . . The French Left are so generous, they defend the *sans papiers* (undocumented immigrants), never the Arabs or blacks, never those who have citizenship. They mobilize for the *sans papiers*. Among all the children of immigrants educated, with diplomas, none have a position of power in France. . . . Until you show force you will not have a political voice, and nothing will change.

A black woman stood up and said, "[T]hose of us from the Antilles know this history. Yet when I speak of the discrimination that I live they tell me no, it isn't true, you exaggerate. They don't know what it is like to be in prison: they never lived it." A young North African interjected, "Here the right and the left speak of the Republic, a universal world of equality, but if you are Arab, Beur, it is 'we don't need you.' I don't give a fuck about the Republic. It is all shit."

"Everyone in the banlieues has a difficult relationship with police," a black lawyer and political activist from Sarcelles told me. "The police will always begin asking for papers and always end humiliating young people. They know someone's name and citizenship after having asked many times, but that doesn't stop them from asking again and again. Do we try to work with police? Yes. Do we work with police? No. They don't want to establish a relationship with us. Their superiors do not want them to have a relationship with us. They say police are here to arrest people, not to make friends."

The day I traveled with my friend (the black lawyer) to Les Bosquets, Montfermeil, we found ourselves unexpectedly in the middle of a large demonstration against the police. Unsure as to what the march was about, we asked a local policeman. "What march?" the white officer responded. We asked if he was a municipal policeman. "Yes," he replied. "Then you don't have weapons?" my friend asked. "Not yet," he said. We had come to interview Madame Caulibali, a middle-aged woman from Mali living in Les-Bosquets-Montfermeil, a neighborhood bordering Clichy-sous-Bois. Her own interaction with the police led to a small neighborhood riot in May 2006. She told us the following story:

Police came to my house and asked me for my son. I asked them, "what did he do?" "None of your business," they said. They then came back again and again and each time asked me for my papers. One time they told me that my son had robbed someone, another time that he had beaten someone. They kept changing the story. The fourth time they asked me for papers, I asked them why they needed my papers, they know who I am, they had been here four times. They said I was going to be sorry. I don't know why, perhaps I don't speak well.

While I was at work, they came again. I came home and found my front door and bedroom door broken and my things everywhere. [I myself saw the broken doors.] But nothing was stolen. My neighbor told me the police had done it. The sixth time they came my son was home. They arrested him and in full view of the neighbors made him pull down his pants. "Why are you pulling down his pants?" I demanded. They yelled at me, and I yelled back, and they sprayed tear gas in my face and arrested us both. They beat me. I don't know why, maybe I don't speak well. We are here because the French went to Mali, and now they say we are not welcome here.[89]

The Riots Begin: Clichy-sous-Bois

Moghdad ran a youth center and had founded a political organization called Association Collectif, Liberté, Égalité Fraternité, Ensemble, Unis (ACLEFEU) in Clichy-sous-Bois. During my visit he pointed to the sharp contrast between the dilapidated buildings on one side of the street and the newly painted, modern buildings and parks on the other side. On one side lived blacks and Arabs, he said, and on the other lived whites. Those who lived on the black and Arab side, according to Moghdad, were often chased by police, arrested, and imprisoned for minor offenses.

He told me the story of a friend of his little sister who was imprisoned for a minor offense. "We don't consider those serving time as criminals," he said. When the young man's father passed away, he was given permission to go to the burial. The police kept him in handcuffs throughout the funeral. They kept him away from his family and stood when they were supposed to sit. Throughout the ceremony the policemen chewed gum loudly. "I hope you understand from this that they did not respect this young man's suffering at this tragic moment. They did [this] deliberately." Moghdad drew a parallel between the indifference of the police to this boy's suffering and the case of the three young men chased into the electric power grid. "The boys had done nothing. They were good kids. They had done well in school. Everyone knew them. Everyone loved them. They were the kind of kids who would always do things for others." One had been a straight A student, the other a high school soccer champion. Running from the police, as the boys had done, he stated, was normal in the *banlieues*. The day the boys were killed, he said, "Banlieue residents heard the police talking on the phone and joking and saying that since the boys had entered the electric grid their skin wasn't worth anything anymore. Then Sarkozy gave that speech saying the police had done nothing wrong. The pain we all felt was now mixed with outrage. About 200 kids from this neighborhood marched in protest. When they saw the police they started yelling and cursing at them and the police shot them with tear gas. The kids threw garbage cans and rocks and anything they could find. It lasted about 3 hours."

The next day the kids from nearby neighborhoods also marched, and now there were also many more police, a policeman for every two kids, he estimated. Again there were confrontations between youths and police. "We tried to keep the kids calm. We told them that there would be an investigation. They should not let things get out of hand." On October 29 more kids arrived, and now there were protests in other neighborhoods in this district as well: "Again police met them in full force and confrontations between the kids and police developed. On October 30, we held a big march in honor of the three boys and accompanied the parents to the funeral. This time people from all over Paris attended, many white French as well. The families were crying."

Later that day police chased two young people to the mosque to ID them. The youths showed them their papers, but a police officer shot his tear gas gun into the mosque, Moghdad told me:

> The place was full of thousands of worshipers. The kids told the police it was a mosque. The police said "Too bad" and shot the tear gas canister into the mosque. There were babies, women and mothers inside. For young Muslims, mothers are very important. And the police shot tear gas at their mothers, their younger brothers, and their sisters. This was a grave, grave offense. Was there an apology? No, Sarkozy got on the radio and said someone else must have shot the tear gas, not the police. When we produced the police canister Sarkozy said he didn't know how it got there. There were hundreds in the hospital and Sarkozy is saying the police did nothing wrong. This time hell broke loose. We couldn't restrain them. Young people were throwing Molotovs, even shooting guns at police. I was shaking. We were all shaking.
>
> They set fire to the cars, because that is what is here. There is nothing else. There are no stores or shops here. What are here are cars, and so they set them on fire. It was like externalizing their internal explosions. Some kids in pain cut themselves. These kids, instead of cutting themselves, set things on fire. It was like getting rid of all this pain inside and throwing it outside.

"If the forms of the revolts were reprehensible they were at the core understandable," Samir Mihi, another local organizer and close personal friend of Siyakha Traoré, said. "What angers young people throughout

France is injustice, discrimination, the police, the prisons, all of that. The country does not care what happens to people like us; they aren't interested in the truth. We are ignored and maligned."

The Riots Spread to Villiers-le-Bel and Garges-lès-Gonesse

The young lawyer described earlier in this chapter stressed the emotional component of the riots. On the night of the riots she and her friends canvassed her neighborhood, Villiers-le-Bel, and several others, speaking to young people. "They didn't know how to explain what they did. They were full of emotion but couldn't put it into words," she told me. "There is strong solidarity among *banlieue* residents." Witnesses, the young pediatrician noted, heard the police joking. "The police had the duty to save the boys. We lost half an hour," she said, while the police did nothing. "In all the discussion of the riots in the press and by the political elite not one of them asked what the police did." Information circulated quickly. "The *banlieues* may be disconnected geographically but [the people] are united as Muslims and as residents of *banlieues*. All the *banlieues* have the same problems, and everyone here has family members in different *banlieues*." Everyone was calling everyone, the lawyer said:

> At first, all of the families were very sad. They went to get their children. But then they got angry. The *banlieues* were so quiet when the police launched the tear gas, as everyone was observing Ramadan. The police had already committed a terrible abuse without provocation, and now they followed it with another—shooting tear gas into a mosque. Only the police seem to have rights here. There were people in the hospital, and the government said nothing. They said the police were not responsible; it was the children who had committed a crime. The entire *banlieue* was horrified at the reaction of the government. Not an ounce of concern was shown for these two young boys who had done nothing. They were now dead and the government was giving the same speech about how the police were just doing their job. These two boys had done well in school and had done nothing wrong.

As in so many other cases, she observed, "the police killed *banlieue* youth without provocation." She blamed Sarkozy first but also de Villepin, the prime minister, who repeated the same story as the police. President Chirac, she said, was "totally silent. This gave the police permission to continue the harassment." It was, she claimed, "as if the political elite wanted to increase the abuse." In contrast, the mayor of Clichy-sous-Bois condemned both the police and the government. He "said it was incredible what Sarkozy had done. It would never have happened in a church or a synagogue." A young law student from Garges-lès-Gonesse told me, while she was handing out campaign literature, that she was not surprised by the riots: "People are trapped. . . . The politics of the police here are oppressive. Police patrols and ID checks make people feel they are being aggressed against. This can lead to a violent reaction."

Muslim/Jewish Tensions in Sarcelles

The riots barely affected Sarcelles, largely because the mayor and local organizers were in the streets all night. Still, police abuse of blacks and Muslims in the neighborhood increased tension between Muslims and Jews. In some ways Sarcelles resembled Williamsburg, Brooklyn. As in Brooklyn, the Jewish community tended to support law-and-order candidates and appeared to have a special relationship with police. There were also important differences between Williamsburg and Sarcelles. Puerto Ricans and Hasidic Jews in Williamsburg did not have major foreign policy differences. The Satmar Hasidim were strong critics of Israeli violations of Palestinian rights. They opposed the construction of a secular Jewish state on holy land. In addition they did not take a position on Puerto Rican independence or Latin American politics, the main foreign policy concern of Puerto Ricans. Although there had been serious conflicts over the distribution of public resources, there had also been more efforts to engage in cross-boundary organizing in Williamsburg. Many members of the predominantly Puerto Rican activist network were Jewish. The former Young Lord activist Luis Garden Acosta organized a joint Hasidic and Puerto Rican protest march against the construction of an incinerator plant in the neighborhood.

In Sarcelles foreign policy differences fueled polarization between the two communities. Aischa, a black Tunisian woman, raised three issues she believed were responsible for the tensions between Muslims and Jews. The first was the social closure of the Jewish community. The Jews looked down on Muslims, she said. The second was that both the French state and the police accorded Jews certain privileges, while engaging in discriminatory actions toward Muslims. The third was the Jewish community's intransigent defense of Israel. The three issues, she believed, were inextricably linked. The Jews were more integrated in France because the French state did not discriminate against them in the same way it did against Muslims. According to Aischa, the Jews thought they were better than Muslims because they were more integrated. The unfair advantages Jews had over Muslims in Sarcelles were similar to the advantages they had over Palestinians in Israel.

She began our interview with an illustration of the first issue, a story about a kosher butcher who would not sell to Arabs. "This butcher told me in Arabic, go buy from the Arabs. I said 'you don't have the right not to sell to me.'" Aischa threatened to call the police. The butcher told her that he still wouldn't sell to Arabs." Aischa then drew a parallel with the situation in the Middle East: "How can you make peace in Palestine and Israel? We have to discuss the problem, we cannot be peaceful without talking about the problem. . . . You can't have peace that way. . . . Forty-four years and [the Palestinians] have no rights."

She then took up the second issue, the privileged status of Jews in France: "I spoke with the Committee Against Discrimination. I asked, 'why don't you keep track of the insults that I receive every day? My whole family is aggressed against. The young are afraid to speak. They feel menaced by the politicians themselves.' Anti-Semitism, racism, it is the same thing. There shouldn't be separate categories for insults. For Jews it is anti-Semitism and for others only racism? To me this is very grave. They trivialize insults against those with all the misery. . . . Now Sarkozy is putting people on planes [referring to his policy of catching immigrants, putting them on planes, and sending them to Africa]." In the United States, she continued, when an immigrant arrives and works, he can succeed:

> There are no black journalists here; there are none on TV or employed by the public sector. It is a hidden racism. In the U.S., blacks can get ahead. Here discrimination is flagrant. A Malian family visited an apartment and was told the apartment is not for you. The landlady says the Malian is dirty. But they [the couple] work, they have four children—they have rights to an apartment. . . . Why do they always take the side of landlords? Animals live better than us.

Why does skin color still matter so? Resumes don't matter. One man was thrown out of his house for being 600 euros behind in his rent—thrown out, with all his furniture. Racism here is very strong and very hidden. When you arrive in the U.S. someone doesn't follow you like the police do here. You have black mayors in the U.S. [The interview was conducted in 2004, well before the election of Barack Obama.]

Aischa blamed Sarkozy for Jewish/Muslim tensions. She said,

Sarkozy reinforces hatred of the other. He talks about the kind of immigrants we want. It is disgusting. . . . When there is an election they speak about immigrants, to satisfy racists and make the French forget all the real problems of government and politicians. They pull "immigration" out of their pocket. The magic word. . . . When the TV and media attack immigrants you can't answer. There are some young people that are pests, but why always focus on them and not the rest of the community? We need a government that brings people together, that celebrates all religious holidays and creates understanding between groups. But as long as the government uses the word "immigrant" to cover up rather than promote dialogue the problem continues.

Patricia, an evangelical, headed a local community group in Sarcelles that helped new immigrants assemble their dossiers and put their identity papers in order. "We help people without a lot of resources," she explained. She told me that she was of Italian and Maltese origins. Only much later in the interview did she tell me that her grandparents were Tunisian. Her husband is from Martinique. She said, "There are 107 ethnic groups here. We have Caribbeans, Bretons, Blacks, [and] Indians. In our church they come from Senegal, Côte d'Ivoire, Cameroon, the Congo, Antilles, Réunion, Madagascar, Cape Verde, Portugal, New Caledonia, Chad, Mauritania, Italy, Malta, Ghana, Morocco, Nigeria, Laos, India, Vietnam, Cuba, Assyria, [and] Chaldon. There are twenty-five ethnicities represented. There are Jews in our church, two messianic Jews."

Patricia's observation about ethnic diversity was a common one among the French. Yet despite the large array of countries, most immigrants came from Africa, the Antilles, or other French territories where they were colonial subjects. This was similar to the ethnic diversity in the South Bronx, where residents were Puerto Rican, Mexican, Dominican, Garifunan, Guatemalan, Jamaican, Senegalese, Guyanese, Guianese, Malian, and so on. But when Patricia discussed the police, she saw a clear us/them boundary: "We do not have a good relationship with the police. The police here are racist, very racist. They behave differently with those of different colors or nationalities. . . . my husband (who is black) knows that he gives them his papers when asked. He doesn't talk back or argue. There are police here that abuse their authority. We have heard of blacks killed by police." But, she said, things could be much worse, as she conjectured it was in other European countries. At least "in France we live in the country of 'the rights of man.'"

Aftermath of the 2005 Riots

At a Ramadan dinner I attended in August 2011, a group of women of Algerian and Moroccan descent and one Palestinian woman currently living in Paris discussed the behavior of the police in the *banlieues* following the 2005 riots. "They are hated," said a French-born woman. The Palestinian woman told me that she had recently seen more North African and black "Caribbean" police but not African police. Another French-born woman pointed out that an Algerian policewoman had told her she had to be tough with young people in the *banlieues* or her boss would come down hard on her. A French-born lawyer from Aubervilliers said, "No one there trusts the police."

I interviewed a group of boys that same evening, as they were gathered in front of a building scrawled with antipolice graffiti. "Yes there are more minorities in the police now but it has not changed the way the police behave at all. If anything they are more aggressive," commented one. "It depends on which neighborhood you are in. In the 93rd [Seine-Saint-Denis, the district where Clichy is located] they are very aggressive. In the richer neighborhoods they are less aggressive," said another. Another pointed out that "there are more black and North African police now, but they behave just the same as the white. The criminal justice system is more and more punitive."

A black truant officer living in a *cité* called La Maladrerie in Aubervilliers told me he tried to understand the policemen's point of view. Referring to the riots, he said, "Why did the kids run? It is not the fault of the police officers that the kids were running. Maybe the kids committed a crime. There are good and bad police, just like there are good and bad kids." Yet when I suggested that the young people might have been afraid of being asked for papers and taken to the station, he responded, "They always ask me for my papers and they know who I am. But they ask me for papers so they can stop and search me; see if I have anything illegal. It is their mentality. Sometimes I say, 'Why are you stopping me? I am a workingman. I am not a kid.' I told them that and they grabbed me by the throat [he gestures how] and slapped cuffs on me. They took me to the station and they treated me badly. I know that at the station they beat people. They also kill people. They kill many here but it is hidden."

The truant officer compared the police to teachers and other truant officers in the neighborhood. He said that coming from the neighborhood gave him a better understanding of the kids, of their problems, and where they came from. The teachers who came from the south could not understand or relate to the children. According to him, it was the same with police officers: "they have in their head[s] all these images that create fear." He pointed out that during a visit to New York (where we first met) he saw police cars with one officer inside each. "You never see that in Paris," he told me, even though in Paris no one in the *banlieues* carried guns. The police "carry around images that frighten them when they are in the *banlieues*," he observed:

> Look how we are sitting here outside a cité in Aubervilliers in the middle of the night and it is quiet. But if you told them you were here in the middle of the night they would think, oh no. It is the image they have. They send up these guys from the south and they are frightened. There are good police and bad police, like good kids bad kids. The police are like a sect. It is not the individual police officer that is the problem. Yes, there are bad kids here that cause problems and do not respect the police. But the police think anyone who is black or Muslim is a criminal.

Why Marseille Did Not Burn

Living in the Panier wasn't something you boasted about. Ever since the nineteenth century it had been a

neighborhood of sailors and whores. A blight on the
city. One big brothel. For the Nazis, who dreamed of
destroying it, it was a source of degeneration for the
Western world. . . . [Later f]ear of Arabs had made the
people of Marseilles flee the downtown area to other
neighborhoods away from the center where they felt
safer. . . . The Arabs had regrouped downtown. They'd
taken over from the whites who'd fled, who'd washed
their hands of Cours Belzunce and Rue 'Aix, and all
the rundown streets. . . . Streets full of hookers.
Buildings unfit for human habitation, flea-ridden
hotels. Successive waves of immigrants had passed
through these streets until redevelopment had pushed
them out to the suburbs. The latest redevelopment was
happening now, and the suburbs had moved to the
very edge of the city. . . . One by one the movie theaters
had closed, then the bars. These days the Canebière
was just a monotonous succession of clothing stores
and shoe stores. One big second hand emporium.
                —*Jean-Claude Izzo*, Total Chaos *(1995)*

Marseille is a city of 1.5 million people, about a quarter the population
of Paris, although its geographic spread is three times greater. Of Marseille's
800,000 residents, over a quarter in 2007 were foreign born: 70,000 Algerians, 65,000 Armenians, 30,000 Tunisians, 15,000 Moroccans, 70,000 Com-
orians, and 7,000 from other sub-Saharan African countries. Religious
diversity is equally great: 190,000 Muslims, 70,000 Jews, 20,000 Buddhists,
and 11,000 Greek Orthodox. Marseille's Jewish community is the third
largest in Europe, and demographers predict that Marseille will be the first
city on the European continent with an Islamic majority. Marseille easily
tops all other French cities in numbers of both immigrants and Muslims.

It also tops all other French cities in poverty and unemployment. In
2004 Marseille's unemployment rate was 20.3 percent, almost twice that of
greater Paris.[90] Official unemployment among youths in 2007 exceeded 40
percent.[91] Despite the racial and ethnic heterogeneity of downtown Marseille, the city ranks, along with Paris and Lille, among the most segregated
in France, exhibiting "great disparities within the population by income,
employment status, and living conditions."[92] In 1999 UNESCO labeled

Marseille's northern arrondissements a "triangle of poverty" and the locale with the highest concentration of poverty and unemployment in France.[93] If immigration, poverty, unemployment, radical Islam, or even large families and polygamy, as the French parliament claimed, were to blame, Marseille should have experienced more riots, not the complete absence thereof. Why did Marseille remain calm while the rest of France burned?

Susanne Stemmler, a French studies expert at the Center for Metropolitan Studies, argues that the answer to that question is Marseille's atypical way of dealing with racial diversity: "If France is a very racist country, Marseilles is its liberated zone."[94] Stemmler's observation is certainly exaggerated, but racial boundaries are less activated in Marseille than elsewhere in France. While it is impossible to do Marseille justice in just a few pages, I argue that four main factors have deactivated Marseille's racial boundaries. The first is the city's more inclusive economic networks and spatial geography. The second is its incorporation and recognition of minority religious and neighborhood organizations. The third is a policing strategy that preferences social peace over the violent enforcement of racial and spatial boundaries. The fourth factor is the role of the Mafia and a closely linked political machine, which incorporates Muslim and black youths at the lower rungs, creating a weblike structure in place of a bifurcated boundary. The Mafia simultaneously metes out punishment to those who strike out on their own.

For twenty-six hundred years Marseille was a central hub of Mediterranean trade. In the thirteenth century the French king Charles of Anjou conquered the independent city-state, but Marseille retained a degree of autonomy, fortified by the ethnic trading networks that were the lifeblood of the city. Networks, social ties, and economic relations, as Katharyne Mitchell observes, "have strong ramifications for spatial organization, especially with respect to the formation of neighborhoods and the location of industries."[95] In Marseille "highly networked ethnicity based capitalism" produced a more spatially inclusive city: "This central city trading node operates on the basis of interethnic ties that involve both older immigrant streams and new arrivals. For every new group that arrives, a different nodal point is added to the web of potential commercial routes through which goods can circulate in the greater Mediterranean region and beyond. The area functions interethnically because of the tremendous advantages that accrue to the neighborhoods as an economic trading zone."[96]

Working-class and immigrant neighborhoods developed around the port, and ethnic commercial enterprises such as restaurants and specialized markets grew in and around those neighborhoods. The wealthy and better-off native French fled the working-class and immigrant port for the city's southern coast and suburbs. Although the majority of North Africans who arrived after the Algerian war were eventually pushed into the impoverished and distant arrondissements in the north, downtown remained an amalgam of immigrant, North African, and African neighborhoods and commerce. A woman I spoke with explained the linkage between the ports and the northern arrondissements: "Marseille is a principal port and that is where industry is located. The only place they could put industry was in front of the sea [explaining to me why there are no beaches in the northern arrondissement despite its geographical proximity to the sea]. But in Marseille people live more liberally than elsewhere. The growth of ethnic business in Marseille is due entirely to the centrality of the port. Here, in the northern arrondissements most of the work is in industry, principally masonry. People do not have a lot of education. The schools are very poor."

The area that stretches from the northern arrondissements to the Panier is a triangle, rather than a clearly demarcated dual city. Patrick Parodi points out that downtown Marseille "is not confiscated by social class: there is a significant community of North African immigrants, often poor."[97] "The fact that the projects are sprinkled through the city," Claire Berlinski observes, "means the inhabitants don't feel cut off from civic life or the traditional life of the city."[98] Miloud, a youth of Moroccan descent, boasted to me when I interviewed him in August 2010, "Just look around, look at the stores, at the restaurants; they are all Maghribin or African. We own this city, it is ours."

Economic disparities are not reinforced by racial or spatial boundaries between downtown and surrounding suburbs. "I can go to the center of the city without thinking I am entering enemy territory," said Abida Hecini, a third-generation immigrant. "We belong to Marseille and Marseille belongs to us."[99] An army commander who grew up in a Parisian *banlieue* and lives now in Marseille told me, "Everyone feels free in Marseille. In the Parisian *banlieues* you feel walled in, trapped. If you take the train or bus into Paris the police make it clear you do not belong there. In Marseille you can always go to the beach or the parks. In the *banlieues* there is only concrete."[100] A young man from one of Marseille's northern arrondissements told me, "We are free in Marseille. Paris is closed in, oppressive, and racist. They stop you five times a day. This city is very poor, but there are things to do and no one stops you. You can go to the beach."

However, immigration, ethnic diversity, and trade did not always bring peace to Marseille. It also brought organized crime and violent conflict. In the 1920s and 1930s Communist longshoremen battled Italian and Corsican mobsters for control of the port. While the two most powerful Corsican gangsters, François Spirito and Paul Bonaventure, worked first as hatchet men for the French fascists in the 1920s and 1930s and then played a similar role for Vichy and the Gestapo, some sectors of the Corsican underworld worked with the resistance. The Communists and their Franc-Tireurs et partisans rejected all alliances with mobsters, but Gaston Deferre, the Socialist leader of the much smaller Mouvement unis de résistance (United Movement of Resistance) joined forces with the Corsican gangsters Antoine and Barthélemy Guerini. This relationship would have long-lasting consequences for Marseille and for the Socialist Party.

When the Nazis were defeated, the Communist Party emerged as the largest party in Marseille. In 1947 the Communist Party candidate Jean Cristofal was, with the support of the Socialists, elected mayor. Cristofal then used the newly formed Compagnies Républicaines de Sécurité, composed largely of former resistance fighters, to circumvent the local police, which were still composed of those who had served Vichy, and rid the city of gangsters.

The U.S. Central Intelligence Agency (CIA) struck a deal with the Socialists and the Guerini mob. When a rise in tramway fares sparked a wave of wildcat strikes, Jules Moch, the Socialist minister of the interior, called eighty thousand reservists and mobilized two hundred thousand regular troops to battle the strikers. United States intelligence services encouraged and funded a Socialist faction of the Confédération générale du travail to form a separate union, La Force ouvrière, and "sent agents and a psychological warfare team to Marseille, where they dealt directly with the Corsican syndicate leaders through the Guerini brothers,"[101] supplying them with arms and money for assaults on Communist strikers and union officials. McCoy notes:

> In the fall of 1947 a month of bloody street fighting, electoral reverses, and the clandestine intervention by the CIA toppled the Communist party from power and brought about a permanent realignment of political power in Marseille. When the strikes and rioting finally came to an end, the Socialists had severed their contacts with the Communists, a Socialist-underworld alliance was in control

of Marseille politics, and the Guerini brothers had emerged as the unchallenged "peacemakers" of the Marseille milieu. For the next twenty years their word would be law in the Marseille underworld.[102]

The police were purged of their Communist members. Marseille became the transit point for all heroin shipped from Turkey to the United States market—what the Americans later called "the French connection." When U.S. drug suppliers turned to the golden triangle for heroin, Marseille's traffickers marketed their product in France. The rise of de Gaulle, combined with U.S. pressure and interdiction efforts in Turkey, resulted in a reversal of fortunes for Antoine and Barthélemy Guerini, one of whom was killed by a rival gang and the other of whom was convicted of murder. Marseille is no longer a heroin or drug-processing capital, but as one journalist points out, "it remains at the centre of the trade in cannabis coming into Europe through Spain from Morocco. The city is also a key point in the cocaine smuggling route into Europe from South America through West Africa. Local police have warned that members of the new generation of criminals are ready to use automatic weapons over the slightest drug trafficking rivalry."[103]

Marseille has had only three mayors since 1953. Gaston Deferre remained in power until his death in 1986. Robert Vigouroux was elected in 1986 by a coalition called the Rassemblement démocratique et social européen, and he resigned in 1995. Jean-Claude Gaudin, a member of the right-wing Union pour une mouvement populaire (UMP, formerly called the Rassemblement pour la République) since he left the Socialists in protest over their coalition with the Communists in the 1980s, has been mayor since 1995. Party differences are not ideological at the local level (or have not been until now), although Marseille mayors have also always served in the national senate. In Marseille party loyalty is, as Mitchell notes, "disciplined by a triad of forces: potential ostracization from the business community. . . .[;] [r]educed access to social housing and other public sector goods controlled and allocated by the mayor and other local political forces; and in some cases by the local mafia, which has been and remains linked to local politicians and their clientelist practices."[104]

During and after the Algerian war Marseille was once again the scene of violent clashes, although this time ethnic as well as ideological. The *pied-noirs*, the Algerian Jews, and the Algerian Muslims (both those who fought with and those who fought against France) all arrived at the same time

from Algeria. Conflict between the city's Muslims and *pied-noirs* (overrepresented among the police) in particular was fierce and unrelenting. In
1973 a North African man knifed a white Marseillaise bus driver. Mobs of
white French marched through the city conducting *ratonades* (rat-killing
raids). The Algerians were the rats.

The violence continued throughout the 1970s. In December 1973 a
group of *pied-noir* terrorists calling themselves "Charles Martel" bombed
the Algerian consulate's offices in Marseille, killing four Algerians and injuring twenty.[105] In 1975 the terrorists bombed Air Algérie offices in Toulouse and Lyon, as well as the Algerian consulate in Paris; no one was hurt
in the attacks. In November 1977 the group kidnapped two Algerians in
Paris. Then on October 18, 1980, the police killed an unarmed youth, La-
houri Ben Mohammed, in the Cité des Flamants. Throngs of North Africans marched down Canabiére Street in nonviolent protest. But police
violence continued unabated. In the summer of 1981 the police raided the
housing project Cité de la Cayolle and injured a large number of women,
children, and elderly residents. Infuriated youths firebombed shopping centers and police stations.[106]

The effort to defuse conflict in Marseille was deliberate. It was not simply an outgrowth of the spatial layout of the city. Rather it developed incre-
mentally out of the resolution of previous conflicts. As a woman social
worker I spoke with in a northern arrondissement recalled,

> In the 1980s they did not simply shoot Mahgrebin in the streets.
> Police went into the housing projects to shoot youth. They came to
> this neighborhood where North Africans, Africans, and Italians live.
> They closed the suburb, controlled the streets, and asked for ID three
> times a day. The conflict between the youth and the police humiliated
> the parents. They could not do anything. They were frightened and
> lacked the language. So it was my generation that began to protest. In
> the 1970s and 1980s there were 150 young people killed by police or
> racist neighbors. There is nothing written about this.

To avoid resistance to his urban renewal program or increasingly violent
clashes between youth and police, Deferre created the Contrat de ville. The
Contrat helped ethnic minorities set up their own community organizations, and the community organizations provided means for the city to
negotiate with the residents. A group of individuals, almost all of North

African extraction and from the northern sections of the city, emerged as interlocutors and served as mediators between public institutions and these communities. By the mid-1990s the city had institutionalized consultation between the mayor's office, these organizations, and their elected leaders as well as imams and community elders.

This experience led Mayor Vigouroux to create Marseille espérance. The original idea was to mediate between Muslims and Jews to avoid an outbreak of violence or interethnic clashes during the Palestinian intifada. However, the concept that the mayor could meet with representatives of minority communities to address issues before a crisis arose was attractive. Marseille espérance has been used to diffuse potentially serious conflicts.[107] For instance, as Trent Buatte notes, when neo-Nazis killed a Camorian in 2002, "the mayor and Espérance condemned the acts and attended local vigils."[108] The gesture was enough to quell unrest. When a white resident, Nicolas Bourgat, was stabbed to death by a Moroccan, the group again calmed city residents. On September 11, 2001, the leaders of Marseille espérance stood with the mayor and the police chief to denounce religious intolerance and call for compassion. In addition, "when Muslims all across France protested the 2003 American invasion of Iraq, the Muslim delegates of Marseille Espérance returned to their mosques and called for calm."[109]

Over the years, notes Buatte, "the group has become a conduit for the mayor to reach immigrant communities and for the communities to reach him. Marseille Espérance may not have formal authority but it has strong influence on the decisions of the mayor and the citizens in the streets of Marseille."[110] During the first week of the 2005 riots the group "met at least once a day, and every night the religious leaders returned to their communities to quell the outrage stewing in the streets. Unlike other French cities Marseille has created a direct line between minorities and local authorities."[111] Since its success in preventing the 2005 riots from erupting in Marseille, the organization has been studied and visited by delegations from Sarajevo, Barcelona, Montreal, Brussels, Anvers, Naples, and Turin. A 2007 survey of French cities found Marseille to be the "only administrative body aimed at maintaining dialogue with resident migrant communities."[112]

Mayor Gaudin has approved the construction of a new Grand Mosque on two acres of land set aside by the city in the northern neighborhood of Saint Louis overlooking the port. Rabbi Charles Bismuth, a member of Marseille espérance, supports the project as well. "I say let's do it! We don't oppose each other. We are all heading in the same direction. That is our message and that is the secret of Marseille."[113] Space, Buatte argues, is important not simply in the layout of the city but also in the arenas opened for discussion and consultation, such as Espace accueil aux étrangers (simply referred to as Espace or Space), Espace jeune, Espace culture, and others. "The concept of space is both psychologically and physically important for foreigners," he says. "It marks a presence in France just for immigrants, a place to meet, organize, and express concerns."[114]

During the first week of the 2005 riots, the group met every day. At night the religious leaders returned to their communities to preempt any disturbance and dispel unrest.[115] It is an exaggeration to claim, however, as one group of Marseille historians have, that Marseille's Antirepublican model has integrated the city.[116] The mayor cultivates and propagates this multicultural Marseillaise identity—a strategy Eleonora Pasotti has called "political branding."[117] The brand has increased Marseille residents' pride and sense of ownership and given the city a certain international cache. Marseille has become an increasingly popular tourist destination and has attracted new private capital and even foreign observers interested in copying the city's success. In 2011 Marseille was designated the European capital of culture for 2013.[118]

Yet there has been little examination of the machine politics that undergird the ties between these religious and community organizations and the mayor. The incorporation of religious organizations is uneven and substitutes for a serious attempt to address the fundamental needs of the city's poorest residents. Racial boundaries may be deactivated, but the mobilization of opposition is also sacrificed. High unemployment and the state's powerful patronage networks make resistance difficult. Sixty-four percent of those employed in Marseille work for the state, compared, for instance, to 47 percent in Lyon.[119] One young man I spoke with told me he had campaigned for the deputy mayor to get a decent job. The night of the riots he got a call from the mayor's office telling him, "Find out what is happening in your neighborhood [in the northern arrondissement] and make sure things remain calm." Everyone he knew, he insisted, received such phone calls, and all the social organizations were in the streets keeping the peace. The social worker I spoke with presented an even more dismal picture:

I get angry when people say Marseille doesn't explode. This is a dream not a reality. There is less conflict here, but also less empowerment. . . . Do you know in the 1990s we still had *bidonvilles* [shantytowns]? Coming from Paris you cannot imagine shanty-towns in the 1990s in Marseille. . . . Everyone says you have organizations, but the aim is social control. You cannot be organized against the political machine. In 1984, Ibraham Ali was shot during a municipal election campaign, by a member of the National Front. . . . Here everyone wants a flat, or a job in a public institution—politics becomes that. We have the poorest representation, and that keeps this sector poor and getting poorer all the time. We have the worst transportation. [It took me hours to get to this district, although it is not very far. I had to take the metro and two buses, and I waited more than an hour for the final and only bus that goes to this neighborhood.] We have the worst schools. We have only two libraries in the entire Northern district—the 13th, 14th, 15th, 16th, and 3rd *arrondissements* (districts). . . .

The locally elected Mahgrebin and black elected leaders are all a part of the politics of the machine. They promise each group something—like jobs—in return for their vote. We cannot organize against the machine without losing jobs and public services. In a district where 40 percent of residents are unemployed? We have very low political empowerment. People think this is how it is everywhere. Yes there is a politics where different groups have spaces for this and that, but it is all part of machine politics. Clientelism is deeply rooted in Marseille. That is the cost we pay for these spaces.

The tapestry that weaves together ethnic and neighborhood organizations, police, and local government also covers a dark underbelly of organized crime and corruption. Gun attacks and murders have grown in number, rising from 58 to 120 a year between 2007 and 2009 alone.[120] Execution-style killings are Marseille's "regrettable specialty," notes one journalist: "On Marseille's northern housing estates, social workers say poverty has worsened the problem. More than 20 percent of the city's population lives below the poverty line. Although Marseille has recovered from the 1990s horror years of industrial decline and acute unemployment, joblessness still exceeds the national average. Local politicians warn that some estates have more than 40 percent youth unemployment and there is an 'underground economy' of drug deals and turf wars."[121]

In 1994 two journalists published a book accusing Mayor Gaudin and another UMP cabinet member of ordering a hit on Yann Piat, a former

National Front and active UMP deputy, who had been conducting an investigation of Mafia influence in Marseille. Piat was shot dead while driving her car along a road near the Riviera. Two Marseille gunmen on a motorcycle fired the fatal shots. It was widely assumed to be a Mafia hit, but no one knew who precisely was behind it. The journalists, Andre Rougeot and Jean-Michel Verne, claimed that François Leotard, the defense minister, and his political ally, Marseille mayor Jean-Claude Gaudin, had ordered the hit.[122] The journalists were convicted of libel and fined. The research was apparently flawed, but the story was credible. While the libel charge may have been justified, everyone who has written about the Mafia or corruption in Marseille has been similarly convicted and fined.

On December 2, 2010, Alexandre Guerini, the manager of waste treatment companies, was indicted for misuse of company property, embezzlement of public property, concealment, bribery, influence peddling, and possession of ammunition. His brother the Marseille senator Jean-Noël Guerini, the président du conseil general parti socialiste de Bouches-du-Rhone, was not indicted. The stain, however, was indelible. Alexandre Guerini had been a key spokesman during his brother's senate campaign and was deeply involved in the running of some of the institutions managed by the Parti Socialist (PS) in Marseille. The indictment alleged that Alexandre and his partner, Philippe Rapezzi, had paid hundreds of thousands of dollars to a consulting firm for nonexistent activity.[123]

Then on March 20, 2011, the Socialist senator Arnaud Montebourg submitted a 170-page report to the Socialist Party leadership claiming that his investigation had found ample evidence of corruption and Mafia influence in Marseille and that the Socialist Party there managed "a feudal system based on intimidation and fear."[124] The report hit the Socialist Party like a hailstorm. Montebourg was accused of leaking the document to the press and publicly embarrassing the party right before the upcoming elections. As was usually the case for those who levied such charges, Montebourg was charged with libel and ordered to pay two thousand euros to Jean-Noël Guerini for violating his presumption of innocence. There has yet to be any serious investigation into Mafia ties and corruption in Marseille, though scandal did lead to the arrest of the owners of a casino in Paris. Those arrests then led to an array of gangland killings: thirty-four people were riddled with bullets between January 2012 and June 2013 in what one journalist calls a style reminiscent of a scene from *The Godfather*:

As in the post-war New York of Francis Coppola's 1972 masterpiece, the real-life contemporary violence in Marseille has its roots in feuds between rival gangs involved in the southern port's drugs trade, police say. Gang-related murders this year have included one last month in which a 17-year-old dealer was shot 20 times with an automatic pistol and a double killing in March that took place in broad daylight and was witnessed by children on a rundown social housing estate. The latter incident sparked a protest movement among local residents who have called on the government to put in place a "Marshall plan" for the city's poorest neighborhoods.[125]

Manuel Valls, the Socialist minister of the interior and a hard-liner on security issues, designated two areas of Marseille as special security zones eligible for extra government funds to fight crime. It is not yet clear what crime-fighting strategy the government plans to employ in these zones. Yet even the Mafia, by incorporating minority youths into the lower rungs of the organization (youths who hope to one day rise or strike out on their own), has helped deactivate racial boundaries.

Police in Marseille are more tolerant than their equivalents in Paris. They accept diversity and ignore low-level delinquency or semi-illicit street sellers. The police chief of Marseille has noted that "if we have had any success it's very relative. It's owed, in part[,] to the geography and ecology of the city. Marseille is a city with space. It's an agglomeration of what we call village nuclei, small neighborhoods that form a complex fabric. What is particularly important is that the banlieue is the city itself."[126] Siyakha Traoré and Samir Mihi found Marseille unlike any other city they visited during their speaking tour: "The city is integrated and there is a strong Marseillaise identity—everyone is Marseillaise. The police know everyone, so they do not need to chase anyone. They know who everyone is."[127] "The police do not act out of line and they always take our concerns seriously," noted the leader of the Algerian council, "because that same officer will have to return the next day and the day after that. Everyone will know if he has done something wrong."[128]

Police are forbidden from storming public housing projects without expressed permission, and they must present reasonable evidence before doing so. Marseille's police force leads the country in diversity training of officers and the incorporation of minorities into its force. Since 2000 the

National School of Police of Marseille (School of Sainte-Marthe) has been leading a pilot program to train new police officers in community awareness. In their courses Marseille police learn "basic knowledge of Islam, the history of immigration and the sociology of the suburbs."[129] A local police chief insisted that the police have permanent contacts with grassroots groups and with the schools: "The police have a permanent dialogue with neighborhood associations—when there's a problem, we go directly to the source. We have personal relationships with the Jewish community, with the Islamic community. We have personal contacts at many levels: Not only the chiefs, but the cops on patrol have regular meetings with community representatives."[130]

However, many black and Arab residents I spoke with believed that the police were simply unconcerned about crime that affected residents of poor African and North African neighborhoods. The social worker I spoke with rolled her eyes at the idea that Marseille had community policing. She said, "The police say we let them do whatever they want in this neighborhood. Police do not enter here, nor can they. Entire families cannot leave their houses out of fear." Others told me that the main enforcers of law and order were the three main Mafia families, who suppressed crimes that might bring unwanted attention to their activities or disrupt their lucrative trade. "It is all the work of the Mafia, the three big families. That is how they control the neighborhoods. The Mayor talks to the Préfet of police, or he talks to the Mafia." There have been several indictments and scandals involving police directly involved or accepting bribes in turning a blind eye to drug trafficking and prostitution.

Yet all of these factors—an integrated downtown with ethnic trading networks and commercial enterprises, a political machine that incorporates and recognizes ethnic and community organizations, a tolerant police force, and the continued power of Sicilian, Corsican, and even North African Mafias—combined to create a weblike structure in marked contrast to the dual city with its sharp boundary separating poor minority suburbs from the largely white city center of Paris. Add a history of violent social, political, ideological, and racial upheavals that have made social peace a priority for both government and law enforcement, and Marseille's relative calm in 2005 is explicable. Racial boundaries were not activated.

Conclusion

The Rise and Fall of Mayor Bloomberg in New York

In 2002 Michael Bloomberg was elected mayor as the Republican Party candidate, although he later declared himself an independent. Bloomberg made Ray Kelly his police commissioner (the same position Kelly had occupied under David Dinkins). The *New York Times* christened Bloomberg "the Freedom Mayor,"[1] and Ray Kelly was chosen as the next mayor by 25 percent of those surveyed in a 2011 Quinnipiac poll, the highest percentage of any candidate.[2] But the NYPD continued to increase its reliance on racial profiling and stop-and-frisks. In 2009 a Rand study commissioned by the mayor concluded that blacks and Latinos were nine times more likely to be stopped than whites, even though they were less likely to be charged with a crime. While 1.7 percent of whites stopped were found to have a weapon, only 1.1 percent of blacks and Latinos were found with one. Of the more than 575,000 blacks and Latinos stopped, only 762 were found with a gun. A buyback program at several Bronx churches had netted 1,186 guns, a far higher number, without infringing on the civil rights of the innocent.[3] Still, the authors of the study concluded that racial profiling was not responsible for the racial disproportion of those stopped, as crime victims described an even higher disproportion of their suspected assailants as black.

In a follow-up study conducted on behalf of the Center for Constitutional Rights, Jeffrey Fagan rejected Rand's conclusion. Fagan cataloged 2.8 million stop-and-frisks between 2004 and 2009. In almost one-third of those stops, "officers either lacked the kind of suspicion necessary to make a stop constitutional or did not include sufficient detail on police forms to determine if the stops were legally justified."[4] In fact Fagan found "a widespread pattern of unprovoked and unnecessary stops and racial profiling in the department's stop-question-and-frisk policy . . . a crime-fighting strategy the department has put more emphasis on over the years."[5] Between 2004 and 2010 alone police stop-and-frisks rose from 313,000 to more than

570,000, most of which occurred in a select number of poor black and Latino neighborhoods:

> The highest proportion of stops occur within police precincts that cover areas with large numbers of black and Hispanic residents. . . . In the quartile of the city with the highest concentrations of black residents, the police stopped people at a rate two to three times as much per criminal complaint than in the quartile of the precincts with the lowest percentage of black residents. . . . The highest concentration of stops in the city was in a roughly eight-block area of Brownsville, Brooklyn, that was predominately black. Residents there were stopped at a rate 13 times as much as the city average.[6]

Fewer guns were discovered (in 0.15 percent of all stops) than were reported in the Rand study.[7] In addition weapons and other contraband were seized nearly 15 percent less often in stops of blacks than in stops of whites and nearly 23 percent less often in stops of Hispanics.[8] For stops that resulted in some form of sanction, blacks were 31 percent more likely than whites to be arrested than to be issued summonses.[9] Force was 14 percent more likely to be used in stops of blacks and 9.3 percent more likely for Hispanics, compared to stops of white suspects.[10]

In 2011 police violence was spotlighted when NYPD officers attacked a group of mostly white youths calling themselves "Occupy Wall Street." Police commanders on the Brooklyn Bridge were filmed pepper-spraying women demonstrators who had been placed inside a pen. Two months later officers were filmed attacking an encampment of young people in Zuccotti Park at one o'clock in the morning. Brendan Fax, of the mayor's Gay, Lesbian, Bisexual, and Transgender Advisory Council, resigned in fury, calling on other members to do the same: "I no longer wish to associate myself with a police agency that evicts in the dark of night, attacks young men and women with pepper spray and batons, destroying personal property. This is a democracy. This is not community policing."[11]

There was an attempt to exclude journalists from filming the events, but this too backfired. Harry Siegel, a reporter for the *Daily News*, noted that "the city doesn't take actions it is proud of at 1:00 A.M., and with the police literally shoving reporters away from the scene 'to protect members of the press' as Bloomberg insisted. That protection applied to at least six journalists who were arrested and many others who were handled roughly, including myself."[12] Eric Alterman noted that "the first thing the police did was clear out the journalists so that they could not see what was going on, just as they routinely do in totalitarian nations."[13] Andrew Sprung at the blog xpostfactoid defended the journalists in no uncertain terms: "You have a gun. I have a camera. You inflict pain. I inflict infamy. Martyrdom is instantaneous and viral. Bearing witness is the keystone of political action. It can also affect the action directly. You shoot, I tweet."[14]

Robert Gangi, founder of the Police Reform Organizing Project, accused the NYPD of bullying: "They do it because they can. There is not enough political pushback to make them pay a price for their harsh, aggressive tactics."[15] The result is a city without any limits placed on the police. The consequence of this impunity can be seen in a series of major corruption scandals involving the NYPD. First, dozens of police officers in the Bronx were caught fixing tickets for friends and family.[16] Second, seven narcotics officers were found to have planted drugs on innocent people after they had stolen multiple bags of cocaine, which they were trafficking themselves. The *New York Times* characterized the NYPD as "a cowboy culture in which anything goes in the war on drugs."[17] Third, twelve officers were convicted for smuggling a million dollars' worth of firearms, cigarettes, and slot machines. The FBI taped a conversation between an officer and a police informant in which the NYPD officer complained to an ostensible arms buyer that the buyer was not paying enough for the arms: "They're risking a lot for a little . . . they know what's going and what trouble they could get in."[18] At a conference to announce the arrests, the U.S. attorney Preet Bharara could not suppress her shock and dismay: "Arresting fellow law enforcers in a corruption case is a heartbreaking thing. It is our duty to enforce the law and to uphold the rule of law—and to do so perhaps most unflinchingly when we come across people who have chosen to breach that sacred duty, because an officer who betrays his badge betrays every honorable officer as well as every member of the public."[19]

In January 2012 it was revealed that the NYPD had been engaged in massive surveillance of mosques and other locations in Muslim communities, not only in New York but in New Jersey as well. In its 2012 report, the New York Civil Liberties Union found that the NYPD had performed 4,356,927 stops during the ten years of the Bloomberg administration, including 685,724 in 2011 alone.[20] For African American males between the ages of fourteen and twenty-four, the number of stops that year was greater than their number in the population.[21] Moreover more than half of those summarily stopped were also searched. Then on August 12, 2013, the federal judge Shira A. Scheindlin (the same judge who had sentenced Francis X. Livoti to seven years for violating the civil rights of Anthony Baez) ruled that New York's stop-and-frisk program was unconstitutional and violated the Fourteenth Amendment's guarantee of equal protections to blacks and Latinos. She argued that the NYPD had adopted "a policy of indirect racial profiling," stopping blacks and Latinos where they would not have stopped whites.[22] She ordered a number of remedies, including a pilot program for police to wear cameras in five precincts and a federal monitor, but stopped short of ordering an end to the process of stop-and-frisk.

Killings of unarmed black and Latino youths continued through 2013. On February 2, 2013, a Bronx NYPD officer, Richard Haste, chased eighteen-year-old Ramarley Graham into his grandmother's apartment in the Bronx and shot him dead in front of his grandmother and a six-year-old boy when he tried to flush a bag of marijuana down the toilet. Despite months of rallies and vigils, the judge dismissed the indictment against Officer Haste, saying that the D.A. had made an error in his instruction to the grand jury. A second grand jury refused to issue a new indictment. Mass protests outside the Bronx District Attorney's Office ensued. As of August 2013, federal prosecutors were looking into bringing civil rights charges against Haste.

On March 9, 2013, two Brooklyn plainclothes police officers fatally shot sixteen-year-old Kimani Gray in East Flatbush. One witness reported hearing Kimani begging for his life, saying, "Please don't let me die."[23] That evening three hundred people showed up for a vigil; "about a hundred of the younger attendees marched down Church Avenue, some of them smashing windows and tossing garbage cans. . . . At a nearby Rite Aid, looters overturned aisles and struck a customer in the head with a wine bottle."[24] Kimani's mother Jummane Williams tweeted, "I'm in the middle of the riot action at Church and Snyder in my district. The youth in this community have no outlets for their anger."[25] Five days of protests and minor skirmishes were contained within a five-block radius by overwhelming police force, the sealing of the neighborhood to the press, and mass arrests. The families of both Ramarley Graham and Kimani Gray are currently considering civil suits.

In September 2013, Bill (born Warren Wilhelm) de Blasio won the Democratic nomination for mayor. During the primary campaign De Blasio promised to raise taxes on the wealthy, increase services for the poor, construct more affordable housing, improve transportation in the Bronx and Brooklyn, and, most relevant to this study, end NYPD's stop-and-frisk policy and hold violent and racist police officers accountable. He understood personally the harm that racial profiling and police violence inflicted on minority youth, he insisted, as his wife and son are black. In November, De Blasio won a landslide election. In December, however, he appointed William Bratton to be his new police commissioner. Many of those interviewed in this book were among the first to publicly express bafflement and dismay.

National Trends

In 2011 police attacked Occupy Wall Street demonstrators across the country. In Seattle an eighty-four-year-old woman, a pregnant nineteen-year-old, and a priest were all pepper-sprayed, and in Portland police pepper-sprayed a young woman at close range in the face. In Oakland police shot a tear gas canister into the head of an Iraqi war veteran and then shot more at those who ran to his aid. At the University of California, Berkeley, police attacked students with batons and pepper spray. Few scenes were as chilling as the response of campus police at the University of California, Davis, where viral videos showed police officers repeatedly spraying students, who were sitting on campus with arms linked, in the face with military-strength pepper spray as they cried in pain. *New York Times* reporter James Fallow could not resist the parallels to authoritarian regimes in "China or Syria," where if Americans had seen the same event, "we'd think: this is what happens when authority is unaccountable and has lost any sense of human connection to a subject population."[26] One woman who aided the protesters noted that "when you protect the thing that you believe in with your body it changes you for good. It radicalizes you for good."[27]

Killings of blacks and Latinos also intensified. In Los Angeles County alone killings by police officers increased by 70 percent between 2010 and 2011, although homicides had hit a historic low. On July 26, 2012, police in Anaheim, California, fatally shot twenty-five-year-old Manuel Diaz while he was on the ground. This was the sixth shooting and the fifth fatal shooting by Orange County police that year. In the days that followed, police unleashed dogs and fired pepper balls and beanbag and rubber bullets into a crowd of Latino women and children. The youngest victim was a five-year-old shot in the eye. Most protests began peacefully, but skirmishes broke out as several protesters set fires and smashed windows. About 250 police were called in to repress five hundred demonstrators. The police met jeers and stones with more rounds of rubber bullets and pepper balls. The confrontations lasted a week.

Police also contributed to the deaths of blacks and Latinos by not protecting them from vigilante violence or not enforcing laws against those who killed minority youths. The most infamous case took place February 26, 2012, in Sanford, Florida, when George Zimmerman, a neighborhood-watch member, followed a seventeen-year-old black teenager wearing a hoodie to a grocery store, where the teenager bought Skittles and iced tea on his way back from his father's house. Although Zimmerman's mother was Peruvian, Zimmerman decided that a black male wearing a hoodie was exhibiting suspicious behavior. When Zimmerman radioed the police to say that he was following the suspicious black male, the police told him to cease and desist. Nonetheless, after Zimmerman fatally shot the teenager, Trayvon Martin, with a concealed weapon, police officers neither arrested Zimmerman nor protected the crime scene. The district attorney charged Zimmerman with second-degree murder, but lack of evidence from the crime scene left the prosecution woefully ill-prepared to win a conviction from an all-white jury. Peaceful vigils were held across the country, although minor skirmishes broke out in Los Angeles. The NAACP asked for federal intervention, and the Martin family was considering a civil suit against Zimmerman, although Florida's "stand your ground law" makes the evidentiary bar for civil suits high.

Mass Incarceration and the War on Immigrants

In 2009 the meteoric rise in American incarceration rates peaked and began to decline. The Rockefeller Laws mandating long prison terms for first-time drug offenders were eliminated, and solitary confinement may also end soon. Five New York prisons have been closed. On March 17, 2010, the disparity in federal sentencing for possession of crack cocaine versus possession of cocaine was reduced from 100 to 1 to 18 to 1. Then, on August 12, 2013, Attorney General Eric Holder announced that he would no longer charge nonviolent drug offenders with crimes that would subject them to long mandatory sentences. He recommended that federal prosecutors write their criminal complaints "when charging low-level drug offenders [so as] to avoid triggering the mandatory minimum sentences."[28] He also recommended the expansion of prison alternatives, such as probation and house arrest, and shorter sentences for the elderly.

Even with the decline in the rate of incarceration, the reduction of federal sentences for low-level drug offenders, and the elimination of mandatory sentences for first-time drug offenders in New York, it will be a long time before all those unjustly imprisoned are released. It will take far longer to reverse the long-term damage inflicted on poor urban neighborhoods. Over the past thirty years, mass incarceration has transformed a generation of black and Latino men into a permanently disadvantaged population: through loss of human capital (work experience, skills, education), erosion of social ties to legitimate employment, and, most significantly, the stigma that permanently repels employers. In 2005 black men were more likely to go to prison than to finish college, and 60 percent of those who failed to graduate from high school spent some time in prison.[29] Studies have demonstrated that even a short stint in prison reduces wages by 26 percent, annual weeks worked by seven weeks, annual earnings by 42 percent, hourly wage growth by 27 percent, and long job tenure by 34 percent.[30]

By eroding living conditions in poor neighborhoods, sharpening the lines of social exclusion, and destroying families and social networks, mass incarceration rolled back a substantial share of the rights won by the civil rights movement. The impact on black children has been especially insidious. Children of prisoners are 50 percent more likely to go to prison. The trauma of their parents' arrests, often in front of the family members; the absence of their parents; the consequent poverty of their families; the role models that the absent parents present for the children; and the lack of male role models in neighborhoods are all risk factors. In 2000, 1.5 million children had a parent in prison and more than half of those children were black. Seven and a half percent of all black children had a parent in prison.[31]

While the war on drugs has begun to wane, the war on immigrants has intensified. Over a million undocumented immigrants were deported between 2009 and 2012, more than double the rate of the previous administration. Another four hundred thousand are still held in detention camps or jails. Families have been torn apart, and undocumented immigrants have been forced to work at half the minimum wage under dangerous working conditions and with no protections, insurance, or ability to protest. The proliferation of draconian anti-immigrant laws at the state level has intensi-fied the targeting of Latinos. In 2010 Arizona enacted legislation requiring police to stop and detain anyone suspected of being in the country illegally. (The Supreme Court placed limitations on the stops. The police could ask for papers, but only after they had stopped someone for another viola-tion.) One of the authors of the Arizona law explicitly used European anti-immigration laws as a model, praising them in an op-ed that conveniently ignored the riots that such identity checks had provoked.[32] Six states fol-lowed Arizona's precedent. Alabama criminalized aiding or failing to report a possible undocumented immigrant, even if that immigrant was, for exam-ple, a child in school or a patient in a hospital. Many churches protested, pointing out that their soup kitchens would be outlawed. On the anniver-sary of Martin Luther King Jr.'s "I have a dream" speech, civil rights activ-ists and church leaders held a mass demonstration in front of the Capitol in opposition to the law.

Although they have suffered the most, racial minorities have not been the only victims of wars on crime, drugs, welfare, and immigration. As Soss, Fording, and Schram note, "[T]he political spectacle constructed around the underclass served the broader effort, not just by using the deviant poor to legitimate broad themes but also by distracting attention from policy changes that were shifting risks onto the backs of working Americans."[33] Under the guise of a war on crime, and the mantra of personal responsibil-ity, the conservative movement won support from the very people who would suffer most from the restructuring and redeployment of state re-sources away from protecting workers' rights and regulating capital and toward protecting banks and large businesses and enforcing labor disci-pline. As Soss et al. note,

> Welfare investments that shield the poor from market pressures have indeed declined. But these resources and far more are being invested in neoliberal governing strategies: policing, incarceration, and parole supervision; aid made conditional on behavior; social programs that emphasize direction, supervision and penalty; poli-cies that use tax dollars to subsidize labor costs; and a host of efforts to incentivize, enable and enforce the placement of labor on the market.[34]

The social safety net has been shredded, wages have stagnated, and mil-lions of workers have been forced to live on less than half the minimum wage (restaurant workers, immigrants, former prisoners, and those dependent on welfare), while the minimum wage itself dropped from 93 percent to 50 percent of the poverty line between 1968 and 2006.[35] Financial crises, housing foreclosures, staggering student debt, jobless recoveries, and steadily widening income inequality have been the inexorable result.

The Rise and Fall of Sarkozy in France

On April 13, 2012, fifteen men filed suit against Claude Gueant, minister of the interior under President Sarkozy of France. The men claimed that they had been regularly stopped and asked for identity cards because of their race and/or origin. Their lawyer, Slim Ben Achour, said, "What they have in common is that they are all black or Arab or perceived as such and have been stopped by police in recent months." They were targeted, he stated, "not because of what they do, but because of what they are[,] black or Arab." A week later, in the Parisian *banlieue* Noicy-le-Sec, a police officer shot a young black man in the back. The police officer claimed that he had found a fugitive and that the shooting was in self-defense. The homicide in Noicy-le-Sec coincided with the first round of the 2012 presidential race between President Sarkozy and François Hollande, his Socialist rival. Ignoring a report indicating that the bullet had entered the young man's back, Sarkozy and Gueant defended the police officer. One should not "put an offender and a police officer" on equal footing, Gueant proclaimed.

In 2007 Sarkozy's strategy of attacking minority youths had helped him trounce Ségolene Royal; he received 53 percent of the vote to Royal's 44 percent. During the campaign he had boasted, "If you want to hear what I really think of the people I called that, *racaille* [scum] is too affectionate."[36] "If we excuse violence we must expect barbarism," he warned.[37] "We have denatured the Republic by saddling it with egalitarianism, social leveling and charity."[38] Those who did not embrace French identity, he insisted, had no place in the republic.[39] France's wealthiest neighborhoods gave Sarkozy his largest margin of victory. In Paris's swanky sixteenth arrondissement, for example, Sarkozy beat Royal with 64 percent to 11.27 percent of the vote in the first round. Sarkozy defeated Royal with 56 percent to 15.35 percent of the vote in the wealthy seventh arrondissement and with 58 percent to 14 percent in the eighth arrondissement.

In poor minority *banlieues,* however, Sarkozy's campaign floundered. Fierce organizing efforts there increased voter registration by 1.8 million. Leading the get-out-and-vote campaign in the *banlieues* was a new generation of grassroots leaders born in the flames of the 2005 riots. In the department of Seine-Saint-Denis, for example, turnout increased by 20 percent, reaching a record-breaking 85 percent of eligible voters. In Clichy-sous-Bois turnout rose by 30 percent, and twenty-five hundred new voters were added to the electoral rolls. "It's the only thing politicians understand," Samir Mihi (interviewed in Chapter 4) told a reporter. "You can be a French citizen, but if you don't vote, they don't take you into account."[40] "We've been telling people," he told another, "that unless they register to vote no politician will ever give a damn about them. We want people to use the ballot box, not boxes of Molotov cocktails."[41]

Sarkozy's Presidency

From the moment of his 2007 victory, Sarkozy's presidency was marked by racial tension. That same evening young people in Paris took to the streets in protest. They clashed with police, set 730 cars aflame, and injured 78 officers. A total of 592 youths were taken into custody. The following night hundreds more marched through the streets, some breaking shop windows and building flaming barricades. If Chirac's government, in the wake of Jean-Marie Le Pen's impressive showing, had assembled a cabinet of harsh punitive ministers, Sarkozy used his cabinet as a battering ram. He named Rachida Dati, a Moroccan woman, as minister of justice. Dati offered Sarkozy cover for his increasingly punitive policies targeting North African youths.

Dati began by questioning a long-standing legal precedent that children lacked the maturity to fully understand the consequences of their acts. Children as young as ten, she claimed, should be held legally and criminally responsible for their actions. Right-wing members of the house pushed for new rules including minimum mandatory sentences and, "for the first time in modern French law, suspended the automatic application of the excuse of minority for sixteen to eighteen year olds and mandated prison for a range of offenses."[42] Eight thousand French judges reacted with alarm, signing a petition that read as follows:

> In the text of the proposed law the theft of a cell phone, committed after two prior infractions, mandates a two-year prison sentence.

This will produce an increase in the number of teenagers in prison. . . . Most have been out of school since the age of fourteen, have no skills and cannot get jobs. Perceiving themselves as useless, humiliated by repeated failures, they "hang out," get into trouble, and commit most of their offenses in groups. Are these the teenagers who will be singled out and treated as adults? Are these the teenagers for whom France will abandon every effort at rehabilitation?[43]

Another draconian measure, the so-called *sûreté* law, allowed judges to extend the sentence of a convicted criminal beyond his original sentence if a judge concluded that he still posed a risk to society.[44]

Within six months of Sarkozy's inauguration riots, Villiers-le-Bel burst into flames when two police officers engaged in a high-speed pursuit of two teenagers on a mini-bike and hit and killed them both. Neighborhood youths claimed that officers had previously threatened the two boys, fifteen-year-old Moushin and sixteen-year-old Larami. Finding themselves surrounded by angry neighbors, the two officers radioed for reinforcements. When the extra officers arrived, a confrontation ensued between the police and close to a hundred young people. The police used tear gas, and the youths responded with stones and garbage and then set cars and local buildings on fire, including the library, the post office, and the police station. One young man held a poster of the two dead boys that read, "25/11/07: Dead for nothing." The riots then spread to Sarcelles, Garges-lès-Gonesse, Cergy, Ermont, and Goussainville. Val-d'Oise burned for two days.

Sarkozy was not above making use of military displays of force to bolster his sagging popularity. In February 2008 a squad of one thousand helmeted and heavily armored officers (accompanied by television cameras and crews) stormed Villiers-le-Bel at dawn, breaking down doors (avoiding the inconvenience of ringing the bells), petrifying small children, and dragging off thirty-seven youths accused of having thrown stones on the day of the riots. Fassin notes:

The disproportionate means used, given the routine nature of the arrests to be made, and the ensuing media spectacle appeared to be aimed less at protecting the police than at producing the dual effect of terrorizing the residents of these neighborhoods by exerting a show of force as they were placed in a state of siege, if for only a few hours, on the one hand, and impressing the mainstream population, who was given to assume that only a quasi-military expedition was capable of reestablishing the authority of the state in territories that threatened to escape it, on the other hand.[45]

Three years later, on April 20, 2010, in Seine-Saint-Denis, Sarkozy promised to fight a "battle without mercy. . . . No district, no neighborhood, no hallway in any building will escape the authority of the law."[46] The occasion was the promotion of Christian Lambert, who headed the Brigade anti-criminalité (BAC) in Seine-Saint-Denis at the time the three teenagers were chased into the electric grid in Clichy-sous-Bois. Sarkozy also promised ever tougher new measures, including the following: a) a slash in benefits to families whose children repeatedly played truant; b) an increase in the deportation of illegal immigrants; and c) a new police unit committed to the discipline of young people under sixteen whose behavior caused problems at school.[47]

In July of that year police fatally shot a young North African man suspected of robbing a casino. Once again the incident sparked two days of riots. Outside Saint-Aignan in southern France, police fatally shot a migrant Roma worker. Again a riot ensued. Sarkozy responded by ordering the Roma encampments obliterated and Roma deported, thereby ignoring European Union statutes recognizing Roma as Europeans legally allowed to settle anywhere inside EU borders. He also announced that any foreign-born French citizen who attacked a police officer would have his or her citizenship stripped and would subsequently be deported: "When one fires upon an agent representing the forces of order, one no longer deserves to be French."[48] This was a violation of centuries of French law and implied a distinction between those born in France and those who acquired citizenship through naturalization.

In contrast to the punitive actions taken against minority youths, "the prevailing mood among police officers," an Amnesty International report noted, was "one of impunity."[49] The main obstacle to combating it, according to a United Nations special rapporteur, was "the conflict of interest inherent in having the same institutions responsible for investigation and prosecution of ordinary law-breaking being also responsible for the same functions in respect of law-breaking by members of those very institutions."[50] As in the United States, attacks on racial minorities were followed by attacks on a wide range of social protections. In September 2010 Sarkozy faced a torrent of protest when he proposed a measure that would increase the retirement age by two years, to sixty-two (after three years of slashing taxes on the wealthy). Four general strikes that were called between September and October of that year began peacefully but grew increasingly violent by October 10. As one journalist observed, "With the support of only 29 percent of the population according to the latest opinion polls and six weeks of strikes and public demonstrations mobilizing millions of people throughout France, hostility to the reform clearly qualifies as the greatest French revolt since the student riots of May 1968."[51]

"In France, we have a big problem with inequality and those of us on the bottom are sick and tired of taking the hit, while those on high get off scot-free," said Pascale Thierse, a teacher. "With this reform the bottom is again getting swindled, while the richest keep getting tax rebates and the like."[52] Over 70 percent of the population expressed support for the strikers in opposition to the government, according to a poll conducted by Le Parisian.[53] At the time nationwide fuel shortages shut schools and oil refineries and virtually paralyzed traffic throughout France. A quarter of the nation's gas stations were closed due to shortages of petrol and supplies. The main airport outside Paris, Charles de Gaulle, cancelled 30 percent of its flights, and the smaller Paris Orly cancelled 50 percent. By evening bus and train drivers had paralyzed the country's high-speed TGV trains.[54] Militant oil refinery workers formed a human chain to prevent strikebreakers from entering a plant at Grandpuits, east of Paris, and Jean-Louis Schilansky, president of the Petrol Industries Association, warned that the alliance of refinery workers and truckers would cause "a very big problem."[55]

On October 20, millions marched through Paris, Marseille, and Lyon. By evening, mass labor protests had given way to student protests. Students occupied schools, universities, and the streets of Paris. The protests were especially fierce in Nanterre, where radical young people from the schools and banlieues joined forces and were met with a hail of rubber bullets and tear gas. The following day the UMP rammed a bill raising the retirement age through Congress, forcing an end to thirty days of demonstrations. But that was not the end of Sarkozy's woes. First, Sarkozy's low popularity was reflected in the cantonal election results in March 2011. In the first round, Sarkozy's UMP ran neck and neck with the National Front, with 16.97 percent against 15.06 percent of the vote. The Socialists easily defeated the UMP with 24 percent of the vote. In the second round a coalition of left-wing parties defeated the governing coalition by 54 percent to 35 percent, routing the UMP from most cantons. The National Front, under Marine Le Pen's leadership, rebounded from its 2007 low, winning 11.57 percent on the average but as much as 20 percent in some regions, such as the northern working-class town of Lille.

Second, a series of scandals came to light implicating the hard-line minister of the interior Brice Hortefaux and several members of his staff (including his chief of staff) from his time as minister of economics under Edoard Balladur. These scandals involved kickbacks and illegal payments to third parties on arms deals—one of which apparently triggered a terrorist attack on French citizens in Pakistan when Chirac called a halt to the illegal payments. President Sarkozy could not be charged, but it did not escape anyone's attention that as minister of finance during the period in which these illicit dealings began, he had to have been aware of such multi-million-dollar deals.

Third, in July 2011 the *cour de comptes* (court of assessment, a quasi-judicial body charged with financial and legislative audits of the government) issued a scathing 250-page analysis of Sarkozy's security policies and his management of some 160,000 police and gendarmes.[56] Attacking Sarkozy's "culture of numbers," the court argued that Sarkozy's goal was not to improve actual performance but rather to give the appearance of fighting crime.[57] Security for the average citizen had declined: between 2002 and 2011, the period in which Sarkozy was either minister of the interior or president, the number of crimes of lesser severity had fallen, but crimes of greater seriousness had increased. Property crimes declined by 28.6 percent, for instance, while violence against persons increased by 21.2 percent.[58]

To meet arrest quotas, police officers had targeted *banlieue* youths for possession of small quantities of cannabis;[59] arrests for cannabis use increased by 76 percent during Sarkozy's presidency. Arrests for selling small amounts of cannabis increased by 30 percent during the same period, while arrests for trafficking (again mostly in cannabis) increased by only 8 percent.[60] Clearance rates for the most serious crimes, in contrast, barely hit 10 percent. Instead of improving their clearance rate, police beefed up their arrest numbers by charging *banlieue* youths with additional crimes including insulting a police officer or resisting arrest, according to two studies conducted in the Bobigny court (for crimes committed in the *banlieues* of Seine-Saint-Denis. One study found that two-thirds of youthful defendants had been accused of either vandalism or insulting the police, and half of those cases were dismissed for lack of evidence. A second study found that over a third of adults arrested for "offenses against persons holding public authority" or property crimes were acquitted of all charges due to the lack of evidence against them.[61] The reason for the low conviction rate was similar to that of the NYPD under Giuliani. The police were being rewarded for high arrest rates even if the charges did not stick or were based on "contradictory testimony, flagrant lies and flimsy arguments."[62]

Arab and black youths constituted the vast majority of rebellion, insult, and resistance cases. In 40 percent of these cases tried in Bobigny, the defendants claimed that police had beaten them (often to provoke a resistance charge).[63] Fassin cites one case in which a young Arab man was beaten with an iron pipe by a white youth (who had accused him of insulting his girlfriend). When the police arrived, all parties declined to press charges. The Arab youth, who had been calm and respectful, despite a mark on his head from the pipe, ended up in the precinct, "half-naked and handcuffed to the bench reserved for those under questioning."[64] He was later released without charges, but not before the officer filed a report on him as a perpetrator of *intentional violence*. The victim was electronically recorded as an offender.[65] Fassin later checked the local Reported Offense Processing System and Canonge databases and found that ten times as many individuals with the first name Mohammed, the most common Arab name, were charged with crimes as those with the first name Pierre, the most common French name.[66]

Not only were police in high crime areas failing to clear most serious crimes, but police were being deployed disproportionately to small towns and wealthy neighborhoods, giving residents the misleading impression that Sarkozy had beefed up security. Marseille, for instance, was assigned the fewest police officers despite its high levels of organized crime and illicit traffic. (The court's report confirms the concerns of those who told me that police never entered Marseille's northern reaches.) Similarly the department of Seine-Saint-Denis was allocated only 55 police officers, while the sparsely populated, low-crime Rhone was rewarded with 155 police officers.[67] Small, relatively crime-free towns were given 1 police officer for every 200 people, and poor urban neighborhoods such as Seine-Saint-Denis were assigned 1 for every 500 people. In addition the least experienced officers were deployed in the poorest *banlieues*.[68]

The *cour de comptes* also criticized Sarkozy's budget-cutting measures, in particular his reliance on municipal police (who depended on the resources of the localities in which they were hired rather than national funds), and his extensive use of video surveillance, an expensive tool that could not compensate for the downsizing of both police and gendarmes. Sarkozy vigorously rejected the charges, accusing the court of being politically motivated. The *cour de comptes*, however, is one of the most reputable and venerated agencies of government, and the report was based on a decade of research, most of which was undertaken by the previous, conservative director of the court. Sarkozy's defensiveness did not boost his standing in France.

As the 2012 elections approached, security took a backseat to economic matters. Angela Merkel campaigned for Sarkozy during her trip to France, unintentionally boosting Hollande's popularity. Hollande mistakenly claimed that he would tax the rich 75 percent, and the mistake also resounded in his favor. In March, however, several incidents put security back on the agenda. First, a young French Algerian man shot to death three Maghrébin soldiers and then burst into a Jewish school, killing the rabbi and three children ages two, six, and eleven. Marine Le Pen reaped the benefit.

In the first round of the presidential race, François Hollande pulled 28 percent of the vote, Sarkozy followed with 27 percent, and Marine Le Pen (the daughter of Jean-Marie Le Pen) boasted a respectable 18 percent, evidence that a large swath of the French electorate was still mobilized by anti-immigrant and anti-Muslim rhetoric. Marine Le Pen beat her father's 2002 showing by distancing herself from the National Front's association with the German occupation. She claimed that unlike her father she had no animus toward Jews and went so far as to meet with Israeli leaders in New York. She singled out the Muslims for reprobation, something that resonated with a substantial portion of the French electorate.

Sarkozy's attempt to win over Le Pen voters in the second round by attacking Muslims and immigrants and calling for a return to France's Christian roots backfired. First, it convinced François Bayrou, a centrist free-market candidate, to endorse Hollande. Second, while the large *banlieue* turnout was not enough to defeat Sarkozy in 2007, in 2012 it gave Hollande the election. In Seine-Saint-Denis, for instance, where three of the neighborhoods I studied were located, Hollande's margin of victory was 72.07 percent to 27.93 percent. Hollande's landslide in poor *banlieues* was enough to put him over the top. In the second round of the general election, Hollande beat Sarkozy 51.6 percent to 48.4 percent. It was the first time since 1981 that a sitting president had failed to win a second term and a Socialist had assumed the presidency. Moreover, in parliamentary elections the following month, the Socialists won a clear majority. Gueant was among those who lost their seats in parliament. Marine Le Pen also failed to win a parliamentary seat, although Jean-Marie Le Pen's granddaughter Marion Maréchal Le Pen won a seat, making her France's youngest parliamentarian.

Ipsos polls following the election were revealing.[69] Sarkozy won approval from 35 percent of those who placed immigration as one of their three main concerns. Le Pen won approval from 62 percent of this group, while Hollande won only 4 percent, and the left-wing candidate Mélenchon won 3 percent.[70] Similarly, Sarkozy won approval from 28 percent of those who listed insecurity (law and order) as one of their main three concerns. Le Pen won approval from 44 percent of those voters, and Hollande and Mélenchon won 7 and 3 percent respectively.[71]

The situation was reversed for those who listed social inequality as among their main three concerns. Fifty percent of these voters chose the left-wing candidate Mélenchon, 38 percent Hollande, 15 percent Le Pen, and only 7 percent chose Sarkozy.[72] The results from voters choosing unemployment as one of their three main concerns were similar, with 42 percent giving their support to Mélenchon, 40 percent to Hollande, 23 percent to Sarkozy, and 21 percent to Le Pen.[73] Purchasing power was also a main concern of most voters. Here Mélenchon led with 55 percent, followed by Hollande with 54 percent, Le Pen with 43 percent, and Sarkozy trailing with 39 percent.[74]

Hollande's first cabinet reflected his debt to Bayrou, however, rather than to the residents of the *banlieues*. His most revealing choices in this regard were those of the budget-conscious Pierre Moscovici as minister of finance and the security hard-liner Manuel Valls as minister of the interior in charge of police. The appointment of Manuel Valls was particularly disappointing to immigrants and residents of the *banlieues*. Residents feared that positions on both crime and immigration were considered to be as hard-line and racially biased as those of Sarkozy. Evidence that these fears were justified was not long in coming. On October 17, 2013, protests spread through 30 high schools in France after a 15-year-old Roma secondary student, Leonarda Dibrani, was arrested during a class picnic and deported to Kosovo along with her five siblings and parents. She had never set foot in the country and did not speak the language. The expulsion was part of the

Valls promise to expel 20,000 Roma, in direct violation of EU directive. Students were also incensed over the deportation of an Armenian high school student the previous week.[75]

Policing the Poor

Most police believe that they have been given a raw deal and have been unfairly blamed for policies that are not of their own making. They are pressured to deal harshly with ethnic and racial minorities and then treated with contempt when they do, even by a public they risk their lives to defend. A shared sense of injustice increases solidarity and a desire to protect their own. Behind the infamous blue wall of silence is a powerful esprit de corps. As one police officer commented, "It is only the other officers that make this job bearable. You know they will be there to watch your back." But this strong feeling of belonging is matched by an equally strong contempt for the communities they are theoretically supposed to serve.

Because police feel undervalued, they embrace law-and-order politicians who defend them from accusations of brutality, praise their performance, and promise to increase their budget. But the price of that support is high. Police answer to police chiefs, who answer to mayors and prosecutors (or in the French case the minister of the interior and the president), who are elected by voters with little stake in the system. As William Stuntz observes, "Voters, for whom crime is usually a minor issue[,] exercise more power over criminal justice. . . . Far from hindering discrimination[,] current law makes discrimination easy. . . . Today, the equal protection guarantee is all but meaningless when applied to criminal law enforcement, one reason why both drug enforcement and enforcement of laws banning violent felonies are so different in black communities than white ones. . . . discretionary power is exercised differently in poor neighborhoods than in wealthier urban and suburban communities."[76]

Residents of poor minority neighborhoods are consequently less willing to provide police the kind of information critical to their work and to the safety of the officers involved. As one NYPD officer told me, "They hate us." The sharper the boundary between police and neighborhoods, the more likely police are to either abuse residents or defend other officers who do so. It is a vicious circle. Racial categories are deeply embedded in police culture and practices, but they are also a fundamental feature of the societies in which police work. Wars on crime put intense pressure on police to show results, measured in quantities of arrests. The politicization of crime control and the system of incentives and penalties in most police departments make racial-category work inevitable.

Riots in Comparative Perspective

In poor minority neighborhoods, but rarely in wealthy neighborhoods, police use violence as a means of intimidation and control. In so doing they sharpen the boundary lines between such communities and the nation at large. Police, as Michael Lipsky observes, represent "government to the people"; their actions influence citizens' perception of the state and their relationship to it.[77] When police engage in violent or indiscriminate attacks on members of minority communities, they polarize social relationships and delegitimize the state. As Mohammed and Mucchielli note, "[T]he very forces charged with reducing insecurity have paradoxically contributed to amplifying it."[78]

In Marseille, a city with extreme poverty and inequality, the willingness of the political elite to recognize minority groups has deactivated racial boundaries. That does not mean that political leaders addressed fundamental inequities or pursued policies to reduce misery and exploitation. Instead, conflict was allayed when political leaders and police consulted with groups representing the aggrieved. Even political machines and mafias, by incorporating poor minority residents into the bottom rungs of their weblike structures, reduced racial polarization, if at the cost of unchecked criminal violence and homicide. Major drug dealers enforced peace, as the French intelligence service reported, because "big dealers did not want trouble in their areas. This may be why Marseille remained riot-free."[79] In contrast, the scandals that have dislodged the most corrupt politicians and led to the arrest of mafia leaders have sparked a violent conflagration for control of the illicit trade, at least for the time being.

Social-movement organizations have a dampening effect on urban unrest. The presence of "disciplined organizations" and "trusted leaders from whom to take guidance" help participants engage in those forms of struggle more likely to succeed, Kurt Weyland notes in his comparison of the Arab

Spring and Latin American anti-dictatorship struggles. In contrast, "[t]he shift to all out confrontation is typical of unorganized contention, which is difficult to sustain over the medium and long run. Once amorphous crowds have started a challenge and encountered resistance they have every incentive to push hard for an immediate victory. . . . Unorganized contention oscillates with particularly high amplitude."[80]

In New York organizations involved with fighting police violence and pursuing justice for victims have developed a standard collective action repertoire. After each police killing, they offer solace to the family. They mobilize mass marches and nonviolent civil disobedience. They try to convince district attorneys to indict, and when that fails, they petition the Justice Department to pursue violations of civil rights charges against the offending officers. They help families find lawyers to pursue civil suits. Only when the injustice is so egregious and irremediable that no other path remains do riots still erupt. That does not mean that social movements are always effective vehicles for social change. Despite the fact that almost every family I interviewed believed that when they marched for justice for their own child, their efforts would lead to greater police accountability in general, their success in the latter arena was quite abysmal. Even so, the possibility of justice was enough to diffuse potentially explosive situations.

A cursory look at a number of recent riots outside of France and the United States suggests that this model may have wider application. While riots have become less common in the United States during the past thirty years, they have grown more common in many European countries. In Great Britain (2011) and Sweden (2013) riots erupted after familiar processes. First, political candidates played to racial fears, inspiring competitive outbidding. Second, in both cases, following elections of conservative leaders, police violence intensified. Third, police killed unarmed members of stigmatized minorities (a black in Great Britain and an immigrant in Sweden), and the government took no action against the police officers involved.

In 2010, David Cameron and the Conservatives came to power in coalition with the Liberal-Democrats, defeating the Labour Party in Great Britain. Within months of his victory, Cameron had cut funds to schools and social programs and intensified the policing of immigrant and minority neighborhoods. On August 6, 2011, riots exploded after police fatally shot Mark Duggan, a black man, as he exited his minivan. Family, friends, and neighbors marched to the police station, called for justice, and demanded that a senior police officer speak with them. When their demands were rejected, several youths began to throw bottles, stones, and garbage at the police. Soon flames rose from empty buildings, windows exploded, and glass rained down on residents as they raced to save their cars. "Pitched battle between lines of riot police officers, some on horses, and hundreds of mostly young black men, in small gangs of four or five," ensued.[81] One young man demanded of a journalist, "How many black people have to die around here? I hate the police."[82] The riots spread to major cities in the United Kingdom and raged for five days.

Similarly in Sweden racially targeted police violence intensified in the years following the election of twenty members of the far-right anti-immigrant Swedish Democrat Party to parliament. During the campaign the mainstream Liberal Party increased its anti-immigrant and anti-Muslim rhetoric. Then on May 21, 2013, Swedish police shot and killed a sixty-nine-year-old immigrant man carrying a knife. Riots began in Husby, a predominantly immigrant area in the northwest suburbs of Stockholm, and spread rapidly to other immigrant suburbs. Youths pelted police with stones and set cars and buildings aflame. The founder of a local youth group told journalists that the riots were a reaction to "police brutality."[83] Rami al-Khamisi, a law student and founder of the youth organization Megafonen, told journalists that he had been racially insulted by police. Black teenagers, he said, had been called "monkeys."[84] A graduate student of African descent told me in an e-mail in 2013 that young people were fed up with police violence and discrimination. A French rapper got it right, she said: "If you are Arab or black it does not matter how long you have lived in Sweden."

Activated categorical boundaries are not always racial. In Athens, Greece, riots erupted in 2010 after police shot an anarchist youth. Riots do not only erupt in stable democratic countries. Police violence triggered a wave of riots in Tunisia in December 2010, for instance, opening opportunities for opposition organizations to press for a transition to democratic rule. In Guadeloupe (2009) police violence triggered riots against colonial French rulers, while in Egypt (2011, 2013), Spain (2011–12), Chile (2011–13), Turkey (2013), and Brazil (2013) police violence increased levels of nonviolent forms of contention, accompanied at times by more unorganized and occasionally violent riots.

Alternative Policing Strategies

It is possible to be an effective police force without activating racial boundaries, killing minority youths, or inciting riots. Some police departments have begun to emphasize problem-solving policing, working with communities to resolve critical community problems. Some officers have concluded that targeting poor minorities for minor nonviolent crimes and remaining silent when other officers use violence and humiliation as means of intimidation and control make police work more dangerous. Community residents are more likely to help police when they believe that the police care about them. Good police work depends on good information.

In both Paris and New York one of the most common complaints is that police act differently in poor minority neighborhoods from the way they do in middle-class white neighborhoods. As Ron Hampton, the president of the National Black Police Association, noted, "[T]he police think the main ingredient of being a criminal is being black. The police working in black communities don't know that part of their job is protecting people's civil rights. They know that when they are working in a white community." Stigmatized minorities see "too little of the kinds of policing and criminal punishments that do the most good and too much of the kinds that do the most harm," Stuntz cogently observes.[85] Many minority women are afraid to call the police when they are victimized. One Muslim woman outside Paris told me about a friend who had reported her car stolen. The woman was beaten by police and threatened with arrest when she went to the station to file the complaint. Kadatou Diallo told me of a friend, a mother whose son was shot and killed by police in her own home after she had called them for help. Allene Person told me how vulnerable she felt knowing that she could not call the police when she needed help.

Violent, race-biased policing sends the message to members of subjugated minorities that they are not equal members of the national community. Such policing undermines democratic governance by "contradicting faith in the principles of justice and equal protection[,] . . . exposing and deepening the racial fault lines that continue to weaken the country and belying its promise as a land of equal opportunity, and it undermines faith among all races in the fairness and efficacy of the criminal justice system."[86]

Police are not independent actors. They carry out the directives of the state and its more powerful constituents. "To the extent that the threats against which a given government protects its citizens are imaginary or are consequences of its own activities," notes Charles Tilly, "the government has organized a protection racket."[87] Elections that are won by creating fear of one category of citizens or residents are such cases. "Created by the wars that required it, the machine now creates the wars it require[s]."[88] As long as politicians win elections by playing to racial fears and voters support candidates who attack racial and ethnic minorities in the name of security, racially targeted police violence will prevail. Where social movement organizations are weak and courts are closed to racial minorities, riots may burst forth.

Notes

Introduction

1. Ben W. Gilbert, *Ten Blocks from the White House: Anatomy of the Washington Riots of 1968* (New York: Praeger, 1968), 1.

2. Marilyn S. Johnson, *Street Justice: A History of Police Violence in New York City* (Boston: Beacon Press, 2003), 235.

3. Hugh Davis Graham, "On Riots and Riot Commissions: Civil Disorders in the 1960s," *Public Historian* 2, no. 4 (1980): 12.

4. The literal translation from the French is "their skins are not worth anything anymore." Jean-Pierre Mignard and Emmauel Tordijman, *L'Affaire Clichy: Morts pour rien* (Paris: Stock, 2006), 105.

5. Molly Moore, "France to End State of Emergency: Violence Has Subsided Since Youth Riots Forced Measures," *Washington Post*, January 4, 2006, A13.

6. Michael Katz, "Why Aren't U.S. Cities Burning?," *Dissent* 54, no. 3, summer (2007): 23.

7. Interview with Roey Cohen, "Word Power," *Haaretz*, December 8,2005, http://www.haaretz.com/news/word-power-1.176149.

8. Charles Tilly, *The Politics of Collective Violence* (Cambridge: Cambridge University Press, 2003), 21. Tilly defines activation as "a shift in social interactions such that they a) increasingly organize around a single us/them boundary and b) differentiate between within-boundary and cross boundary interactions."

9. Eric Wolf, *Envisioning Power: Ideologies of Dominance and Crisis* (Berkeley: University of California Press, 1999), 273.

10. Adolph Reed Jr., "Marx, Race and Neoliberalism," *New Labor Forum* 22, no. 1 (2013): 49.

11. Tilly, *The Politics of Collective Violence*, 10.

12. Reed, "Marx, Race and Neoliberalism," 49.

13. Anibal Quijano, "'Raza,' 'etnia,' 'nación' en Mariategui: Cuestiones abiertas," in *Jose Carlos Mariategui y Europa: El otro aspecto de descubrimiento*, ed. R. Forgues (Lima, Peru: Empresa Editora Aumata, S.A., 1993), 167–69; Ramon Grosfoguel and Chloe S. Georas, "'Coloniality of Power' and Racial Dynamics: Toward a Reinterpretation of Latino Caribbeans in New York City," *Identities* 7, no. 1 (2000): 96.

14. Charles Tilly, *Durable Inequality* (Berkeley: University of California Press, 1998), 88–89.

15. Ibid., 71–72.

16. David Theo Goldberg, ed., *Anatomy of Racism* (Minneapolis: University of Minnesota Press, 1990), xii.

17. Anthony Marx, "Contested Citizenship: The Dynamics of Racial Identity and Social Movements," *International Review of Social History* 40, supplement S3 (December 1995): 159.

18. Niall O Dochartaigh and Lorenzo Bosi, "Territoriality and Mobilization: The Civil Rights Campaign in Northern Ireland," *Mobilization* 15, no. 4 (2010): 408.

19. Sebastien Roché, *Le frisson de l'émeute* (Paris: Seuil, 2006), 104.

20. David Jacobs and Robert M. O'Brian, "The Determinants of Deadly Forces: A Structural Analysis of Police Violence," *American Journal of Sociology* 103, no. 4 (1998): 844.

21. Clifford Rosenberg, *Policing Paris: The Origins of Modern Immigration Control Between Wars* (Ithaca, N.Y.: Cornell University Press, 2006), 40.

22. Cited in ibid., 148. See also Chautemps, AN F7 13, 412, quoted in Faithi Bentabet and Catherine Rodier Bentabet, "L'immigration Algériérienne et l'hôpital Franco Musulman dans la région Parisienne entre les deux guerres, 1915–1947" (matrîse, Université de Paris I, 1981), 40.

23. Simon Holdaway, "Constructing and Sustaining 'Race' Within the Police Force," *British Journal of Sociology* 48, no. 1 (1997): 24.

24. Jeffrey A. Fagan, Amanda Geller, Garth Davies, and Valerie West, "Street Stops and Broken Windows Revisited: The Demography and Logic of Proactive Policing in a Safe and Changing City," in *Race, Ethnicity and Policing: Essential Readings*, ed. Stephen K. Rice and Michael D. White (New York: New York University Press, 2010), 312.

25. Ó Dochartaigh and Bosi, "Territoriality and Mobilization," 108. See also Robert D. Sack, *Human Territoriality: Its Theory and History* (New York: Cambridge University Press, 1986).

26. Tilly, *Durable Inequality*, 86.

27. Didier Fassin, *Enforcing Order: An Ethnography of Urban Policing* (Boston: Polity Press, 2013), 158 (translated from the original French, Didier Fassin, *La Force de L'ordre: Une anthropologie de la police des quartiers* [Paris: Seuil, 2011]).

28. French police officer interviewed in March 2001. It is noteworthy that I conducted this interview five years before the riots and six months before the 9/11 attacks in New York and Washington, D.C.

29. Pieter Spierenburg, *Spectacle of Suffering* (Cambridge: Cambridge University Press, 1984), 2.

30. Paul Chevigny, *Edge of the Knife: Police Violence in the Americas* (New York: New Press, distributed by Norton, 1995), 12.

31. Fassin, *Enforcing Order*, 134–35.

32. Donatella Della Porta and Herbert Reiter, *Policing Protest: The Control of Mass Demonstrations in Western Democracies*, vol. 6, *Social Movements, Protest, and Contention* (Minneapolis: University of Minnesota Press, 1998), 9.

33. Fassin, *Enforcing Order*, xvii.

34. Kerner Commission, "The 1968 Report of the National Advisory on Civil Disorders" (1968), 1.

35. Ibid., 6.

36. Ibid., 1.

37. Ibid., 7–8.

38. Susan Olzak, Suzanne Shanahan, and Elizabeth H. McEaney, "Poverty, Segregation and Race Riots: 1960–1993," *American Journal of Sociology* 61, no. 4 (1996): 590–613.

39. Ibid.

40. Stanley Lieberson and Arnold Silverman, "The Precipitants and Underlying Conditions of Race Riots," *American Sociological Review* 30, no. 6 (1965): 897.

41. Ibid., 895–96.

42. Ibid.

43. Harlan Hahn and Joe T. Feagan, "Riot-Precipitating Police Practices: Attitudes in Urban Ghettos," *Phylon* 31, no. 2 (1970): 183–86.

44. Robert Fogelson, "From Resentment to Confrontation: The Police, the Negroes and the Outbreak of the Nineteen-Sixties Riots," *Political Science Quarterly* 83, no. 2 (1968): 86.

45. Edward H. Ransford, "Isolation, Powerlessness and Violence: A Study of Attitudes and Participation in the Watts Riot," *American Journal of Sociology* 73, no. 5 (1968): 583.

46. Melvin Seeman, "The Signals of '68: Alienation in Pre-Crisis France," *American Sociological Review* 37, no. 4 (1972): 401.

47. Lord Scarman, *The Scarman Report: The Brixton Disorders, 10–12 April 1981* (London: Penguin, 1986), 78.

48. "Race Riots Not New to Britain," CNN.com/World, July 10, 2001, http://edition.cnn.com/2001/WORLD/europe/UK/07/09/riot.timeline/.

49. David Waddington, *Policing Public Disorder: Theory and Practice* (Collumpton, Devon: Willan Publishing, 2007), 49–59; see also David Waddington, "Applying the Flashpoints Model of Public Disorder to the 2001 Bradford Riot," *British Journal of Criminology* 50, no. 2 (2010): 342–59.

50. Clive Norris, Nigel Fielding, Charles Kemp, and Jane Fielding, "Black and Blue: An Analysis of the Influence of Race on Being Stopped by the Police," *British Journal of Sociology* 43, no. 2 June (1992): 207–24.

51. Ibid.

52. Holdaway, "Constructing and Sustaining 'Race' within the Police Workforce," *British Journal of Sociology* 48, no. 1 (March 1997): 26.

53. Robert Reiner, "Police Research in the United Kingdom: A Critical Review," *Crime and Justice* 15, Modern Policing (1992): 490–91.

54. Hugues Lagrange, "Socialisation des adolescents et délinquance: Les enfants issus des familles Africaines noires" (paper presented at the Migration and Policing Conference, Maison Science de l'Homme, Paris, France, June 9, 2006).

55. Fabien Jobard, "Rioting as a Political Tool: The 2005 Riots in France," *Howard Journal* 48, no. 3 (2009): 235–44; Fabien Jobard, "The 2005 French Urban Unrests: Data-Based Interpretations," *Sociology Compass 24* 2, no. 4 (2008): 1–13.

56. Jobard, "Rioting as a Political Tool," 237.

57. Ibid., 239.

58. Fabien Jobard, "Police, justice et discriminations raciales," in *De la question social à la question raciale? Représenter a Société Française*, ed. Didier Fassin and Éric Fassin (Paris: La Découverte, 2006), 221.

59. Fabien Jobard and René Lévy, *Profiling Minorities: The Study of Stop and Search Practices in Paris* (New York: Open Society Institute, 2009), 9.

60. Didier Lapeyronnie, "Révolte primitive dans les banlieues françaises: Essaie sur les émeutes de l'automne 2005," *Déviance et société* 30, no. 4 (2006): 431–48.

61. Robert E. Park, "The City: Suggestions for the Investigation of Human Behavior in the City Environment," *American Journal of Sociology* 20 (1915): 608; Nicole P. Marwell, *Bargaining for Brooklyn: Community Organizations in the Entrepreneurial City* (Chicago: University of Chicago Press, 2007), 15.

62. Marwell, *Bargaining for Brooklyn*, 17.

63. Didier Lapeyronnie, "L'ordre de l'informe," *Eurozine* 36 (2001): 7, http://www.eurozine.com/pdf/2001-06-28-lapeyronnie-fr.pdf.

64. Didier Lapeyronnie, *Ghetto urbain: Ségrégation, violence, pauvreté en France aujourd'hui* (Paris: Laffont, 2008); Lapeyronnie, "Révolte primitive."

65. Lapeyronnie, *Ghetto urbain*.

66. Lapeyronnie, "Révolte primitive," 439.

67. Sack, *Human Territoriality*, 32.

68. Elizabeth Jean Wood, *Insurgent Collective Action and Civil War in El Salvador* (Cambridge: Cambridge University Press, 2003), 19.

69. Michel Kokoreff, *Sociologie des émeutes* (Paris: Parot, 2008), 208.

70. Sophie Body-Gendrot, "Police Marginality, Racial Logics and Discrimination in the Banlieues of France," *Ethnic and Racial Studies* 33, no. 4 (2010): 659.

71. Ibid., 663.

72. Roché, *Le frisson de l'émeute*, 110.

73. Laurent Bonelli, *La France a peur* (Paris: La Découverte, 2008); Farhad Khosrokhavar, *L'Islam dans les prisons* (Paris: Éditions Balland, 2004); Marwan Mohammed and Laurent Mucchielli, "La police dans les 'quartiers sensibles': Un profond malaise," in *Quand les banlieues brûlent*, ed. Laurent Mucchielli and Véronique Le Goaziou (Paris: La Découverte, 2006); Laurent Mucchielli and Véronique Le Goaziou, *Quand les banlieues brûlent* (Paris: La Découverte, 2006); Laurent Mucchielli and Christian

Mouhanna, "Rapport de la cour des comptes sur la politique de sécurité: Où est le problème?," in *Vous dit sécurité,* ed. Laurent Mucchielli (Paris: Le Monde, 2011); Didier Fassin, *La force de l'ordre: Une anthropologie de la police des quartiers* (Paris: Seuil, 2011); Fassin, *Enforcing Order.*

74. Laurent Bonelli, "Governing the Police: Political Bargaining and Organizational Outputs in the French Police Reforms (1982–2010)," in *International Political Science Association Annual Conference,* 5 (Madrid, Spain, 2012). See also Bonelli, *La France à peur.*

75. Khosrokhavar, *L'Islam dans les prisons,* 10–25, 280.

76. Mohammed and Mucchielli, "La police dans les 'Quartiers Sensibles,' " 98–99.

77. Marwan Mohammed and Laurent Mucchielli, "La police dans les 'quartiers sensibles': Un profond malaise," in *Quand les banlieues brûlent,* ed. Laurent Mucchielli and Véronique Le Goaziou (Paris: La Découverte, 2006).

78. Fassin, *Enforcing Order: An Ethnography of Police,* translated from the original French, Fassin, *La force de l'ordre: Une anthropologie de la police des quartiers.*

79. Fassin, *Enforcing Order,* 87.

80. Ibid., i.

81. Loïc Wacquant, *Urban Outcasts* (London: Polity Press, 2007); Janet Abu-Lughod, *Race, Space and Riots in Chicago, New York and Los Angeles* (Oxford: Oxford University Press, 2007); Katz, "Why Aren't U.S. Cities Burning."

82. Wacquant, *Urban Outcasts,* 9.

83. Ibid., 152.

84. Ibid.

85. Ibid., 5.

86. Ibid.

87. Ibid., 23.

88. Ibid.

89. Ibid., 33.

90. Ibid., 23.

91. Abu-Lughod, *Race, Space and Riots.*

92. John Iceland, Daniel H. Weinberg, and Erika Steinmetz, *Racial and Ethnic Residential Segregation in the United States 1980–2000,* ed. U.S. Census Bureau (Washington, D.C.: U.S. Government Printing Office, 2000), 1–151. Iceland et al. categorize racial segregation using five indexes. The first is the dissimilarity index, which they claim is the most commonly used to measure segregation (8). New York is the third most segregated city in the country according to that index alone, following Detroit and Milwaukee-Waukesha (69). They use four other indices—the isolation index, the Delta index, the absolute centralization index, and the spatial proximity index—to come up with an overall ranking on segregation (14). Averaging the five indexes puts New York in a tie for the sixth most segregated city in the country, while Los Angeles does not even make the top ten (68).

93. Michael B. Katz, "Why Don't American Cities Burn Very Often?," *Journal of Urban History* 34, no. 2 (2008): 185–208; Katz, "Why Aren't U.S. Cities Burning," 23–29; Michael Katz, *Why Don't American Cities Burn?* (Philadelphia: University of Pennsylvania Press, 2012).

94. Katz, *Why Don't American Cities Burn*, 81.

95. Paul Jargowsky, "Stunning Progress, Hidden Problems: The Dramatic Decline in Concentrated Poverty in the 1990s," in *Redefining Urban and Suburban America: Evidence from the Census 2000*, ed. Alan Berube, Bruce Katz, and Robert E Land (Washington, D.C.: Brookings Institution, 2005), 3: 138, cited in Katz, *Why Don't American Cities Burn*, 80–81.

96. Tilly, *The Politics of Collective Violence*, 75, cited in Katz, *Why Don't American Cities Burn*, 82.

97. Katz, *Why Don't American Cities Burn*, 83.

98. Ibid.

99. Ibid., 83–84.

100. Ibid., 85.

101. Ira Katznelson, *City Trenches: Urban Politics and the Patterning of Class in the United States* (Chicago: University of Chicago Press, 1982), 179, cited in Katz, *Why Don't American Cities Burn*, 87.

102. Katz, *Why Don't American Cities Burn*, 88.

103. Ibid., 97.

104. Ibid.

105. Raymond Augustine Bauer, Ithiel de Sola Pool, and Lewis Anthony Dexter, *American Business and Public Policy*, Atherton Press Political Science Series (New York: Atherton Press, 1963), 420; Robert Jervis, *System Effects: Complexity in Political and Social Life* (Princeton, N.J.: Princeton University Press, 1997), 57.

106. Fassin, *Enforcing Order*, 40.

107. Katz, "Why Aren't U.S. Cities Burning," 28.

108. Gary Goertz and James Mahoney, *A Tale of Two Cultures: Qualitative and Quantitative Research in the Social Sciences* (Princeton, N.J.: Princeton University Press, 2012), 42.

109. Ibid., 68. Goertz and Mahoney call this "asymmetry of explanation."

110. Pamela Oliver, "Repression and Crime Control: Why Social Movement Scholars Should Pay More Attention to Mass Incarceration as a Form of Repression," *Mobilization* 13, no. 1 (2008): 10.

111. Ibid., 14.

112. Gregg Carter, personal communication over e-mail, June 25, 2011.

113. While civil rights activists had long used federal courts to overturn decisions reached by lower courts in the Deep South, the 1965 Civil Rights Act enabled the federal Department of Justice to intervene to protect civil rights even in local jurisdictions throughout the country.

114. Rogers Smith and Desmond King, "Racial Policy Alliances and Partisan Polarization: A Synthetic Analysis" (unpublished paper presented at seminar on 20th Century American Politics, Columbia University, December 2011), 13.

115. Human Rights Watch and Allyson Collins, *Shielded from Justice: Police Brutality and Accountability in the United States* (New York: Human Rights Watch, 1998), 107, http://www.hrw.org/legacy/reports98/police/uspo107.htm:

"Former Transit Officer Paolo Colecchia, who had been convicted for second-degree manslaughter for fatally shooting Nathaniel Levi Gaines, Jr. in July 1996, was sentenced to one and one half to four and one half years in prison in July 1997. A New York housing authority officer was convicted of criminally negligent homicide in August 1995, for a fatal shooting that occurred in March 1992, before the housing authority merged with the NYPD. In 1977, Thomas Ryan was convicted of criminally negligent homicide for the beating death of Israel Rodriguez in July 1975; the Ryan homicide conviction was the first recorded in the city of an on-duty policeman. Judith Cummings, *New York Times*, November 6, 1977."

116. Andy Humm, "Crackdown on Protest Could Spark More Scrutiny of Police," *Gotham Gazette*, November 21, 2011.

117. Tilly, *The Politics of Collective Violence*, 142–50.

118. Ibid., 227.

119. Thomas J. Sugrue, *Sweet Land of Liberty: The Forgotten Struggle for Civil Rights in the North* (New York: Random House, 2008), 326–27.

120. Roger Karapin, *Protest Politics in Germany: Movements on the Left and Right Since the 1960s* (University Park: Pennsylvania State University Press, 2009).

121. Tilly, *The Politics of Collective Violence*, 142–50.

122. Ashutosh Varshney, "Ethnic Conflict and Civil Society: India and Beyond," *World Politics* 53, no. 3 (2001): 363.

123. Personal conversation with Donald Horowitz at George Washington University, November 15, 2010.

124. Donald Horowitz, *The Deadly Ethnic Riot* (Berkeley: University of California Press, 2001), cited in Tilly, *The Politics of Collective Violence*, 144–49.

125. Tilly, *The Politics of Collective Violence*, 148.

126. Ulf Hannerz, *Soulside: Inquiries into Ghetto, Culture and Community* (New York: Columbia University Press, 1969), 173.

127. Tilly, *The Politics of Collective Violence*, 144.

128. Cited in Sidney Fine, *Violence in the Model City: The Cavanagh Administration, Race Relations and the Detroit Riot of 1967* (Ann Arbor: University of Michigan Press, 1989), 352; Tilly, *The Politics of Collective Violence*, 147.

129. Tilly, *The Politics of Collective Violence*.

130. Robert Curvin and Bruce Porter, *Blackout Looting!* (New York: Gardner Press, 1979), 3–19. See also Harold M Rose, *The Black Ghetto: A Spatial Behavioral Perspective* (New York: McGraw Hill, 1971), 94–101.

131. Curvin and Porter, *Blackout Looting!*, 37–77.

132. Goertz and Mahoney, *A Tale of Two Cultures.*

133. Sidney Tarrow, "The Strategy of Paired Comparison: Toward a Theory of Practice," *Comparative Political Studies* 43, no. 2 (2010): 240.

134. Javier Auyero, *Routine Politics and Violence in Argentina: The Grey Zone of State Power* (Cambridge: Cambridge University Press, 2007).

135. Ramiro Martinez Jr., "Revisiting the Role of Latinos and Immigrants in Police Research," in *Race, Ethnicity and Policing,* ed. Stephen K. Rice and Michael D. White (New York: New York University Press, 2010), 435.

136. Ibid., 436.

137. Tilly, *Durable Inequality,* 8–9.

Chapter 1

1. Janet Abu-Lughod, *Race, Space and Riots in Chicago, New York and Los Angeles* (Oxford: Oxford University Press, 2007), 136.

2. Joseph McLaren, ed., *Autobiography: The Big Sea (The Collected Works of Langston Hughes)* (Columbia: University of Missouri Press, 2002), 178.

3. W. E. B. Du Bois, Editorials, "Our Special Grievance," and "The Reward," *Crisis* 16, no. 3 (1918): 217, cited in Ira Katznelson, *When Affirmative Action Was White: The Untold History of Racial Inequality in Twentieth-Century America* (New York: Norton, 2005), 84.

4. Katznelson, *When Affirmative Action Was White,* 85.

5. Marilyn S. Johnson, *Street Justice: A History of Police Violence in New York City* (Boston: Beacon Press, 2003), 184.

6. Ibid., 185.

7. Ibid.

8. Ibid., 186.

9. Ibid., 187.

10. LaGuardia Commission Report, 115, 121, cited in ibid., 188.

11. Johnson, *Street Justice: A History of Police Violence in New York City,* 187.

12. Ibid., 189.

13. Letter to LaGuardia from [Commissioner] Lewis Valentine, April 30, 1935, reel 76, frames 1505–10, and letter to LaGuardia from Uptown Chamber of Commerce, August 14, 1935, reel 76, frames 1075–79, LaGuardia Papers; Thomas Kessner, *Fiorello H. LaGuardia and the Making of Modern New York* (New York: McGraw-Hill, 1989), 375; Johnson, *Street Justice,* 189.

14. Letter to LaGuardia from Valentine, April 30, 1935, and letter to LaGuardia from Uptown Chamber of Commerce, August 14, 1935, LaGuardia Papers; Kessner, *Fiorello H. LaGuardia,* 375; Johnson, *Street Justice,* 189.

15. Johnson, *Street Justice,* 191.

16. Thomas J. Sugrue, "The Unfinished History of Racial Segregation," unpublished ms., July 15, 2008, 1. http://www.prrac.org/projects/fair_housing_commission/chicago/sugrue.pdf.

17. Ibid., 2.

18. Ibid.

19. Johnson, *Street Justice*, 190.

20. Ibid., 98.

21. Katznelson, *When Affirmative Action Was White*, 101.

22. Johnson, *Street Justice,* 196.

23. Ibid.

24. Adam Clayton Powell Sr., *Riots and Ruins* (New York: Richard R. Smith, 1943), 47.

25. Johnson, *Street Justice,* 199.

26. Ibid.

27. Ibid., 191–92.

28. Ibid., 203.

29. Ibid., 200.

30. Abu-Lughod, *Race, Space and Riots*, 129.

31. Larry Long, *Migration and Residential Mobility in the United States* (New York: Russell Sage Foundation, 1988), 151.

32. Katznelson, *When Affirmative Action Was White*, 29.

33. Ibid., 138.

34. Ibid.

35. Ibid.

36. Dennis R. Judd, "Segregation Forever?," *Nation*, December 9, 1991, 740–43.

37. Thomas Sugrue, *The Origins of the Urban Crisis: Race and Inequality in Postwar Detroit* (Princeton, N.J.: Princeton University Press, 1996), 8–9.

38. Ibid., 41.

39. Evelyn Gonzalez, *The Bronx* (New York: Columbia University Press, 2003), 118.

40. Michael Katz, *Why Don't American Cities Burn?* (Philadelphia: University of Pennsylvania Press, 2012), 152.

41. Ibid.

42. Eric Schneider, *Smack: Heroin and the American City* (Philadelphia: University of Pennsylvania Press, 2009), 42.

43. Ibid., 100.

44. Thomas J. Sugrue, *Sweet Land of Liberty: The Forgotten Struggle for Civil Rights in the North* (New York: Random House, 2008), 329–30.

45. Ibid., 328.

46. Ibid.

47. Katz, *Why Don't American Cities Burn?*, 84.

48. Gonzalez, *The Bronx*, 148.

49. Ibid., 149.

50. Schneider, *Smack*, 115.

51. Ibid.

52. Ibid.

53. Ibid.

54. Ibid., 135.

55. Sugrue, *Sweet Land of Liberty*, 327.

56. Johnson, *Street Justice*, 232. See also *New York Times*, February 24, 28, and May 7, 1964.

57. Daniel J. Monti, "Patterns of Conflict Preceding the 1964 Riots," *Journal of Conflict Resolution* 23, no. 1 (1979): 50–51.

58. James Baldwin, "A Report from Occupied Territory," *Nation* (1966), http://www.thenation.com/article/159618/report-occupied-territory.

59. Ibid.

60. Ibid.

61. James Baldwin, "Fifth Avenue Uptown," *Esquire* (July 1960). TAlso cited in Sugrue, *Sweet Land of Liberty*, 327.

62. Sugrue, *Sweet Land of Liberty*, 325.

63. Frank J. Donner, "Aftermath to Harlem Riot: The Epton Anarchy Trial," *Nation* 201, no. 14 (November 15, 1965): 356.

64. Kenneth B. Clark, "The Wonder Is There Have Been So Few Riots," *New York Times*, September 5, 1965, 10, 38, 45, 48.

65. Donner, "Aftermath to Harlem Riot," 355–57.

66. "Russell Is Quoted on Riots in Harlem," *New York Times*, April 7, 1965.

67. Paul Good, "Nothing Worth Saving," *Nation* 206, no. 4 (April 14, 1967): 101–2.

68. Sugrue, *Sweet Land of Liberty*, 325.

69. Ibid.

70. Sol Rubin, "Cops, Guns and Homicides," *Nation* 201, no. 15 (December 27, 1965): 527–29.

71. Sugrue, *Sweet Land of Liberty*, 325.

72. Gregg Carter, "Hispanic Rioting During the Civil Rights Era," *Sociological Forum* 7, no. 2 (1992): 301–22.

73. Schneider, *Smack*, 140.

74. Roberto P. Rodriguez-Morazzani, "Political Culture of the Puerto Rican Left in the United States," in *The Puerto Rican Movement*, ed. Andres Torrres and Jose A. Velazquez (Philadelphia: Temple University Press, 1998), 32.

75. Johnson, *Street Justice*, 256.

76. Ibid.

77. Ibid.

78. Ibid.

79. Sugrue, *Sweet Land of Liberty*, 328.

80. Good, "Nothing Worth Saving," 101–2.

81. Joe Soss, Richard C. Fording, and Sanford F. Schram, *Disciplining the Poor: Neoliberal Paternalism and the Persistent Power of Race*, ed. Benjamin I. Page et al.,

Chicago Studies in American Politics (Chicago: University of Chicago Press, 2011), 30–31.

82. Ira Katznelson, *City Trenches: Urban Politics and the Patterning of Class in the United States* (Chicago: University of Chicago Press, 1982), 177, 99.

83. Sugrue, *Sweet Land of Liberty*, 358.

84. The New York Young Lords Party was modeled on the Young Lords of Chicago. The Chicago Lords had been founded by Jose "Cha Cha" Jimenez, the leader of a politicized street gang. Jimenez had been influenced by Ron Hampton, the Black Panther he had met in prison. When he left prison, he converted his street gang into a political organization and Puerto Rican partner to the Black Panthers.

85. Sarah Ferguson, "Second Suspect Pleads Guilty in Armando Perez Killing," http://thevillager.com/villager_52/closureas2nd.html.

86. The Tenant Interim Lease program (TIL) was modeled on the Real Great Society's Adopt-a-Building program. It gave tenant associations the right to buy out the contracts to city-owned buildings.

87. Miguel "Mickey" Melendez, *We Took to the Streets* (New Brunswick, N.J.: Rutgers University Press, 2005), 84.

88. Ibid., 105.

89. Gonzalez, *The Bronx*, 125.

90. Schneider, *Smack*, 138.

91. Gonzalez, *The Bronx*, 124.

92. Schneider, *Smack*, 129.

93. Ibid.,146.

94. Ibid., 187.

95. Ibid.

96. Harold M. Rose, *The Black Ghetto: A Spatial Behavioral Perspective* (New York: McGraw-Hill, 1971); Ernest H. Wohlenberg, "Geography of Civility," *Economic Geography* 58, no. 1 (1982): 29–44.

97. Wohlenberg, "Geography of Civility," 31.

98. Interview with Spike Lee in "The Bronx Is Burning," public television series directed by Jeremiah S. Chechik (2007).

99. Jonathan Mahler, *The Bronx Is Burning: 1977, Baseball, Politics and the Battle for the Soul of a City* (New York: Picador, 2005), 186.

100. Ibid., 200.

101. Ibid.

102. Ibid., 189.

103. Ibid., 211.

104. Ibid., 198.

105. Robert Curvin and Bruce Porter, *Blackout Looting* (New York: Gardner Press, 1979), 168.

106. Ibid.

107. Ibid.

108. Mahler, *The Bronx Is Burning*, 122–23.

109. This argument has been put forth in Pamela Oliver, "Repression and Crime Control: Why Social Movement Scholars Should Pay More Attention to Mass Incarceration as a Form of Repression," *Mobilization* 13, no. 1 (2008): 1–24; Loïc Wacquant, *Urban Outcasts* (London: Polity Press, 2007); Katz, *Why Don't American Cities Burn?* (Philadelphia: University of Pennsylvania Press, 2012).

110. Soss et al., *Disciplining the Poor*, 33.

111. Cited in William J. Chambliss, *Power, Politics, and Crime* (Boulder: Westview Press, 2001), 14.

112. Nixon cited in Dan T. Carter, *From George Wallace to Newt Gingrich: Race in the Conservative Counterrevolution, 1963–1994* (Baton Rouge: Louisiana State University Press, 1999), 30. See also John E. Roemer, Woodjin Lee, and Karin Vander Straeten, *Racism, Xenophobia and Distribution: Multi-Issue Politics in Advanced Democracies* (New York: Russell Sage Foundation; Cambridge, Mass.: Harvard University Press, 2007), 60.

113. Soss et al., *Disciplining the Poor*, 31.

114. O'Neill quoted in ibid., 33.

115. Craig Reinerman and Harry G. Levine, "The Crack Attack: America's Latest Drug Scare, 1986–1992," in *Images of Issues: Typifying Contemporary Social Problems*, ed. Joel Best, Social Problems and Social Issues (New York: A. De Gruyter, 1995), 152, 51.

116. Robert Jervis, *System Effects: Complexity in Political and Social Life* (Princeton, N.J.: Princeton University Press, 1997), 164.

117. Eric Sterling, "Tales of a Recovering Drug Warrior," in *Under the Influence*, ed. Preston Peet (New York: Disinformation Company, 2004), 92.

118. Ibid., 93.

119. Todd Clear, *Imprisoning Communities: How Mass Incarceration Makes Disadvantaged Neighborhoods Worse* (New York: Oxford University Press, 2007), 54.

120. Eva Bertram, *Drug War Politics: The Price of Denial* (Berkeley: University of California Press, 1996), 39.

121. Phillip Thompson III, *Double Trouble: Black Mayors, Black Communities, and the Call for a Deep Democracy* (Oxford: Oxford University Press, 2006), 221–22; Joseph B. Treaster, "Brooklyn Businessman Strangled in a Struggle with Police Officers," *New York Times*, June 17, 1978, A25.

122. Thompson, *Double Trouble*, 190.

123. Ibid.

124. Clarence Lusane, "In Perpetual Motion: The Continuing Significance of Race and America's Drug Crisis," *University of Chicago Legal Forum* 83 (1994): 97.

125. Thompson, *Double Trouble*, 189.

126. Ibid., 199; Asher Arian, Arthur Goldberg, John Mollenkopf, and Edward Rogowsky, *New York City Politics* (New York: Routledge, 1991).

127. Violent crime and homicide rates in New York peaked in 1990 and began a steady decline from that year on. All other crimes began their decline in 1989. http://www.disastercenter.com/crime/nycrime.htm. In 1990, a man set the Happy Land social club on fire in vengeance against a woman who had rejected him. Eighty-seven people died in the flames, raising the murder rate for that year. See also George James, "New York Killings Set a Record, While Other Crimes Fell in 1990," *New York Times,* April 23, 1991, http://www.nytimes.com/1991/04/23/nyregion/new-york-killings-set-a-record-while-other-crimes-fell-in-1990.html?pagewanted = all&src = pm.

128. Peter Pringle, "Riots Report Puts Pressure on Dinkins; New York Mayor Responded 'Poorly' to Flare-up Between Blacks and Jews," *Independent,* July 21, 1993, http://www.independent.co.uk/news/world/riots-report-puts-pressure-on-din kins-new-york-mayor-responded-poorly-to-flareup-between-blacks-and-jews-1486 152.html.

129. Ibid.

130. Chrisena Coleman and Austin Fenner, "Blacks Say Mayor Being Unfair," *Daily News,* April 3, 1998, http://www.nydailynews.com/archives/news/blacks-mayor -unfair-article-1.801452.

131. Ibid.

132. Ibid.

133. Twenty-five blacks were killed, sixteen Latinos, eight whites, two Asians, one Algerian, and one Indian or Middle Eastern. Eleven were shot by police, four by shop owners, sixteen by other seen and arrested shooters, and five by unseen shooters. Four died from arson; five were beaten, stabbed or strangled; and eight were hit by a car or died in traffic accidents. See Pamela Oliver, "Deaths in the L.A. Riots," http://www .ssc.wisc.edu/~oliver/soc220/Lectures220/AfricanAmericans/LA%20Riot%201992% 20Deaths.htm.

134. Manuel Pastor, "Latinos and the Los Angeles Uprising: The Economic Context" (Claremont, Calif.: Tomas Rivera Center, 1993), 28.

135. Wacquant, *Urban Outcasts,* 32; Mike Davis, "In L.A., Burning All Illusions," in *Inside the L.A. Riots: What Really Happened and Why It Will Happen Again,* ed. Don Hazin (New York: Independent Publisher's Group, 1992).

136. The actual incident was as follows: A Korean merchant, Soon Ja Du, saw Latasha Harlins putting a bottle of orange juice in her backpack but did not pay attention to the money Harlins had in her hand and was giving her for it. Thinking the girl was stealing a bottle of orange juice, Du grabbed the girl by the sweater and took her backpack. Harlins then hit back, knocking Du to the ground, and backed away. Du followed the girl and threw a stool at her. Harlins then picked up the orange juice that had fallen, put it on the counter, and turned to leave. Du picked up a shotgun she had illegally tampered with to make it trigger sensitive and shot the girl in the back of her head, from a distance of three feet, as the girl was leaving the store. The girl died with the two dollars in her hand for the purchase of the orange juice. The jury convicted Du of manslaughter and recommended a sixteen-year sentence.

The judge dropped the sentence to a five-year suspended sentence and a five-hundred-dollar fine.

137. Ronald Sullivan, "Washington Heights; A Policeman Is Cleared and Street Violence Defused," *New York Times,* September 13, 1992, http://www.nytimes.com/1992/09/13/weekinreview/sept-6-12-washington-heights-a-policeman-is-cleared-and-street-violence-defused.html?ref=josegarcia.

138. Guy Halverson and Lucia Mouat, "Calm Sought after N.Y. Police Shooting," *Christian Science Monitor,* July 10, 1992.

139. Ibid.

140. Ibid.

141. Ibid.

142. Ibid.

143. Ibid.

144. Ibid.

145. "Washington Heights Violence Has Deep Roots," *New York Times,* July 22, 1993, http://www.nytimes.com/1993/07/22/opinion/l-washington-heights-violence-has-deep-roots-798493.html.

146. Halverson and Mouat, "Calm Sought After N.Y. Police Shooting," *Christian Science Monitor,* July 10, 1992, http://www.csmonitor.com/1992/0710/10032.html.

147. Ian Fisher, "O'Connor Again Praises Dinkins for Actions in Washington Heights," *New York Times,* August 21, 1992, http://www.nytimes.com/1992/08/21/nyregion/o-connor-again-praises-dinkins-for-actions-in-washington-hts.html.

148. Alan Finder, "The Washington Heights Case: In Washington Heights, Dinkins Defends Actions after Shooting," *New York Times,* September 11, 1992, http://www.nytimes.com/1992/09/11/nyregion/washington-heights-case-washington-heights-dinkins-defends-actions-after.html.

149. Ibid.

150. Ibid.

151. Fisher, "O'Connor Again Praises Dinkins."

152. Ibid.

153. The City of New York, Milton Mollen (Chair), Harold Baer Jr., Herbert Evens, Roderick C. Lankler, Harold R. Tyler Jr., "Commission to Investigate Allegations of Police Corruption and the Anti-Corruption Procedures of the Police Department" (1994), 1.

154. Ibid., 1–2.

155. Stolen Lives Project, ed., *Stolen Lives: Killed by Law Enforcement* (New York: Stolen Lives Project, 1999); Stolen Lives Project, ed., *Stolen Lives: Killed by Law Enforcement,* rev. ed. (New York: Stolen Lives Project, 2006).

Chapter 2

1. Michelle Lamont, *The Dignity of Working Men: Morality and the Boundaries of Race, Class and Immigration* (Cambridge: Cambridge University Press, 2000), 242.

2. Ibid.

3. Patrick Weil, "La politique française d'immigration," *Pouvoirs*, no. 47 (1988): 45–60. Patrick Weil, *Qu'est-ce qu'un français? Histoire de la nationalité française de la révolution á nos jours* (Paris: Grasset et Fasquelle, 2002); Patrick Weil, *La république et sa diversité: Immigration, intégration, discrimination*, La république des idées (Paris: Seuil, 2005).

4. Loïc Wacquant, *Urban Outcasts* (London: Polity Press, 2007); Pierre Bourdieu and Loïc Wacquant, "On the Cunning of Imperialist Reason," *Theory, Culture & Society* 16, no. 1 (1999): 247–73.

5. Fabien Jobard, "The 2005 French Urban Unrests: Data-Based Interpretations," *Sociology Compass 24* 2, no. 4 (2008): 1287–1302.

6. Maxim Silverman, *Deconstructing the Nation: Immigration, Racism and Citizenship in Modern France* (London: Routledge, 1992), 3.

7. Gérard Noiriel, *The French Melting Pot: Immigration, Citizenship, and National Identity*, vol. 5, *Contradictions of Modernity* (Minneapolis: University of Minnesota Press, 1996), 5.

8. Didier Fassin, *Enforcing Order: An Ethnography of Urban Policing* (Boston: Polity Press, 2013), 45.

9. As described in David Lapoutre, *Coeur de banlieue* (Paris: Éditions Odile Jacob, 2001), 84.

10. Ibid., 83.

11. Todd Shepard, *The Invention of Decolonization: The Algerian War and the Remaking of France* (Ithaca, N.Y.: Cornell University Press, 2006), 7.

12. Ibid., 47.

13. Fassin, *Enforcing Order*, 149.

14. Ibid.

15. Ibid., 152.

16. "L'indigène musulman est français; néanmoins il continuera à être régi par la loi musulmane. Il peut être admis à servir dans les armées de terre et de mer. Il peut être appelé à des fonctions et emplois civils en Algérie. Il peut, sur sa demande, être admis à jouir des droits de citoyen français; dans ce cas, il est régi par les lois civiles et politiques de la France" [The indigenous Muslim is French; nevertheless he continues to be governed by Islamic law. He may serve in the armies of land and sea and may be called upon to serve as a civil employee in Algeria. He may, upon request, be allowed to enjoy the rights of a French citizen: In this case, he would be governed by political and civil laws of France] (article 1 of the 1865 *Code de l'indigénat*).

17. Clifford Rosenberg, *Policing Paris: The Origins of Modern Immigration Control Between Wars* (Ithaca, N.Y.: Cornell University Press, 2006), 111.

18. Shepard, *The Invention of Decolonization*, 31.

19. Ibid., 34.

20. Mahfoud Bennoune, "Maghribin Workers in France," *Middle East Research and Information Project Reports*, no. 34 (January 1975): 2.

21. Mahfoud Bennoune, "Origins of the Algerian Proletariat," *Middle East Research and Information Project Reports*, no. 94, *Origins of the Working Class: Class in the Middle East* (February 1981): 363; Myron Echenberg, "'Morts pour la France': The African Soldier During the Second World War," *Journal of African History* 26, no. 4 (1985): 363–80. Bennoune puts the number of Algerians who served at 175,000, but the Exhibition at the Musée de l'Armée, "Algérie 1830–1962, with Jacques Ferrandez," May 16 to July 29, 2012, puts the number at 250,000.

22. Bennoune, "Maghribin Workers in France," 2.

23. Alec G. Hargreaves, *Immigration, "Race" and Ethnicity in Contemporary France* (London: Routledge, 1995), 15.

24. Bennoune, "Maghribin Workers in France," 2.

25. Robert Wilde, "Casualties of the First World War," http://europeanhistory.about.com/cs/worldwar1/a/blww1casualties.htm, October 24, 2013.

26. Tony McNeill, "Immigration in Postwar France," http://www.unc.edu/depts/europe/francophone/Muslim_women/eng/Immigration_lecture2.pdf, The University of Sunderland, GB, last updated February 19, 1998.

27. Kimberly Hamilton, "The Challenge of French Diversity," http://www.migrationinformation.org/Profiles/display.cfm?id=266, November 2004.

28. Hargreaves, *Immigration, "Race" and Ethnicity in Contemporary France*, 9.

29. Bennoune, "Maghribin Workers in France," 2.

30. Rosenberg, *Policing Paris*, 19.

31. Ibid., xiii.

32. Ibid., 19.

33. Ibid., 161.

34. François La Roque's Croix de feu and Jacques Doriat's Parti popular française disavowed the fascist label, fearful that the links to Germany would undermine their nationalist credibility. But both organizations had more than a passing resemblance to their counterparts in Italy, Spain, and Germany and were equally brutal.

35. Peter Fysh and Jim Wolfreys, *The Politics of Racism in France* (New York: Palgrave Macmillan, 2003), 96–99.

36. Rod Kedward, *France and the French: A Modern History* (Woodstock and New York: Overlook, 2005), 214.

37. Ibid.

38. Ibid.

39. Ibid., 217.

40. Bennoune, "Maghribin Workers in France," 2.

41. Kedward, *France and the French*, 266.

42. Ibid., 249.

43. M. R. Haberfeld and Ibrahim Cerrah, *Comparative Policing: The Struggle for Democratization* (Thousand Oaks, Calif.: Sage, 2008), 249.

44. Jim House and Neil MacMaster, *Paris 1961: Algerians, State Terror and Memory* (New York: Oxford University Press, 2006), 35.

45. Ibid.

46. Ibid., 34.

47. Echenberg, "Morts pour la France," 365.

48. Ibid.

49. Ibid., 373.

50. Ibid.

51. Cited in Shepard, *The Invention of Decolonization*, 41.

52. Kedward, *France and the French*, 319.

53. Ibid., 333.

54. Andre Siegfried, *Le Figaro*, January 3, 1950, cited in ibid., 325.

55. Kedward, *France and the French*, 328.

56. Ibid., 331.

57. Shepard, *The Invention of Decolonization*, 47–48.

58. Ibid., 51.

59. Kedward, *France and the French*, 336.

60. Ibid., 335.

61. Abdelmalek Sayad, *The Suffering of the Immigrant* (London: Polity Press, 2004), 45.

62. Kedward, *France and the French*, 409.

63. Amit Prakash, *Empire on the Seine: Surveillance, Citizenship, and North African Migrants in Paris (1925–1975)* (New York: Columbia University Press, 2010), 87.

64. "Préfet de police a M le Ministre de Interior," November 1946, in Archives de la Prefecture de Police D/A 768: Indigenes nord-africains (1931–1954), cited in Prakash, *Empire on the Seine*, 87.

65. Rosenberg, *Policing Paris*, 207.

66. Ibid.

67. Ibid., 90.

68. House and MacMaster, *Paris 1961*, 38.

69. Ibid.

70. Ibid., 40.

71. Rosenberg, *Policing Paris*, 207.

72. Laurent Bonelli, "Governing the Police: Political Bargaining and Organizational Outputs in the French Police Reforms (1982–2010)" (paper presented at the International Political Science Association Annual Conference, Madrid, July 5, 2012), 5. See also Laurent Bonelli, *La France a peur* (Paris: La Découverte, 2008).

73. Emmanuel Blanchard, "Police judiciaire et pratiques d'exception pendant la guerre d'Algéri," *Vingtième siècle: Revue d'histoire* 90 (Avril-Juin 2006): 63.

74. Ibid., 63–64.

75. Emmanuel Blanchard, "La goutte d'or, 30 juillet 1955: Une émeute au coeur de la métropole coloniale," *Actes de la recherche en sciences sociales*, no. 195 (2012): 98–111. See also Blanchard, "La goutte d'or, 30 july 1955: A riot in the heart of the

colonial city," *Les Mots son Importants,* July 30, 2013, http://lmsi.net/La-Goutte-d-Or
-30-juillet-1955.

76. House and MacMaster, *Paris 1961,* 43.

77. Ibid., 44.

78. Ibid.

79. Ibid., 98.

80. Ibid., 99.

81. Hargreaves, *Immigration, "Race" and Ethnicity in Contemporary France,* 70.

82. Prakash, *Empire on the Seine,* 194.

83. House and MacMaster, *Paris 1961,* 95.

84. Ibid., 107; Jean Luc Einaudi, *October 1961: Un massacre á Paris* (Paris: Librarie
Arthéme Fayard, 2001), 363–65.

85. House and MacMaster, *Paris 1961,* 107.

86. John Bowen, *Why the French Don't Like Headscarves: Islam, the State and
Public Space* (Princeton, N.J.: Princeton University Press, 2007), 36.

87. Cited in Kristin Ross, *May '68 and Its Afterlives* (Chicago: University of Chicago Press, 2002), 43.

88. Daniel A. Gordon, "World Reactions to the 1961 Pogrom," *University of Sus-
sex Journal of Contemporary History,* issue 1 (2000): 2.

89. Ross, *May '68,* 43.

90. James J. Napoli, "A 1961 Massacre in Paris: When the Media Failed the Test,"
Washington Report on the Middle East Affairs (March 1997): 36, http://www.wrmea
.org/wrmea-archives/185-washington-report-archives-1994–1999/march-1997/2464
-a-1961-massacre-of-algerians-in-paris-when-the-media-failed-the-test-.html.

91. Cited in Ross, *May '68,* 43; Paulette Péju, *Les ratonnades à Paris* (Paris:
Maspero, 1961).

92. Ross, *May '68,* 43.

93. Kedward estimates the number killed at two hundred; Kedward, *France and
the French,* 345. Einaudi estimates the number killed at 325. He includes legally registered deaths, legal claims pursued for those missing, and deaths listed by medical-legal
authorities; Einaudi, *October 1961,* 347, 349–70. This figure is a revision upward of his
original estimate of 142 in Jean Luc Einaudi, *La bataille de Paris, 17 Octobre 1961*
(Paris: Seuil, 1991), 266–68. The official figure is forty.

94. Napoli, "A 1961 Massacre in Paris."

95. House and MacMaster document 105 North Africans violently killed that
month but estimate that the number was at least 121 given the large number who
never reached the morgue (House and MacMaster, *Paris 1961,* 107). Einaudi, *October
1961,* 347–70; Gordon, "World Reactions to the 1961 Pogrom," 36; Ross, *May '68,* 43;
Kedward, *France and the French,* 345; Rosenberg, *Policing Paris,* 19; Napoli, "A 1961
Massacre in Paris," 36.

96. Exhibition at the Musée de l'Armée, "Algérie 1830–1962."

97. House and MacMaster, *Paris 1961,* 134.

98. Ibid.

99. Rosenberg, *Policing Paris*, 206.

100. William Gardner Smith, *The Stone Face* (New York: Farrar, Straus, 1963), cited in Ross, *May '68*, 44.

101. Smith, *The Stone Face*, 38, cited in Ross, *May '68*, 46.

102. Ross, *May '68*, 45.

103. Einaudi, *October 1961*, 232–33.

104. Kedward, *France and the French*, 345.

105. The Exhibition at the Musée de l'Armée, "Algérie 1830–1962, with Jacques Ferrandez," May 16 to July 29, 2012, puts the number between 300,000 and 430,000.

106. Shepard puts the number at 16,000; Shepard, *The Invention of Decolonization*, 6. The Exhibition at the Musée de l'Armée, "Algérie 1830–1962, with Jacques Ferrandez," May 16 to July 29, 2012, puts the number at 12,000.

107. Shepard, *The Invention of Decolonization*, 6.

108. Ibid., 75.

109. Ibid.

110. Ibid., 170.

111. Ibid.

112. Ibid., 234–35.

113. Cited in ibid., 194.

114. Sayad, *The Suffering of the Immigrant*, 44.

115. Perry Anderson, "Union Sucreé," *London Review of Books* 26, no. 18 (2004): 14, http://www.lrb.co.uk/v26/n18/perry-anderson/union-sucre.

116. Bennoune, "Maghribin Workers in France," 3.

117. Silverman, *Deconstructing the Nation*, 43.

118. Prakash, *Empire on the Seine*, 291.

119. Ibid.

120. Ibid., 293.

121. Ibid., 295.

122. Bennoune, "Maghribin Workers in France," 3.

123. Silverman, *Deconstructing the Nation*, 52.

124. Philip Gourevitch, "No Exit: Can Nicolas Sarkozy—and France—Survive the European Crisis?" *New Yorker*, December 12, 2011, http://www.newyorker.com/reporting/2011/12/12/111212fa_fact_gourevitch?currentPage = all.

125. Kedward, *France and the French*, 419.

126. Ibid.

127. Ibid.

128. Georges Séguy, cited in Michael Seidman, "Workers in a Repressive Society of Seductions: Parisian Metallurgists in May–June 1968," *French Historical Studies* 18, no. 1 (1993): 258.

129. André Malterre, cited in Seidman, "Workers in a Repressive Society of Seductions," 258.

130. Ibid.

131. Ibid., 364.

132. Ibid., 258.

133. Ibid., 268.

134. Ibid.

135. Philip E. Converse and Roy Pierce, "Basic Cleavages in French Politics and the Disorders of May and June 1968," paper presented at the 7th World Conference of Sociology, Varna, Bulgaria, September 1970, 23, cited in Melvin Seeman, "The Signals of '68: Alienation in Pre-Crisis France," *American Sociological Review* 37, no. 4 (1972): 400.

136. Edward H. Ransford, "Isolation, Powerlessness and Violence: A Study of Attitudes and Participation in the Watts Riot," *American Journal of Sociology* 73, no. 5 (1968): 581–91.

137. Kurt Weyland, "The Arab Spring: Why the Surprising Similarities with the Revolutionary Wave of 1948?," *Perspectives on Politics* 10, no. 4 (2012): 924.

138. Fysh and Wolfreys, *The Politics of Racism in France*, 108.

139. Prakash, *Empire on the Seine*, 299.

140. Fysh and Wolfreys, *The Politics of Racism in France*, 109.

141. Ibid., 110.

142. Antonis A. Ellinas, *The Media and the Far Right in Western Europe: Playing the Nationalist Card* (Cambridge: Cambridge University Press, 2010), 174–75.

143. Azouz Begag, *Ethnicity in the Balance* (Omaha: University of Nebraska Press, 2007), 12.

144. Ellinas, *The Media and the Far Right in Western Europe*, 172.

145. Silverman, *Deconstructing the Nation*, 57; Weil, "La politique française d'immigration," 10.

146. Begag, *Ethnicity in the Balance*, 12.

147. Silverman, *Deconstructing the Nation*, 49–50.

148. Begag, *Ethnicity in the Balance*, 13.

149. A. Peyrefitte, "Réponses à la violence" (rapport à M. Président de la République présenté par le Comité d'Etudes sur Violence, la Criminalité, et la Délinquance, 1977) [State-commissioned Report on Delinquency], cited in Susan Terrio, *Judging Mohammed: Juvenile Delinquency, Immigration and Exclusion at the Paris Hall of Justice* (Palo Alto, Calif.: Stanford University Press, 2009).

150. Ibid., 69.

151. Ibid., 70.

152. Begag, *Ethnicity in the Balance*, 13.

153. Ibid., 15.

154. Ibid.

155. Silverman, *Deconstructing the Nation*, 55.

156. Hargreaves, *Immigration, "Race" and Ethnicity in Contemporary France*, 69.

157. Ibid., 70.

158. Renee Zauberman and René Lévy, "Police, Minorities and the French Republican Ideal," *Criminology* 41, no. 1 (November 2003): 1065.

159. Paul A. Silverstein, "Postcolonial Urban Apartheid" (paper presented at the Social Science Research Council [SSRC] conference on "Riots in France," New York City, 2006).

160. Bonelli, "Governing the Police," 5. See also Bonelli, *La France a peur*.

161. Ibid.

162. Ibid., 6.

163. Fassin, *Enforcing Order*, xiv.

164. Ellinas, *The Media and the Far Right in Western Europe*, 172–73.

165. Ibid., 173.

166. Fassin, *Enforcing Order*, 216.

167. Paul A. Silverstein, "Urban Violence in France" (Middle East Report Online, 2005), http://www.merip.org/mero/interventions/urban-violence-france, last accessed October 25, 2013.

168. Fassin, *Enforcing Order*, 9.

169. Ellinas, *The Media and the Far Right in Western Europe*, 176.

170. Ibid., 177.

171. Paul A. Silverstein, *Algeria in France* (Bloomington: Indiana University Press, 2004), 160.

172. Ellinas, *The Media and the Far Right in Western Europe*, 178.

173. Ibid.

174. Ibid.

175. Ibid., 181–82.

176. Silverman, *Deconstructing the Nation*, 64.

177. Ibid., 65.

178. Ibid., 64.

179. Sayad, *The Suffering of the Immigrant*, 264–65.

180. Pamela Irving Jackson, "Minority Group Threat, Crime and Mobilization of Law in France," in *Ethnicity, Race and Crime*, ed. Darnell Hawkins (Albany: State University of New York Press, 1995), 354. See also "France Takes a Tough Stance on Crime and Immigration," *New York Times*, April 9, 1993, A2.

181. Silverman, *Deconstructing the Nation*, 65.

182. Jacques Chirac, "Meeting Electoral," cited in Pierre Tevanian and Sylvie Tissot, eds., *Mots à Maux* (Paris: Éditions Dagorno, 1990), 77.

183. Silverstein, "Postcolonial Urban Apartheid," http://riotsfrance.ssrc.org/Silverstein_Tetreault/.

184. Fassin, *Enforcing Order*, 216.

185. Philip Booth and Bernard Jouve, eds., *Metropolitan Democracies: Transformations of the State and Urban Policy in Canada, France and Great Britain* (Aldershot, Hampshire: Ashgate, 2005), 191.

186. Silverman, *Deconstructing the Nation*, 67; Silverstein, "Urban Violence in France," http://www.merip.org/mero/interventions/urban-violence-france; Fabien Jobard, "Les voies a venir des conflits urbains: Premièrs analyses sur la mobilisation politique de dammarie-ès-lys" (unpublished working paper, 2002); Amnesty International, "France: The Search for Justice," hhtp://web.amnesty.org/library/Index/ENG EUR210012005?open&of = ENG-FRA.

187. Pierre Tournier, "Nationality, Crime and Criminal Justice in France," in *Ethnicity, Crime and Immigration*, ed. Michael Tonry (Chicago: University of Chicago Press, 1997), 533, 40.

188. Terrio, *Judging Mohammed*, 75.

189. Fassin, *Enforcing Order*, 91.

190. Ibid., 179.

191. Silverstein, "Urban Violence in France"; Fabien Jobard, "Les violences policieres," in *Crime et securite l'état des savoirs*, ed. Laurent Mucchielli and Philippe Robert (Paris: Édicions la Découverte, 2002); Amnesty International, "France," hhtp://web.amnesty.org/library/Index/ENGEUR210012005?open&of = ENG-FRA.

192. Hélène Franco, "Prévention de la délinquance amalgames et réalités" (paper presented at the French Senate conference on "Prévention de la délinquance," Senat, Palais de Luxembourg, Paris, 2005).

193. Sebastien Roché, *Le frisson de l'emeute* (Paris: Seuil, 2006), 100.

194. Michel Wieviorka, Philippe Bataille, Karine Clémént, Olivier Cousin, Farhad Khosrokhavar, Séverine Labat, Éric Macé, Paola Rebughino, and Nikola Tietze, *Violence en France* (Paris: Seuil, 1999), 98–114, 330–44.

195. http://hudoc.echr.coe.int/sites/eng/pages/search.aspx?i = 001–58287#{"ite mid":["001–58287"].

196. Amnesty International, "France," http://www.amnesty.org/en/library/asset/EUR21/002/2010/en/01aea6d5–0a23–47fe-8d58–8a8fad707605/eur210022010en.pdf.

197. Ibid., 24.

198. "Rapport au gouvernment de la république française relatif à la viste en France effectuée par le du 14 Au 26 Mai 1990" (Direction generale des droits de l'homme, comité européen pour la prévention de la torture, Strasbourg, France, 1991); "Rapport au gouvernment de la république française relatif à la viste en France effectuée par le comité Européen pour la prévention de la torture et des peines ou traitements inhumains ou dégradants du 14 Au 26 Mai 1995" (1996); "Rapport au gouvernement de la république française relatif à la visite en France effectuée du 14 Au 26 Mai 2000" (Comité européen pour la prévention de la torture et des peines ou traitements inhumains ou dégradants, Strasbourg, France, 2001).

199. "French Police Protest at Jailing of Colleagues for Beatings," *Irish Times*, April 2, 1999, 10.

200. Jobard, "Les voies a venir des conflits urbains." It is extremely difficult to get accurate statistics on police killings. The government does not release them, and

nongovernmental organizations are too small to collect them. It is equally difficult in most American cities.

201. European Commission, Eurobarometer 47.1, 1997.

202. Terrio, *Judging Mohammed,* 73.

203. Fassin, *Enforcing Order,* 182.

204. *Le Monde,* September 4, 1998, cited in Terrio, *Judging Mohammed,* 80.

Chapter 3

1. Evan Thomas and Suzanne Smalley, "Rudy's Roots: Growing up Giuliani," *Newsweek* (December 3, 2007): 31.

2. Kevin Baker, "A Fate Worse than Bush: Rudolph Giuilani and the Politics of Personality," *Harper's* 315, no. 1877 (August 1, 2007): 31–39.

3. Susan Jacoby, "Respect," in *America's Mayor, America's President: The Strange Case of Rudy Giuliani,* ed. Robert Poiner (New York: Soft Skull Press, 2007), 153.

4. Pamela Oliver, "Repression and Crime Control: Why Social Movement Scholars Should Pay More Attention to Mass Incarceration as a Form of Repression," *Mobilization* 13, no. 1 (2008): 10.

5. Baker, "A Fate Worse than Bush," 35.

6. Robert Stutman in Robert M. Stutman and Richard Esposito, *Dead on Delivery: Inside the Drug Wars, Straight from the Street* (New York: Warner Books, 1992), 148.

7. Robert M. Entman and Andrew Rojecki, *The Black Image in the White Mind: Media and Race in America, Studies in Communication, Media, and Public Opinion* (Chicago: University of Chicago Press, 2000).

8. CBS News/New York Times, *New York City Mayoral Election Exit Polls* (New York: CBS News/New York Times, 1993).

9. Ibid.

10. Ibid.

11. Ibid.

12. Ibid.

13. Todd S. Purdum, "Police Gaining a Community Role," *New York Times,* May 10, 1987, http://www.nytimes.com/1987/05/10/weekinreview/police-gaining-a-community-role.html.

14. George L. Kelling and James Q. Wilson, "Broken Windows: The Police and Neighborhood Safety," *Atlantic* (March 1, 1982), http://www.theatlantic.com/magazine/archive/1982/03/broken-windows/304465/. See also G. Kelling and W. Bratton, "Declining Crime Rates: Insiders' Views of the New York City Story," *Journal of Criminal Law and Criminology* 88, no. 4 (1998).

15. William Bratton, presentation on the panel "Regional Spotlight Session: Broken Windows Policing in New York City 20 Years On," at American Sociology Association Annual Conference, New York, N.Y., August 12, 2013.

16. Robert E. Moffitt and Edwin Meese III, *21 Steps Public Officials Can Take to Support Pittsburgh's Police* (Pittsburgh: Allegheny Institute for Public Policy, 1999);

Bernard E. Harcourt and Jens Ludwig, "Broken Windows: New Evidence from New York City and a Five-City Social Experiment," *University of Chicago Law Review* 73, no. 1 (2006).

17. Luc Sante, "Order," in *America's Mayor, America's President*, ed. Poiner, 66.

18. William J. Stuntz, *The Collapse of American Criminal Justice* (Cambridge, Mass.: Harvard University Press, 2011), 3–4.

19. Alison Mitchell, "With Defense of Police at Mosque, Giuliani Moves to Isolate 2 Critics," *New York Times*, January 15, 1994, http://www.nytimes.com/1994/01/15/nyregion/with-defense-of-police-at-mosque-giuliani-moves-to-isolate-2-critics.html.

20. Ibid.

21. Ibid.

22. Ibid.

23. In his paper delivered on the panel "Regional Spotlight Session: Broken Windows Policing in New York City 20 Years On," at American Sociology Association Annual Conference in New York, August 12, 2013, Tom Tyler argued that youth who viewed the police negatively were twice as likely to engage in violence. See also Tom R. Tyler, "Legitimacy and Cooperation: Why Do People Help Police Fight Crime in Their Communities?" Yale Law School Faculty Scholarship Series, January 1, 2008; Andrew Gelman, Jeffrey Fagan, and Alex Kiss, "An Analysis of New York City Police Department's 'Stop and Frisk' Policy in the Context of Claims About Racial Bias," *Journal of the American Statistical Association* 102, no. 479 (2007): 813–23.

24. Jeffrey A. Fagan, Amanda Geller, Garth Davies, and Valerie West, "Street Stops and Broken Windows Revisited: The Demography and Logic of Proactive Policing in a Safe and Changing City," in *Race, Ethnicity and Policing: Essential Readings*, ed. Stephen K. Rice and Michael D. White (New York: New York University Press, 2010), 314.

25. Mathew Purdy, "In New York the Handcuffs Are One-Size-Fits-All," *New York Times*, August 24,1997, http://www.nytimes.com/1997/08/24/nyregion/in-new-york-the-handcuffs-are-one-size-fits-all.html?pagewanted = all&src = pm.

26. Ibid.; Editorial, "Examining Marijuana Arrests," *New York Times*, April 1, 2012, http://www.nytimes.com/2012/04/02/opinion/examining-marijuana-arrests.html.

27. Todd R. Clear, *Imprisoning Communities: How Mass Imprisonment Makes Impoverished Communities Worse* (New York: Oxford University Press, 2007), 64.

28. Donna De La Cruz, "Giuliani Rips Allegations of Profiling," *Washington Post*, October 6, 2000, A3.

29. Ibid.

30. Marilyn S. Johnson, *Street Justice: A History of Police Violence in New York City* (Boston: Beacon Press, 2003), 292.

31. Kevin McCoy, "Police Misconduct Mess," *New York Daily News*, July 16, 2000, 6; "United States of America: Police Brutality and Excessive Force in the New York City Police Department" (Amnesty International, June 1996), http://www.amnesty.org/en/library/asset/AMR51/036/1996/en/7b6bf842-eb05-11dd-aad1-ed57e7e5

470b/amr510361996en.pdf, 1; Richard Emery and Illann Margalit Maazel, "Why Civil Rights Lawsuits Do Not Deter Police Misconduct: The Conundrum of Indemnification and a Proposed Solution," *Fordham Urban Law Journal* 28, no. 2 (2000): 590.

32. Kevin McCoy, "Police Misconduct Mess," 6.

33. Amnesty International, "United States of America: Police Brutality and Excessive Force in the New York City Police Department," 11.

34. Ibid.

35. Ibid., 13.

36. Cited in Fox Butterfield, "Drop in Homicide Rate Linked to Crack's Decline," *New York Times*, October 27, 1997, http://www.nytimes.com/1997/10/27/us/drop-in-homicide-rate-linked-to-crack-s-decline.html.

37. Jeffrey Fagan, Franklin E. Zimring, and June Kim, "Declining Homicide in New York City: A Tale of Two Trends," *Journal of Criminal Law and Criminology* 68, no. 4 (1998): 1277.

38. Michael Jacobson, *How to Reduce Crime and End Mass Incarceration* (New York: New York University Press, 2005); Franklin Zimring, *The Great American Crime Decline* (New York: Oxford University Press, 2007), 120–22, 195–206; William J. Stuntz, *The Collapse of American Justice* (Cambridge, Mass.: Belknap Press of Harvard University Press, 2011), 1–8, 274–312; John Tierney, "Prison Populations Can Shrink When Police Crowd Streets," *New York Times*, January 25, 2013, http://www.nytimes.com/2013/01/26/nyregion/police-have-done-more-than-prisons-to-cut-crime-in-new-york.html?_r=1&hp=&adxnnl=1&adxnnlx=1359212493-BdRB/ZbPqByhz0yooOETWw&.

39. Robert Sampson, *The Great American City: Chicago and the Enduring Neighborhood Effect* (Chicago: University of Chicago Press, 2012), 35–39, 135–233, 420–26.

40. Tyler, "Legitimacy and Cooperation."

41. Lori Fridell, Robert Lunney, Drew Diamond, and Bruce Kubu, with Michael Scott and Colleen Laing, *Racially Biased Policing: A Principled Response* (Washington, D.C.: Police Executive Research Forum, 2001), 13–16.

42. These include the Audre Lorde Project, Organizing Asian Communities, the Immigrant Justice Solidarity Project, Make the Road New York, the Malcolm X Grassroots Movement, the National Hip Hop Political Convention, and Nodutdol for Korean Community Development.

43. "Yes, a Police Riot," *New York Times*, August 26, 1988, http://www.nytimes.com/1988/08/26/opinion/yes-a-police-riot.html.

44. Howard W. French, Michael Wines, and Todd S. Purdum, "Melee in Tompkins Sq. Park: Violence and Its Provocation," *New York Times*, August 14, 1988, http://www.nytimes.com/1988/08/14/nyregion/melee-in-tompkins-sq-park-violence-and-its-provocation.html?pagewanted=all&src=pm.

45. Ibid.

46. Andy Humm, "Crackdown on Protest Could Spark More Scrutiny of Police," *Gotham Gazette*, November 21, 2011, http://www.gothamgazette.com/index.php/civil-rights/867-crackdown-on-protests-could-spark-more-scrutiny-of-police.

47. Benjamin Weiser, "U.S. Asserts Police Officers Planned to Lie," *New York Times*, June 25, 1998.

48. Kelly Anderson and Tami Gold, *Every Mother's Son* (New York: Independent Television Service, 2004). I was unable to talk directly with Iris Baez as she moved her family to Florida after police beat her other son in an alley. Instead I spoke with Panama Alba, a close friend of Iris Baez, and the leader of the mobilization efforts to help get justice for her son.

49. Ibid.

50. David Stout, "Judge's Hypothetical Question Is Cited in Bronx Officer's Acquittal," *New York Times*, October 11, 1996, http://www.nytimes.com/1996/10/11/ny region/judge-s-hypothetical-question-is-cited-in-bronx-officer-s-acquittal.html.

51. Ibid.

52. David Gonzalez, "For a Mother, Vindication and Sorrow," *New York Times*, February 8, 1997, http://www.nytimes.com/1997/02/08/nyregion/for-a-mother-vindi cation-and-sorrow.html.

53. "Deeper Failures in the Livoti Case," *New York Times*, October 15, 1998, http://www.nytimes.com/1998/10/15/opinion/deeper-failures-in-the-livoti-case.h tml.

54. Benjamin Weiser, "Former Officer Gets 7 1/2 Years in Man's Death," *New York Times*, October 9, 1998, http://www.nytimes.com/1998/10/09/nyregion/former -officer-gets-7-1-2-years-in-man-s-death.html.

55. Eric Lipton, "Mayor to Sign Bill Renaming Street for Police Choking Victim," *New York Times*, April 17, 2000, http://www.nytimes.com/2000/04/17/nyregion/ mayor-to-sign-bill-renaming-street-for-police-choking-victim.html.

56. Julio Marsh, "Court Date for Officers in Cop on Cop Bash," *New York Post*, July, 16, 2013, http://nypost.com/2013/07/16/court-date-for-officers-in-cop-on-cop -bash/. Barbara Ross and Dareh Gregorian, "Court Hears Former NYPD Officer's Suit 22 Years After Bar Beating Left Him Brain-Damaged," *New York Daily News*, July 15, 2013, http://www.nydailynews.com/news/crime/court-hears-ex-officer-suit-22-years- bar-beating-article-1.1399554#ixzz2imIw2mFQ.

57. Richard Emery and Ilann Margalit Maazel, "Why Civil Rights Lawsuits Do Not Deter Police Misconduct: The Conundrum of Indemnification and a Proposed Solution," *Fordham Urban Law Journal* 28, no. 2 (2000).

Chapter 4

1. This type of gun, which was invented in France, fires large rubber bullets that do not pierce the body. While it is less lethal than a regular gun, it can cause the loss of an eye or severe organ damage, and in rare instances it can prove fatal.

2. Jean-Pierre Mignard and Emmanuel Tordjman, *L'affaire Clichy: Morts pour rien* (Paris: Stock, 2006), 105. Translation mine.

3. Ibid., 47.

4. Keith Richberg, "The Other France, Separate and Unhappy," *Washington Post*, November 13, 2005, http://www.washingtonpost.com/wp-dyn/content/article/2005/ 11/11/A R200511110227 7.html.

5. Alec G. Hargreaves, "The Emperor with No Clothes?" (paper presented at the Social Science Research Council [SSRC] conference on "Riots in France," New York, New York, October 24, 2006).

6. Hugues Lagrange, "Socialisation des adolescents et délinquance: Les enfants issus des familles africaines noires" (paper presented at the conference on "Migration and Policing," Maison Science de l'Homme, Paris, France, June 9, 2006).

7. Dror Mishani and Aurelia Smotriez, "What Sort of Frenchmen Are They? Interview with Alain Finkielkraut," *Ha'aretz Magazine*, November 16, 2005. Finkielkraut, on a trip to Israel in March 2007, claimed that he was misrepresented in that interview and denied using the word "barbarian." Mishani and Smotriez point out that the word was "savage" and insist that Finkielkraut used it. See Yair Sheleg, *A Racist Attack* (www.haaretz.com, 2007 [cited March 28, 2007]), available from http://www.haaretz .com/print-edition/features/a-racist-attack-1.216822. Also see Daniel Ben-Simon, "French Philosopher Alain Finkielkraut Apologizes After Death Threats," *Haaretz*, November 7, 2005, http://www.haaretz.com/print-edition/news/french-philosopher -alain-finkielkraut-apologizes-after-death-threats-1.175186. Both articles were accessed October 26, 2013.

8. Cited in Hargreaves, "The Emperor with No Clothes."

9. Mohammed Rebzani, *Des Jeunes dans la discrimination* (Paris: Paris Presses Universitaires de France, 2002). High school and university graduates of immigrant parentage are also twice as likely (11 percent) as those with French parentage (5 percent) to be unemployed; see Bertrand Bissuel, "Les étrangers particulièrement touchés par la misère," *Le Monde*, February 8, 2002. Testers using identical resumes with different French, Arabic, and African names consistently find those with European names eight times more likely to get an interview.

10. See, for example, Stéphanie Giry, "France and Its Muslims," *Foreign Affairs* 85, no. 5 (2006). For an excellent non-Marxist analysis of France's unemployment crisis, see Timothy B. Smith, *France in Crisis: Welfare, Inequality and Globalization Since 1980* (Canbridge: Cambridge University Press, 2004).

11. This approach is similar to that of William J. Wilson, *The Truly Disadvantaged: The Inner City, the Underclass, and Public Policy* (Chicago: University of Chicago Press, 1987).

12. Olivier Roy, "The Nature of the French Riots" (paper presented at the Social Science Research Council [SSRC] conference on "Riots in France," New York, New York, October 26, 2006).

13. Laurent Mucchielli, "Autumn 2005: A Review of the Most Important Riot in the History of French Contemporary Society," *Journal of Ethnic and Migration Studies* 35, no. 5 (2009): 738.

14. Hugues Lagrange, "Autopsie d'une vague émeutes," in *Émuetes urbains et protestations: Une singularite français*, ed. Hugues Lagrange and Marco Oberti (Paris: Science-po, 2006); Hugues Lagrange, "La structure et l'accident," cited in Fabien Jobard,

"The 2005 French Urban Unrests: Data-based Interpretations," *Sociology Compass* 2, no. 4 (2008).

15. International Crisis Group, "La france face à ses musulmans: Emeutes, jihadisme et dépolitisation," Rapport Europe de Crisis Group, N° 172, March 9, 2006, ii.

16. Ibid.

17. Mucchielli, "Autumn 2005," 739.

18. John Lichfield, "Sarkozy Offers Deportation of Foreign Rioters," *Independent (London),* November 10, 2005, 24.

19. Susan Terrio, *Judging Mohammed: Juvenile Delinquency, Immigration and Exclusion at the Paris Hall of Justice* (Palo Alto, Calif.: Stanford University Press, 2009), 290.

20. Sebastien Roché, *Le frisson de l'émeute* (Paris: Seuil, 2006), 111.

21. Jobard, "The 2005 French Urban Unrests," 1292.

22. Ibid.

23. Mucchielli, "Autumn 2005," 739.

24. Wage disparities are twice as low for those of African or North African origin, and poverty rates are four times higher; see Phillipe Bernard, "L'immigration au fil de besoins de marché du travail," *Le Monde,* April 16, 2002; Bissuel, "Les étrangers particulièrement touchés par la misère."

25. Mignard and Tordjman, *L'affaire Clichy;* Paul A. Silverstein, "Urban Violence in France" (Middle East Report Online, 2005), http://www.merip.org/mero/interventions/urban-violence-france; Paul A. Silverstein, "Postcolonial Urban Apartheid" (paper presented at the Social Science Research Council [SSRC] conference on "Riots in France," New York, New York, October 26, 2006).

26. Lagrange, "Autopsie d'une vague émeutes"; Lagrange, "La structure et l'accident."

27. Mucchielli, "Autumn 2005," 739.

28. Forty percent of youths cited police; 60 percent were coded as other, which was the biggest category for all those who were interviewed. Thirty-three percent of inhabitants cited Sarkozy; 34 percent were coded as other. Neither group mentioned any of the other causes cited by the vast majority of the speakers. See Donatella Della Porta and Bernard Gbikpi, "The Riots: A Dynamic View," in *Violent Protest, Contentious Politics, and the Neoliberal State,* ed. Hank Johnston and Seraphim Seferiades (Farnham: Ashgate Publishing, 2012), 95–96.

29. Mucchielli, "Autumn 2005," 740.

30. Ibid., 742.

31. Ibid.

32. Marwan Mohammed and Laurent Mucchielli, "La police dans les 'quartiers sensibles': Un profond malaise," in *Quand les banlieues brûlent,* ed. Laurent Mucchielli and Véronique Le Goaziou (Paris: La Découverte, 2006), 111.

33. Didier Fassin, *Enforcing Order: An Ethnography of Urban Policing* (Boston: Polity Press, 2013), 216.

34. For instance, Martine Aubry, *Petit dictionnaire pour lutter contre l'extreme roite* (Paris: Editions du Seuil, 1995).

35. Antonis A. Ellinas, *The Media and the Far Right in Western Europe: Playing the Nationalist Card* (Cambridge: Cambridge University Press, 2010), 194.

36. Ibid.

37. Ipsos, *1er tour presidentielle 2002: Comprendre le vote des français. Qui a voté quoi? Les motivations de vote* (Paris: Ipsos, 2002).

38. Ibid.

39. Ibid.

40. "Sécurité: Ce que veulent les français," *Le Figaro*, March 18, 2002.

41. Ipsos, *1er tour presidentielle 2002.*

42. Fassin, *Enforcing Order*, xv.

43. Marie-Beatrice Baudet, "Les nouvelles frontières de l'insécurité sociale," *Le Monde*, May 14, 2002.

44. Commission nationale consultative des droits de l'homme, "Sondage exclusif: Quel sont vos sentiments personnells à l'égard des differents groups suivants," *Marianne*, May 24, 2002.

45. Kimberly Morgan, "The Gendered Politics of Immigrant Integration Policy in France" (paper presented at Comparative Politics Workshop, George Washington University, September 13, 2013), 24.

46. Discours de M Jacques Chirac, Président de la République à l'issue de son déplacement à Troyes(Aube)," NEWS Press, October 16, 2002, cited and translated by Morgan, "The Gendered Politics of Immigrant Integration Policy in France," 24.

47. Laurent Bonelli, "Governing the Police: Political Bargaining and Organizational Outputs in the French Police Reforms (1982–2010)" (paper presented at the International Political Science Association Annual Conference, Madrid, 2012), 4. See also Laurent Bonelli, *La France à peur* (Paris: La Découverte, 2008).

48. Laurent Bonelli and Gilles Sainati, *La machine à punir*, 2nd ed. (Paris: L'esprit Frappeur, 2004).

49. Fassin, *Enforcing Order*, xvi.

50. Ibid., 78.

51. Ibid.

52. Ibid.

53. United Nations Committee Against Torture, 44th session, Observatoire international des prisons—French section, information on the treatment of individuals detained in French prisons (consideration of France's fourth to sixth periodic reports), April 2010, 35, http://www2.ohchr.org/english/bodies/cat/docs/ngos/OIP_France44_en.pdf.

54. Tracy McNicoll, "French Prisons Are Becoming an Embarrassment," *Newsweek*, filed August 1, 2008, updated March 13, 2010, http://www.newsweek.com/french-prisons-are-becoming-embarrassment-87695.

55. Sarkozy speech delivered June 9, 2005, cited in Éric Fassin, "La démocratie sexuelle et le conflit des civilisations," *Multitudes* 3, no. 26 (2006): 123–31, and cited and translated by Morgan, "The Gendered Politics of Immigrant Integration Policy in France," 27.

56. Farhad Khosrokhavar, *L'islam dans les prisons* (Paris: Editions Balland, 2004).

57. Amnesty International, *Public Outrage: Police Officers Above the Law in France* (London: Amnesty International, 2009). See also Bruce Crumley, "Amnesty Report: French Police Above the Law," *Time*, April 3, 2009, http://content.time.com/time/world/article/0,8599,1889349,00.html.

58. Amnesty International, *Public Outrage*.

59. Fassin, *Enforcing Order*, 72.

60. Ibid.

61. Crumley, "Amnesty Report"; Amnesty International, *Public Outrage*.

62. Ibid.

63. Alain Salles, "Les 'sages' censurent le régime de la garde à vue," *Le Monde*, August 2, 2010; La conseil constitutionnel, "Decision N 2010–14/22 Qpc du 30 Juillet 2010 [*garde à vue*]," in *12030*, ed. Cour de cassation, Paris (2010), http://www.conseil -constitutionnel.fr/decision/2010/2010-14/22-qpc/decision-n-2010-14-22-qpc-du-30 -juillet-2010.48931.html.

64. Jacqueline Hodgson, "The French Garde À Vue Declared Unconstitutional (August 31, 2010)" (Warwick School of Law Research Paper, forthcoming), available at SSRN: http://ssrn.com/abstract = 1669915, http://www.conseil-constitutionnel.fr/ conseil-constitutionnel/francais/les-decisions/acces-par-date/decisions-depuis-1959/ 2010/2010-14/22-qpc/decision-n-2010-14-22-qpc-du-30-juillet-2010.48931.html.

65. Renee Zauberman and René Lévy, "Police, Minorities and the French Republican Ideal," *Criminology* 41, no. 1 (November 2003): 1092.

66. Dominique Monjardet, "La culture professionnelle des policiers," *Revue française de sociologie* 35 (1994): 121, cited in Zauberman and Lévy, "Police, Minorities and the French Republican Ideal."

67. Fassin, *Enforcing Order*, xv.

68. Piotr Smolar, "Une lente amélioration dans las police," *Le Monde*, January 23, 2006. See also Sophie Body-Gendrot, "Police Marginality, Racial Logics and Discrimination in the Banlieues of France," *Ethnic and Racial Studies* 33, no. 4 (2010): 666.

69. Body-Gendrot, "Police Marginality, Racial Logics and Discrimination," 666.

70. Ibid.

71. Fassin, *Enforcing Order*, 172.

72. Ibid.

73. Bonelli, "Governing the Police," 5. See also Bonelli, *La France à peur*.

74. M. R. Haberfeld and Ibrahim Cerrah, *Comparative Policing: The Struggle for Democratization* (Thousand Oaks, Calif.: Sage, 2008), 268.

75. Ibid., 256.

76. Ibid., 260.

77. Tyler Stovall, *The Rise of the Paris Red Belt* (Berkeley: University of California Press, 1990), 21.

78. Herve Veillard-Baron, "Les banlieues: Des singularites françaises aux realites mondiales (Paris; Hachette, 1999), 150–51, cited in Zauberman and Lévy, "Police, Minorities and the French Republican Ideal," 170.

79. Zauberman and Lévy, "Police, Minorities and the French Republican Ideal."

80. Ibid., 1070.

81. Michel Wieviorka et al., *La France raciste* (Paris: Seuil, 1992), 219–76.

82. Zauberman and Lévy, "Police, Minorities and the French Republican Ideal," 1072.

83. Roché, *Le frisson de l'émeute*, 108.

84. Fassin, *Enforcing Order*, 121.

85. Ibid., 43.

86. December 2001.

87. Lydie Hervieux, "Evaluation du module dialogue citoyen en milieu fermé: 23, 24, 25 Octobre 2001, Bois d'Arcy," Bois d'Arcy (2001). These were a series of focus groups conducted with prisoners in the juvenile detention center Bois d'Arcy.

88. Interviewed June 5, 2006.

89. Interviewed June 10, 2006.

90. Eurostat news release, "Urban Audit: Geographic, Economic and Social Data on 258 Cities Across Europe" (European Commission, Brussels, 2004).

91. Michael Kimmelman, "In Marseille, Rap Helps Keep the Peace," *New York Times*, December 19, 2007; Eurostat news release, "Urban Audit."

92. André Donzel and Alain Moreau, eds., *Ville et intégration: Le creuset marseillais*, vol. 5, *Fair Saviors: Science humaines et social en La Region Paca* (2005), http://www.amares.org/index.php/les-sommaires/17-fsnd5-ville-et-integration.

93. Damian Moore, "Multicultural Policies and Modes of Citizenship in European Cities: Marseille," in *UNESCO-MOST Programme* (Paris: UNESCO, 1999).

94. Cited in Andrew Purvis, "Marseille's Ethnic Bouillabaisse: Some View Europe's Most Diverse City as a Laboratory of the Continent's Future," *Smithsonian Magazine* 30, no. 9 (December 2007), http://web.ebscohost.com.proxyau.wrlc.org/ehost/detail?vid=3&sid=384363f4-43fb-4f0e-af18-ab53c889f9c3%40sessionmgr113&hid=117&bdata=JnNpdGU9ZWhvc3QtbGl2ZQ%3d%3d#db=aph&AN=27637820.

95. Katharyne Mitchell, "Marseille's Not for Burning: Comparative Networks of Integration and Exclusion in Two French Cities," *Annals of the Association of American Geographers* 101, no. 2 (2011): 408.

96. Ibid., 412.

97. Patrick Parodi et la grupe La Durance, "Citoyenneté et intégration: Marseille, modèle d'intégration?," Site académique Aix-Marseille Histoire et Géographie (2002), https://www.ac-aix-marseille.fr/pedagogie/upload/docs/application/pdf/2011-08/ppa033_integration.pdf.

98. Claire Berlinski, "The Hope of Marseille," *Azure* (January 2005).

99. Cited in Daniel Williams, "Long Integrated Marseilles Is Spared," *Washington Post*, November 16, 2005, http://www.washingtonpost.com/wp-dyn/content/article/2005/11/15/AR2005111501418.html.

100. Interview I conducted in August 2010.

101. Alfred W. McCoy, *The Politics of Heroin: CIA Complicity in the Global Drug Trade* (New York: Lawrence Hill Books, 1991), 60.

102. Ibid., 61.

103. Angelique Christafis, "All over for Tomcat and Gremlin as New Breed of Gangster Takes Hold in Marseille," *Guardian*, February 13, 2009.

104. Mitchell, "Marseille's Not for Burning," 412; Cesare Mattina, "Changes in Clientelism and Urban Government: A Comparative Case Study of Naples and Marseilles," *International Journal of Urban and Regional Research* 31, no. 1 (2007).

105. The group was called the Charles Martel Club, after the Frankish king who famously repelled the Umayyad caliphate's advance into Europe at the Battle of Tours in 732.

106. Silverstein, "Urban Violence in France"; Adil Jazouli, *Les années banlieues* (Paris: Seuil, 1992), 21–22.

107. Trent Buatte, "Space, Race, and the City: How Marseille, France, Escaped the 2005 Riots" (paper presented at the 7th annual Honors Capstone Research Conference, American University, April 14, 2010).

108. Ibid.

109. Ibid.

110. Ibid.

111. Ibid.

112. Maren Borkert, Wolfgang Bosswick, Friedrich Heckmann, and Doris Lüken-Klaßen, "Local Integration Policies for Migrants in Europe," a report of the European Foundation for the Improvement of Living and Working Conditions, 2007, 50.

113. Cited in Buatte, "Space, Race, and the City."

114. Ibid.

115. Ibid.

116. Jocelyne Cesari, Alain Moreau, and Alexandra Schleyer-Lindenmann, *Plus marseillais que moi, tu meurs!* (Paris: L'Harmattan, 2001).

117. Eleonora Pasotti, *The Decline of Machine Politics in Bogota, Naples and Chicago*, ed. Margaret Levi, Cambridge Studies in Comparative Politics (Cambridge: Cambridge University Press, 2010).

118. Cesari et al., *Plus marseillais que moi, tu meurs*.

119. Winifred Tate, *Counting the Dead: The Culture and Politics of Human Rights Activism in Colombia*, California Series in Public Anthropology (Berkeley and Los Angeles: University of California Press, 2007).

120. Angelique Chrisafis, "A New Breed of Gangster Takes Hold in Marseilles," *Guardian*, February 13, 2009.

121. Ibid.

122. Ben Macintyre, "Dubious Tale of Murder in High Places Rocks France," (London) *Times*, October 11, 1997; Agence France-Presse, "A Marseille, Alexandre Guérini écroué dans une affaire de marchés publics," *Libération*, December 2, 2010.

123. Michel Henry, "Alexandre Guérini arrêté pour corruption," *Libération*, December 3, 2010; "A Marseille, Alexandre Guérini écroué dans une affaire."

124. Arnaud Montebourg, *Rapport de constatation sur les pratiques de la Federation socialiste des Bouches-du-Rhone* (Paris: Premier secrétariat du Parti Socialiste, 2010).

125. Agence France-Presse, "Godfather Style Slaying Lifts Marseille Murder Toll," *New York Daily News*, 2013, http://www.hurriyetdailynews.com/godfather-style-slaying-lifts-marseille-murder-toll.aspx?pageID = 238&nID = 49298&NewsCatID = 351.

126. Mitchell, "Marseille's Not for Burning," 415.

127. Cited in Cathy Lisa Schneider, "Police Power and Race Riots in Paris," *Politics and Society* 366, no. 1 (2008).

128. Mallah Ben Bella interview, in Buatte, "Space, Race, and the City."

129. Open Society Institute, *Muslims in Europe: A Report on 11 European Cities* (New York: Open Society Institute, 2010).

130. Berlinski, "The Hope of Marseille."

Conclusion

1. Tim Stelloh, "Detective Is Found Guilty of Planting Drugs," *New York Times*, November 1, 2011, http://www.nytimes.com/2011/11/02/nyregion/brooklyn-detective-convicted-of-planting-drugs-on-innocent-people.html?_r = 0.

2. Ibid.

3. Al Baker, "New York Minorities More Likely to Be Frisked," *New York Times*, May 12, 2010, http://www.nytimes.com/2010/05/13/nyregion/13frisk.html?pagewanted = all.

4. Cited in Al Baker and Ray Rivera, "Study Finds Street Stops by N.Y. Police Unjustified," *New York Times*, October 26, 2010, http://www.nytimes.com/2010/10/27/nyregion/27frisk.html?pagewanted = all.

5. Ibid.

6. Ibid.

7. Ibid.

8. Ibid.

9. Ibid.

10. Ibid.

11. Quoted in Andy Humm, "Crackdown on Protest Could Spark More Scrutiny of Police," *Gotham Gazette*, November 21, 2011, http://www.gothamgazette.com/index.php/civil-rights/867-crackdown-on-protests-could-spark-more-scrutiny-of-police.

12. Ibid.

13. Eric Alterman, "Think Again: Billionaire Media Moguls vs. Occupy Wall Street," *Center for American Progress*, November 17, 2011, http://www.americanpro gress.org/issues/media/news/2011/11/17/10668/think-again-billionaire-media-moguls -vs-occupy-wall-street/.

14. Andrew Sprung, "I Record Therefore We Are," Xpostfactoid, November 20, 2011, http://xpostfactoid.blogspot.com/2011/11/i-record-therefore-we-are.html.

15. Humm, "Crackdown on Protest Could Spark More Scrutiny of Police."

16. AP, "Gun Smuggling Sting Nabs 5 NYPD Cops," *CBS News*, October 25, 2011, http://www.cbsnews.com/8301-201_162-20125153/gun-smuggling-sting-nabs-5-nypd -cops/; Humm, "Crackdown on Protest Could Spark More Scrutiny of Police."

17. Stelloh, "Detective Is Found Guilty of Planting Drugs"; Humm, "Crackdown on Protest Could Spark More Scrutiny of Police."

18. AP, "Gun Smuggling Sting Nabs 5 NYPD Cops"; Humm, "Crackdown on Protest Could Spark More Scrutiny of Police."

19. AP, "Gun Smuggling Sting Nabs 5 NYPD Cops"; Humm, "Crackdown on Protest Could Spark More Scutiny of Police."

20. http://www.nyclu.org/content/stop-and-frisk-data.

21. Ibid.

22. Joseph Goldstein, "Judge Rejects New York's Stop-and-Frisk Policy," *New York Times*, August 12, 2013, http://www.nytimes.com/2013/08/13/nyregion/stop-and -frisk-practice-violated-rights-judge-rules.html?_r = 0. See also "On the Stop and Frisk Decision: Floyd v City of New York," *New York Times*, August 12, 2013, http://www .nytimes.com/interactive/2013/08/12/nyregion/stop-and-frisk-decision.html.

23. Robert Fischer, "Protect and Serve," *New Yorker*, March 18, 2013, http://www .newyorker.com/online/blogs/newsdesk/2013/03/protect-and-serve-the-aftermath-of -the-kimani-gray-shooting.html.

24. Ibid.

25. Ibid.

26. Cited in Ariana Huffington, "Pepper-Spraying Occupy: An Assault on Our Democracy," *Huffington Post*, November 21, 2011, http://www.huffingtonpost.com/ arianna-huffington/occupy-wall-street-pepper-spray_b_1106535.html.

27. Ibid.

28. Dylan Mathews, "Eric Holder Is Cutting Federal Drug Sentences," *Washington Post wonk blog*, August 12, 2013, 2:30, http://www.washingtonpost.com/blogs/wonk blog/wp/2013/08/12/eric-holder-is-cutting-federal-drug-sentences-that-will-make-a -small-dent-in-the-u-s-prison-population/.

29. Bruce Western, *Punishment and Inequality in America* (New York: Russell Sage Foundation, 2006), 73–75.

30. Ibid.

31. Patillo et al., *Imprisoning America*, 9.

32. Kris W. Kobach, "Why Arizona Drew a Line," *New York Times*, April 28, 2010, http://www.nytimes.com/2010/04/29/opinion/29kobach.html.

33. Joe Soss, Richard C. Fording, and Sanford F. Schram, *Disciplining the Poor: Neoliberal Paternalism and the Persistent Power of Race* (Chicago: University of Chicago Press, 2011), 36.

34. Ibid., 39.

35. Ibid., 40.

36. Philip Gourevitch, "Sarkozy and the European Crisis," *New Yorker*, December 12, 2011, 52–53.

37. Nicolas Sarkozy, "Conference de presse sur sécurité, l'aménagement du territoire et immigration," http://www.interieur.gouv.fr/Archives/Archives-de-Nicolas -Sarkozy-2005-2007/Interventions/11.01.2007-Conference-de-presse (2007), 52, cited in Susan Terrio, *Judging Mohammed: Juvenile Delinquency, Immigration and Exclusion at the Paris Hall of Justice* (Palo Alto, Calif.: Stanford University Press, 2009), 14.

38. Gourevitch, "Sarkozy and the European Crisis," 53.

39. Ibid., 55.

40. "Immigration Helps Define French Presidential Election," *Chicago Tribune*, April 21, 2007, http://www.popmatters.com/article/immigration-helps-define-french-presidential-election/.

41. Mathew Campbell, "French Suburbs Threaten Riotous Dawn for the Reign of Sarkozy," *Sunday Times*, May 6, 2007, http://www.thesundaytimes.co.uk/sto/news/ world_news/article64199.ece.

42. Terrio, *Judging Mohammed*, 15.

43. Ibid.

44. After encountering strong opposition, the UMP agreed to allow indeterminate sentencing only for those given that penalty at the time of sentencing.

45. Didier Fassin, *Enforcing Order: An Ethnography of Urban Policing* (Boston: Polity Press, 2013), 41.

46. "Sarkozy Promises to Fight Crime in Paris Suburbs," *Washington Times*, April 20, 2010, http://www.washingtontimes.com/news/2010/apr/21/world-scene-84170632/ ?page = all.

47. Ibid.

48. Gourevitch, "Sarkozy and the European Crisis."

49. Amnesty International, *Public Outrage: Police Officers Above the Law in France* (London: Amnesty International, 2009), 10.

50. United Nations Economic and Social Council Commission on Human Rights, Report of the special rapporteur on torture, E/CN, 4/2001/66, para. 1310, cited in ibid., 14.

51. Rodney Crisp, "The French Retirement Revolt," *On Line Opinion: Australia's E-journal of Social and Poltical Debate* (2010), http://www.onlineopinion.com.au/view .asp?article = 11145&page = 0. Last accessed October 29, 2013.

52. "Growing Revolts in France," in *Kasama: Great Chaos under Heaven—The Situation Is Excellent* (2010), http://kasamaproject.org/2010/10/21/france-rocked-by -clashes-over-pensions/. Last accessed October 29, 2013.

53. Daily Mail Reporter, "French Strikes Ablaze: Britons Warned to Stay Away as Violence Spirals," *Mail Online*, October 19, 2010, http://www.dailymail.co.uk/news/article-1321730/France-strikes-Paris-streets-ablaze-Britons-warned-stay-away-violence.html. Last accessed October 29, 2013.

54. Ibid.

55. Ibid.

56. Patricia Tourancheau, "Un rapport de la cour des comptes dévoilé hier critique la gestion des forces de sécurité depuis 2002," *Libération*, July 8, 2011, http://www.liberation.fr/societe/2011/07/08/le-mauvais-bilan-du-policier-sarkozy_747966.

57. Laurent Mucchielli and Christian Mouhanna, "Rapport de la cour des comptes sur la politique de sécurité: Où est le problème?," in *Vous avez dit sécurité? Saison 1*, ed. Laurent Mucchielli (Paris: Edicions Champ social, 2012), 118–22.

58. Tourancheau, "Un rapport de la cour des comptes."

59. "Insécurité: La cour des comptes accuse, Sarkozy récuse," *Marianne*, July 8, 2011, http://www.marianne.net/sarkofrance/Insecurite-la-Cour-des-Comptes-accuse-Sarkozy-recuse_a501.html; Mucchielli and Mouhanna, "Rapport de la cour des comptes sur la politique de sécurité"; Tourancheau, "Un rapport de la cour des comptes."

60. Tourancheau, "Un rapport de la cour des comptes."

61. Fassin, *Enforcing Order*, 195.

62. Ibid.

63. Ibid.

64. Ibid., 166.

65. Ibid.

66. Ibid.

67. Tourancheau, "Un rapport de la cour des comptes."

68. Ibid.

69. Ipsos, *Les enjeux du vote: Quels sont, parmi les suivants, les trois thèmes qui compteront le plus dans votre choix de vote Dimanche?* (Paris: Ipsos, 2012).

70. Ibid.

71. Ibid.

72. Ibid.

73. Ibid.

74. The numbers add up to more than 100 percent because individuals listed three main concerns.

75. Associated Press, "Father of Roma girl expelled from France says he claimed they were from Kosovo to gain asylum," *Washington Post*, October 18, 2013, http://www.washingtonpost.com/world/europe/tensions-between-students-police-at-paris-protest-over-immigrant-expulsions/2013/10/18/d0412828-37ef-11e3-89db-8002ba99b894_story.html.

76. William J. Stuntz, *The Collapse of American Criminal Justice* (Cambridge, Mass.: Harvard University Press, 2011), 6–7.

77. Michael Lipsky, "Introduction," in *Law and Order, Police Encounters*, ed. Michael Lipsky, Trans-Action Books ([Chicago]: Aldine, 1970).

78. Marwan Mohammed and Laurent Mucchielli, "La police dans les 'quartiers sensibles': Un profond malaise," in *Quand les banlieues brûlent*, ed. Laurent Mucchielli and Véronique Le Goaziou (Paris: La Découverte, 2006), 98–99.

79. Alex Duval Smith, "Playing with Fire," *Observer*, February 5, 2006, http://www.theguardian.com/world/2006/feb/05/france.features.

80. Ipsos, *Les enjeux du vote*," 923–24. Kurt Weyland compares the organized social movements of the Latin American Southern Cone countries with the unorganized mass demonstrations during the Arab Spring. He points out that in the former, activists were able to sustain mobilization over time, responding strategically to regime strengths and weaknesses, while in the latter, people took to the streets, often misread their own strengths or likelihood of success, and pushed for immediate resolution. See Kurt Weyland, "The Arab Spring: Why the Surprising Similarities with the Revolutionary Wave of 1848?" *Perspectives on Politics* 10, no. 4 (2013): 917–34. In my book on the Chilean shantytowns targeted by the Pinochet dictatorship, I reach a similar conclusion. Residents of communist neighborhoods did not riot but sustained and organized (sometimes underground) protests over a three-year period, eventually achieving victory with the fall of Pinochet. See Cathy Lisa Schneider, *Shantytown Protest in Pinochet's Chile* (Philadelphia: Temple University Press, 1995).

81. Caroline Davies, "Deaths in Police Custody since 1998: 333; Officers Convicted: None," *Guardian*, December 3, 2010, http://www.theguardian.com/uk/2010/dec/03/deaths-police-custody-officers-convicted.

82. Ravi Somiya and Sarah Maslin Nir, "Riots Flare in London against Police Violence," *New York Times*, August 7, 2011.

83. BBC, "Sweden Riots Spread Beyond Stockholm Despite Extra Police," *BBC News Europe*, May 25, 2013, http://www.bbc.co.uk/news/world-europe-22656657.

84. Ibid.

85. Stuntz, *The Collapse of American Criminal Justice*, 5.

86. Human Rights Watch, "Punishment and Prejudice: Racial Disparities in the War Against Drugs" (2000), 5.

87. Charles Tilly, "State Making as Organized Crime," in *Bringing the State Back In*, ed. Peter B. Evans, Dietrich Rueschemeyer, and Theda Skocpol (Cambridge and New York: Cambridge University Press, 1985), 171.

88. Joseph Shumpeter, *Imperialism, Social Classes* (Cleveland: World Publishing, 1955), 25, cited in Robert Jervis, *System Effects: Complexity in Political and Social Life* (Princeton, N.J.: Princeton University Press, 1997), 55.

Index

Acknowledgments

All those who shared their stories, read drafts of this manuscript, or provided me a home or home base in a foreign country are owed a debt of gratitude. My research began in New York (although I had no idea, at the time, of the direction it would take) when I was an Aaron Diamond Fellow at the Hunter College Center on AIDS, Drugs and Community Health in the mid-1990s. The Center had been founded and directed by Nicholas Freudenberg, my coauthor on the grant. Working with syringe exchange programs and Música against Drugs in the South Bronx, Brooklyn, and Lower East Side drew my attention to the negative impact of racial profiling and police violence. My first article based on this research discussed the destructive impact that the racially biased drug war had on the concentration and spread of AIDS in poor minority neighborhoods. Life was hard and often short in the areas where I worked. Several of those who breathed life into this manuscript died tragically before its completion. Armando Perez of CHARAS–El Bohio Cultural and Community Center and Coalition for a District Alternative (CODA), and a former district leader on the Lower East Side, was murdered. David Santiago of South Side Political Action Committee in Williamsburg died during surgery for hepatitis C. Manny Maldonado and Augie Rivera of Música Against Drugs, also in Williamsburg, died of AIDS. Chris Lanier, also of Música, died of cancer.

Their insights and those of Margarita Lopez, Allan Clear, Harry De-Rienzo, Joyce Rivera Beckman, Juan Gonzalez, Jessica Clemente, and particularly Vincente "Panama" Alba, director of the Coalition Against Police Brutality, were invaluable. I want to thank my dear friend Angelo Falcon at the National Institute of Latino Policy, which in the 1990s was still the Institute for Puerto Rican Policy. I owe another debt to my former student and outstanding research assistant Ramon Gonzalez. Ramon's father had been one of the original Young Lords, and Ramon interviewed several former Young Lords leaders for me. His interview with Micky Melendez figures prominently in this book. Thanks go to the police officers who gave generously of their time and helped me grasp the nuts and bolts of policing. Special thanks go to Ron Hampton, director of the National Police Accountability Project; Drew Diamond of the Police Executive Research Forum; Nicholas Pastore, former police chief of New Haven; and Anibal Diaz, formerly of the New York Police Department. Thanks to Phil Mauceri too, for inviting Nicholas and me to be keynote speakers at a drug policy conference and in so doing introducing us. Finally, I am deeply obliged to the mothers and fathers of young people killed by police. Nicholas Heyward, Margarita Rosario, Kadiatou Diallo, Juanita Young, and Allene Person thoughtfully and courageously shared their stories.

I began my research in Paris as a Columbia University Fellow at Reid Hall on September 10, 2001. I was fortunate to have been among the first group of fellows to grace that beautiful hall. Huge thanks go to Micah Bacou and Danielle Haase-Dubosc, who were fantastic hosts. Arriving in a new country and navigating in a new language, I would have been lost without a coterie of good friends. Eros Sana, one of my earliest and closest friends, introduced me to the realities of *banlieue* life and to many of the people who populate this book. He generously shared his home on numerous occasions as well. He also introduced me to Julien Pitinome, the photographer who contributed my powerful cover shot. Audrey Debah, another dear friend, put me in contact with many of the individuals featured prominently in this book. She did not simply introduce me; she accompanied me on interviews, helped interpret and translate some of my more linguistically difficult ones, invited me into her home, and shared her insights. Audrey also introduced me to Siyakha Traoré, the brother of Bouna (whose death set off the 2005 riots), and I owe a heartfelt thanks to Siyakha and Samir Mihi as well. Maria Benali, another friend and *banlieue* resident, gave generously of her time, invited me into her home, and introduced me to many of those who grace the pages of this book. Maria's sister even drove me to the airport. I want to thank my cherished friend Nadia Arraiz, without whom I would have had a difficult time in Paris. Nadia opened her home to me more times than I can count. Laurent Bonelli and Anastassia Tsoukala were two of the first scholars I met in Paris, and both gave me a critical introduction to the security issue in France. Vincent Delbos and Gilles Sainati shared their perspectives as judges. Vincent, in particular, gave me the benefit of his wisdom and experiences from a wide variety of judicial appointments over the years. My cousin Sandra Lippenholtz, who moved from Buenos Aires to Paris over thirty years ago, opened her home and helped me manage when I first arrived in Paris. Maria Antoinelle Joubert invited me to stay with her and her daughter in Marseille during nearly a month of comparative research. Jim Cohen was one of my first friends in Paris, and he introduced me to his former students and their friends in Marseille. They in turn kindheartedly shared their stories and made it possible for me to meet others. I am especially grateful to Miloud, who treated a perfect stranger as a friend. Many of the voices in this book belong to people who prefer to remain, or I have left, anonymous, including residents of Parisian *banlieues*, residents and social workers in Marseille, French police officers, New York police officers, and residents of Mott Haven, Williamsburg, and the Lower East Side. Their time and participation are no less valued.

Finding people willing to read a book-length manuscript is trying. In the early days this project benefited immensely from the kindness, perseverance, and brilliance of Robert Jervis and Charles Tilly. Robert and his wife, Kathy, even helped me get my luggage to the airport outside Paris when my brother was taken gravely ill and I needed to fly to his hospital bed in Los Angeles. Chuck Tilly had the most influence on the development of this book. *Durable Inequality* and *The Politics of Collective Violence* were the intellectual genesis, but I also had the immense joy of receiving feedback from Chuck on everything I sent him between 1985, when we first met, and 2008, when he passed. It was a bit like wandering in the wilderness after that. My first article on police violence and riots in Paris benefited enormously from the comments and encouragement of Gay Seidman, Eric Olin Wright, David Plotke, and the editorial board of *Politics and Society*. I profited immensely from the willingness of Gay Seidman, Carmenza Gallo, Michelle Egan, Ernesto Castaneda, Michael Katz, Sidney Tarrow, David Ost, and Peter Andreas to read either the proposal or the initial introductory chapter. Carmenza, Ernesto, and Michelle read substantially more than the introduction, and Carmenza read multiple drafts. Diarmuid Maguire read the entire manuscript twice and gave me needed feedback. I enjoyed a long e-mail dialogue with Michael Katz early in the project, shortly after he published his first take on why American cities did not burn and I published my first take on why French cities did. The Protest and Politics workshop at City Graduate Center (the legacy of Charles Tilly's workshop at the New School and Columbia) gave me useful feedback just as my ideas were beginning to gel. Special thanks go to Randa Serhan, who later became a colleague at American University and has been an unwavering source of encouragement. I was fortunate to have several skilled research assistants. John Cappel translated or summarized some of the French literature on riots, policing, and *banlieues*. John was actually Dean James Goldgeier's research assistant, but Jim charitably shared John's time with me during the final stages of the manuscript. Micah Johnston and Andi Sullivan carefully proofread earlier incarnations of the manuscript, particularly the French orthography. Jaeda Harmon plotted the criminal justice graphs. Trent Buatte, my undergraduate honors student, introduced me to Marseille; we wrote a chapter together for an edited book on policing divided societies. Emma Fawcett, my brilliant research and teaching assistant, freed some of my teaching preparation time so I could devote more time to the manuscript, provided the index, and put a herculean effort into tracking down references, proofreading, and otherwise getting the manuscript ready for press. I thank my wonderful editor at the University of Pennsylvania Press, Peter Agree, and my amazing readers, Eric Schneider and Jacqueline Ross, without whose acumen and contributions this book would have been much impoverished.

Final thanks go to family and friends who provided support throughout this long process and made my time in New York a labor of love. Particular thanks go to my aunt Molly Starkman, my niece Naomi Simchi, my cousin Linda Powell, and friends who have become family: Desmonique Bonet; Carina Sinclair and her daughter Christina Sinclair Jones; Donna Anderson Wright and her son Greg Anderson; and Manny and Christine Resto. This book is also dedicated to the memory of my sister-in-law Masako Van Dresser and my friend Tulia Camacho.